YASUO KUNIYOSHI

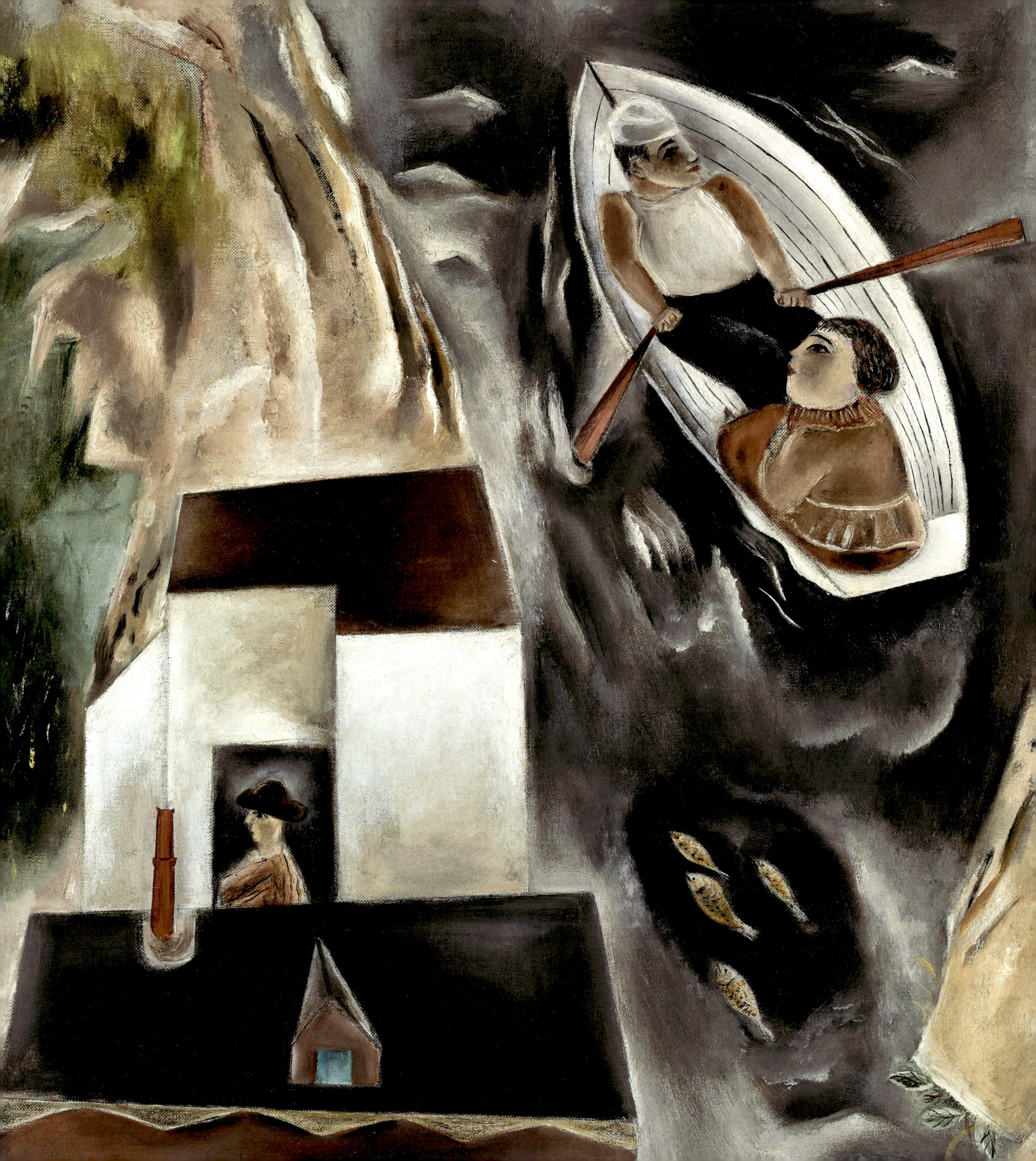

The Artistic Journey of
YASUO KUNIYOSHI

Tom Wolf
with an introduction by Elizabeth Broun

Smithsonian American Art Museum, Washington, DC
in association with D Giles Limited, London

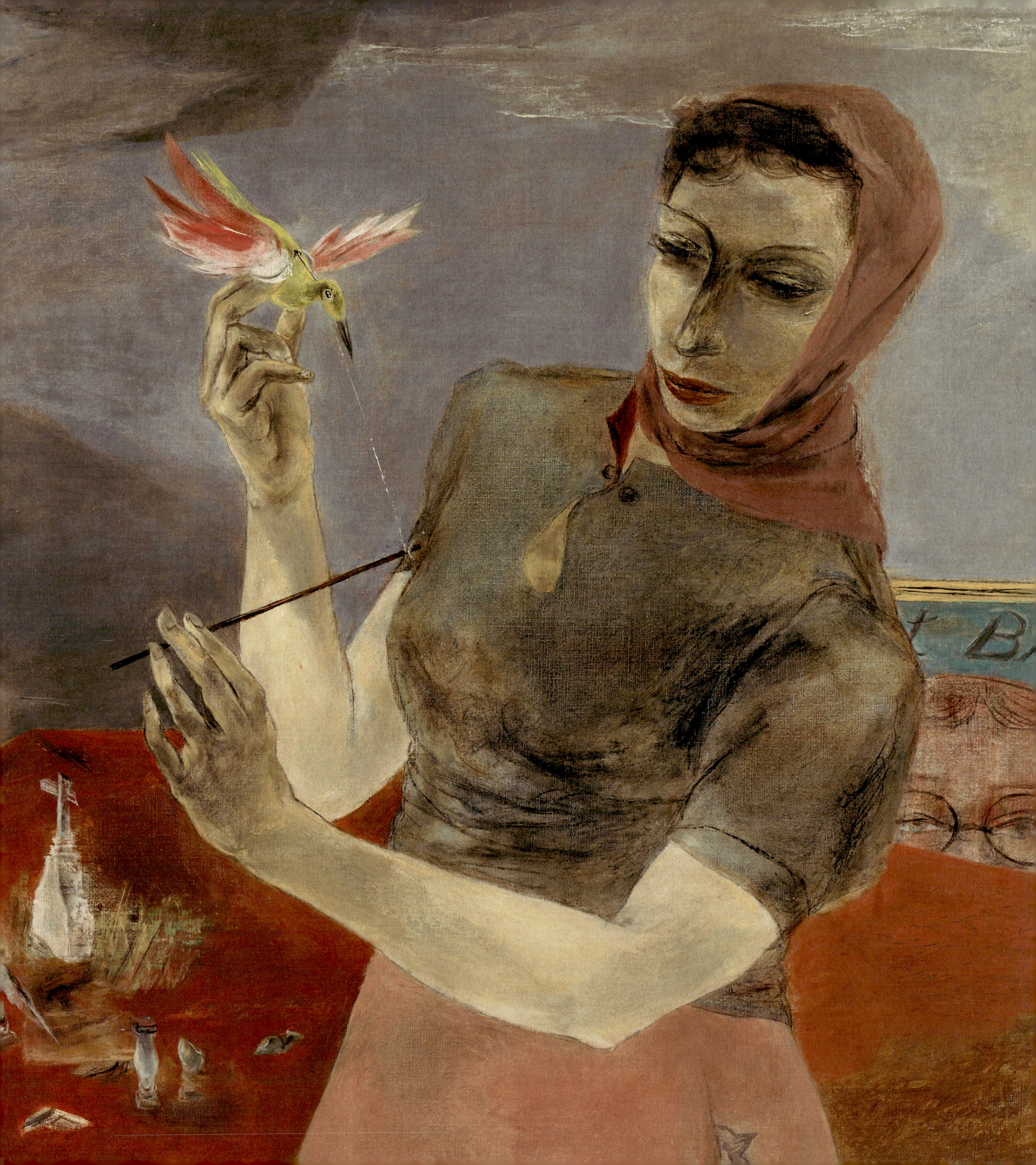

The Artistic Journey of
YASUO KUNIYOSHI

is organized by the
Smithsonian American Art Museum.

American Honda Motor Co., Inc., provided leadership support for the exhibition.

We are especially grateful to Mr. Soichiro Fukutake for his major support of the book and exhibition, for his generosity in lending artworks from the Fukutake Collection in Okayama, and for his long advocacy for this artist.

Additional generous contributions have been provided by:
All Nippon Airways Co., Ltd.
E. Rhodes and Leona B. Carpenter Foundation
Fukutake Foundation
Raymond J. and Margaret Horowitz Endowment
Japan-United States Friendship Commission
Peter and Paula Lunder
Friends of Franklin Riehlman
Sara Roby Foundation
Share Fund
Yasuda Fine Arts Inc.

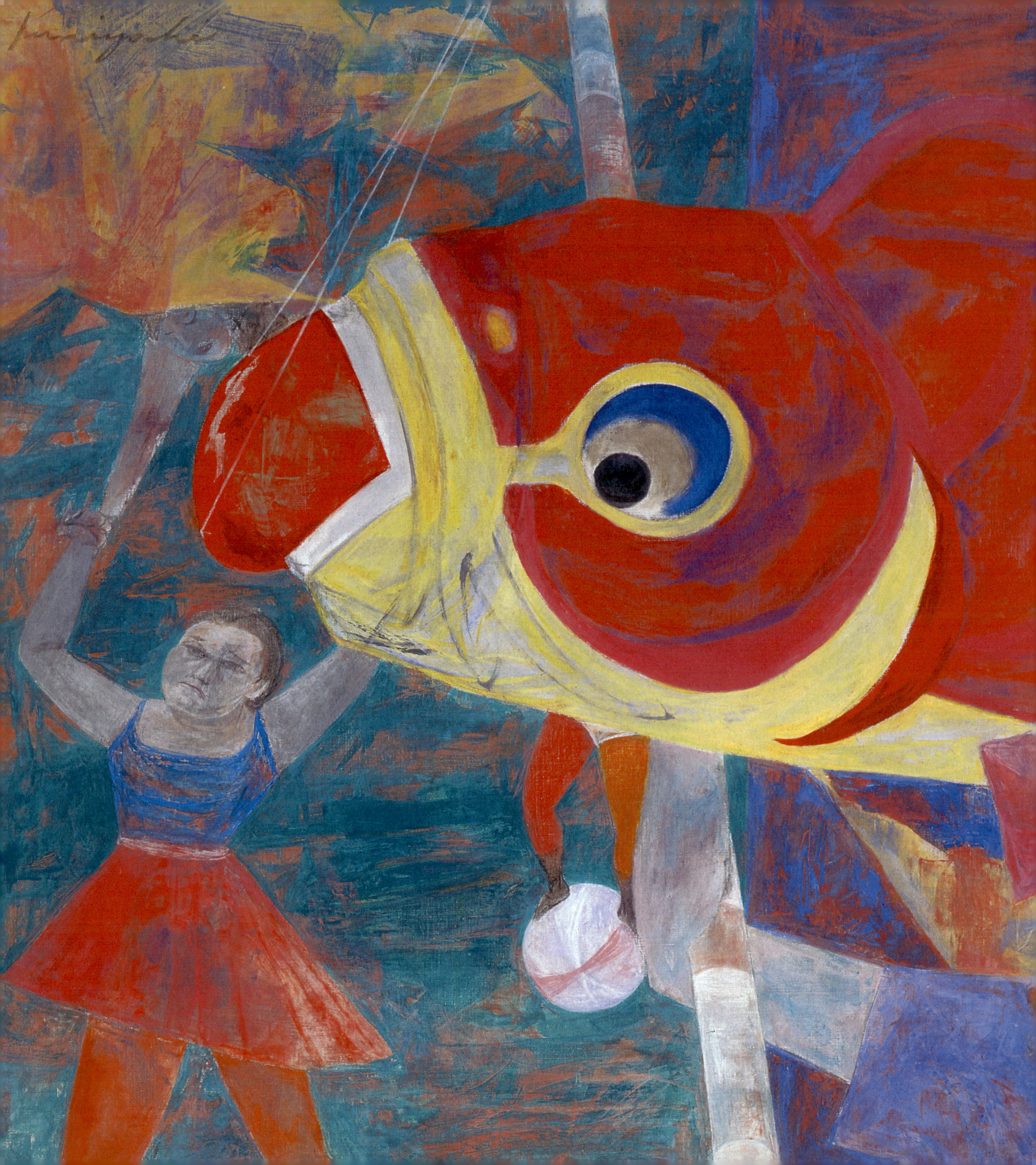

The Smithsonian American Art Museum is grateful to the following lenders to the exhibition:

Amon Carter Museum of American Art, Fort Worth

Arizona State University (ASU) Art Museum, Tempe

Brooklyn Museum, New York

Carnegie Museum of Art, Pittsburgh

John Cassara

Cincinnati Art Museum, Ohio

The Cleveland Museum of Art, Ohio

Columbus Museum of Art, Ohio

Crystal Bridges Museum of American Art, Bentonville, Arkansas

Currier Museum of Art, Manchester, New Hampshire

Delaware Art Museum, Wilmington

Denver Art Museum, Colorado

Fine Arts Museums of San Francisco, California

Fukutake Collection, Okayama, Japan

Gallery Nii, Osaka, Japan

Hirshhorn Museum and Sculpture Garden, Smithsonian Institution, Washington, DC

Indianapolis Museum of Art, Indiana

Menard Art Museum, Komaki, Aichi, Japan

The Metropolitan Museum of Art, New York

Modern Art Museum of Fort Worth

Museum of Contemporary Art, Tokyo

The Museum of Modern Art, New York

Norton Museum of Art, West Palm Beach, Florida

Ogunquit Museum of American Art, Maine

Okayama Prefectural Museum of Art, Japan

The Phillips Collection, Washington, DC

Private collectors

Saint Louis Art Museum, Missouri

Santa Barbara Museum of Art, California

Jule Collins Smith Museum of Fine Art, Auburn University, Alabama

Syracuse University Art Galleries, New York

University of Iowa Museum of Art, Iowa City

University of Tsukuba, Ibaraki, Japan

Wadsworth Atheneum Museum of Art, Hartford, Connecticut

Whitney Museum of American Art, New York

The Artistic Journey of YASUO KUNIYOSHI

Published on the occasion of the exhibition *The Artistic Journey of Yasuo Kuniyoshi*, presented at the Smithsonian American Art Museum, Washington, DC, April 3–August 30, 2015.

Chief of Publications Theresa J. Slowik
Edited by Mary J. Cleary
Designed by Jessica L. Flynn
Permissions coordinated by Amy Doyel

Printed in Slovenia.

Smithsonian American Art Museum

The Smithsonian American Art Museum is home to one of the largest collections of American art in the world. Its holdings—more than 42,000 works—tell the story of America through the visual arts and represent the most inclusive collection of American art of any museum today. It is the nation's first federal art collection, predating the 1846 founding of the Smithsonian Institution. The Museum celebrates the exceptional creativity of the nation's artists, whose insights into history, society, and the individual reveal the essence of the American experience.

For more information or a catalogue of publications, write: Office of Publications, Smithsonian American Art Museum, MRC 970, PO Box 37012, Washington, DC 20013-7012.

Visit the Museum's website at AmericanArt.si.edu.

Library of Congress Cataloging-in-Publication Data

Wolf, Tom (Tom M.) author.
The artistic journey of Yasuo Kuniyoshi / Tom Wolf; with an introduction by Elizabeth Broun.
pages cm
Issued in connection with an exhibition held Apr. 3-Aug. 30, 2015, Smithsonian American Art Museum, Washington, DC.

Includes bibliographical references and index.

ISBN 978-1-907804-63-2 (hardback)
ISBN 978-0-937311-77-6 (softcover)

1. Kuniyoshi, Yasuo, 1889-1953—Criticism and interpretation. I. Broun, Elizabeth, writer of introduction. II. Kuniyoshi, Yasuo, 1889-1953. Works. Selections. III. Smithsonian American Art Museum. IV. Title.
N6537.K83W65 2015
740.92–dc23

2014043181

Image details
Cover: *Self-Portrait as a Photographer*, 1924, (pl. 23); frontispiece: *Upstream*, 1922 (pl. 10); p. 4: *Look, It Flies!*, 1946 (pl. 53); p. 6: *Fish Kite*, 1950 (pl. 61); p. 10: *Child Frightened by Water*, 1924 (pl. 22); p. 14: *Self-Portrait as a Golf Player*, 1927 (pl. 29); p. 158: *Circus Girl Resting*, 1925 (pl. 25); p. 164: *Disturbing Dream*, 1948 (pl. 59); p. 166: *The Swimmer*, 1924 (pl. 21); p. 174: *Little Joe with Cow*, 1923 (pl. 12).

Chronology, pp. 159–61, adapted from Bert Winther, chronology in *Yasuo Kuniyoshi [100th Anniversary of His Birth…]*, essays by Susan Lubowsky, Alexandra Munroe, Takeo Uchiyama, and Tom Wolf ([Japan]: Nippon Television Network Corp., 1989); used by permission.

Contents

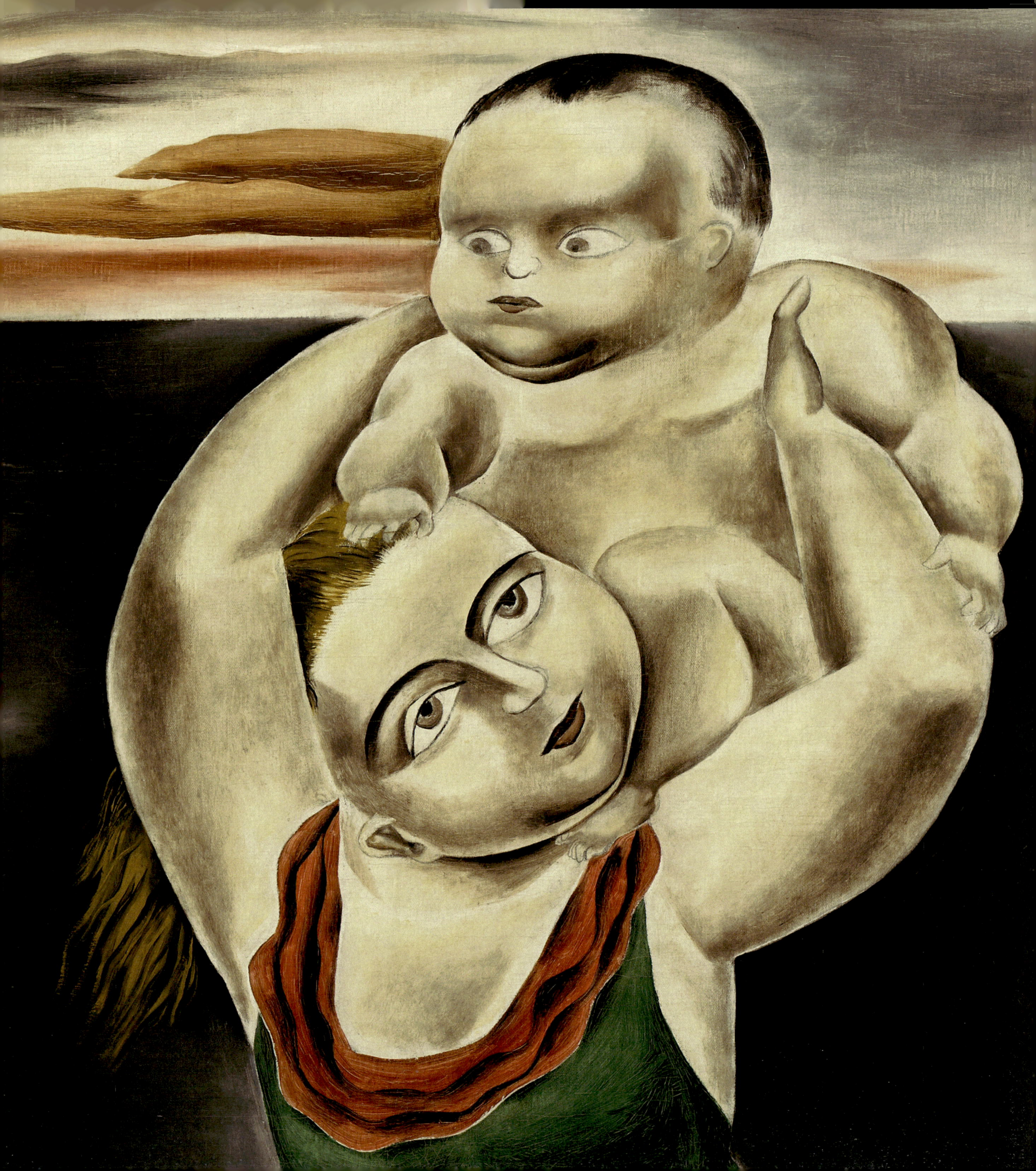

A Stony Journey
YASUO KUNIYOSHI IN AMERICA

The life and career of Yasuo Kuniyoshi (1889–1953) seem to embody every immigrant's dream of upward mobility, rewarding work, and great success in the adopted homeland. He arrived on the West Coast as an impoverished teenager, coming by himself from Japan to make a new life in America. Sympathetic mentors and patrons guided his early career and his amiable personality helped him make a circle of friends in the emerging modern art community. He married an American and showed his art in good galleries; he traveled in France and found buyers for his paintings. He was often chosen for prestigious art juries, and he was appointed the first president of Artists Equity. The Whitney Museum celebrated his work in 1948 with a big show, the first retrospective the museum gave to a living artist. Surely his was a career to be envied!

Yet Kuniyoshi's life was also clouded by constant anxiety related to his immigrant status, and this is evident in his art, if one looks closely enough. Eager to make his way, he spoke only obliquely about his circumstances, and in his paintings he used charm or symbolic references to cloak a deeper, more troubled expression. Even now, eighty or ninety years later, we must search carefully to find those points of apprehension in his art and life, but like dots on a graph they chart the back story of this immigrant's experience.

Six paintings from the early 1920s are about fear, including *Boy Frightened by Snake* (1921–22) with its crucifixion imagery, and *Child Frightened by Water* (1924) with its sense of vulnerability in an engulfing environment. Is it fair to suggest they reflect uncertainties about the anti-immigrant sentiment spreading like a fever across America in those same years? So-called nativist racism pervaded the country, a pseudo-scientific movement that sought to preserve America's Anglo-Saxon or Nordic majority and prevent the debasement of society by intermarriage with Asians and "swarthy" immigrants from Eastern Europe or Africa. Fabricated racial theories poured from the scientific establishment, and organizations such as the Immigration Restriction League and the Race Betterment

Foundation called for banning all immigration from East Asia and sharp restrictions on non-Nordic immigrants. This ban was enacted in 1924, just one of the punitive aspects of the Immigration Act passed that year at the height of those passions. How could Kuniyoshi not have felt concern about what next was coming?

And how did this widespread anti-Japanese sentiment affect his life with Katherine Schmidt, the lively young artist he married in 1919? Katherine was only twenty when she defied her conservative parents of German ancestry by marrying "Yas." They disowned her for it, not speaking to the young couple for six years. Is it too extreme to see in *Boy Stealing Fruit* (1923) an allegory of the marriage, where a sly boy sneaks a juicy peach from a distinctly "early Americana" bowl? Kuniyoshi's frequent use of Americana objects and his style so reminiscent of early folk art have been linked to the revival of colonial American culture in the 1920s, a revival that led to the founding of Colonial Williamsburg, Winterthur, and the Shelburne Museum. But it's also possible to understand his colonial-influence style and Americana references as a way of more closely presenting himself as a "real" American.

Anti-immigrant hostility fed a robust eugenics movement in the United States in those same years; it is discredited today and seldom referenced in our history books. But America's eugenics movement of the 1920s—with its elaborate racial hierarchies and gene pool theories, and forced sterilization and euthanasia programs—thrived in academic and scientific communities, fueled by such books as Madison Grant's *The Passing of the Great Race* (1916) and Lothrop Stoddard's *The Rising Tide of Color Against White World-Supremacy* (1920). Any children born to Kuniyoshi and Katherine would have been viewed as "mongrels," products of miscegenation and a debasement of the "pure American stock." What then should we make of his statement, "People think that babies are beautiful, but I thought otherwise"? In *The Baby* (1921), *Child* (1923), and *Two Babies* (1923), Kuniyoshi made sure that the children were all emphatically early colonial Anglo-Saxon American kids. Kuniyoshi and his wife had no children.

One can trace similar threads throughout Kuniyoshi's career, especially the troubled chapter during World War II, when he was declared an "enemy alien" by the U.S. government; his movements were restricted and his camera was confiscated. Friends rallied to his defense, and his work as a poster artist for the Department of War helped him assert his loyalty as a true American, despite his Japanese ancestry. But the postwar years brought more unwelcome attention. In 1946, his participation in an international touring exhibition organized by the State Department called *Advancing American Art* attracted intense criticism from the Hearst newspapers, various congressmen, and President Truman for its "communistic" tendencies; Kuniyoshi's *Circus Girl Resting* (1925) was singled out again and again as the most offensive work in the show. Joseph McCarthy's witch-hunts began in earnest in 1950, ensnaring artists, including Kuniyoshi's good friends. It's one possible way of understanding the bitter late circus paintings with bright "acid" colors such as *Mr. Ace* (1952), showing a paunchy clown wearing an evil mask, or *Fakirs* (1951), where the evil clown blows a trumpet while small clowns dangle from his arm and body. Despite his disillusionment, Kuniyoshi still hoped to apply for citizenship as the McCarran-Walter Act was passed, which finally permitted the naturalization of Asian immigrants, but his death cut short this decades-long dream.

A still deeper current—a profound distrust of military aggression—coursed through Kuniyoshi's life in key ways. Perhaps his departure from Japan at sixteen was intended to avoid service in the Japanese army that was, at the turn of the twentieth century, launching aggressive campaigns such as the First Sino-Japanese War (1894–95) and the Russo-Japanese War (1904–5). His several reflective paintings from the 1930s of studio nudes reading newspapers, and his contributions to Chinese victims of the Second Sino-Japanese War (1937–45), reveal that Japanese militarism continued as a concern. When his native country attacked his adopted homeland at Pearl Harbor, Kuniyoshi was eager and affirmative in placing his allegiance squarely with America. But we are left wondering how he felt when the United States then dropped the first atomic bombs on Japan, a dramatic escalation of the military capacity for annihilation. Kuniyoshi donated to relief programs for Hiroshima victims, underscoring his lifelong concern for lives impacted by military action. These deep currents may help explain the extraordinary bitterness of such late works as *Fish Head* and *Work at Dawn*, both from 1952.

Connecting all these dots involves leaps of faith and speculation, but even when details are blurry, it is clear that his choice as a teenager to come to the land of freedom placed him on a stony journey with many twists and obstacles. Now, more than half a century after his death, it is fitting that this museum, which is dedicated to the American experience as revealed through art, should present Kuniyoshi's life and art for a new generation to assess and enjoy.

My sincere thanks go to Professor Tom Wolf of Bard College for curating this exhibition and authoring the book. Special thanks also to Dr. Joann Moser, deputy chief curator of the Smithsonian American Art Museum, for co-curating and helping secure loans. The lenders themselves are heroes for allowing their prized paintings to be part of this major exhibition. We are particularly grateful to the Japanese lenders for sending their artworks over the ocean. Mr. Fukutake is owed a most particular debt of gratitude for his many loans, and for initiating this study with a grant to Bard College for the release of Tom Wolf's time, so he could concentrate on the project. And American Honda Motor Co., Inc., generously offered early support that guaranteed the exhibition could go forward. To all my colleagues in this wonderful Smithsonian museum, I offer heartfelt thanks. Our publications team headed by Theresa Slowik, our design team headed by Claire Larkin, the registration group headed by Melissa Kroning, the development staff headed by Donna Rim, and many more have collaborated to bring all together.

Elizabeth Broun
The Margaret and Terry Stent Director

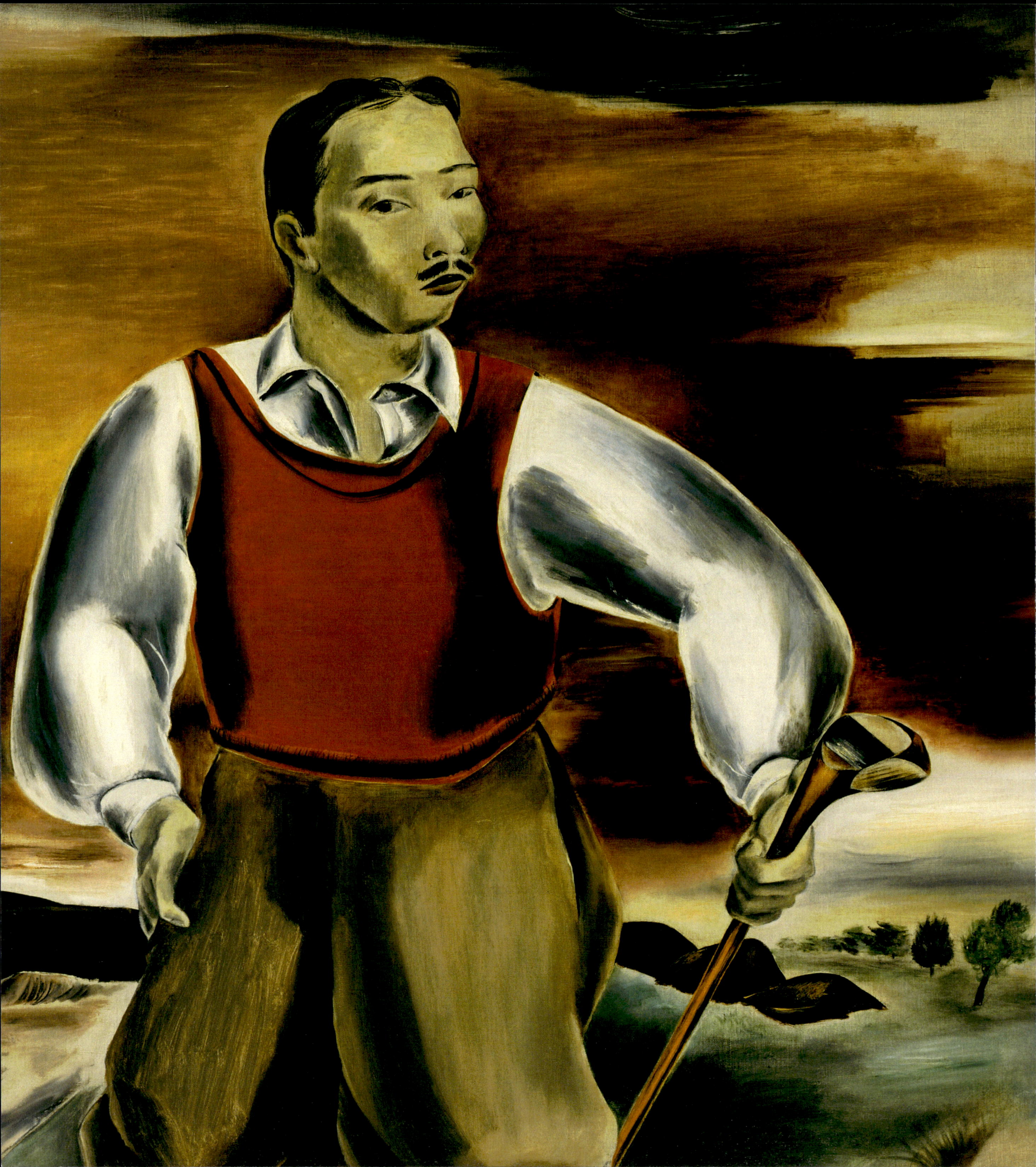

Tom Wolf

The Artistic Journey of YASUO KUNIYOSHI

To Franklin Riehlman

Yasuo Kuniyoshi had no intention of becoming an artist when he came to the United States from his native Japan in 1906, only sixteen years old. Encouraged by a high school teacher in Los Angeles to pursue his artistic talent, he went on to become one of the most esteemed painters in the New York art world in the years between the two world wars. Kuniyoshi's art is subtle and sophisticated, idiosyncratic and unique. During the course of his career it ranged from deadpan humor through erotic sensuality to deep tragedy. It is rich and profound, and should be better known.

This book and the exhibition at the Smithsonian American Art Museum surveying the highlights of his career will be a revelation to the art world, as his work has not been seen at its best in the United States since his retrospective exhibition at the Whitney Museum of American Art in 1948—the first that museum ever devoted to a living artist.

After his early student work Kuniyoshi's artistic career can be divided into roughly three periods. In the 1920s he made peculiarly humorous, highly original paintings that incorporate the influence of American folk art, a popular avant-garde enthusiasm at the time, and melded it with elements from Japanese art, and American and European modernism. After two extended visits to Paris in 1925 and 1928 he began painting from reality instead of, as he put it, "almost entirely from imagination and my memories of the past."[1] What resulted were lushly brushed images of sensual women, often deep in thought, and complexly personal still lifes, painted with refined, understated color.

The years leading up to and through World War II were difficult times for Kuniyoshi. Despite his desires, immigration law made it impossible for someone born in Japan to become an American citizen until 1952, the year before his death. After the Japanese bombing of Pearl Harbor on December 7, 1941, he was classified an "enemy alien" by the U.S. government and subjected to prejudice and harassment, although, living on the East Coast, he was not confined to an internment camp. He was devoted to the United States and its democratic system, but also felt compassion for his native land. During these years his art took on a moodier aspect, and he made violent drawings for the American propaganda effort. In his postwar paintings he often rendered disillusioned subjects with paradoxically hot, brilliant color.

Kuniyoshi's career as an artist concluded with the profound and intense black ink drawings he made in his last years, in counterpoint to his vividly colored paintings of the same time. He frequently made preparatory studies for these drawings, which he regarded as finished works of art, echoing the artistic practices of Japan and China. He had developed a personal style of ink drawing in the 1920s, juxtaposing areas of white paper with fine lines played against passages of thick ink that he scratched into for highlights. At the end of his career, his black ink drawings, with their physical handling and tragic subjects, paralleled the art being produced by the new generation of abstract expressionist artists.

Kuniyoshi's artistic output was limited. He started painting relatively late; he supported himself partly by teaching; he painted slowly; he spent a lot of time as an activist in artists' organizations, and he died fairly young. His catalog lists only around 350 paintings.[2] The Smithsonian exhibition focuses on forty-one paintings and twenty-five ink drawings that comprise the best of this immensely talented and individualistic artist's production. It traces the career of a painter who was esteemed during his time, and whose life was closely linked to some of the major historical events of the twentieth century. The evolution of Kuniyoshi's art from his strangely cheerful works in the 1920s, through his sensual and worldly paintings of the 1930s, to the richly troubling works of his last years is a deeply human story, and the opportunity to see it in all its visual eloquence is a rewarding one.

Kuniyoshi was an activist in the New York art world in both politics and art politics. He was the central figure among the Japanese artists who were active in the city between the world wars. During his career critics in the United States regularly claimed that there was something "Oriental" about his painting, while the art public in Japan saw it as "European." In fact its uniqueness sprang from his singular sensibility, plus his ability to merge the artistic practices of East and West in ways that were original and integrated, unlike many of his Japanese American contemporaries who often veered from one tradition to the other.[3] As he wrote, his aim was "to combine the rich traditions of the East with my accumulative experiences and viewpoint of the West."[4] In my discussion I seek to define how this statement was actually manifested in his art and his career. To do so runs the risk of being labeled "essentialist" for trying to define aspects that descend from Japanese artistic traditions versus those that the artist learned through his artistic schooling in the United States and his travels in Europe. But I believe that this approach is essential (not essentialist) to understanding how he defined himself as an American artist while at the same time remaining very aware that his Asian origins played an important role in his identity and in his artistic practices. For his complex art Kuniyoshi drew from Japanese, European, American, and American folk traditions. The Parisian modernism that inspired him was itself in part inspired by Japanese art, so the issue quickly becomes multifaceted rather than dualistic. What set Kuniyoshi apart from his contemporaries was the sophisticated way that he used these various traditions and expressed them through a distinctive vision. This uniqueness, which lifted him to the top of the art world in his time, may ultimately be impossible to describe in words, but I believe that I can articulate some of the diverse factors that went into it, and the artist's dual identity between Japan and the United States is central. All his life he was Japanese identified, due to his appearance, his manner of speech, and his citizenship. The fact that he was an American artist unable to become an American citizen played a crucial role in his career. His entire life as an artist took place in the United States; in addition I will also suggest that after his single trip back to Japan, in 1931, he also played a role in the Japanese art world.

A photograph from 1922 shows a group of Japanese artists who organized an exhibition of their works at the Civic Club in New York; Kuniyoshi is at the far right (fig. 1). Five years later a photograph documents a similar group, again exclusively artists of Japanese origin, who organized another show in New York, sponsored by the English-language newspaper, the *Japanese Times* (fig. 2). Now Kuniyoshi is seated in the middle of the group, testimony to his rapidly rising reputation in the New York art world. In contrast a photograph from the 1930s depicts a lively group of artists at a party in Woodstock, New York (fig. 3). Where the previous two photographs show Kuniyoshi exclusively in the company of his fellow countrymen, here he is probably the only person of Asian descent among some forty revelers. These images illustrate the alternate worlds Kuniyoshi inhabited, the shifting contexts he participated in, which I will argue are key to understanding his career as an artist in New York.

FIG. 1
Japanese Artists Society in New York, 1922, gelatin silver print, photographed by Laquan Studio. Ishigaki Memorial Museum, Taiji, Wakayama, Japan

FIG. 2
First Annual Exhibition, Japanese Artists in New York, 1927, black-and-white photo paper, photographed by Laquan Studio. Ishigaki Memorial Museum, Taiji, Wakayama, Japan

FIG. 3
Woodstock party, 1930s. Historical Society of Woodstock, New York; Gift of Sara Kuniyoshi

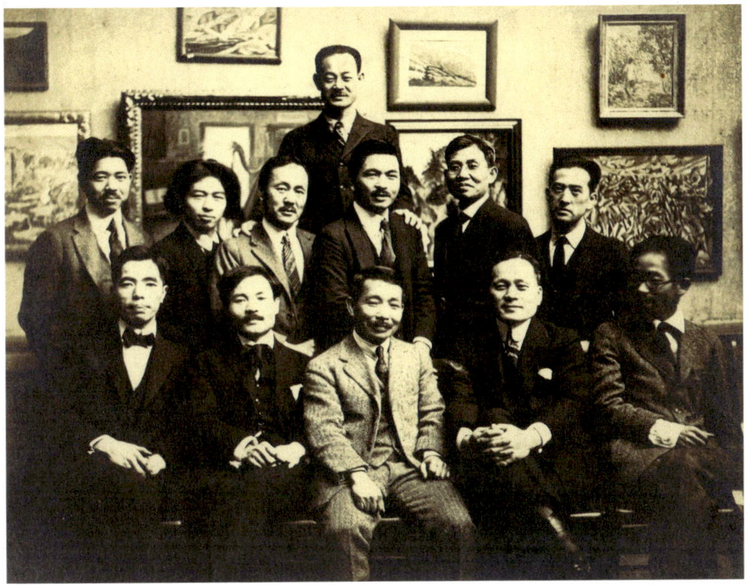

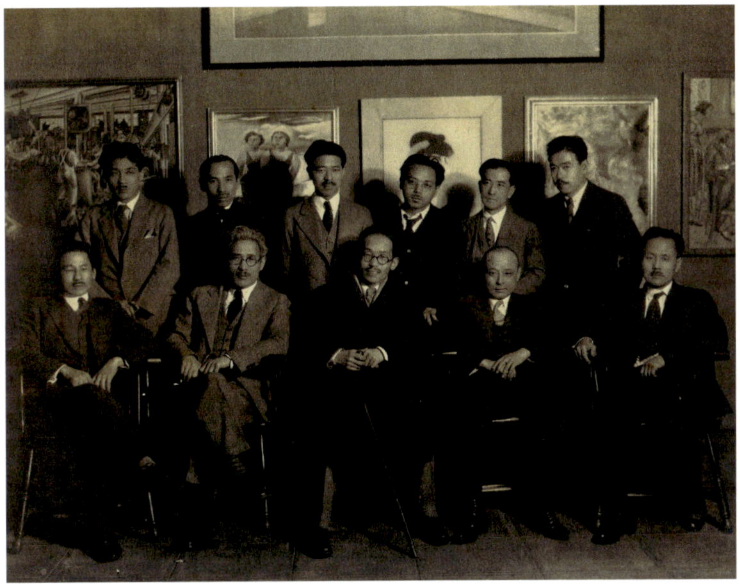

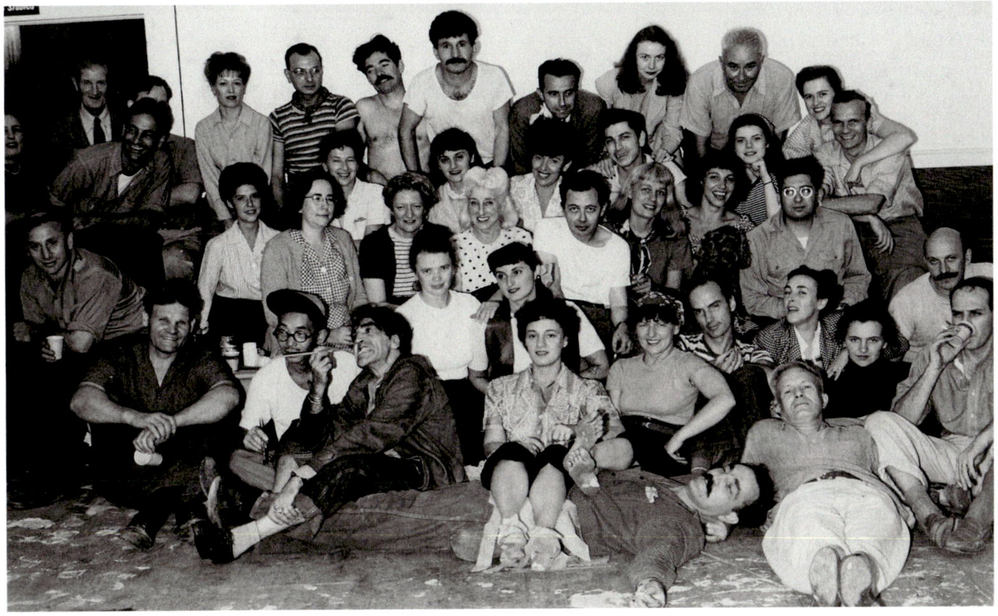

COMING TO THE UNITED STATES AND BECOMING AN ARTIST

Raised in his hometown of Okayama, Kuniyoshi had never even been to Tokyo when, in 1906, age sixteen, he left Japan for the United States. His father was a man of modest means who went through several professions before becoming the head of a rickshaw men's union.[5] His son received a conventional education and then studied at a school of weaving, dyeing and textile design, which familiarized him with styles of Japanese decorative arts and also with traditional techniques of drawing. In later years he remembered being impressed by a painting in the Western style: "It was a realistic panorama of a battle scene. It stirred me greatly because it was so real and life-like, a factor that I had not been aware of in the works of art that surrounded my childhood."[6] That he saw it as a contrast to what he was used to makes it clear that he was familiar with Japanese artistic traditions.

The teenager decided that rather than go into the army he would seek his fortune in the United States, a decision that foreshadowed his later antimilitarist politics. He optimistically assumed wealth would come easily to him, and that he would return to his native country in a few years. "I thought nothing of money, expecting to pick it up practically from the streets."[7] He arrived in Vancouver, where he stayed in a Japanese hotel, and getting rich fast turned out to be less easy than he expected. To survive he began working a series of menial jobs, including picking fruit in the fields and working as a hotel bellhop. Seeking a more pleasant climate, he worked his way south to Los Angeles. There he enrolled in high school, where a teacher told him he had artistic talent, which led him to take classes at the Los Angeles School of Art and Design. Founded in 1887 as the city's first art school, it was progressive for its day: the impressionists were respected, and the building, which overlooked Westlake Park (today MacArthur Park), had a rooftop garden specifically so that the students could paint outdoors.[8] Japanese students were a regular presence at the school, but Kuniyoshi was ambitious and restless, and in 1910 he headed for New York, the artistic capital of the United States.

Although there were far fewer Japanese in New York than on the West Coast, he knew a Japanese commercial artist, a friend of his father's, who gave him room and board in return for the youngster's cleaning out his studio. His impecunious restlessness continued as he attended three different art schools over the next few years, living with almost no income. "But by this time I had definitely decided to continue studying art. Somehow that aim was firm enough so that no matter what I did it was always bearable."[9] As he shopped around for schools he attended the prestigious National Academy of Design for part of one semester, and then some classes taught by the charismatic Robert Henri. Next he tried the Independent School, run by Homer Boss. Today Boss is best known for Western scenes, but in the 1910s he was considered a radical young painter. He had exhibited at the famous Armory Show in 1913, which explosively introduced several generations of avant-garde European art to an unprepared American audience. Boss briefly adopted the cubist style and attracted progressive-minded students. Kuniyoshi did not personally see the Armory Show—he was off working in a hotel in Syracuse—but he heard about it at the Independent School, where he met several young painters who would become lifelong friends, including Stuart Davis.

After two years of study in this radical milieu, Kuniyoshi made another change, enrolling in 1916 in the Art Students League, the school he would be identified with for the rest of his life, first as a student, then as teacher. At the time of his studies, the League was a more progressive school than the National Academy, but less avant-garde than the Independent School. The faculty included academic painters like Frank Vincent DuMond and George Bridgeman, as well as progressives who were members of the socially concerned group, the Ashcan school, including Robert Henri, George Bellows, and John Sloan, all dedicated to painting scenes of rugged urban life. Kuniyoshi studied there four years, started to find his own voice as an artist, and made friends who would sustain him throughout his life: "I had a great hunger for friends and companionship as a natural reaction from my lonely wanderings. At the League I found warmth and kindness which I sorely needed."[10]

He was still very poor, taking care of the League's cloakroom at night in exchange for free tuition and a scholarship that paid $15 per month. By 1918 he was augmenting his tiny income by selling small paintings and watercolors to fellow students. In contrast to his practice for most of his career, during these student years he was painting fast. He also started making prints, encouraged by Peggy Bacon, a fellow student. Her later drypoint print, *The Ardent Bowlers*, from 1932, pays tribute to the relaxed camaraderie among this group of artists whose lasting friendships were founded at the League in the 1910s (fig. 4). The gathering around the bowling match includes Kuniyoshi, with a pipe right of center; Katherine Schmidt, the fellow art student whom he married in 1919, seated left of the bowling figure; and Reginald Marsh, Wood Gaylor, Robert Laurent,

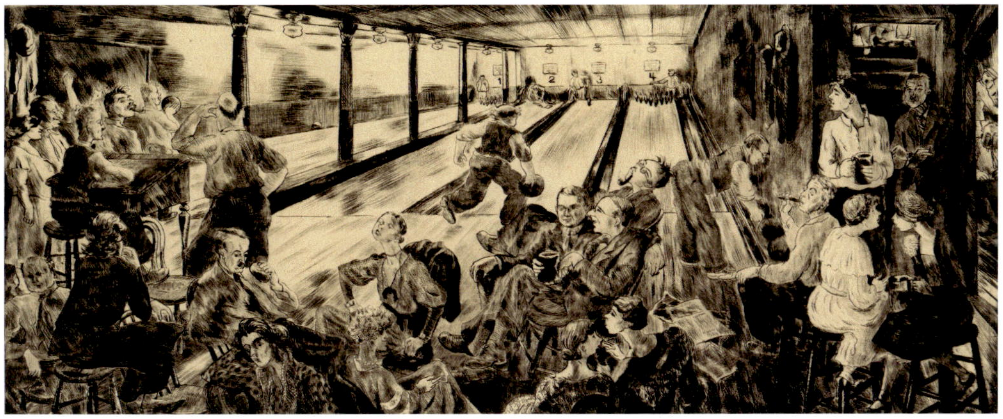

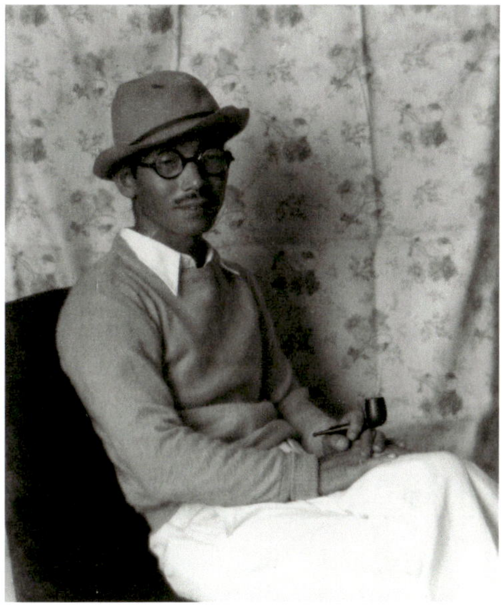

FIG. 4
Peggy Bacon, *The Ardent Bowlers*, 1932, drypoint; plate: 6 × 13 15⁄16 in., sheet: 11 3⁄8 × 18 5⁄8 in. Whitney Museum of American Art, New York; purchase

FIG. 5
Peter A. Juley & Son, *Yasuo Kuniyoshi*, 1910s, Archives & Special Collections, Smithsonian American Art Museum, JUL J0001796

Bernard Karfiol, Niles Spencer, Emil Ganso, and Alexander Brook, all part of Kuniyoshi's circle of artist friends. Kuniyoshi still wears the round, dark-framed glasses that he sported more than a decade earlier, in a photograph of him by Peter Juley, where he is dapper and fashionable as usual, and in his earliest painted *Self-Portrait*, 1918 (fig. 5; pl. 1). This is the first of four self-portraits he painted during his career, and it already gives a sense of his talent. Executed with the warm, muted colors, sensuous brushwork, and shallow space that will characterize much of his art, it is modest but subtle, as he developed a composition of rhyming curves in his hat and shoulders, complemented by rhythmic repeats in the wings of his bowtie, his moustache, and the circles of his glasses. He looks out at us impassively, but the round disks of his glasses evoke a sense of innocence, and his head is haloed with light.

When Kuniyoshi started at the Art Students League he wanted to study with the popular George Bellows, but Bellows's class was full so he turned to Kenneth Hayes Miller, who would be the only teacher he worked with during his entire time as a student at the League. Miller had a great influence on Kuniyoshi. He was a legendary teacher, respected for his knowledge of art history and his passion for the Old Masters, and he inspired his students with his enthusiasm for artists such as Honoré Daumier and El Greco, who would remain important to Kuniyoshi.

Today Miller is not very well known, and those who are interested in his art think mainly of paintings where he represented scenes of contemporary life, often women shoppers on Fourteenth Street, whom he rendered as statuesque, volumetric figures in clear, perspectival settings. But in the early 1910s, Miller had been working in a symbolist mode, painting imaginary scenes of seminude figures in mystical landscapes (fig. 6). Miller was impressed by the great visionary artist Albert Pinkham Ryder, and despite Ryder's reclusiveness he was able to befriend Ryder in his late years. He passed on his admiration for Ryder to Kuniyoshi, and it is reflected in some of the small, dark, brooding landscapes the latter painted in the 1910s.[11] Miller's greatest enthusiasm was for the European Old Masters, whose art he praised for its volume and plasticity, which he felt was more profound than what he found in Asian art. In a lecture from the 1920s he argued that

> Painting in its most complete form of communication is a development from the decoration of useful objects to the fullest embodiment of expression in three-dimensional substance.
>
> In the East this step was never taken.[12]

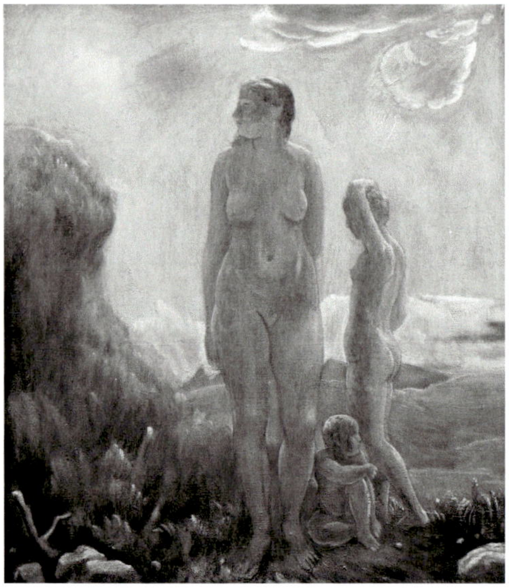

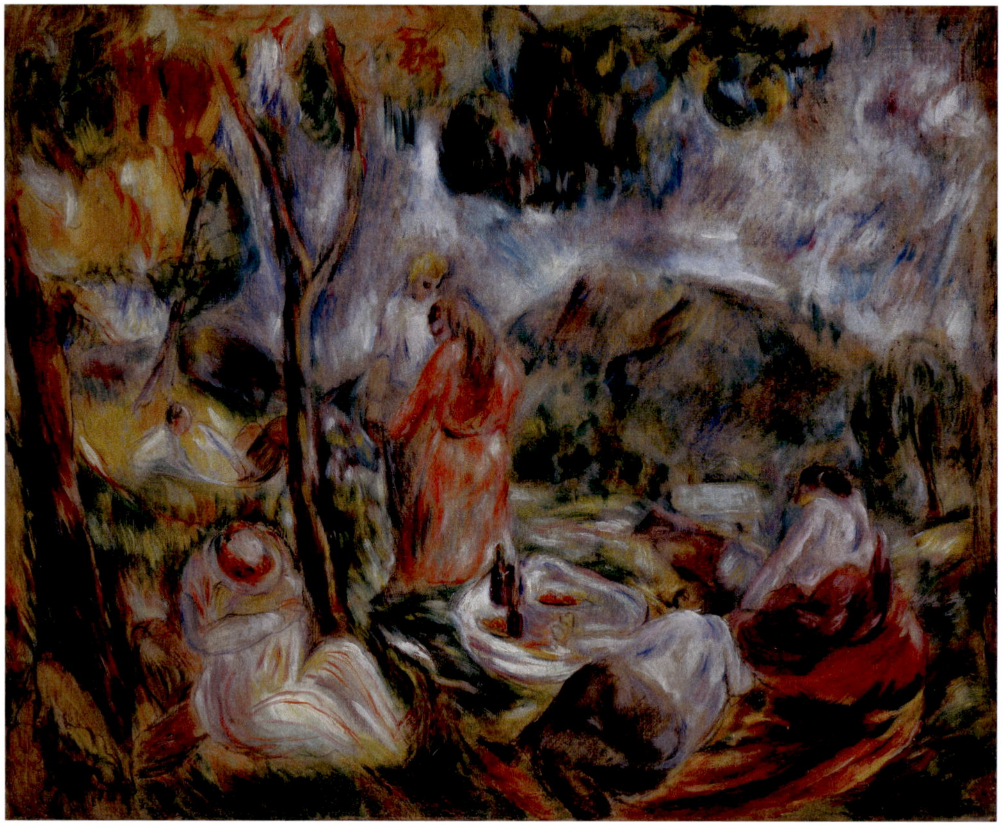

FIG. 6
Kenneth Hayes Miller, *Landscape with Figures*, 1914, oil on canvas, 20 × 17 in. Metropolitan Museum of Art, New York; Gift of students and admirers of the artist, 1927

FIG. 7
Yasuo Kuniyoshi, *Picnic*, 1919, oil on canvas, 30 ⅛ × 36 in. Fukutake Collection, Okayama, Japan

According to Lloyd Goodrich, Miller's former student, he believed that

> the widespread influence of Oriental art, coming to us through Whistler, Degas, Gauguin, Matisse and Picasso, helps to explain why so much contemporary painting, in spite of its cleverness, gaiety and zest, seems thin and slight compared to the work of those two ancestors of modernism, Renoir and Cézanne, and their predecessors.[13]

Here he paid tribute to two artists Kuniyoshi admired, Renoir and Cézanne, and was condescending about Asian art, blaming it for the decline of solid form and three-dimensionality in the works of a group of modern artists Kuniyoshi also admired. Nevertheless, Goodrich, in notes from his interviews with Kuniyoshi in 1948, quoted the artist's view that he "had been brought up seeing and feeling things in the Oriental way, that is in a two-dimensional way...Then Miller taught him to see things in depth."[14]

Kuniyoshi and Miller had their studios in the same building on Fourteenth Street, but once they were both teaching at the League they were not greatly fond of each other. Kuniyoshi's art would significantly depart from Miller's neo-Renaissance ideals, and while he often acknowledged his debt to Miller's teaching, the older artist still felt slighted. Artist Richard Lahey recalled that Miller complained that when the two met in the hall Kuniyoshi would just grunt, which Miller explained by saying, "You can never understand Orientals."[15] An example of the casual prejudice Kuniyoshi often encountered, this also demonstrates the bitterness Miller sometimes expressed in his later years. As the art writer Harry Salpeter put it, "He would have to be a saint not to wince, at least in private, at the way in which youngsters who have sat at his feet as students have shot up into public esteem and have eclipsed him."[16] Even during his lifetime Miller's hard, bulky shoppers and nudes had detractors, but his teachings effectively conveyed his enthusiasm for traditional European painting to his students. In today's art historical climate he can be associated with the *rappel à l'ordre* (return to order), the movement toward classicizing realist painting by many European modernists in the 1920s, after the trauma of World War I—although his work was always traditionalist, unlike the radical painters who turned conservative in the 1920s.[17]

After his early symbolist period and before developing his trademark Fourteenth Street paintings, in the mid-1910s when Kuniyoshi was studying with him Miller practiced figurative painting that reflected his admiration for Renoir. Kuniyoshi was further exposed to the impressionists and to their devotion to plein-air painting in 1917, when he enrolled in the League's summer school in landscape painting in Woodstock, New York. There he got to know the art colony where he would build a home in 1929. He studied with the esteemed but conservative John Carlson, and painted very quickly, often two paintings a day, in contrast to the slow process that would characterize his mature practice. As he recalled later: "It was in the style of the Impressionistic school and we never believed any other way than painting out in the field in the broiling sun."[18]

Katherine Schmidt reminisced about the talk among the students in those years: "I remember we used to argue who was the really key influence—Cézanne or Renoir? And we divided just in two. Some for Renoir, some for Cézanne."[19] Kuniyoshi juggled the influence of both artists in a series of paintings from his student days (fig. 7). The League students would see works by these masters at Paul Durand-Ruel's gallery, while they also regularly visited Alfred Stieglitz's 291 gallery to see avant-garde art.

EARLY WORKS AND EXHIBITIONS

Kuniyoshi had a typical immigrant's experience, in that he continually found support from people from his native country to help him deal with his new environment. This included staying in a Japanese hotel in Seattle, and attending art schools in Los Angeles and New York that had Japanese students. At the Art Students League in New York he met the painters Eitaro Ishigaki and Toshi Shimizu, who became lifelong friends. In New York he was given lodging from a Japanese friend of his father's, and he helped support himself by selling small works to the Japanese American Church. At the same time, the dominant culture repeatedly reminded him of his foreign origins. At the Art Students League he found a group of genuine friends, and he also met his first wife, artist Katherine Schmidt. But by law he could not become an American citizen and there was debate among the students as to whether it was right for her to marry someone Japanese. When she did she lost her American citizenship and her family stopped talking to her or helping her financially for six years.[20]

Meanwhile Kuniyoshi had begun exhibiting his art in 1917. His first showing was in April 1917, at the debut exhibition of the Society of Independent Artists. The Society was created to give artists opportunities to exhibit outside the restrictive juried shows dominated by the conservative artists from the National Academy of Design. Today the 1917 show is best known for the fact that Marcel Duchamp (one of the founders of the Independents) using a false name submitted the urinal he titled *Fountain*, and despite the group's open policy it was not exhibited. The show itself was a huge hodgepodge, with hundreds of artists of all types exhibiting a vast array of works of varying degrees of competence. Kuniyoshi, who was twenty-seven years old, showed two paintings there, taking on a central subject in the history of Euro-American art with his *Crucifixion*. Its generalized figures in a barren landscape recall Miller's symbolist landscapes (fig. 8). In February 1918 he showed at the McDowell Club, another exhibiting society devoted to openness; its policy was that any self-organized group of artists could exhibit there. In this case the group was the Japanese Artists Association, with Kuniyoshi showing twelve works, far more than any other exhibitor. Here he went from the totally heterogeneous Society of Independents to another open venue, but one where he was in the company of exclusively fellow Japanese—as was the case again in the two shows in the 1920s (see figs. 1, 2).

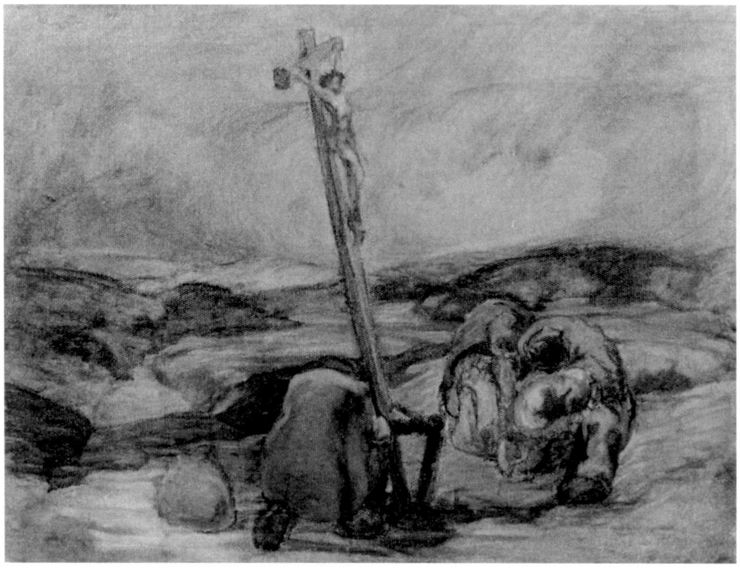

FIG. 8
Yasuo Kuniyoshi,
Crucifixion, 1917,
location unknown

In 1917 he also exhibited with the Penguin Club, a boisterous, progressive group of young artists led by Walt Kuhn, one of the organizers of the Armory Show. The Penguins were a loose, playful bunch: no officers, no dues, no membership. Like the Dadaists in Europe, they were blowing off tension in reaction to World War I, though they were less confrontational. A writer for the *New York Sun* in 1917 observed, "there is a real necessity, the Penguins feel, for a little tonic nonsense."[21] But the group did more than party: they rented the floor of a building at Eight East Fifteenth Street in Greenwich Village, and held figure drawing classes and ambitious art shows, supported by art auctions and joyous annual costume parties. The figure classes usually featured a nude female model who was sketched by an audience of male artists. As Katherine Schmidt observed, the Penguin was "just the boys," although eventually there would be a complementary group of Penguinettes.[22] Kuhn was assisted by a core of stalwarts, including Louis Bouché and Wood Gaylor, as well as Albert Gleizes and Jules Pascin, members of the Parisian art world who were sitting out the war in New York. The exhibitions featured some of the most progressive artists in New York, and European modernists as well. One significant exhibition was of the Vorticists, the British avant-garde group, including pieces by sculptor Henri Gaudier-Brzeska, with Wyndham Lewis contributing more than half the seventy-five works. Kuniyoshi wrote about the Penguin years later: "I was terribly excited to be asked to show my work there, along with such artists as Kuhn, Weber, Pascin and several other noteworthy painters. This small but fertile group helped establish the roots of contemporary American painting."[23]

In 1919 he participated in a big Penguin show, and his etching was singled out as "one of the gems of the exhibition" by artist Horace Brodzky, in *Playboy*, a Greenwich Village magazine self-described as "A Portfolio of Art and Satire." Brodzky wrote that Kuniyoshi's print of "a number of old topers around a table is a clever character rendering significantly drawn."[24] This describes Kuniyoshi's etching *Figures around a Table* (about 1916–18), which depicts a scene of alcoholic dissipation with an astonishing economy of line (fig. 9). The tilted space and the drastic cropping of the figure at the top left already manifest some of the eccentricity that characterizes the artist's work of the 1920s. In this small, early work we can see the diagonal spatial construction that is common in Japanese prints, perhaps transmitted through a European modernist like Edgar Degas, combined with the European perspective tradition, seen in the small size of the background figure compared to the seated drinkers. Ashcan school painters, with their love of gritty urban realism, sometimes painted bar scenes, like John Sloan's *McSorley's Bar* (1912), but Kuniyoshi's modest print is closer to Degas's great *Absinthe* (1875–76), with its diagonal construction and dissolute characters (figs. 10, 11). These two well-known paintings present a classic contrast between a clear, Renaissance-derived illusionistic spatial construction and a Japanese-influenced, off-center diagonal composition. Comparing a small, early print with two major paintings may be questionable, but it makes a visual point that will be relevant throughout Kuniyoshi's career. He knew John Sloan, who was a prominent personality at the Art Students League and the teacher of several of Kuniyoshi's friends, while he was also very aware of the impact of Japanese art on Degas's work: "Degas learned a great deal from the Orientals. He had an extraordinary sense in constructing. He used big floor spaces, had faces half cut off."[25] In another early drawing, *Brawl in a Tavern* (1917), Kuniyoshi's line whips around, defining four figures with great spontaneity, as with a few rapid strokes he articulated the two antagonists and the distressed reaction of the woman on the left (fig. 12).

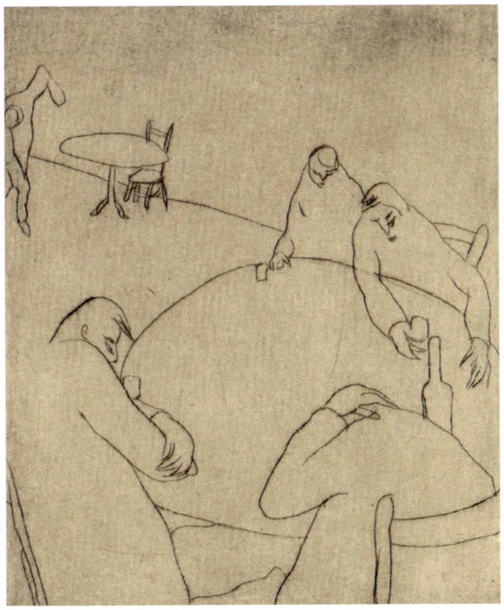

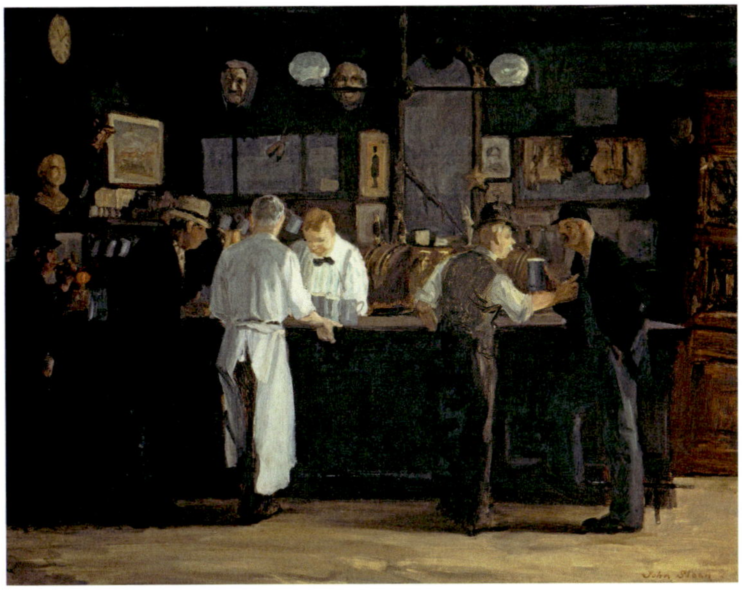

FIG. 9
Yasuo Kuniyoshi, *Figures around a Table*, about 1916–18, etching, 4 15⁄16 × 4 in. Fukutake Collection, Okayama, Japan

FIG. 10
John Sloan, *McSorley's Bar*, 1912, oil on canvas, 26 × 32 in. Detroit Institute of Arts, Founders Society Purchase, General Membership Fund

FIG. 11
Edgar Degas, *In a Café*, also called *Absinthe (Ellen Andrée and Marcellin Desboutin)*, 1875–76, oil on canvas, 36 ¼ × 26 ¾ in. Musée d'Orsay, Paris; Bequest of Count Isaac de Camondo, 1911

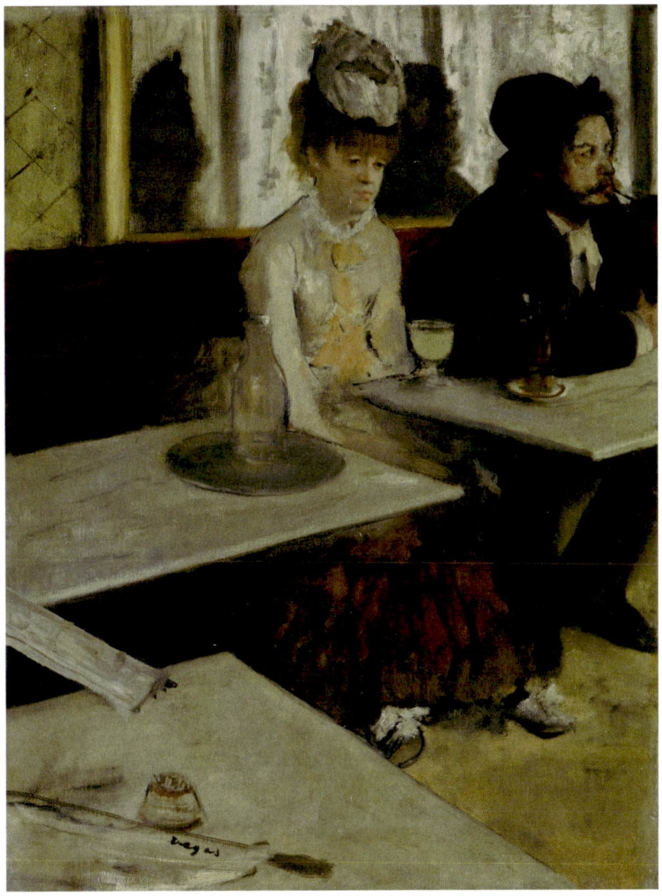

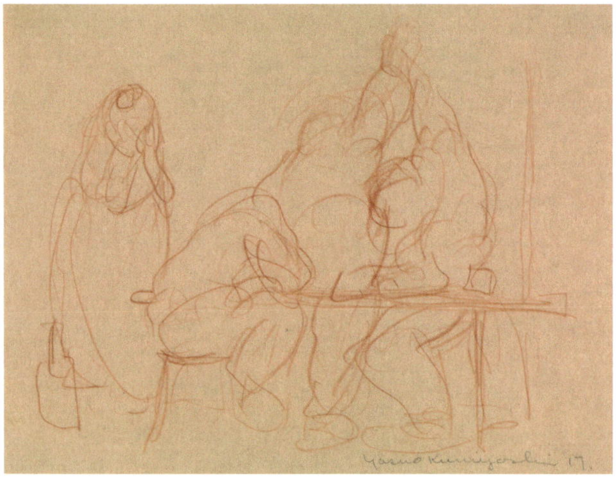

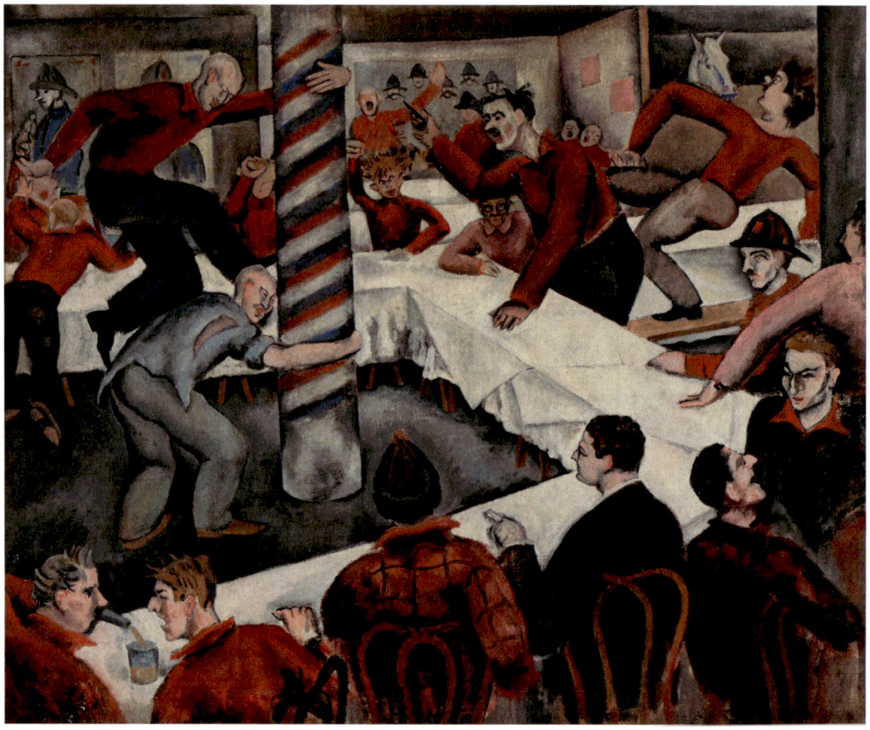

FIG. 12
Yasuo Kuniyoshi, *Brawl in a Tavern*, 1917, sepia crayon on paper, 8 ½ × 11 in. Metropolitan Museum of Art, New York; Bequest of Dorothy Varian, 1986

FIG. 13
Alexander Calder, *Firemen's Dinner for Brancusi*, 1926, oil on burlap, 36 × 42 ⅛ in. Whitney Museum of American Art, New York; Gift of the artist

The Penguin group lasted through 1919 and then revived with an event in 1926, the Firemen's Dinner for Brancusi, memorialized in a painting by the young Alexander Calder (fig. 13). The party, in honor of the Romanian sculptor's visit to New York, was held at the Tip Toe Inn, and judging from accounts and from Calder's painting it was closer to a food fight than a quiet gathering. For the event Penguin artists painted collaborative portraits of firemen and of a famous fire horse, and partiers dressed in firemen's costumes, complete with helmets. When things got rowdy—someone threw a grapefruit and two men started swinging on a fire pole—Bouché rose to reprimand them, which is the moment Calder chose to record. Kuniyoshi, with his characteristic round spectacles, is visible under Bouché's arm, while others in the group include Alexander Brook, Calder (lower left corner), Walt Kuhn, Marsden Hartley, and Art Young.[26]

HAMILTON EASTER FIELD

At his debut at the 1917 Independents exhibition Kuniyoshi met Hamilton Easter Field, an artist, critic, and collector who would have an even greater impact on his career than Kenneth Hayes Miller. Among his many activities, Field was a patron of young artists and an expert about Japanese art. Born to a wealthy

Quaker family, he studied in France in the late nineteenth century, where his relatives included the Havilands, who ran Haviland China in Limoges, a successful business that was early to incorporate Japanese designs into its ceramics. Another relative was Philippe Burty, art critic and member of the impressionist circle, who collected Japanese prints and, around 1872, coined the term "Japonisme."[27] Field caught their enthusiasm, and studied and collected Japanese art in Paris.

When Field returned to the United States he brought around a thousand Japanese prints with him, and established himself as one of the leading experts on Japanese art in the country. In 1920 he founded the *Arts Magazine*, and ran it up to his death from pneumonia two years later. The magazine covered the New York art scene, but Field also saw to it that each issue included an article about Japanese art. Ecumenically responsive to all sorts of art, from the Old Masters to non-Western, he was also very involved with contemporary art. In 1909 he daringly commissioned Picasso to paint a cubist mural for his house, and he actively supported progressive American artists.[28] He was an early appreciator of American folk art; Edith Halpert, who would be Kuniyoshi's dealer in the later part of his career, gave Field credit, calling him "undeniably the pioneer" of the appreciation of American folk art.[29] He recognized the parallels between the flat spaces and unrealistic figures of the folk artists and those in works by avant-garde modernists—for example, writing in 1921 about the eighteenth-century portrait *Catalina Schuyler* by an anonymous artist, Field claimed that it "might almost be a late example of Pablo Picasso."[30]

Field's center of activity was the group of three buildings that he owned overlooking the East River in Brooklyn Heights; he lived there and gave spaces to artists to live and work, including Kuniyoshi and Katherine Schmidt. In one building he created Ardsley Studios, a teaching and exhibition space where he organized innovative shows, including several that juxtaposed Japanese prints with works by American artists, including Winslow Homer, Childe Hassam, John Sloan, and Max Weber. Most of the important contemporary American artists of his time showed at Ardsley Studios, bridging generations from John La Farge to Man Ray, from Childe Hassam to Abraham Walkowitz. Field exhibited prints by Odilon Redon, the late-nineteenth-century fantasist, and paintings by Albert Gleizes, the pioneering French cubist who was active with the Penguin Club in New York.

By coincidence one of Field's favorite Japanese printmakers was also called Kuniyoshi (although the two artists' names are written differently in Japanese): Utagawa Kuniyoshi, the great nineteenth-century ukiyo-e printmaker. Field exhibited twenty-five prints by the elder Kuniyoshi in his Ardsley Studios in 1918, with works by Americans in a neighboring room, advocating a synergy between the two traditions that he would encourage in the younger Kuniyoshi's art as well. Field believed that it was essential for contemporary art to draw on the traditions of non-European cultures: "Surely we are not all so jaded but that we shall find inspiration from these riches, just as the artists of the Renaissance were quickened by the discovery of a few Hellenic originals. . . . For our modern man is no longer a creature of local tradition but a citizen of the world."[31] Kuniyoshi became an exemplar of the melding of traditions that Field advocated, and Field praised Kuniyoshi's achievement: "He has expressed the ideal of modern Japan and of modern America as he has read them fused together in his own heart."[32]

Field's openness to all kinds of art was an example to the Kuniyoshis, reinforced by the fact that the older man was in large part supporting them. He provided the struggling artists with crucial financial assistance for several years, giving them lodging and studio space not only in Brooklyn, but also during the summers in his artists' colony in Ogunquit, Maine, where he presided at Kuniyoshi and Schmidt's wedding in 1919. Around 1910, Field had bought land by the ocean that included a group of fishing shacks, and in subsequent years he let artists use them. The picturesque fishing village was already the site of an art school, created by painter Charles Hawthorne and dating back to 1898. After Field and his protégé, sculptor Robert Laurent, established their Thurnscoe School of Modern Art, it represented the progressive forces of American art in contrast to the more conservative landscape tradition practiced at Hawthorne's establishment; Field's guests included Max Weber, Marsden Hartley and Niles Spencer, among many others.

THE EARLY 1920S

Maine provided a great summer escape, a healthy environment with distinctive scenery and abundant antiquing for inexpensive American folk art and crafts objects. Many of Kuniyoshi's paintings in this period were inspired by the Maine landscape: the sea, the flora and fauna, the bathers, and the architecture all featured in his artistic breakthrough to his first individual style that happened in the early 1920s. By the time he hit his style Kuniyoshi was highly art literate. Kenneth Hayes Miller had taught him to value the Old Masters, and Field had added appreciation of Asian art. In addition, Kuniyoshi was constantly exposed to European modernism and to the most progressive tendencies in the New York art world through Field, the Society of Independent Artists, the Penguin Club, and his fellow students from the Art Students League. Kuniyoshi's *Landscape*, from 1920, is a transition piece (pl. 2). Here we can see him continuing to reconcile Renoir and Cézanne, with the soft, caressing brushwork of the former, and the spatial paradoxes of the latter. The mountain at the top of the composition could be an homage to one of Cézanne's best-known motifs, Mont Sainte-Victoire, or alternatively to Mount Fuji, which appears so frequently in the history of Japanese art, most famously in Katsushika Hokusai's *Thirty-six Views of Mount Fuji* that some art historians point out anticipated Cézanne's extensive series of views of a specific mountain.[33] The cow in the foreground would become one of Kuniyoshi's trademark images in the 1920s, but here it is still rendered more realistically than those with wedge-shaped heads seen in *Little Joe with Cow* (1923; pl.12). The small woman with the umbrella hovering at the left edge of the canvas introduces an element of fantasy that will continue in Kuniyoshi's art in the 1920s.

Maine Family (about 1922–23) is an example of his new style, where he firmed up the soft forms of *Landscape* and introduced curiously proportioned figures, stocky with tiny appendages (pl. 11). He ignored the rules of Renaissance perspective, disregarding the teachings of Miller and his disciples to create an uptilted space articulated with hard-edged geometric shapes that parallel the modernist simplifications of his contemporaries like Hartley and Spencer. The subtle palette of earth colors will become distinctively Kuniyoshi's, as will the curious mood, slightly comical, slightly wistful. The mother, with her formal hat and dress, stares into space. The big-headed girl holds a hoop to skip with, but instead opts to look directly at us from the middle of the painting, while the crawling baby glances grimly across the scene to the toy animal on the other side. There is no father, as is the case in several paintings about familial subjects Kuniyoshi painted in this period (*Three Generations*, 1918–20, and *Sisters*, 1920, both in Gallery Nii, Osaka). He was in his early thirties and had not seen his family in fifteen years. He had also started taking four years off his age, claiming to be born in 1893 instead of 1889.

Over the next few years Kuniyoshi embarked on an extraordinary creative run, painting a series of unique works that continue the stylistic characteristics developed in *Maine Family*. *Dream* (1922) features a snake looped around an outsize bush

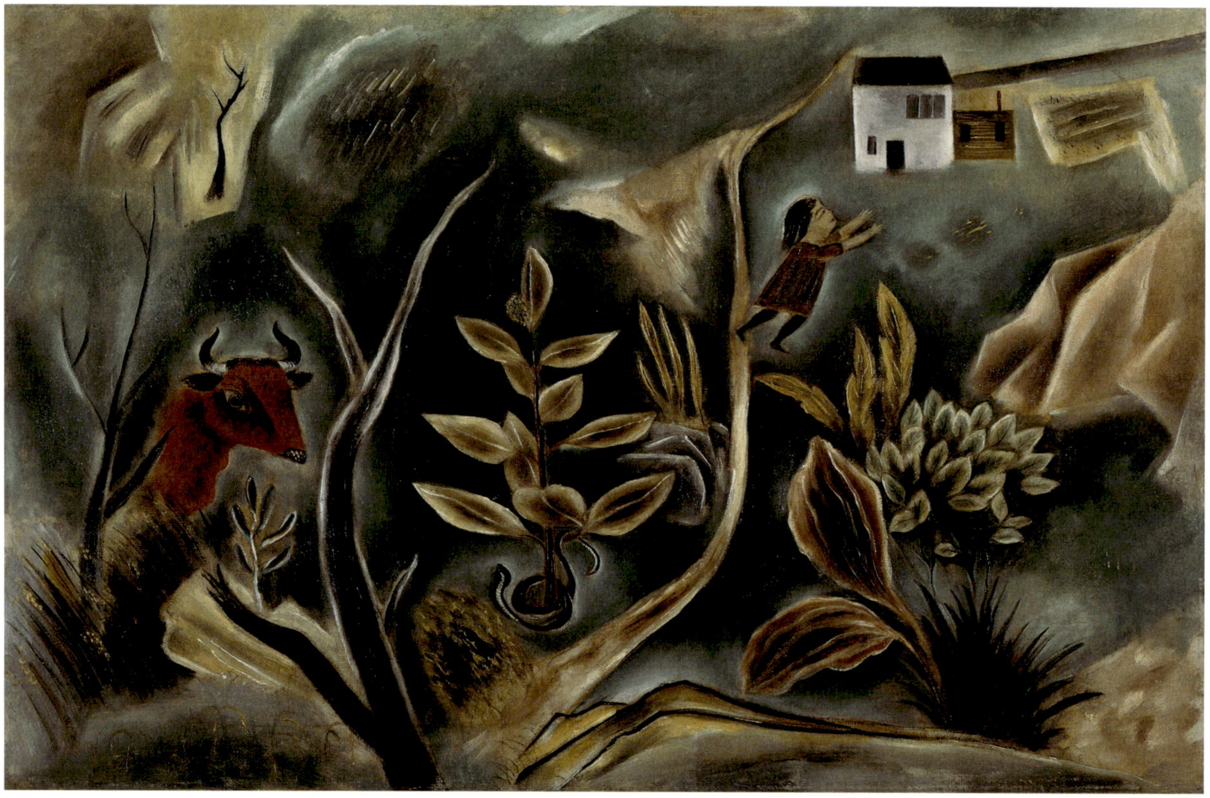

FIG. 14
Yasuo Kuniyoshi, *Dream*, 1922, oil on canvas, 20 ¼ × 30 3/16 in. Bridgestone Museum of Art, Ishibashi Foundation, Tokyo

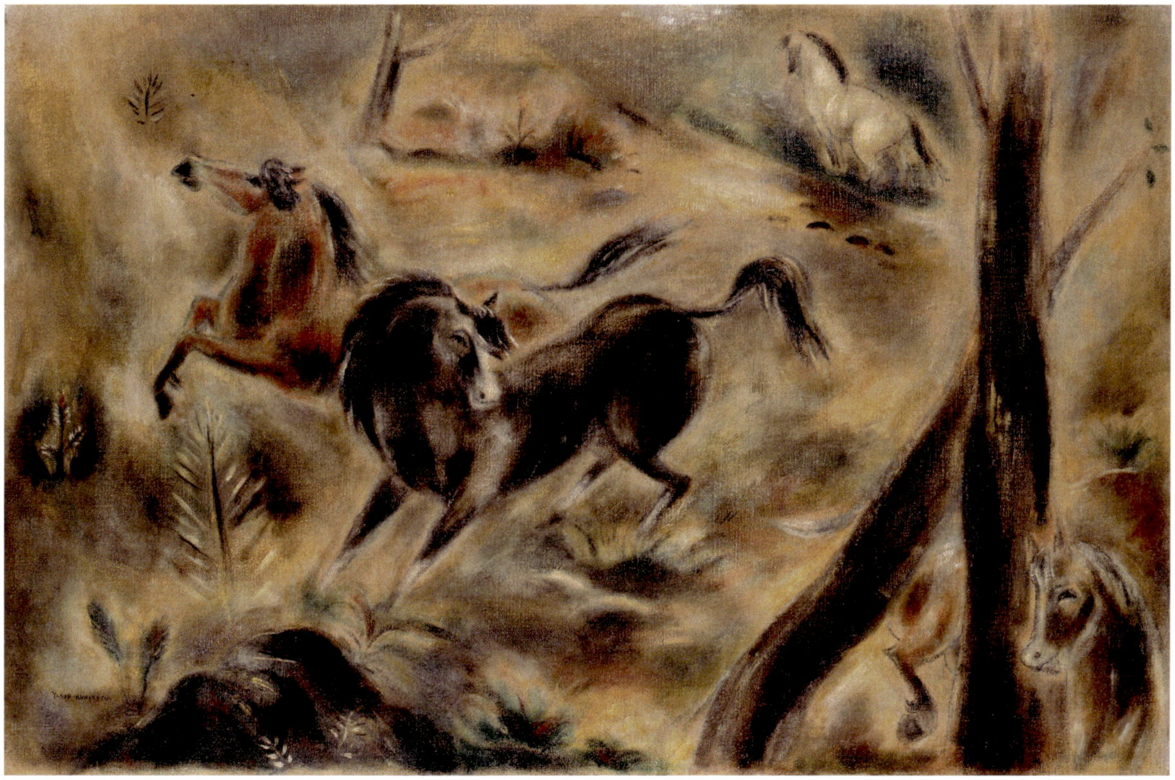

FIG. 15
Yasuo Kuniyoshi, *Wild Horses*, 1921, oil on canvas, 20 1/16 × 30 1/16 in. Fukutake Collection, Okayama, Japan

in the center, and a small girl floating as if sleepwalking on the right, both the subject of the dream and its dreamer (fig. 14). A Kuniyoshi cow with a trowel-shaped head and human eye emerges out of an undefined space on the left, a benign presence presiding over this unreal scene. *Upstream* (1922) depicts a stolid couple rowing improbably up a vertical stream, surrounded by fish, which will be a recurrent presence in Kuniyoshi's work (pl. 10). For example, in *Adam and Eve (The Fall of Man)*, Kuniyoshi took on a venerable subject of European religious art and promptly broke with tradition by having Adam half-immersed in a pond, holding a fish in his hand (1922; pl. 9); the first man seems to debate if he wants to let it go to take the fruit Eve is offering. Besides the fish, Kuniyoshi's Eden is populated with various swimming and crawling creatures, from the grasshopper at Eve's feet to the amphibians swimming around Adam—not the staffage of a traditional Temptation scene. A bird dive-bombs Adam, as if to warn him of what is coming, while a two-headed snake slithers toward Eve. At the right a typical Kuniyoshi cow looks on: it has a pointed back and a spade-shaped head with a human eye. Because of its small size we understand it is in the background, but otherwise there are no spatial cues to locate it. The cow, literally smaller than the bush at the bottom center, contributes to the strange space that Kuniyoshi constructed for this painting.

Adam and Eve evinces a new confidence and firmness of form in Kuniyoshi's art, reflecting the respect he was getting after his first one-person exhibition in 1922 at the Daniel Gallery, the gallery that would represent him for ten years. The exhibition of ten paintings and several drawings, mostly inspired by rural life in Maine, was widely reviewed, with comments that ranged from negative to very positive. As would be the case for the rest of Kuniyoshi's career, most critics found ways to relate the works to the artist's Japanese identity. Several noted the confluence of modernist and Asian elements: "With true Asiatic subtlety, and at the same time in perfectly frank and guileless sincerity, he has applied the dynamics of 'cubism' to the flat perspective and synthetic abstraction of Oriental drawing," wrote the critic in the *New York World*.[34] *Wild Horses* (1921) was the painting that got by far the most attention, because its space and subject were more traditional than some of the other paintings, and because the image could be related to a centuries-old theme in Chinese painting (fig. 15).

In tribute to the artist's independence, art critic Henry McBride singled Kuniyoshi out from other Japanese painters working in New York: "It is for one thing, unusual and encouraging to meet with a Japanese who does not paint after the style of Cézanne."[35] The writer in the *Evening Sun* felt "the whole hearted appreciation" Kuniyoshi's show was receiving from hard-to-please art students approached the popularity of Toulouse-Lautrec among connoisseurs in the late nineteenth century.[36]

In *Boy Stealing Fruit* (1923) the artist boldly depicted a subject that may be novel in the history of art (pl. 13). Before a window that looks out onto a landscape of simplified, geometric shapes inspired by Maine's colonial architecture, the boy, who has already grabbed a banana, reaches a greedy hand into the fruit bowl while looking out to check if anyone is watching. Originally titled *Boy Stealing Forbidden Fruit*, it is a secular *Fall of Man* with no Eve necessary to tempt this hungry Adam. A similarly large-headed boy appears again in *Little Joe with Cow*. This was probably the last and the largest of around sixty paintings, drawings, and prints featuring Kuniyoshi's characteristically misshapen cows. The wide-eyed animal with its udder hanging almost to the ground dominates the composition, while two unrealistically large seedpods float behind her hindquarters. Joe, wearing a suit with short pants, is surrounded by images of fecundity; he almost seems to be growing from a cluster of healthy plants as he distractedly pats the cow. Here the artist combined many of the features that made his work from these years so unusual and appealing: the warm earth tones, golds and greens; the peculiar space, where an entire tree to the left of the cow is dwarfed by a leafy plant next to it; the simplified, pristinely geometrical buildings that contrast with the organic forms around them; and the intriguing mixture of innocence and sophistication in the same commanding painting.

He suggested that he had an innate closeness to the cow: "You see I was born, judging by the Japanese calendar, in a 'cow year.' According to legend I believed my fate to be guided, more or less, by the bovine kingdom." His art was nurtured in the New York art world, but here he offered an explanation rooted in his exotic Asian origins, as he took subjects that were often portrayed as idyllic, such as cows in pastoral landscapes, and distorted them into something unusual and distinctive. Cows were seldom farmed in Japan during his youth. Japanese and Japanese American literature afford recurrent examples of beef being associated with non-Japanese cultures and cows rarely appeared in Japanese art, which made their ungainly proportions that much more intriguing to him.

In his memoir Kuniyoshi explained how he first painted cows and then switched to babies:

> I was interested in the cow because I thought it decorative as well as ugly and so I painted cows constantly until I was exhausted. Following that I turned to babies. People think that babies are beautiful, but I thought otherwise and so I painted babies and babies.[37]

In the small painting *Child* (1922) a serious infant with an improbably large head and tiny extremities pushes a curtain (fig. 16). The stubby proportions of the child contrast with the linear delicacy of the black-and-white decoration of the vase in front of it, which the artist studied in an independent, finished ink drawing. A second painting titled *Child* (1923) evokes American folk art more overtly than most of Kuniyoshi's paintings (fig. 17).[38] The formally posed, sharply outlined youth resembles any number of stiff nineteenth-century portraits of children. The white stoneware vase on the table is an anonymous nineteenth-century collectible, one of many that appear in Kuniyoshi's works of the 1920s. Folk art was rapidly becoming popular among progressive American artists. In 1924 the first exhibition of folk art in the United States was held at the Whitney Studio Club; organized by Henry Schnakenberg, it included loans from both Kuniyoshi and Katherine Schmidt. It was one of a series of artist-curated exhibitions at the galleries that would become the Whitney Museum of American Art. They included a show curated by Alexander Brook that marked the first time José Clemente Orozco exhibited in the United States (Brook paired him with the caricaturist Miguel Covarrubias), and Charles Sheeler curated a show that included major paintings by Marcel Duchamp, as well as works by Marius de Zayas and Picasso. Kuniyoshi also curated a show on view in April 1924: an exhibition of portraits and religious paintings. It was a strange choice for him, since he did few portraits or religious paintings. The religious works were by an outsider artist from New Jersey, John Mauro, whose contributions included a floor-to-ceiling *Crucifixion*. The portraits were a heterogeneous group, featuring several works by Parisians, including Matisse and Raoul Dufy, as well as Americans such as Vincent Canade and Joseph Stella; seven women artists were included among the portrait painters.[39] In later years Kuniyoshi acknowledged the connection between European avant-garde painting and folk art that played a role in his taste in the 1920s: "I liked decorative work of Campendonk, Kandinsky, Chagall then, and early

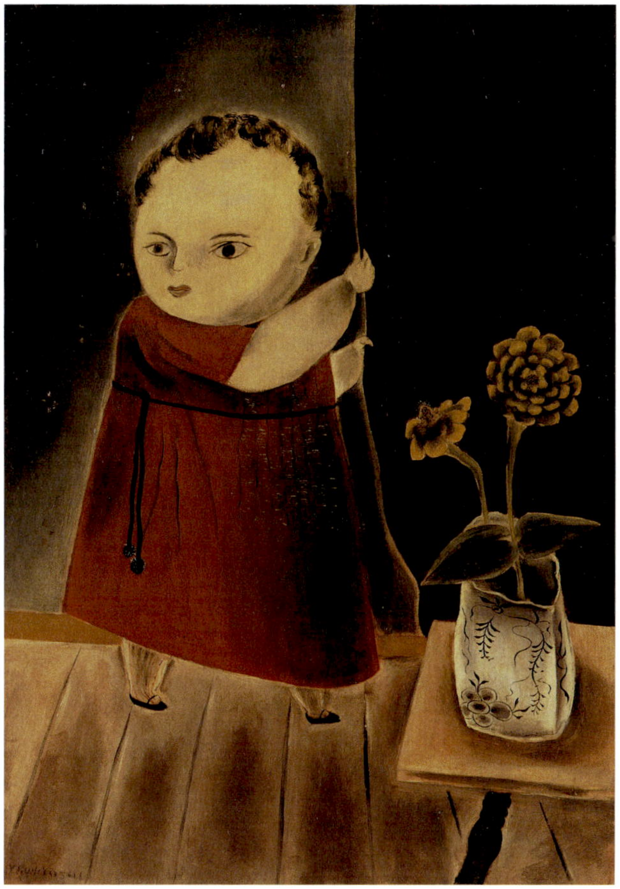

FIG. 16
Yasuo Kuniyoshi, *Child*, 1922, oil on canvas, 22 ¼ × 15 3⁄16 in. Okayama Prefectural Museum of Art, Japan

FIG. 17
Yasuo Kuniyoshi, *Child*, 1923, oil on linen, 30 ⅛ × 24 3⁄16 in. Whitney Museum of American Art, New York; Gift of Mrs. Edith Gregor Halpert

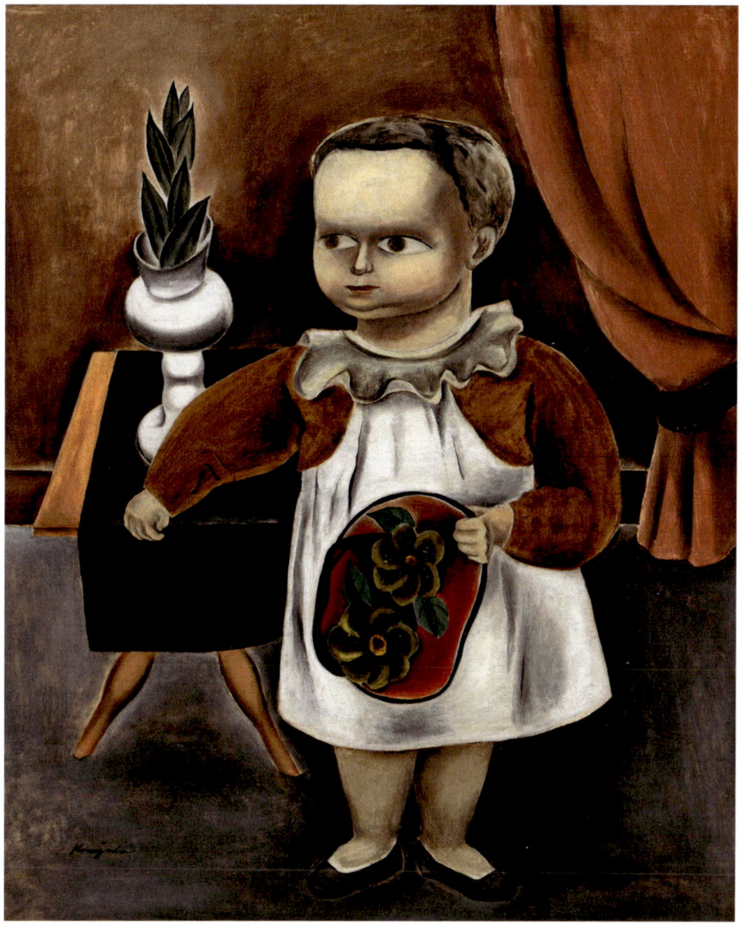

American painting, its design and color."[40] This was not the first time Kuniyoshi's early work had been associated with German Expressionism as well as folk art. At the time of his first show at Daniel in 1922 several critics saw a relationship with the distorted figures in the paintings of Albert Bloch, an American living in Germany and affiliated with Der Blaue Reiter group, whose exhibition at Daniel immediately preceded Kuniyoshi's.[41]

Although he was commanding a lot of respect and had Field's support, Yasuo and Katherine still had little money. She managed at the Art Students League lunchroom for two years, and then became an assistant to Juliana Force, the energetic deputy of Gertrude Vanderbilt Whitney, at the Whitney Studio Club. Katherine ran the sketch club there, and helped Force manage the institution that would evolve into the Whitney Museum of American Art. Yasuo taught himself photography and worked as an art photographer, lugging his heavy camera equipment to galleries and artists' studios. His remarkable *Self-Portrait as a Photographer* (1924) is the second of the four

FIG. 18
Yasuo Kuniyoshi, *Boy Frightened by Snake*, 1921–22; location unknown

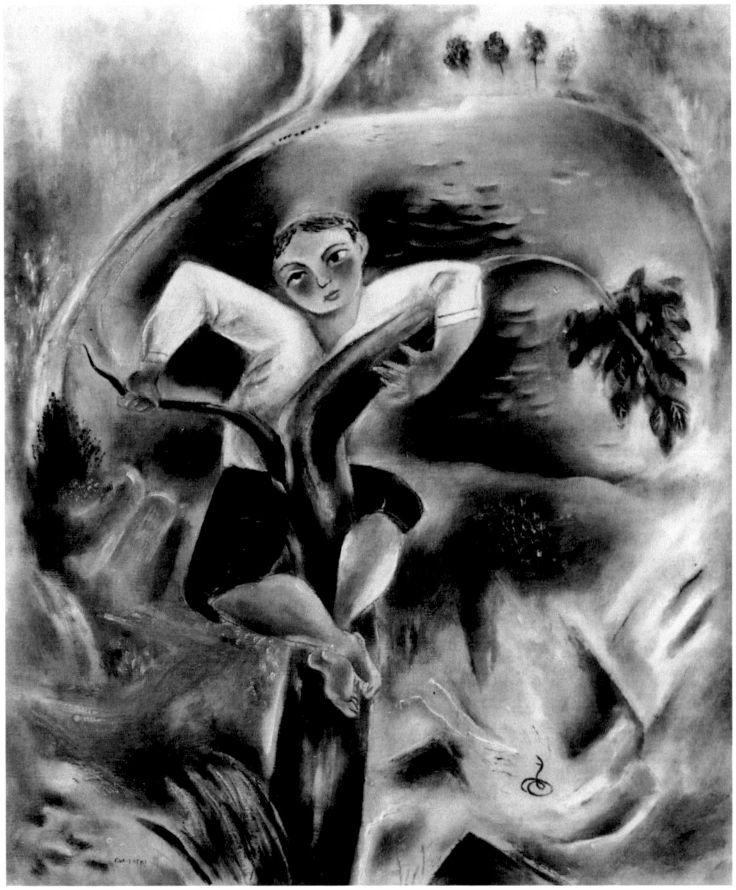

FIG. 19
Yasuo Kuniyoshi, *The Shore*, 1923; location unknown

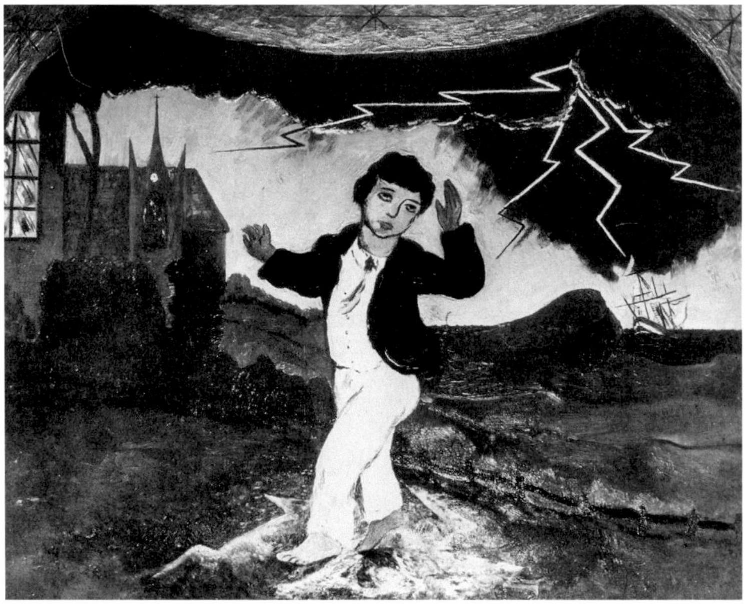

self-portraits he would paint during his career (pl. 23). He stands behind his camera ready to snap a photo, his head twisted to look out at us, his right hand above his head inexplicably pointing forward. In contrast to contemporary photographs of him, he boldly exaggerated his Asian facial features, particularly the prominent cheekbones (see fig. 5). Critics at the time likened his hooded appearance to a priest or a monk, yet he is involved with the modern technology of the camera.[42] He set up a complex pun in the painting: the camera points at a landscape, but it is unclear whether Kuniyoshi is photographing the view outside a window, or photographing a painting of a landscape, as he did professionally. In addition, he rendered the landscape in monochrome shades of gray, as if to forecast the black-and-white photograph he is in the process of taking. Although Kuniyoshi has often been thought of as a straight, unintellectual painter, this is only one example of the conceptually intricate subjects we will see in his art.

In addition to such brainteasing images, Kuniyoshi also explored emotion, in a series of paintings he made in the 1920s on the subject of fear. Several important pieces are lost, which is the case for a surprising number of his early works. These include *Boy Frightened by Snake* (1921–22; fig. 18) and the drawing *Boy Frightened by Lightning*. The latter relates to a lost painting, *The Shore*, known only by a reproduction from an art magazine from 1923 (fig. 19).[43] Here Kuniyoshi drew the boy, alarmed by a storm, with his face, body, and extremities in normal proportions, unlike the swollen heads and diminutive appendages that were so distinctive in paintings like *Child Frightened by Water* (1924), another of his works about fear (pl. 22). The stocky mother and son are half-submerged in the ocean, the lighthouse behind them inspired by Maine landscapes. The child's fright is understated, expressed mostly by his wide eyes and tight mouth; we are made aware of it mostly thanks to the title of the painting. Marcel Duchamp said that adding a title to a work of art is like adding another color, and in these works Kuniyoshi's titles contribute an essential layer of meaning. With *Sisters Frightened by a Whale* (1923) he again came up with a subject unique in the history of art (pl. 15). Two nude young women, a bit misshapen but definitely curvy, hold hands while standing in the water, while the whale swims by in the distance. The subject is the remote descendant of some of the most dramatic and terrifying ancestors in the history of American art and literature, paintings like John Singleton Copley's *Watson and the Shark* (1778), Albert Pinkham Ryder's *Jonah* (about 1885–95), and Herman Melville's novel *Moby-Dick* (1851). The distance from them to Kuniyoshi's quirky sisters serves to illustrate the idiosyncratic peculiarity of his art. While one cannot determine with certainty what motivated him to create these unusual scenes of fear, they coincide with his sudden emergence from anonymity to becoming well known in the art world. In general, reviews of his work were positive, but there were also hostile ones. His anxious subjects also appeared at the time that the U.S. government was enacting the Asian Exclusion Act of 1924, which made it illegal for people from Asia to immigrate to the United States, responding to the advocates of eugenics who believed that the innate superiority of white races who descended from northern European countries would be compromised by intermarriage. Immigration for Asians was already limited, and now it was entirely restricted, marooning Kuniyoshi and his small band of Japanese artist friends in New York, with no more colleagues coming from Asia to join them. While these were grim aspects to his life in the United States, his career was on the rise, and he was a fun-loving person with a sense of humor who liked to party—as suggested by a photograph of him laughing at a costume party, a whiskey glass in one hand and Katherine Schmidt perched on his knee, a cutout replica of his painting of a rooster above them (fig. 20).

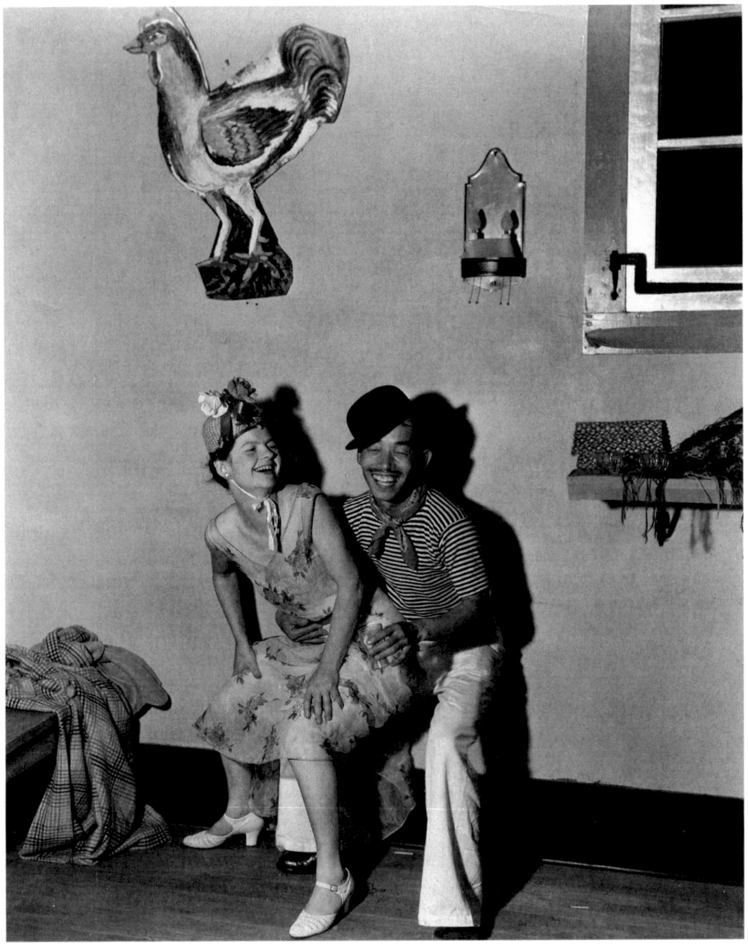

FIG. 20
Stowall Studios, *Yasuo Kuniyoshi and Katherine Schmidt*, mid-1920s, photographic print, 10 1/5 × 7 4/5 in. Rosalie Berkowitz collection of photographs, Archives of American Art, Smithsonian Institution

When Kuniyoshi wrote that after painting cows "I painted babies and babies," he could have added that after babies he turned to babes—voluptuous, if peculiarly proportioned, women began appearing in his art in 1923. As we have seen, the artist often created images that he depicted only a few times, unlike, for instance, his esteemed older contemporary, John Marin, who painted seascapes over and over during these years. Kuniyoshi's *Island of Happiness* (1924) is an image of a stocky nude, floating as if in a dream (pl. 24). She is encircled by a womb-like island and surrounded by undulating plants and moist marine creatures in a compelling evocation of fertility; a slender tree issues from her protruding belly like an umbilical cord. In an interior scene, *Girl on a Sofa* (1925) stares coolly at us as she reclines on a chaise, seemingly unconcerned that her slip has come off her shoulder exposing her breast (pl. 28). The diagonal, off-center perspective, reminiscent of compositional practices in Japanese prints, and the abrupt cropping of her legs by the bottom edge of the painting set her apart from the more conventional nudes painted by Kuniyoshi's contemporaries like John Sloan, Alexander Brook, and Bernard Karfiol, to name a few. The pack of Camel cigarettes at the right adds a proto-pop image of twentieth-century advertising culture to the scene, comparable to the billboards in paintings by the artist's friend Reginald Marsh, while the cigarette that thrusts out of the pack, plus the three erect pears next to it, add a suggestively male element to the ensemble.

Circus Girl Resting (1925) also has her slip coming off, as she smiles a faint smile while inexplicably holding up the curtain behind her (pl. 25). Perhaps she is preparing to tip over the bowl of curvaceous fruit that rests on it? More than twenty years later her heavy proportions would make her the target of conservative right-wing politicians, but in 1925 she was a calmly bemused sister to the girl on the sofa. The two paintings share the rich palette of warm earth colors for which the artist was known, and also exemplify his evolution from the innocence of his earlier works into something racier—as critic Forbes Watson wrote about *Circus Girl Resting*, "Mr. Kuniyoshi has painted a pair of stockings that may bring him orders from sources not strictly artistic."[44]

Kuniyoshi's shows at Daniel received steady attention in the press, usually favorable. The artist later stated in his memoir that he was amazed that people saw him as a humorist, but critics of Kuniyoshi's 1920s Daniel Gallery shows frequently complimented the humor they found in his work, a subtle, understated wit that is difficult to articulate but which still communicates to viewers today. As Alexander Brook wrote, "What actually motivates his thoughts is difficult to ascertain but no conjecture seems too far-fetched."[45] Kuniyoshi's 1921 drawing *The Widow* is an adult joke: its uneasy, properly dressed figure stands under her parasol while in the space above her, two dogs copulate—an image of what the widow is missing (pl. 4)? It is rendered with his customary finesse—a decorative play of patterns and spatial cues—but the contrast between the serious woman and the uninhibitedly carnal dogs gives a shock that is funny, if off-color. Many friends and acquaintances experienced Kuniyoshi's humor in person, and commented that he was great fun to be with. Humor is famously hard to pin down, and in Kuniyoshi's case his critics' attempts sometimes reveal the arbitrariness of racial, national, or ethnic stereotypes: the *Evening Post* declared, "The wall between the Orient and the Occident is especially firm where humor is concerned and no sort of osmosis seems to go on. It is regrettable . . . that I do not get the humor in his work," blaming Kuniyoshi's Asian origins for the writer's lack of response. In direct contrast the critic in the *Brooklyn Eagle* described the art as having an "illusive quality of Japanese technique combined with American humor."[46]

Reviews, no matter how short, mentioned that the artist was Japanese, and the writers usually tried to characterize Japanese elements in his art, often resorting to generalizations such as "aloofness," "detachment," "subtlety," "refinement," and "attention to detail." The critic in the Sunday *World* felt "His art could not come from a Western mind."[47] Critics described their impressions of the melding of cultures in Kuniyoshi's art in various ways. Some recognized a similarity between Asian nonrealist artistic traditions and modernist abstraction, and some cited the confluence of Asian practices and folk art ("half Japanese, half Early American").[48] Many also pointed out the originality of his art, for example the critic for the *Tribune* who wrote, "The modernist point of view was never more curiously personal in its manifestations."[49] In 1922, writer William Murrell included Kuniyoshi in a series of small monographic books he published about contemporary artists. He argued, accurately in my opinion, "Yasuo Kuniyoshi is perhaps the only Japanese now painting in America whose work is free from both Oriental and Occidental influences as such; the single instance of a selective blending of dynamic elements from two great traditions into a style distinctly original."[50] Kuniyoshi was getting a lot of encouragement for his cross-cultural fusion, starting with his patron, Hamilton Easter Field. The critics also usually agreed that Kuniyoshi's remarkable black ink drawings were among his most accomplished works.

INK DRAWINGS OF THE 1920s

One group of these striking monochromatic pieces is made up of sensuous still lifes of fruit or plants. In *Squash* (1924) the artist created a monumental image of the lumpy vegetable, modeling its light and shade with sensitive gradations of graphite that play against the deep black ink that encircles them (pl. 16).

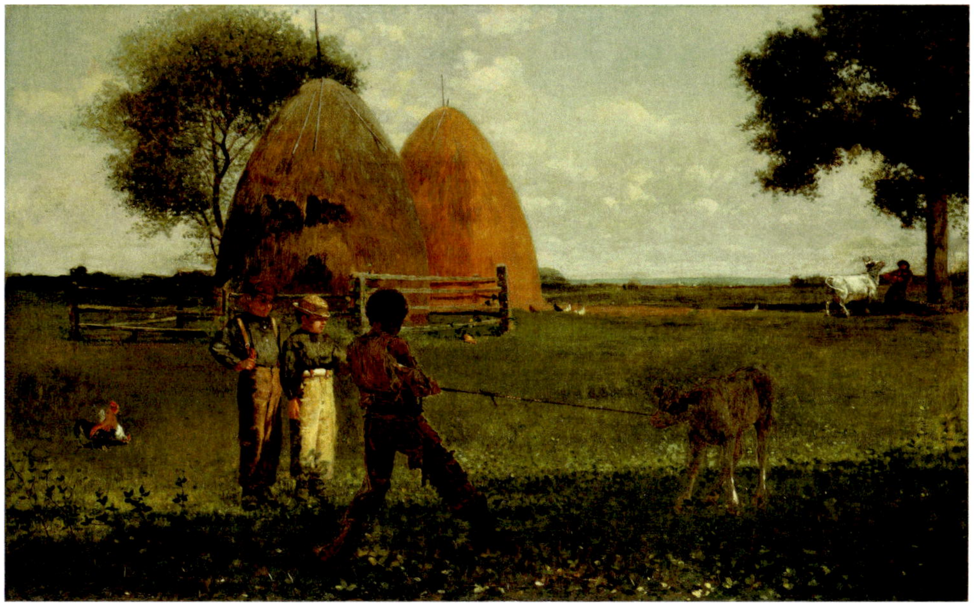

FIG. 21
Winslow Homer,
Weaning the Calf, 1875,
oil on canvas, 24 × 38 in.
North Carolina Museum
of Art, Raleigh;
Purchased with funds
from the State of North
Carolina

Its rotund bumpiness floats against the absolute whiteness of the paper, a distilled statement that sets the three-dimensional illusionism of the European Renaissance against the flatness characteristic of Japanese art, American folk art, and European modernism. In some of these drawings, such as *Squash* and *Orange* (1925), the artist added a touch of warm color (pl. 26). In *Orange* he played the fruit's weighty corporeality against a dramatic single line, which sweeps across the top of the composition to define a round table. *Remains of Lunch* (1922), with its elegant plate and dainty dessert spoon, includes a cigarette butt stubbed out on the delicate dish and two pears leaning into each other, a still life redolent of bohemian life in Greenwich Village, far from the farms of Maine (pl. 6). Here, as in most of these drawings, Kuniyoshi used a visceral technique of putting down areas of thick black ink and then scratching through them to the white paper underneath to create tactile highlights. He may have seen this method in some of the drawings of George Bellows, who taught at the Art Students League, but Kuniyoshi brought it to new heights of refinement and sensuality.

In addition to still lifes, the artist made ink drawings of plants seen close-up in landscapes. In *Lady Slipper* (1924) he emphasized the erotic heat of the plant's engorged sac by tinting it yellow in contrast to the monochrome of the rest of the scene (pl. 19). His space is also expressive: the plant seems enormous as it dwarfs an entire tree in the background. Typically he vignetted the scene—no form touches the edges of the white expanse of paper; everything floats in the middle, subverting traditional realist landscape practices. These drawings are highly developed, and the artist made preparatory sketches for them, just as he did for his paintings. Finished black-ink brush paintings are common in centuries of Chinese and Japanese art, and by treating an ink drawing on paper with as much seriousness as an oil painting, Kuniyoshi continued East Asian practices.

The Calf Doesn't Want to Go (1922) is a quirky example of his cow subjects, though he made one painting on the same theme (pl. 8). Again, in the drawing no part of the image touches the edge of the paper, as the stubborn tug-of-war between man and animal is suspended in an imaginary space. Despite the rustic subject, Kuniyoshi rendered the scene with great decorative finesse. The delicate black lines ornamenting the boy's sleeves are reversed in the fine white lines scratched into the black ink of his overalls, and these elegant linear rhythms are echoed in the syncopated treatment of the plants that surround the figures. The boy leans impassively forward as he pulls on the rope, while the cow braces her legs to resist, in a contest that seems specific to Kuniyoshi's art—except in this case there are precedents, such as Winslow Homer's *Weaning the Calf* (1875; fig. 21).[51] Homer was one of the nineteenth-century American artists most esteemed by Hamilton Easter Field, who owned two great watercolors by him that he sometimes showed in his Brooklyn space.[52] Homer's and Kuniyoshi's treatment of the same subject—with the former's defined horizon and clear foreground,

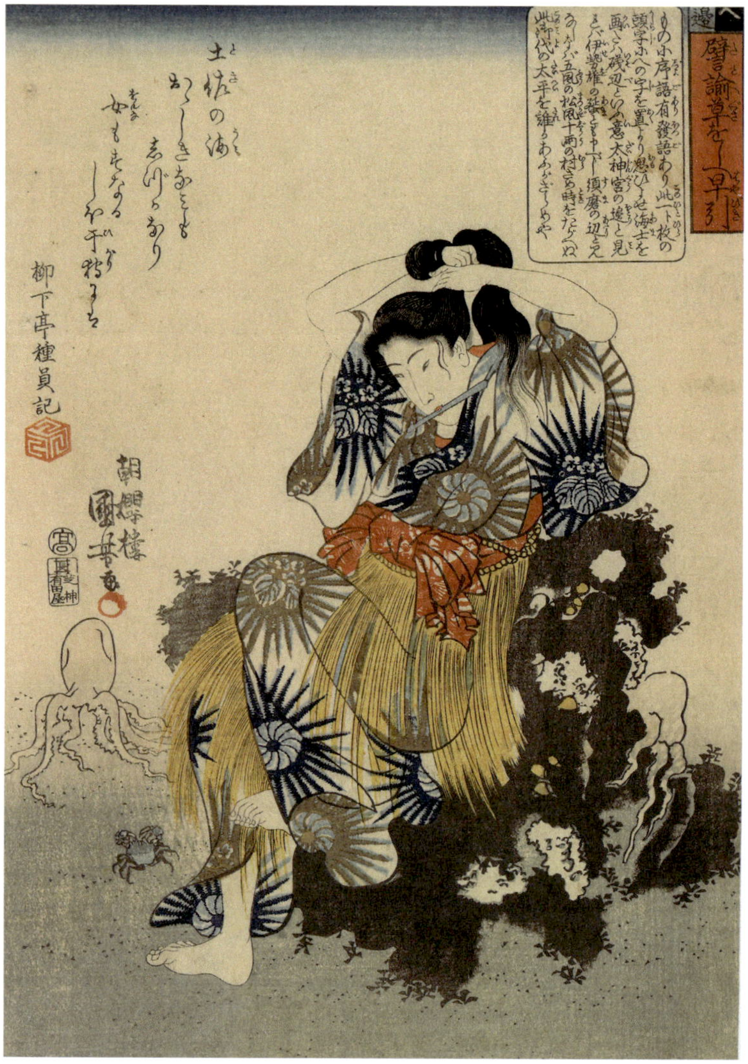

FIG. 22
Utagawa Kuniyoshi, *Fisherwoman on the Shore, An Analogical Dictionary Tatoe gusa no hayabiki Iribe,* about mid-1840s, woodblock print; ink and color on paper, 14 ⅛ × 9 ⅝ in. Arthur M. Sackler Gallery, Smithsonian Institution, Washington, DC; The Anne van Biema Collection

middle ground and sky progression into space, plus the different media—should make it clear why commentators felt there was something Japanese about Kuniyoshi's drawings.

His two largest black ink paintings from the 1920s, *Bad Dream* and *Fisherman,* both from 1924, offer totally different moods (pls. 18, 20). *Bad Dream* is an absurd nightmare: a smiling nude woman in the center is partially immersed in water and surrounded by monstrous, metamorphic creatures enacting semicomic scenes of abduction. It looks forward to surrealism and back to Hieronymus Bosch, but Kuniyoshi added two figures directly taken from Japanese culture. The demon levitating at the right, blowing vapor from his mouth, and the one at the top, emitting lightning and surrounded by a ring of cylindrical drums, are the gods of wind and of thunder who appear frequently in Japanese art, most famously in Tawaraya Sōtatsu's seventeenth-century screens in Kyoto, a National Treasure of Japan.

Fisherman is another wonderfully complex drawing, featuring an astonishing variety of drawing techniques, for example the long, sweeping linear strokes that make up the patch of grass at the far right, juxtaposed with the compressed zigzag lines that render a fuzzy caterpillar crawling on one blade. The floating mountain at top is a staple of Chinese and Japanese landscape painting that will appear many times in Kuniyoshi's art. The fisherman works above a marvelously diverse anthology of sea creatures, as Kuniyoshi's recurrent use of marine imagery links him again to Japanese cultural and artistic traditions. Of course fish appear frequently in Euro-American art, but Japan is an island country, and sea life is commonplace in Japanese imagery and culture in a way that it is not in the West. We have seen that the Venus figure in *Island of Happiness* (see pl. 24) is surrounded by creeping marine animals, a juxtaposition more emphatic in her black ink counterpart, *Sleeping Beauty* (1924), where the recumbent nude is being approached by an octopus whose tentacle is about to touch her breast (pl. 17). You do not find many erotic encounters between women and octopi in Euro-American art, but Kuniyoshi's nineteenth-century predecessor Utagawa Kuniyoshi depicted several in his series about a young ama, a woman pearl diver (fig. 22); the unlikely lovers are also represented in Katsushika Hokusai's well-known erotic print *Girl Diver and Octopi* (1814).[53]

FIRST TRIP TO EUROPE

By 1925 the young Kuniyoshis had gotten together enough money to travel to Europe for over six months, joining many of their American contemporaries who were flocking to Paris. As he wrote to art dealer and print expert Carl Zigrosser, "Anybody that you can think of is here in Paris at present."[54] He had already shown in the big *Exhibition of American Art* there in 1924, organized by the Art Patrons of America to bring recent American art to the attention of the French art public.[55] The exhibition included more than three hundred works, with respected artists like George Bellows and Arthur B. Davies extensively represented. Kuniyoshi showed a baby painting and *Cows in a Pasture* (1923), which featured two of his eccentrically shaped cows juxtaposed with farm buildings flattened out into geometric shapes. Writing about the Paris show, critic Forbes Watson commented,

> I am bound to add that during the course of a dozen visits to the galleries at different times of the day I saw exactly one French person looking with dubious interest at the pictures. The small audience was nearly always made up entirely of Americans.

He concluded that it would have been a better idea to travel the show in the United States, where the same number of French could see it, plus many more Americans.[56] The School of Paris was dominant, and artists from all over the world traveled there to partake of its artistic dynamism. The Kuniyoshis set off for Paris after a raucous farewell party sponsored by Juliana Force. They took an extensive tour of Italy, looking at art of the Old Masters, and then spent the winter in the South of France, in Vence, where they had painting studios, and also visited England. Because of their extensive travels Kuniyoshi produced relatively few paintings in this period, but he had enough for a strong show at Daniel after he returned in 1926. *St. Cloud* (1925) is one of his works inspired by the French countryside (fig. 23). It shares the style of his *Landscape* from the year before: a few architectural forms, rendered as simplified modernist geometries, are lodged among undulant plant shapes and juxtaposed with some contradictory perspectival cues (fig. 24).

St. Cloud is lost and known only through reproductions, but its sky may well have exuded the same uneasy warmth as in *Landscape*, thanks to Kuniyoshi's distinctive brown color scheme. He had developed an individual landscape type, and it influenced some of the lesser-known Japanese American contemporaries who were part of his circle in New York, as is evident in Kiyoshi Shimizu's *Landscape* from around the same time (fig. 25). Shimizu is quite forgotten today, while his brother, Toshi, who was a friend of Kuniyoshi's, has a reputation in Japan because he returned there after working in New York and Paris, and after his death many of his paintings were acquired by the Tochigi Prefectural Museum of Fine Arts, outside Tokyo, where they are often on view. Kiyoshi on the other hand seems to have vanished, but several of his landscapes remain, and they depict the contemporary American scene in subdued colors, with modest buildings simplified to rectangular geometries echoing the modernism of Kuniyoshi's landscapes in the 1920s.

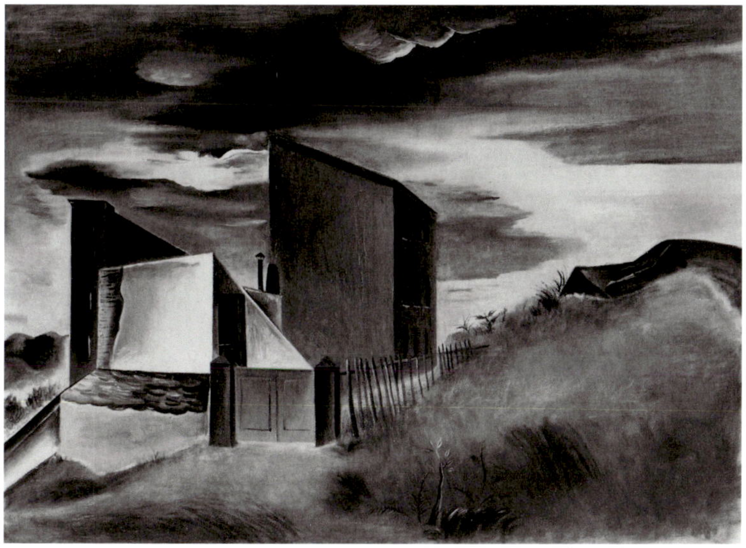

FIG. 23
Yasuo Kuniyoshi,
St. Cloud, 1925;
location unknown

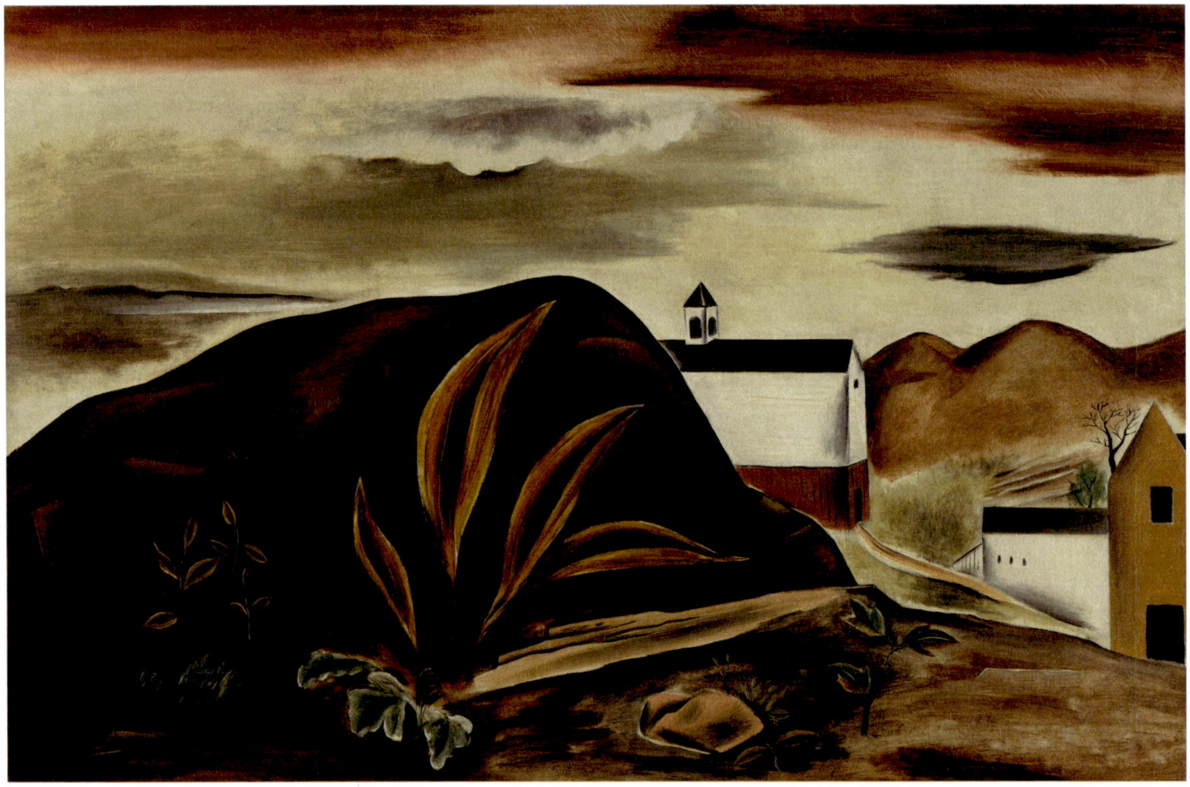

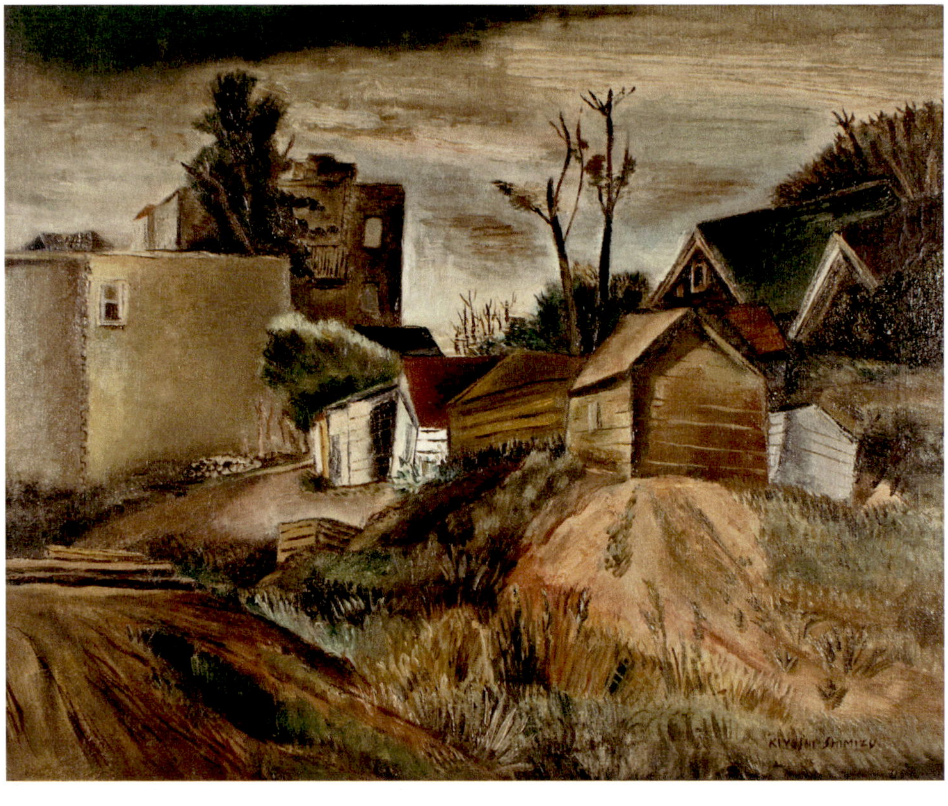

FIG. 24
Yasuo Kuniyoshi, *Landscape*, 1924, oil on linen, 20 ¼ × 30 ⅛ in. Whitney Museum of American Art, New York; purchase

FIG. 25
Kiyoshi Shimizu, *Landscape*, about 1930, oil on canvas, 20 × 24 in. Private collection

FIG. 26
Installation view of *The Circus in Paint* exhibition at the Whitney Studio Galleries, 1929. Photograph by Soichi Sunami

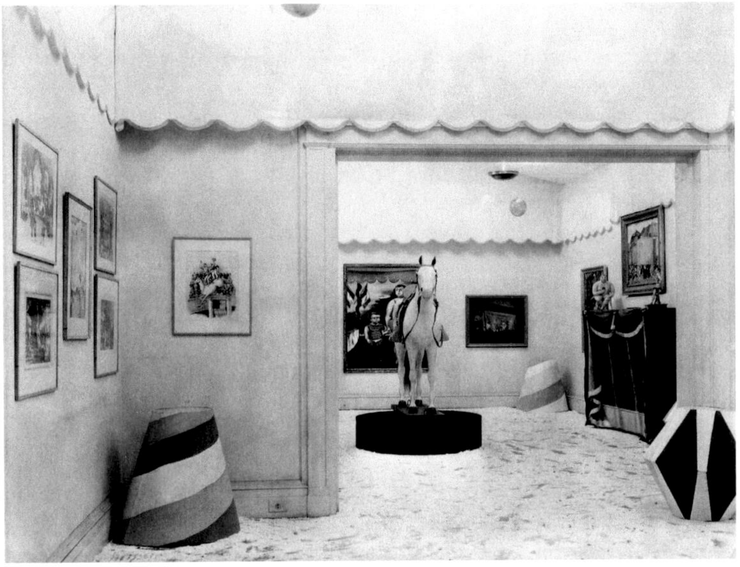

Strong Woman with Child (1925) features one of Kuniyoshi's corpulent women, standing upright with a big barbell between her and a husky boy whose hand she holds, suggesting he is her son, as themes of family and childhood continue in the artist's work (pl. 27). They stand on a platform, with small mansard-roofed buildings appearing abruptly at the right edge of the painting, in homage to French architecture, while the artist toned down the red-white-and-blue French flags hanging at the left with his characteristically muted color. Along with *Circus Girl Resting*, *Strong Woman with Child* introduced the subject of circus performers into Kuniyoshi's art, where it would reappear in many moods and guises for the rest of his career. The circus was an established theme in modern art, and it had an autobiographical element for Kuniyoshi, since during his early days scrambling in New York he sometimes made money by doing a vaudeville act on Broadway, drawing caricatures of Woodrow Wilson.[57] The image of the performer, an alter ego for the artist, either sensitive and alienated or an exemplar of professional skill and daring, descended from paintings of *commedia dell'arte* figures in the eighteenth century. After the circus became popular in the early nineteenth century it became a common theme for artists, including Daumier, with his street performers, Seurat, Toulouse-Lautrec, Picasso, Rouault, and members of the Brücke group of German Expressionists. Among Kuniyoshi's New York contemporaries, Walt Kuhn, the spirit behind the Penguin Club and an organizer of the Armory Show who was in many group shows with Kuniyoshi, was known for his circus subjects. Kuhn became increasingly involved with circus themes in the mid-1920s, as did Alexander Calder, who began his famous *Circus* performances in Paris in 1926. Although Kuniyoshi and Calder were acquaintances rather than friends, and their subjects were realized in different media, their imagery shared a lighthearted mood and a modernist freedom from the realism of earlier generations.

Both Kuniyoshi and Kuhn participated in *The Circus in Paint* exhibition in 1929 at the Whitney Studio Club, which featured Kuniyoshi's *Strong Woman and Child* prominently displayed in a setting that today could be called installation art (fig. 26). The floor was covered with sawdust, the walls painted with circus scenes by Louis Bouché, and brightly decorated circus stands, balloons and a wooden horse were interspersed among the paintings and sculptures, while barrels offered peanuts and popcorn, prefiguring relational aesthetics.[58]

Kuniyoshi's *Self-Portrait as a Golf Player* (1927), third of his four self-portrait paintings, the only full-length and the largest of them, is a major statement of identity—and it is typically original: what other artist in the history of art painted a self-portrait in a golfing outfit (pl. 29)? He dominates the canvas, extending almost its entire height, standing on the golf course, club in hand, golf ball on one side and a sand trap on the other, before a brushy, unrealistically brown sky. His stocky proportions make him seem weighty, but he casts little shadow. A contemporary portrait of the most famous golfer of the time, *Bobby Jones* (1926), by Wayman Adams, who like Kuniyoshi studied briefly with William Merritt Chase and Robert Henri, provides a revealing contrast (fig. 27). Jones stands in the traditional, relaxed *contrapposto* pose that dates back to the ancient Greeks, against a blue sky with white clouds. Kuniyoshi stands with legs akimbo, a stiff pose that recalls traditional Japanese images of actors or samurai. But to claim that these were Kuniyoshi's source is overly simple. It is just as valid to liken *Self-Portrait as a Golf Player* to the sixteenth-century portrait *Vincenzo Anastagi* by El Greco, a painting that entered the Frick Collection in New York in 1913,

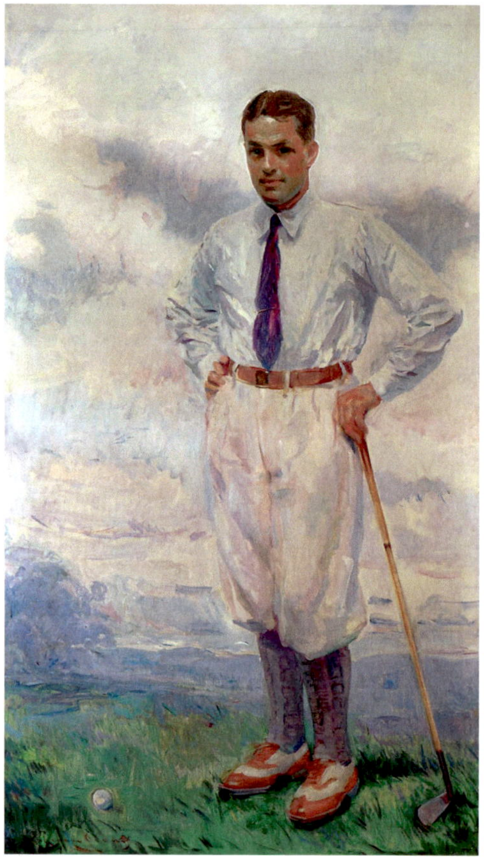

FIG. 27
Wayman Adams, *Bobby Jones*, 1926, oil on canvas, 83 × 52 in. Atlanta Athletic Club, John's Creek, Georgia

FIG. 28
El Greco, *Vincenzo Anastagi*, about 1575, oil on canvas, 74 × 49 ⅞ in. The Frick Collection, New York; Henry Clay Frick Bequest

FIG. 29
Kyohei Inukai, *Self-Portrait with Sword*, 1927, oil on canvas, 72 × 48 in. Private collection

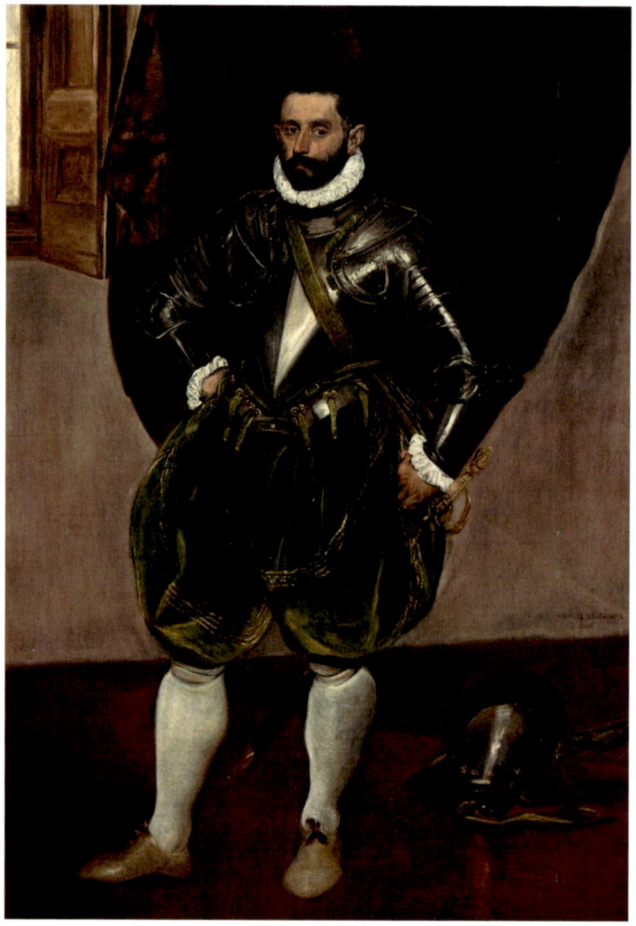

by an artist Kuniyoshi admired greatly (fig. 28). He would tell his students, "You can imitate somebody but don't you ever imitate me because I'm a small fry beside a big guy like El Greco, like Picasso maybe or Matisse."[59] El Greco's reputation was revived in the early twentieth century by the modernists, who admired his expressive departures from Renaissance realism, and he was one of Miller's enthusiasms. His *Anastagi* stands without casting a shadow against a background of warm earth colors, an improbable curtain coming down from the top of the painting to frame him. Kuniyoshi was art historically erudite, and did not favor one tradition or another—the value of his work is in the way it effectively relates to many traditions and still makes an individual statement.

In his *Self-Portrait as a Golf Player*, Kuniyoshi curiously forecast the passion for golf that took over Japan after World War II, depicting himself wearing the conventional golfing attire of the time: a vest and plus fours. In his case, although he enjoyed playing golf in Ogunquit and Woodstock, due to his nationality he "would largely have been excluded from country club life

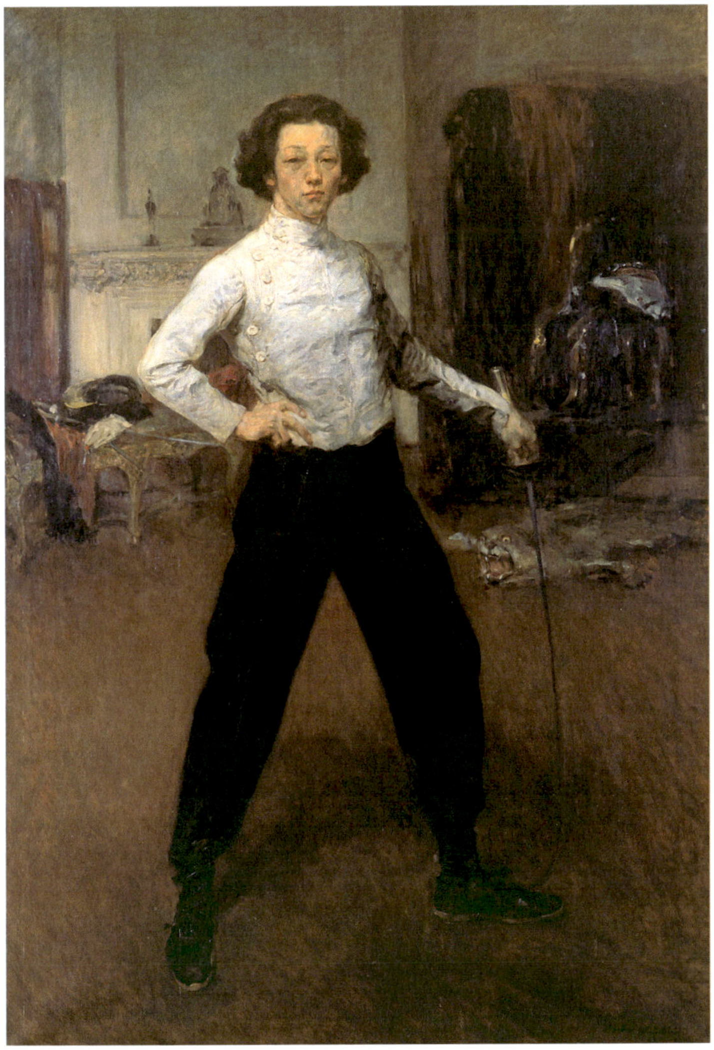

or professional or amateur golf associations either by law or custom."[60] In Woodstock he did not belong to the golf club, but often went as the guest of his fellow painter Eugene Speicher.[61] In the painting Kuniyoshi complicated his American subject by exaggerating his Japanese physiognomy almost to the point of caricature: his cheekbones protrude and his skin is a tawny color that includes the "whites" of his eyes, in contrast to the ruddy pinks and reds of Bobby Jones in Adams's painting. Several commentators at the time pointed out that the deep red-brown of his vest, which dominates the center of the painting, is one of the traditional colors of Japanese lacquer.[62]

Contemporary with Kuniyoshi's painting, Kyohei Inukai's glamorous, large-scale *Self-Portrait with Sword* from 1927 rivals *Self-Portrait as a Golf Player* for assertiveness and ambition (fig. 29). Inukai was an artist in Kuniyoshi's Japanese American circle who delighted in painting self-portraits. Born a year after Kuniyoshi, also in Okayama, he studied art in Chicago, moved to New York, and exhibited with Kuniyoshi in the exhibitions of Japanese artists in New York in the 1920s. Their self-portraits both have autobiographical components: Kuniyoshi enjoyed golf, and Inukai was an expert fencer. But the comparison of the two highlights the strangeness of Kuniyoshi's. Inukai's painting is a bravura exercise in the virtuoso portrait style of John Singer Sargent. His cast shadow locates him clearly in the space of the room; the dramatic tiger skin rug recedes into the distance, creating conventional perspective. The only hints of Asia are in the artist's physiognomy and the sketchily indicated sculpture on the mantel in the background. It is a self-dramatizing and dashing painting, but by the 1920s it represented expert workmanship in an established style deriving from Sargent that progressive artists had moved beyond, unlike Kuniyoshi's more individualistic work.

RETURN TO PARIS

In 1928 the Kuniyoshis returned to Europe for their second extended stay, a trip that would lead to decisive changes in Kuniyoshi's art. He was already a good friend of Jules Pascin, a celebrated School of Paris painter who had spent the years of World War I in the United States. Unlike Kuniyoshi, as a European he could become a U.S. citizen, which he did. He lived for a while in New York, a neighbor to the Kuniyoshis in the Columbia Heights apartments formerly owned by Hamilton Easter Field. Pascin, who was active with the Penguin Club, was a famous party animal, generously using the proceeds from his many exhibitions to finance late-night outings to bars and cabarets. He befriended the madam of a brothel when he was a teenager, and started publishing caricatures in the German satirical magazine *Simplicissimus* around the same time. His art took the bars, brothels, and women of Paris as its subject, in the tradition of Toulouse-Lautrec, and Degas before him. He drew and painted constantly, and, like many School of Paris artists, he often worked from a posed model. A typical Pascin painting would be of a scantily dressed young woman (or two, or three) lounging on a chair or a couch (fig. 30). He also made elaborate, multifigured compositions, sometimes satirical, sometimes erotic, often both. That Kuniyoshi was impressed by Pascin is evident in his new interest in working from life, and in his increased concern with bohemian and erotic subjects in this phase of his career.

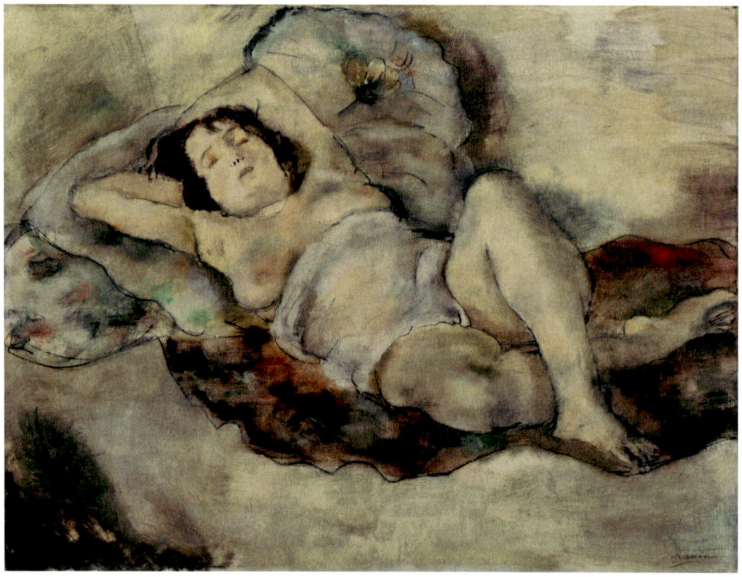

Kuniyoshi stayed in Paris for more than half a year, with some side trips, and devoted himself mostly to making lithographs. He was already experienced with printmaking, having made a group of etchings in 1917–18 at the Art Students League, but lithography would become his chosen print medium; its soft, sensuous marks fit his painterly sensibility. He drew his first lithograph in 1923 in New York, and in 1927 he made twenty-two more, mostly tabletop still lifes of flowers or fruit, printed by George Miller at the League. In Paris in the 1920s many American artists were drawn to the print shop of Edmond Desjobert, including Stuart Davis, Adolf Dehn, Louis Lozowick, Reginald Marsh, and Andrée Ruellan. At Desjobert lithographs were printed from stone, not the zinc plates used by George Miller, and they characteristically were *chine-collé*—prints on very fine sheets of paper that were then adhered to a thicker, supporting paper. Kuniyoshi responded to the hospitality of the atelier and the delicacy of the stone medium and made twenty-four prints during his Parisian sojourn. Pascin urged him to move to Paris permanently, and Katherine Schmidt explained the appeal of this idea to interviewer Paul Cummings:

> Schmidt: Well, there was Foujita who was making a darn good living in Paris. And it was easier to live there. In those years there was a great deal of anti-Japanese feeling in this country. And if you were married to a Japanese you were quite aware of this feeling.
> Cummings: Really? I didn't know that.
> Schmidt: Oh boy, yes![63]

But she was not fond of their bohemian lifestyle in Paris and returned to New York after six months; Kuniyoshi stayed for several months more, before he decided that his real home was in the United States. A year and a half later he was shocked and saddened to learn of Pascin's suicide.

FIG. 30
Jules Pascin, *Reclining Model*, about 1925, oil on canvas, 28 ¾ × 36 ¼ in. Museum of Modern Art, New York; Gift of A. Conger Goodyear

FIG. 31
Tsuguharu Foujita, *Nude Stretching Out with a Cat*, 1921, oil on canvas. Petit Palais, Geneva

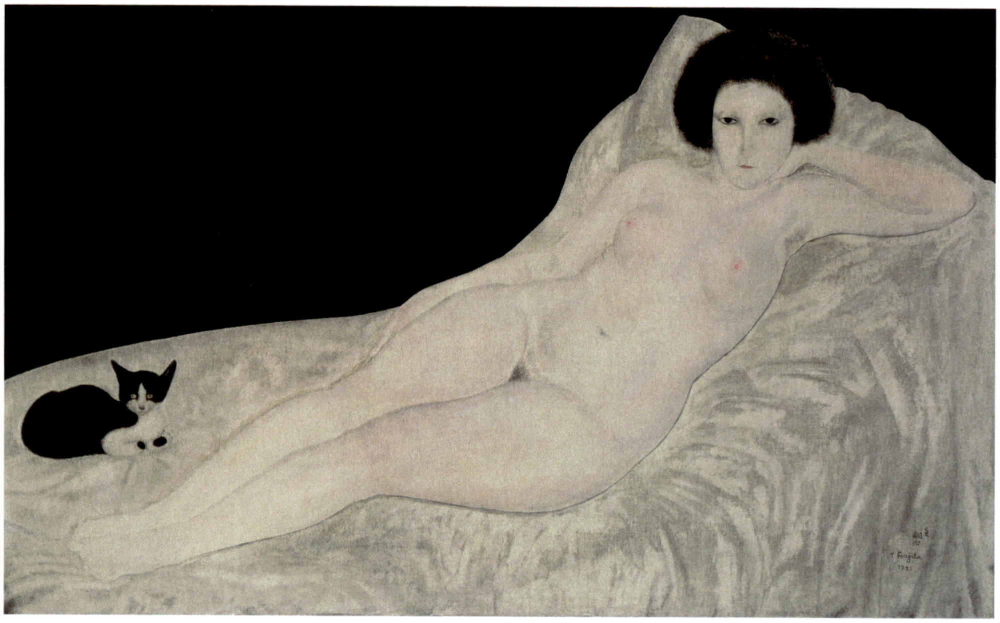

When I interviewed artist Andrée Ruellan at her home in Woodstock, New York, in 1986 about her times in Paris in the 1920s, she remembered walking through the Tuileries Garden with Kuniyoshi and two young Japanese artists who spoke Japanese with him the entire time. Artists from around the world were drawn to Paris, and Kuniyoshi again found himself in the company of fellow countrymen, some of them there by way of New York. He was fast becoming the center of a group of expatriate Japanese artists in New York, and in Paris Tsuguharu Foujita occupied a similar role, as the most esteemed Japanese artist in the city, a magnet for others. So it was natural for Kuniyoshi to get to know Foujita, who specialized in paintings of cats and sensuous, erotic nudes (fig. 31). Few details of their acquaintance have come to light, but Kuniyoshi introduced Foujita to Alexander Calder, and Foujita would go on to assist the American sculptor with some of the early performances of his famous *Circus*. A few years later, in 1931, when Kuniyoshi took his one trip back to Japan, Foujita helped him with a supportive letter of introduction, as the international network of Japanese expatriate artists again went into action.

When Katherine Schmidt returned to New York, she took with her prints of all twenty-four lithographs Kuniyoshi had made at Atelier Desjobert for a show at the Daniel Gallery. The exhibition was well received on the whole, critics appreciating the nuanced tonal values in the black-and-white lithographs, though quite a few were taken aback by his images of French prostitutes. *Dancing* (1928) features an accordion player serenading a woman wearing just a slip, and a lumpy nude woman dancing with a man in a bowler hat, an item of clothing associated with Pascin (fig. 32). There were several prints of solitary sultry women, and critic Murdock Pemberton wrote in the *New Yorker*, "The American, reared to the Puritan ideal of womanhood, will find himself somewhat shocked at the grosser manifestations of nature as chronicled by Kuniyoshi," a prediction borne out by the critic in the *American* who complained about Kuniyoshi's "deplorable lack of taste."[64] Such subjects comprised fewer than half of the twenty-four, the rest of which consisted of handsome still lifes, images of confident women circus performers, several Parisian cityscapes with railroad tracks, and two bullfight scenes inspired by a visit to Spain that the critics found particularly appealing.

FIG. 32
Yasuo Kuniyoshi, *Dancing*, 1928, lithograph, composition: 11 ⅝ × 10 ¼ in.; sheet: 18 ¼ × 12 13/16 in. Museum of Modern Art, New York; Given anonymously

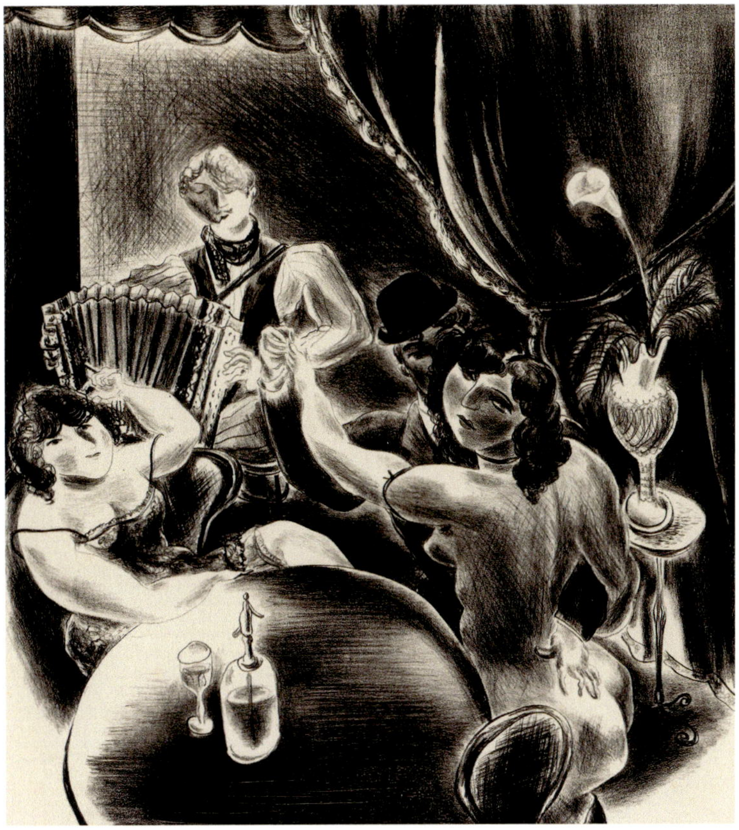

BACK IN THE U.S.A.

By the late 1920s, Kuniyoshi had gone from being an unknown painter at the start of the decade to being accepted as an important artist even by his detractors. His prestige was further enhanced when Julius Meier-Graefe, the influential German critic, came to the United States and included him as one of the four artists he chose to write about (along with Charles Demuth, Preston Dickinson, and John Marin), describing him as "an outsider," comparable to the Russian Marc Chagall in Europe. Others had made that comparison in the past, due to the elements of fantasy in the works of both artists, although their styles were quite different, Kuniyoshi's characterized by weightier figures, his distinctive color sensibility, and unusual subject matter. Meier-Graefe described Kuniyoshi as "the

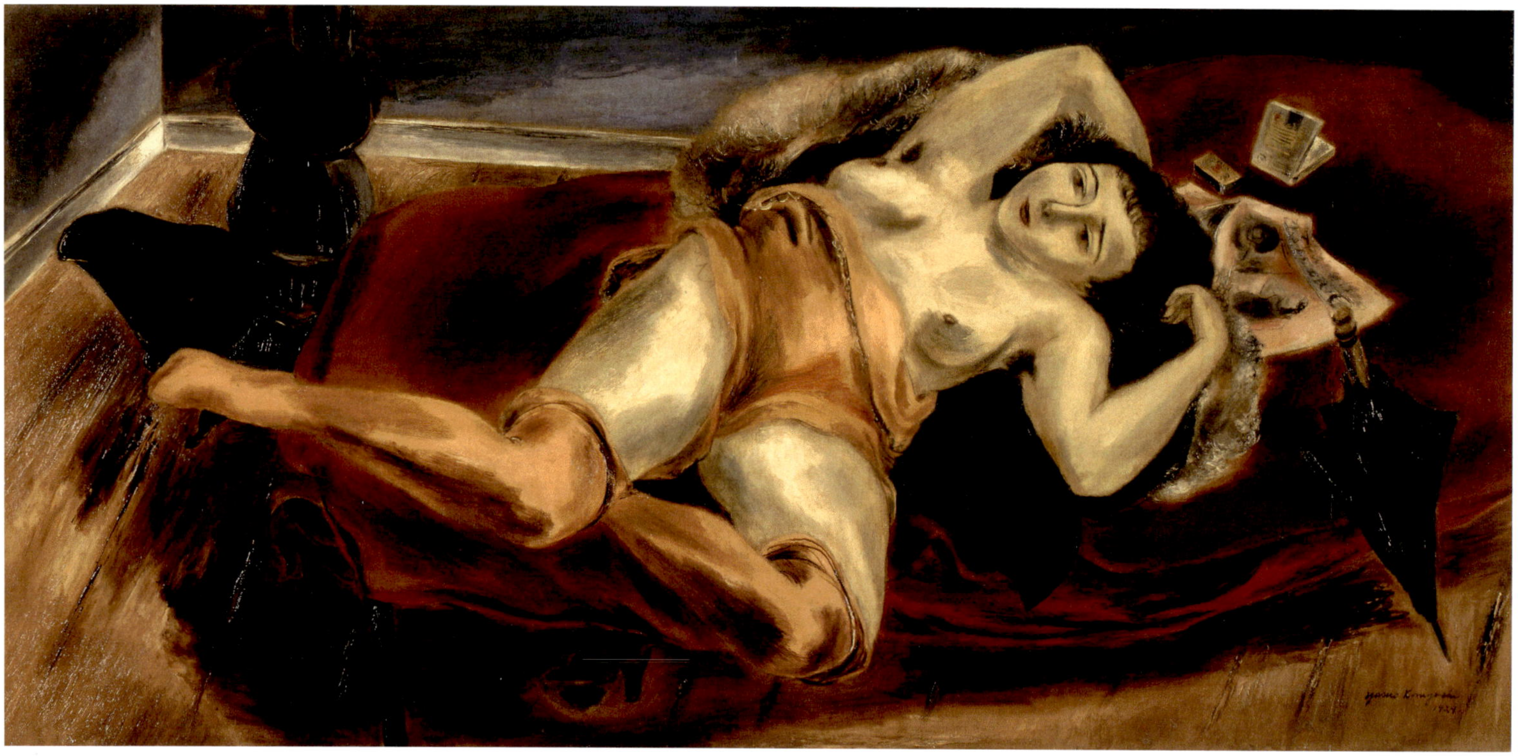

most gifted modern Japanese I have ever seen," viewing him in terms of his national origins as critics always did, but also in the context of modernism and implicitly valuing him higher than Foujita.[65]

Undaunted by those who condemned his imagery as too racy, Kuniyoshi exhibited a confrontational painting of a nude in the highest profile exhibition of his career to date, *Paintings by 19 Living Americans* at the Museum of Modern Art in 1929 (fig. 33). The second show ever at the new institution, it was the type of project that still ignites debate and controversy: a selection of a small group of artists from all those active in the United States. It followed the inaugural exhibition that focused on the fathers of modernism: Cézanne, Gauguin, Seurat and Van Gogh, a much-lauded show that set up its immediate successor for criticism. Kuniyoshi showed five paintings, including a Maine landscape, a still life, the charming *Boy Stealing Fruit*, and the majestic *Self-Portrait as a Golf Player* (which the museum subsequently acquired). His *Nude* is a large horizontal canvas of a half-dressed woman sprawled out on a low bed, seen from above, her crotch pointing toward the viewer from the center of the painting. She is painted with the artist's typical warm reds, browns, and golds. Her thighs are bare, her upraised arms reveal her underarm hair, and her slip is pulled down to expose her breasts, which include nipples, a detail Kuniyoshi often omitted from his topless women, making them less literally naked. She rests upon a coat with a fur collar, next to an umbrella leaning on the bed; both suggest that she has a cosmopolitan, fashionable life outside the studio. The cigarettes and matches in the still life above her indicate that she is bohemian, as proper women did not smoke in the 1920s, and the open newspaper next to them shows that, even if it is an illustrated tabloid, she reads and has a life of the mind. She is not simply a sex object, though she is that as well. Kuniyoshi's friend from the Ogunquit years, Bernard Karfiol, also showed paintings of nude women in the show, and they were much praised—but today their classical poses and conventional compositions seem timid and proper compared to the refined languor of Kuniyoshi's *Nude*, and they make it clear how expressive and confrontational his skewed spaces are (fig. 34).

The organizers of the *19 Living Americans* show took pains to state that this was not a selection of those they considered the "best" American painters. They claimed it was intended to be a group of American artists representing both conservative and progressive tendencies, and it would be followed by many

FIG. 33
Yasuo Kuniyoshi, *Nude*, 1929, oil on canvas, 40 × 80 in. Hokkaido Museum of Modern Art, Sapporo, Japan

FIG. 34
Bernard Karfiol, *Seated Nude*, 1929, oil on canvas, 40 × 30 in. Museum of Modern Art, New York; Gift of Abby Aldrich Rockefeller

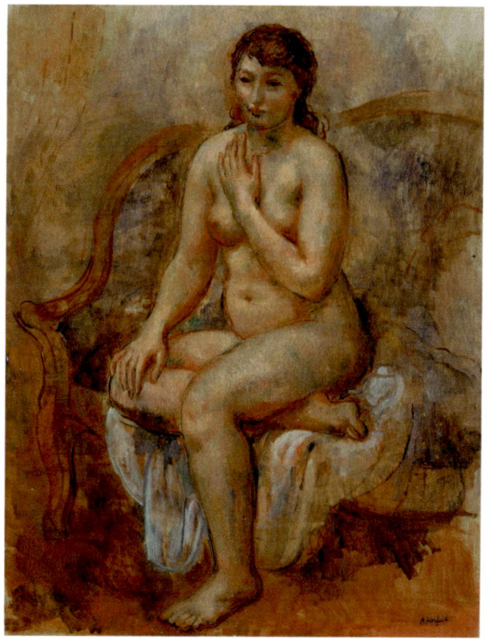

more exhibitions of contemporaries, which was true. The exhibition still drew vociferous criticism, much of it centered on the definition of "American." Here Kuniyoshi was a primary target, drawn into an issue that ran through his entire career, due to his not being eligible for citizenship in the United States. Singled out with him were his friend Jules Pascin, whose artistic identity was linked to the School of Paris, where he lived most of the time, although he was legally an American citizen, and Lyonel Feininger, whose artistic career was in Germany, where he lived, although he too was an American citizen, having been born in Chicago. Audrey McMahon wrote, "The absurd query as to what constitutes an American painter has been asked more frequently concerning no one than Kuniyoshi," although in the same paragraph she also cited "the profoundly un-American character of his work and his outlook" due to the unusual and caustic sense of humor she found in it.[66] Forbes Watson likened the outcry to an "aesthetic Ku Klux Klan" and reported about Kuniyoshi, "his friends tell me that doubts about his legitimacy as an American painter are exceedingly irritating to this artist," as his training and career took place entirely in the United States.[67] Around the same time Kuniyoshi wrote to Samuel Kootz, who was preparing a book called *Modern American Painters*, "I have wished to express the thought of the East, my race, using the tradition of expressing the inner thoughts through the full realization of the matter of my experience," the final clause signifying the Western realist tradition. He also wrote Kootz, "My preferences among artists have been: Sesshu, Korin, Chinese sculptures, Courbet, Signorelli, Daumier and Delacroix," listing Asians as well as Europeans, another way of proclaiming his identity as one where Eastern and Western traditions meet.[68] In his view he was an American painter, one with Asian origins. Despite the citizenship issue, almost every critic praised the power and originality of Kuniyoshi's paintings, and he was given great respect as one of the progressives in the show, along with Charles Demuth, Preston Dickinson, Lyonel Feininger, John Marin, Georgia O'Keeffe (the only woman), and Max Weber.

A measure of Kuniyoshi's success by 1929 was that he and Katherine bought land and built a house for a summer residence in Woodstock, New York. Woodstock was a flourishing art colony, larger and closer to the New York art world than Ogunquit, and Kuniyoshi was familiar with it from his months at the Art Students League summer school in 1917. Woodstock's identity as a place for artists dates back to 1902, when Ralph Radcliffe Whitehead, a wealthy British student of John Ruskin, established the Byrdcliffe Arts and Crafts colony there. In 1906 the Art Students League started its summer school in Woodstock, bringing scores of young students there annually. By 1919 the artistic life was so established in the community that a group of artists bought land in the middle of town and created an exhibition facility, the Woodstock Artists Association, which is still active today. The divisions between the conservatives and the modernists in Woodstock reflected the New York art world, with artists like George Bellows and Eugene Speicher on one side and Andrew Dasburg and Konrad Cramer on the other. There were disputes, though both sides could work together on projects like creating the Artists Association, and there was a steady flow of parties and events that fostered a social community of artists, especially during the summers.

Kuniyoshi was one of the few artists who could afford to have a residence in Woodstock and an apartment in New York. He and Katherine bought land on Ohayo Mountain, overlooking

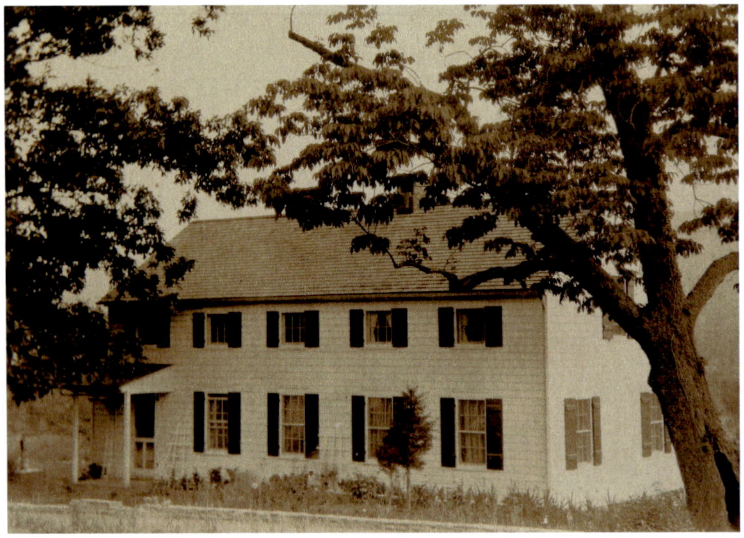

the former farming village below, and built a simple, elegant two-story shingled white house in the American colonial style, inspired by the Maine architecture he loved (fig. 35). It had studio space for her in the house, and a small, freestanding studio building up the hill for him. Kuniyoshi was an avid gardener, who favored Asian plants uncharacteristic of the region: a Japanese maple tree flourished in front of the house as once again he brought East and West together.[69] He would spend most summers in his Woodstock home for the rest of his life.

RETURN TO JAPAN

In 1931, Kuniyoshi made his only return visit to his native country, to be with his ailing father who frequently wrote asking him to visit, and whom he had not seen for twenty-five years. He brought his letter of introduction to the Japanese art world from Foujita, and in Japan he spent time with artists he knew from Los Angeles, New York and Paris, men like Toshi Shimizu who had left Japan to explore the art and culture of other places. Although many returned to their native country, they were a self-selected group of independent-minded, worldly individuals who supported each other through their interconnectedness.

Kuniyoshi traveled to Japan by boat across the Pacific, after taking a train across the United States to Seattle. Throughout his trip he wrote chatty, affectionate letters to Katherine, which have been preserved, and which are a major source of my information about his voyage.[70] On his train trip he took photographs for his own interest, as opposed to photographing works of art as a paying job, an early example of a practice he would continue in the 1930s. The empty landscapes he passed in Montana, including "vast flat space and a dark funny looking house," inspired a photograph and also a critical remark about his contemporary, Edward Hopper: "I think Hopper ought to see what America look like before he was called an American painter" (fig. 36).[71] His Montana photograph recalls some of Hopper's

FIG. 35
Kuniyoshi's house in Woodstock, New York, about 1931–35, gelatin silver print, 3 9/16 × 4 11/16 in. Okayama Prefectural Museum of Art, Japan

FIG. 36
Yasuo Kuniyoshi, *Midwest*, 1931, gelatin silver print, 3 5/8 × 5 in. Philadelphia Museum of Art, Archives, Yasuo Kuniyoshi Papers

paintings of monumental isolated buildings, but the small scale of the house in the photograph emphasizes the magnificent emptiness of the surrounding space, a feeling Kuniyoshi would try to recapture in the landscapes inspired by the southwestern United States he painted from the late 1930s into the 1940s.

Arriving in Japan, to his surprise he was met at the dock by a group of photographers and journalists, who had notice that a well-known Japanese American artist was coming to their country. During his visit he divided his time between visiting his ailing father, seeing his divorced mother on the sly due to family tensions, and having exhibitions, which got considerable attention and were celebrated by social events thrown by artists in his honor. At the end of his trip he had achieved a substantial reputation as an artist in Japan, but had sold only a few paintings and lithographs, a cause of concern back in New York. Charles Daniel, his dealer, who would soon close his gallery, owed him money and Katherine had bills to pay. His stay was partly consumed by social activities, but he also enjoyed revisiting places from his youth, particularly the beautiful Korakuen Park, a twenty-eight acre eleventh-century strolling park a few blocks from the house where he grew up. He found it "exquisite" and unchanged, and visited it repeatedly during his stay: "It is really the picture of Japan everybody paints. I have taken walks here many times and thought about you Katherine and wish that you were with me."[72] His childhood experiences of the park could have influenced his adult fondness for gardening, as well as the imagery of plants and insects that occurs frequently in his art, culminating in his last works.

Kuniyoshi exhibited lithographs in Okayama, and twenty-nine paintings plus lithographs in Tokyo and Osaka. This represented a cross section of his work over the past decade: cows, children, still lifes, women and nudes. He wrote Katherine about the Tokyo show, "Police department here has been very strict about nude painting and always examine the show just before open."[73] Four of his paintings, including the large *Nude* exhibited in the *19 Living Americans* show at the Museum of Modern Art, required two visits from the police, until Kuniyoshi resolved the issue by covering the questionable areas with white chalk, which apparently made them acceptable so all were allowed to remain on view. When asked to describe his art to the press, Kuniyoshi said, "Briefly mine is a modified expressionist school—Kuniyoshism, if you will."[74]

Having spent three months in Japan, much of it in the company of Japanese artists, Kuniyoshi wrote of his impressions of the contemporary art scene to Katherine, and in a short article, "Art and Artists in Japan," for *Arts Weekly*. To Katherine he wrote that he felt that much of the art was not so good, though it was executed with "amazing" technical ability, often in works of impressive size. He was also surprised that the Japanese artists were unfamiliar with lithography; the prints he brought from the United States were the first exposure for many of them. And he felt that they had no awareness of American art. Both to Katherine and in his article he wrote that the artists in Japan had it easier than in the United States, because people in general were more interested in art and there was a broader support system: "The artist lives in Japan with comparative ease, sustained by patrons, teaching, or by the sale of his pictures."[75] He described the existence of art societies which sponsored large group shows—in fact, while he was there several societies competed for his membership, and after stalling for a while he finally agreed to join Nikakai, an organization formed in 1914 that had become prestigious by the 1920s from its promotion of the progressive Yōga painting that had been discouraged in government-sponsored exhibitions. In his article he described the existence of two schools of painting, the traditional (Nihonga), which he felt was unable to compete with the achievements of the earlier masters but was still in touch with the roots of Japanese taste, and the Western school (Yōga), derived principally from the School of Paris, which he felt had more vigor but needed to develop new means to connect with native impulses. While in Japan, Kuniyoshi made brush paintings that are the most Nihonga works of his career; several ink brush on kimono silk paintings that Kuniyoshi made in 1931 exist, depicting clusters of grapes, or an octopus (fig. 37). In his letters to Katherine he complained several times that people he hardly knew were asking him to do drawings for them for remembrances—"very funny and same time make me very angry because they never think of buying (people of this kind)," but he still generously drew several, including one for the family who lived next door to his childhood house.[76]

He had been away for twenty-five years, and no longer felt at home: "I was criticized for not observing the elaborate Japanese formality and etiquette of dealing with people," he reported, and an encounter with a policeman where he was rebuked for not removing his hat and showing the proper respect also left him feeling alienated.[77] He returned to New York certain that the United States was the right place for him: "I sailed back in February 1932 firmly convinced that my adopted home was my home." By the time he got to New York

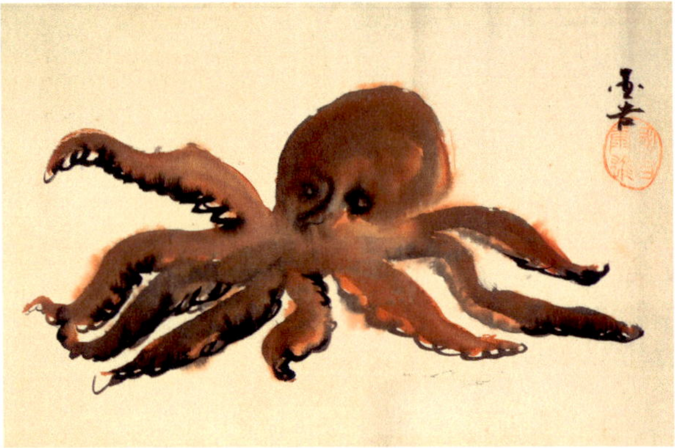

FIG. 37
Yasuo Kuniyoshi, *Octopus*, 1931, ink on kimono silk, Yumeji Art Museum (Ryobi Cultural Foundation), Okayama, Japan

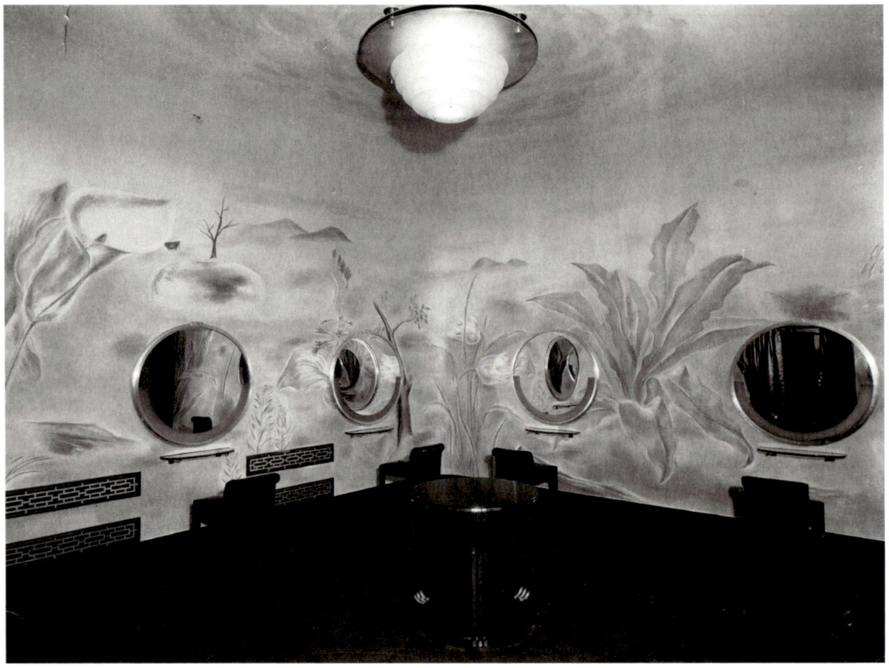

FIG. 38
Yasuo Kuniyoshi, murals for Ladies' Powder Room, Radio City Music Hall, New York, 1932

his father had died, and after his mother died the next year, "The deepest ties with my native land had been broken."[78] But at the same time, his artistic links with his native country had been strengthened: he befriended several artists and stayed in contact with them once he returned to the United States, and this also was the case with his stepsisters, the daughters of his father's second wife, who were taking care of his father while Kuniyoshi visited. In fact, the Japan trip has great significance for an evaluation of Kuniyoshi's career, because from then on he was involved with contemporary Japanese as well as American art. Once his art was exposed in Japan he was seen as the American parallel to Foujita in Paris. His work was frequently reproduced in Japanese magazines, and as we will see he increasingly acted as a liaison between the contemporary art worlds of his native country and the United States.

THE RADIO CITY MUSIC HALL MURAL

Once back in New York, Kuniyoshi undertook a commission that would result in the largest of all his paintings by far: to paint the four walls and ceiling of the second-floor ladies' powder room in the new Radio City Music Hall in Rockefeller Center (fig. 38). The project was a collaboration with the designer Donald Deskey, who was in charge of the decoration of the entire building. Deskey designed the room with nine round mirrors mounted on the walls, complementing his sleek, round black Bakelite art deco tables and black leather and lacquer chairs. To harmonize with Deskey's circular motifs Kuniyoshi painted a magical environment of immense plants in a dreamlike landscape space, with the mirrors reflecting the floral forms back on themselves. He painted the room in pale earth tones and muted greens and blues—a viewer is surrounded by a landscape filled with huge leaves and flowers. The scheme transitions from the immense plants to floating perspectival passages and small misty mountains above. As the walls curve into the ceiling (there are no right angles) the warm colors turn into pale blues that culminate with Deskey's stepped beehive light fixture. Rather than carefully constructing his composition to fit around Deskey's mirrors and the doorways, Kuniyoshi treated his gigantic plants as if they were growing behind the mirrors that abruptly overlap them. The viewer is immersed in an insect's point of view, looking up at the tall flowers that loom over the small trees and mountains beyond. Deskey designed the space so that a woman would put on her make-up in the bathroom to the right of Kuniyoshi's interior, and exit the main room through a curtained doorway which had a mirror facing it, so leaving the room, looking her best, she saw herself reflected in front of a large Kuniyoshi plant.

The artist, assisted by Woodstock painter Judson Smith, finished the entire mural in an amazing four or five weeks. He had received the commission on short notice, because Deskey had first offered it to Georgia O'Keeffe. She was eager to take it; it would have been the largest painting of her career, as it was for Kuniyoshi. But Alfred Stieglitz, her husband and dealer, opposed the venture, which led to great stress in their relationship. Her biographers point out that Stieglitz's new girlfriend, Dorothy Norman, was already in his life, adding to the tension, and in the end O'Keeffe withdrew from the commission, broke down, and was hospitalized.[79] Once O'Keeffe quit, Deskey called Kuniyoshi, who accepted and got to work. Subsequent writers have suggested that Kuniyoshi's murals, dominated by large flowers, were inspired by O'Keeffe's famous floral imagery—which could be the case. He certainly knew her work—she exhibited with him in the *19 Living Americans* show at the Museum of Modern Art in 1929, and Stieglitz admired Kuniyoshi's art. But to suggest that her work influenced his murals leads to a winding path, since she had studied with Arthur Wesley Dow, a major advocate of Japanese art in the United States. And we have seen that Kuniyoshi frequently created images of large plants set against evocative distant landscapes in his own ink drawings from the 1920s, like *Lady Slipper* (see pl. 19). The floating mountains in the backgrounds of the mural import a convention from Asian landscape traditions, one that Kuniyoshi had frequently adopted in his black ink drawings.

Over the years the room deteriorated due to constant use, and graffiti appeared on Kuniyoshi's walls. They were restored in 1979 and look good today, and they include a characteristic Kuniyoshi visual joke: the tiny hindquarters of a cow, its head overlapped by a huge calla lily, floats high on one wall.

Deskey hired twenty-one painters and sculptors to work on decorating Radio City Music Hall. Soon after it opened to the public, critic Philippa Gerry Whiting wrote of Kuniyoshi's mural, "This is really mural decoration, conceived architecturally and with some knowledge of mural requirements. Most of the other so-called murals are merely large easel paintings."[80] Rockefeller Center was an optimistic monument to America built in the middle of the Depression. Soon the federal government would sponsor hundreds of public murals by American artists, devoted to socially uplifting themes, populated by monumental working figures. Coming at the beginning of this renaissance of mural painting, Kuniyoshi's ladies' powder room murals are little-known treasures of art deco New York.

KUNIYOSHI'S STILL LIFES

In the 1930s, Kuniyoshi's reputation continued to rise. Critics for the most part were in favor of his change to working from reality instead of from his imagination, and praised his innate artistic talent. Edward Alden Jewell, the critic for the *New York Times*, exemplified the new appreciation: "It used to be much more difficult for some of us to be enthusiastic about Kuniyoshi's work. Queer mannerisms were always getting in the way."[81] While they acknowledged Kuniyoshi's individuality, the critics frequently cited Pascin as an influence on his figure paintings, and invariably they discussed him in terms of his Japanese origins, with many different versions of what this meant. In the early 1930s, Kuniyoshi began to win awards and prizes at prestigious group exhibitions, and his winning works were usually still-life paintings, a genre that he explored with a complexity of meaning that has rarely been acknowledged.[82] *Watermelon, Fruit and Cigars*, from 1927, is an example of the multileveled statements he was able to incorporate into his still-life paintings. Like a surprising number of his important early works, today its location is unknown, and it is available only in black-and-white reproductions (fig. 39). He presented a stately grouping of objects on a table in skewed perspective, in front of a window that opens to a light-infused segment of a landscape, the foreground dominated by a variety of fruits, including grapes and peaches. Kuniyoshi acknowledged that the fruits, especially the grapes, evoked memories of his early days in the United States when he worked harvesting in the fields:

> When I paint a bowl of grapes in my studio, I do it because grapes mean something to me. When I was a boy I spent many long hot summer days picking them. I used to go to the field very early, before sunrise, the air is cool then and the vines and grapes are wet with dew. The big black bunches hang down so heavily, one on top of another. The first thing I did was grab a soft slippery bunch and stuff as many into my mouth as it would hold. They were so juicy and cold.
>
> I don't think about this when I paint grapes, but it is part of the feeling I have about grapes which I try to put into my painting.[83]

Peaches are closely associated with Kuniyoshi's birthplace, Okayama, known as the hometown of Momotaro, the peach boy famous in Japanese folklore. In the painting a reproduction of a portrait of a woman by Goya hangs on the wall,

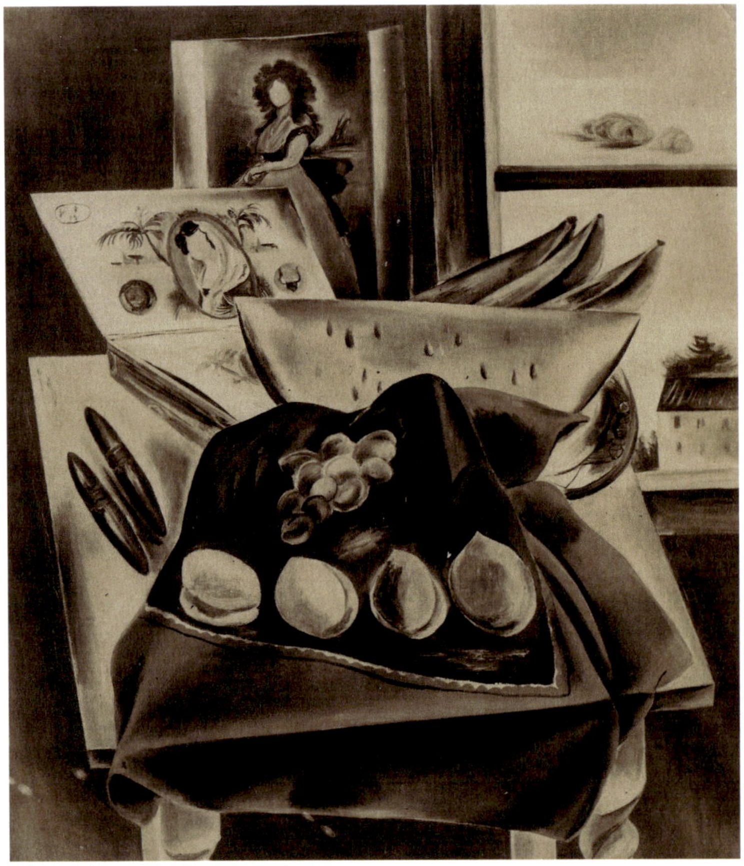

FIG. 39
Yasuo Kuniyoshi, *Watermelon, Fruit and Cigars*, 1927, oil on canvas, 25 × 30 in.; location unknown

above the fruit, and it also has autobiographical resonance, since Kuniyoshi was still working as a photographer of works of art. In addition the Goya refers to his love of the European Old Masters, who were a continual inspiration for him.[84] Below it an open box of cigars reveals its inside cover, decorated with the bust of a woman wearing a shawl, flanked by palm trees. Clearly the Goya is the ancestor of the cigar box image as Kuniyoshi juxtaposed the great Old Master tradition with its appropriation into commercial advertising. The palm trees and the clothing of the cigar box woman indicate that the cigars are from Cuba, where fine cigars are produced, a country colonized by Goya's Spain, as Kuniyoshi set up a visual conversation about multiculturalism and global exchange. He has generally not been given credit for this sort of conceptual sophistication in his art, but it is there in the imagery of his painting, and the idea that it just happened by chance is belied by other of his still-life paintings that incorporate images of paintings within them, and also raise complicated issues of interpretation.

Goya's woman appears again six years later in *Weathervane and Objects on a Sofa* (1933), another one-of-a-kind title (pl. 31). While this painting is ostensibly from Kuniyoshi's return-to-reality phase, it is still eccentric compared to the many straightforward still lifes being painted by his American contemporaries in the 1930s, thanks to the peculiarity of the objects he selected and his distinctive abstract swirls of thick oil paint in the background. The off-kilter composition is anchored by the curvy white vertical object in the center of the still life whose downward point acts like a wedge holding the composition together. This mysterious object that suggests a pallid human profile is an upside-down mold of a bust by sculptor Paul Fiene, part of Kuniyoshi's Woodstock circle of artists.[85] The history of painting is full of still lifes that include sculptures, but a mold is unusual. Kuniyoshi gave himself the challenge of painting the negative of a three-dimensional face in the center of his composition, and below it he placed a totally flat sculpture, a folk art weather vane representing a galloping horse. The horse, frozen in motion as it appears to race across the scene, makes a disturbing juxtaposition with the reverse head—an arbitrary irrationality that evokes the contemporary works of the surrealists in Paris.[86] The apparently random collection of objects actually constitutes an anthology of artistic traditions that shaped the artist: Goya represents the Old Masters; Paul Fiene, contemporary American art; the weather vane, American folk art; and a copy of *Cahiers d'Art*, the French magazine of contemporary art, lies below the horse's tail, representing the School of Paris. What about Japanese traditions? They, perhaps filtered through Parisian modernism, underlie the off-kilter composition, supported by its boldly cropped sofa, seen on a diagonal.

Other Kuniyoshi still lifes incorporate quotations of paintings by Titian and Rubens, and Matisse's famous *Woman with a Hat* (1905), one of the paintings that launched the color revolution of the Fauves (fig. 40). It would be fascinating to see how Kuniyoshi dealt with Matisse's radical color, but again the painting is lost and we have only a monochrome photograph. From the reproduction we can see that Kuniyoshi treated Matisse's image casually, almost cruelly, using it as a place mat

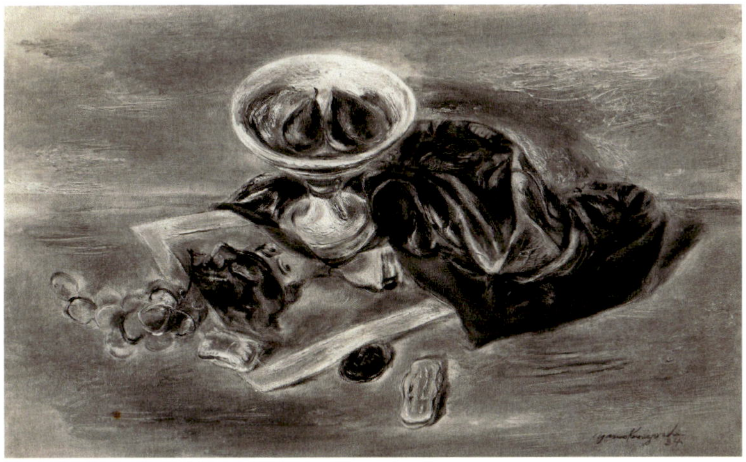

FIG. 40
Yasuo Kuniyoshi, *Still Life*, 1934; location unknown

FIG. 41
Max Weber, *Still Life with Challah*, about 1930, oil on canvas, 23 ½ × 28 ½ in. The Jewish Museum, New York; Gift of Joy S. Weber, 1994-59

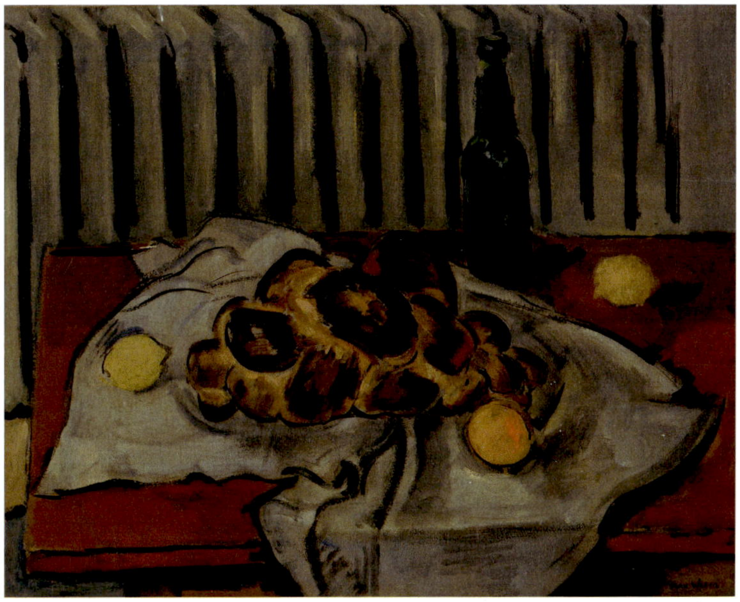

for the conventional still-life objects. Several other paintings get similarly rough treatment in Kuniyoshi's still lifes, including *End of Juanita* (1942; pl. 40), where everyday objects including a pitcher stand on top of an unstretched painting of watermelon halves, and *Things on an Iron Chair* (1936), where a similar painting is uncomfortably bent into a near cylinder to fit into a vessel. "Juanita" was the name Yasuo and Sara, his second wife, gave to a pitcher they purchased on their honeymoon in Mexico in 1935. It broke during their three-year separation, during which the artist painted his still life featuring the damaged vessel, weaving personal imagery into what appears to be a neutral assemblage of objects.[87]

The watermelon paintings Kuniyoshi incorporated into *End of Juanita* and *Things on an Iron Chair* could be his own, as the fruit featured frequently in his still lifes, and several years later he painted a work titled *Watermelon* (1938; pl. 36). Together these paintings create a fascinating dialogue, between the actual painting featuring the lush fruit, and the still lifes that include the melon paintings within them—different levels of reality that spur meditations on the nature of creation and the art of painting. *Watermelon*, apart from its provocative relationship to these works, illustrates the other extreme of Kuniyoshi's still-life practice: the simple, straightforward representations of everyday objects as such. Its stark directness gives *Watermelon* its power. Kuniyoshi represented the fruit halves against a caramel-brown background. Their sensuous, fleshy modulations of red herald his move toward bright color that will follow in the years after World War II, but also evoke flesh and blood and include a suggestion of suffering along with the hedonism of the succulent subject. The painting titled *The Twist Loaf* (1930) is another example of Kuniyoshi's large-scale, straightforward still lifes, where a single loaf of bread sits on an improbably supported table, set against clouds of black and gray paint (pl. 30). The loaf itself is challah, the traditional bread of Jewish ritual, which the artist depicted again in *Odd Objects on a Couch* and *Rolls on a Chair*, both of 1930. The cloth, which pours out of the painting from under the loaf, could refer to the uncovering of the shrouded bread before cutting it, part of the Sabbath ceremony. A challah loaf appeared around the same time in a painting by Max Weber, the esteemed American modernist, eight years Kuniyoshi's senior, who frequently showed in group exhibitions with Kuniyoshi (fig. 41). Weber's painting shares the out-of-perspective table with Kuniyoshi's, but beyond that is smaller and more conventional. It was part of Weber's artistic program to paint subjects that affirmed his Jewishness, but the subject is more of a leap for Kuniyoshi, whose second wife would be Jewish, but he was not yet involved with her. It perhaps reflects the social milieu

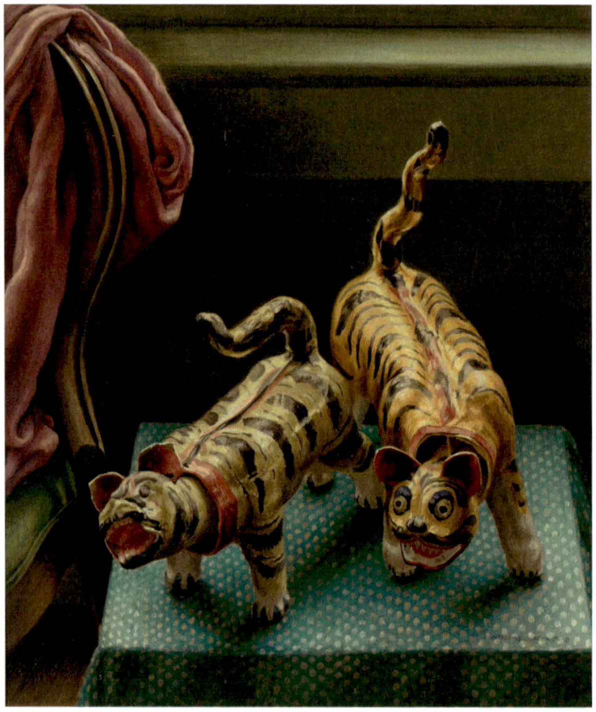

he increasingly found himself in, a society of politically leftist artists that included many Jews. But it is not clear that the artist knew the religious significance of this type of bread, and during his lifetime the painting passed under the title *The Twist Loaf*, or was described as "a loaf of French bread."[88] The artist himself said about his still-life paintings: "I picked up all kind of materials—cigars and toys and weathervanes and the old sofa in Woodstock... I picked them for shapes, colors, textures—but sometimes when they were all together they take on symbolism for me."[89]

When he returned from Japan in 1931, Kuniyoshi brought two Japanese toy tigers with him, and he and his wife painted them into two complementary still lifes (figs. 42, 43). Katherine and Yasuo had parallel careers as artists. His reputation was greater than hers, but she also exhibited at the Daniel Gallery, though not as frequently as he. Her work rarely ventured into areas of eccentricity like Kuniyoshi's; it remained rooted in the realism she had learned at the Art Students League. Her *Tiger, Tiger* (1933) is a forcefully realistic rendering of two strongly lit toy animals seen from above, receding into space. The objects

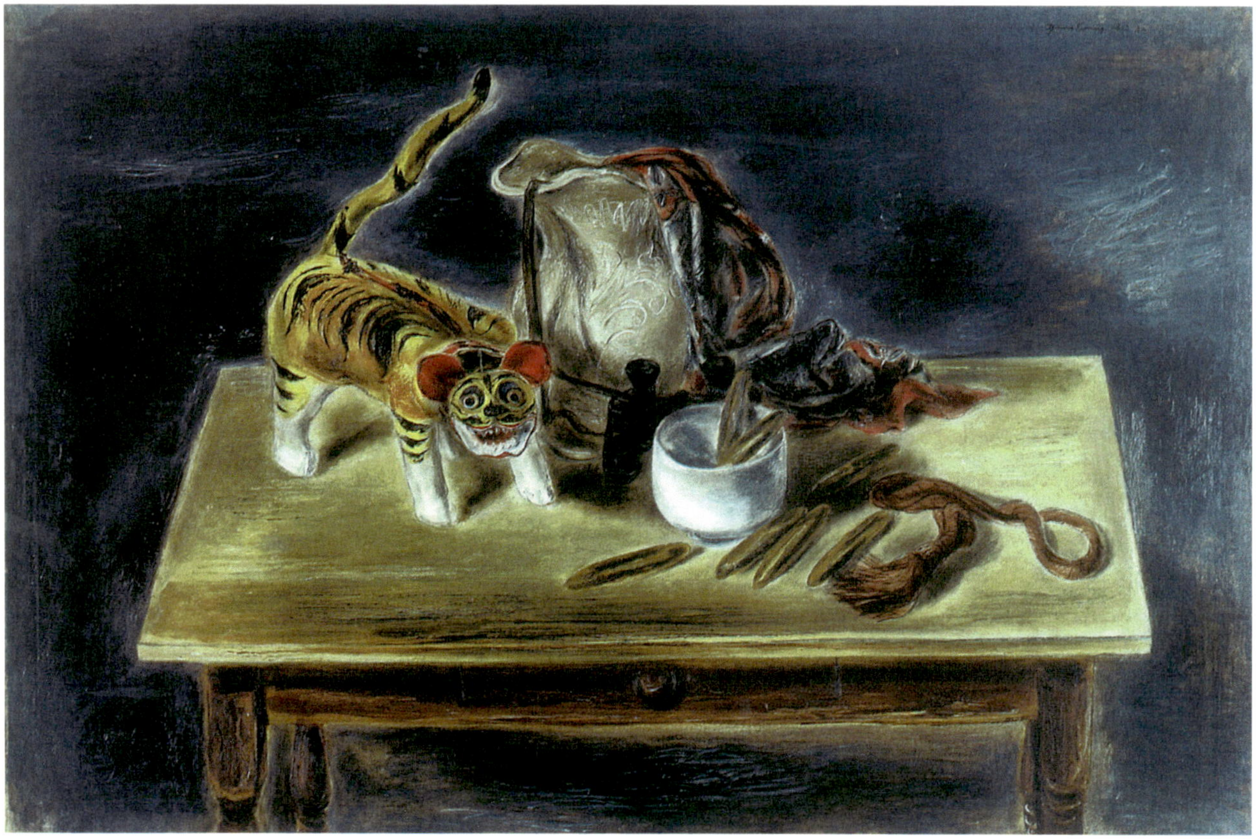

FIG. 42
Katherine Schmidt, *Tiger, Tiger*, 1933, oil on canvas, 30 × 25 in. Whitney Museum of American Art, New York; Katherine Schmidt Shubert Bequest

FIG. 43
Yasuo Kuniyoshi, *Japanese Toy Tiger and Odd Objects*, 1932, oil on canvas, 33 9/16 × 49 1/2 in. Fukutake Collection, Okayama, Japan

are Japanese but the realistic perspective is Renaissance, and the title quotes the first words of one of William Blake's most famous poems while the toys playfully enact its "fearful symmetry." Kuniyoshi's version is characteristically more sensually painted, less precisely realistic, and populated with curious objects: a pitcher, a scattering of cigars, a pair of binoculars, and the tiger itself, which is enlivened in that it seems to return our gaze directly, unlike her two, which are exotic objects for us to scrutinize. Kuniyoshi's still life can seem like an arbitrary accumulation of objects, but the stare of the tiger, coupled with the binoculars, suggests ideas about looking, essential to the art of painting, and the apparently random objects again seem to offer some sort of narrative meaning. For example, might the lone tiger accompanied by the masculine cigars be a comment on the changing nature of his relationship with his wife, in contrast to the two united figures in her painting?

Kuniyoshi and Schmidt divorced amicably in 1932. She had a strong personality, while over the course of their relationship he became increasingly confident as his career flourished. In his autobiographical writings from the 1940s Kuniyoshi described how his upbringing in Japan made him uncomfortable with women:

> I never felt easy about the other sex, and never knew anything about it until I was about twenty-five years old. Perhaps this was due to the way I was brought up not to associate with the other sex. Traditionally, the people of Japan are taught to look down on females. In the public schools, or any other place, from childhood on, we were forbidden to associate with the girls...
>
> It was rather difficult for me to adjust to a new angle after I came to the United States. I was still clinging to the ideas I had been taught, and it was rather difficult to get used to associating with the other sex. Even after being here some time, I felt awkward and any association naturally was a superficial one, because somehow at the bottom of my mind I regarded talking to a woman as difficult and shameful.... My contact with women was slowly developed, but by today I have the reverse of my former attitude, and not only that, I believe that women should have equal rights in every way.[90]

In a manuscript for a speech to a Japanese Americans group he used his marriage as an example of reticence that is best conquered:

> When I was first married, quite inexperienced and shy, I took no part in any expressive action. Perhaps I was not interested. In any case I was exceedingly retiring and in time the attitude represented practically non-existence. I felt that my wife spoke my ideas and that she expressed them with greater clarity than I could...if one fails in expressing one's own idea and becomes dependent on another one loses his self-respect. Today we as Japanese Americans are facing the same challenge.[91]

That Katherine was the spokesperson for the relationship is borne out by Woodstock artist Florence Ballin Cramer, who described a visit from the Kuniyoshis in a diary entry from 1932: "mostly Katherine who talks about him to us." Katherine had been uncomfortable with the licentious lifestyle of Kuniyoshi's crowd in Paris, which prompted her coming back to the United States without him. Once they were reunited, many women were attracted to him as a young, famous, charismatic artist. A year after their divorce Katherine married lawyer Irvine Shubert and she remained a close friend of Kuniyoshi. He married aspiring dancer Sara Mazo, twenty-one years his junior, in 1935. After Kuniyoshi's death his ex-wife and his widow continued their friendship until Katherine's death in 1978.

ACTIVITIES IN THE 1930S

In the 1930s the Depression deepened in the United States, with worldwide repercussions as nationalism grew in many countries, including Japan. During his trip there Kuniyoshi witnessed the rising militarism as Japan was invading Manchuria, a manifestation of its increasing military aggression against China, which would lead to the Second Sino-Japanese War in 1937 and then to World War II. Kuniyoshi wrote Katherine about a group of men he saw running nude to a temple to pray for their friends at war in Manchuria, and about getting up at 5:00 a.m. to watch a ceremony inducting young men into the army.[92] Unlike many artists in New York, he was strongly aware of Japanese imperial ambitions through the 1930s, while in the United States people were jobless and suffering, and many artists were involved with labor politics. Kuniyoshi was increasingly active both in the political and the art-world arenas, often assuming positions of leadership, a sign of the respect given to him by his fellow artists. He suggested to Lloyd Goodrich that these involvements also gave him a sense of belonging.[93] Already in the late 1920s he had served as secretary of the Hamilton Easter Field Foundation and as an officer in the Salons of America, an exhibiting organization created by Field. As we will see, he continued to take positions of art-world leadership for the rest of his career, including being an officer in the American Artists' Congress, the president of An American Group (an organization of progressive figurative painters), and the president of Artists Equity. These civic activities in the art world took up increasing amounts of his time, and stole time from his painting—and he worked slowly. He told an interviewer in 1940 that it took him a year to complete a painting, and that he hoped to finish fifteen a year, while having around a dozen going at one time.[94] His working method involved periodically putting a painting aside and then returning to it, painting and repainting until he was satisfied. Late in his career he explained to a student: "I draw for two weeks on a canvas with charcoal before I start to paint. The drawing is fixed on the canvas. Then as I paint, if I need to, I scrape down to the drawing—it's always there. I never paint over." He advocated the use of a palette knife: "You put it on, then take if off—not thick, but thin."[95]

He also took occasional outside projects, such as illustrating two short stories for *Harper's Bazaar*.[96] In 1934, Samuel Kootz, who was working in the textile business before making the transition to being an art dealer, commissioned fabric designs from Stuart Davis, Arthur Dove, and Kuniyoshi. Kuniyoshi put his early training in fabric design in Japan to use, creating several inventive, soberly hued patterns.[97]

The issue of Kuniyoshi's not being an American citizen kept coming up. In 1935, after Diego Rivera's murals in Rockefeller Center, which included a prominent portrait of Lenin, were controversially destroyed, there was a movement to create a Municipal Art Center, which would show works by contemporary American artists. With the support of Mayor LaGuardia a building on Fifty-Third Street was temporarily turned over to artists for exhibitions organized by self-selected groups. But to exhibit artists had to be citizens of the United States, and when it became clear that this excluded Kuniyoshi a protest letter was signed by sixty-five artists, and eventually this condition was withdrawn. The signers of the letter included Kuniyoshi's usual friends and affiliates, such as Alexander Brook, Niles Spencer, Bernard Karfiol, Raphael Soyer, and Stuart Davis.

Another side of Kuniyoshi's art world was brought to light in Ruth Benjamin's October 1935 article in *Parnassus*: "Japanese Painters in America," a review of an exhibition of Japanese artists living in New York held at the liberal ACA Gallery. The piece began with Kuniyoshi, "the best known . . . undoubtedly," and then went on to consider other Japanese artists in his circle, including his friends Bumpei Usui and Chuzo Tamotzu, plus the young Isamu Noguchi, bringing this little-known enclave of twentieth-century New York art temporarily to light.[98] The ACA show was another instance of these artists exhibiting together in New York, a practice that we have seen dated back to at least 1922 and which would continue sporadically, with a shifting cast of characters, to a 1947 exhibition at the Riverside Museum. Several critics felt that the paintings in the ACA exhibition were too dependent on French prototypes and did not sufficiently reflect the Japanese origins of their artists: "For the most part the exhibitors are tricked out in Western attire, through which native traits occasionally show rather awkwardly."[99] Several of these artists, including Kuniyoshi, showed again at ACA in 1937 in conjunction with a number of Chinese artists as a protest against the exclusion of Asian-born artists from the WPA artist relief projects, an exhibition which also was a gesture of solidarity in the face of increasing Japanese aggression against China.

When Kuniyoshi married Sara Mazo in 1935 she was a twenty-four-year-old dancer and actress who had trained with Martha Graham. They met when she was acting in a Maverick Theatre production in Woodstock, and her boyfriend, American surrealist painter James Guy, suggested she pose for Kuniyoshi. After he wooed her and they wed, she gave up her performing career; eventually she would work at the Museum of Modern Art for several decades, mostly as the assistant to the renowned curator Dorothy Miller. The Kuniyoshis spent most summers in Woodstock, and the rest of the year in New York City, where he had his studio on Fourteenth Street. They lived in a modest walk-up apartment at 118 Waverly Place. A photograph of their living room shows that they favored simple, early American furnishings, including the Shaker box in front of the fireplace, the stemmed white fruit bowl that appeared in many of Kuniyoshi's works, and the large, carved wooden eagle over the mantel, a patriotic symbol of the United States (fig. 44).

When progressive artists in New York, concerned about the distressing international situation, created the American Artists' Congress in 1936, Kuniyoshi became an officer. He headed the exhibitions committee, which that year sponsored *Against War and Fascism*, a show of art past and present, including works by historic artists such as Goya and Callot. In 1937 the committee organized *In Defense of World Democracy: Dedicated to the Peoples of Spain and China*, which included almost two hundred artist members of the congress, plus antifascist drawings by schoolchildren of Madrid

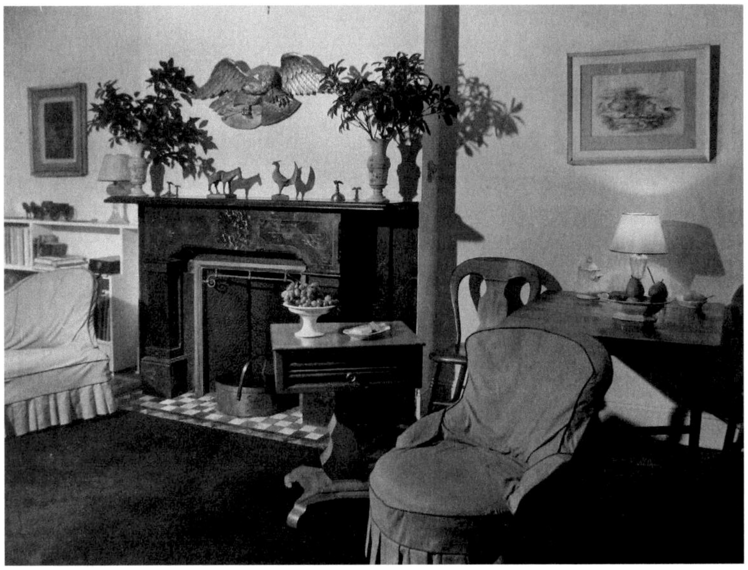

FIG. 44
Eliot Elisofon,
Kuniyoshi home on Waverly Place,
November 27, 1946,
photograph, 11 × 14 in.

and Picasso's etchings, *The Dream and Lie of Franco*. (In 1939 the Artists' Congress would help to get Picasso's monumental antiwar painting, *Guernica* (1937), shown in New York.) In conjunction with the 1937 *In Defense of World Democracy* exhibition the congress organized an evening at Carnegie Hall that included a message of support from Picasso, a speech by Thomas Mann delivered by his daughter, and speeches by Mayor LaGuardia, dancer Martha Graham, and painters Philip Evergood, Rockwell Kent, and Kuniyoshi, among others. In Kuniyoshi's presentation, "Alien Discrimination," he discussed the fact that although he was a widely exhibited artist in the United States, his work could not be purchased by the Hearn Fund of the Metropolitan Museum of Art because he was not an American citizen, and he criticized the fact that he and his fellow Japanese artists were dropped from the government art programs for the same reason.[100]

While most of the works in the exhibition focused on the rise of fascism and war in Spain and Germany, Kuniyoshi's Japanese colleagues, with their heightened sensitivity to what was going on in East Asia, exhibited art that took Asian conflicts as their subjects. Chuzo Tamotzu showed *Beware of Militarism* (1939), a painting of a giant saber-wielding Japanese general rampaging over a landscape with peaceful farmworkers while Mount Fuji erupts in the background (fig. 45).[101] Eitaro Ishigaki's *Flight* (about 1937; fig. 46) depicts a Chinese peasant family fleeing a city in flames, and Sakari Suzuki submitted a visual allegory of War with a skeleton wearing the uniform of a military commander towering over a Chinese soldier. Kuniyoshi exhibited a print. He rarely resorted to the propagandistic imagery of his colleagues—until after the Japanese attack on Pearl Harbor in December 1941. At this point in his career he was becoming a leader among politically active artists, but the one illustration he published in the aggressively leftist magazine, *Art Front*, seems closer to a critique of political art than an example of it (fig. 47). It appeared above an article by Jacob Burck, a communist artist, who criticized remarks from an earlier issue by Thomas Hart Benton, the prominent Regionalist painter. Kuniyoshi's illustration depicts a drawing class, like the ones he taught at the Art Students League since 1933, except the students are seriously working on drawing a gas pump. Perhaps it is a comment on Regionalism's dedication to portraying Americana, or a satire of artists like Stuart Davis and Charles Sheeler and their involvement with mechanization as subject matter. In any case, the students have turned away from the nude model at the right, who seems to be leaving her modeling platform because she has been displaced by the pump. It is quite remote from the debates about communism raging in the magazine text below it, and it seems to be a statement of the artist's belief in sensuality and the human figure as the just subject for art.

Unlike some of his colleagues in the Artists' Congress, for example William Gropper and Louis Lozowick, in this period Kuniyoshi rarely created overtly literal political images. But there were some exceptions, like his *Deserted Brickyard* (1938), where he painted a ruined landscape inhabited by one lonely man sleeping on the ground, a clear reference to homelessness in the midst of the Depression (fig. 48). He also made a drawing, and a lithograph, of men sleeping on the floor, and his *Refugees*, a casein painting of 1939 depicting a man, woman, and child struggling across a desolate landscape took up a theme common among leftist artists of the time, like Gropper, who were expressing their empathy for those dispossessed by the war in Europe.

FIG. 45
Chuzo Tamotzu, *Beware of Militarism*, 1939, sumi brush, watercolor, and pen on paper, 13 × 14 ½ in., 000-609-0065, Chuzo Tamotsu Pictorial Collection, Center for Southwest Research, University Libraries, University of New Mexico, Santa Fe

FIG. 46
Eitaro Ishigaki, *Flight*, about 1937, gelatin silver print of painting (location unknown). Ishigaki Memorial Museum, Taiji, Wakayama, Japan

FIG. 47
Yasuo Kuniyoshi, "From Asso. to Esso," about 1934–37, for *Art Front* magazine. Yasuo Kuniyoshi Papers, Archives of American Art, Smithsonian Institution

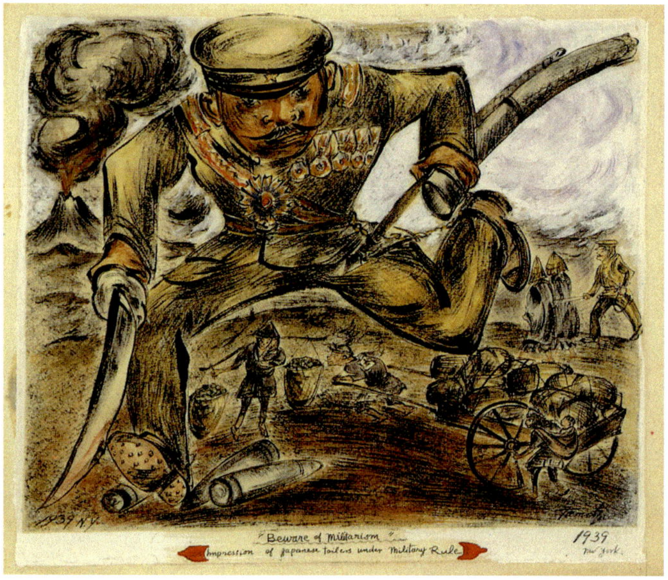

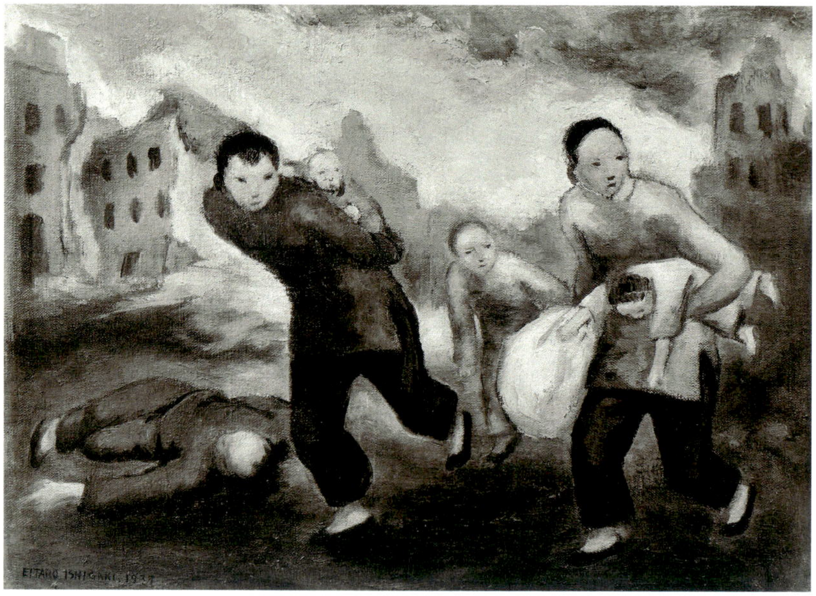

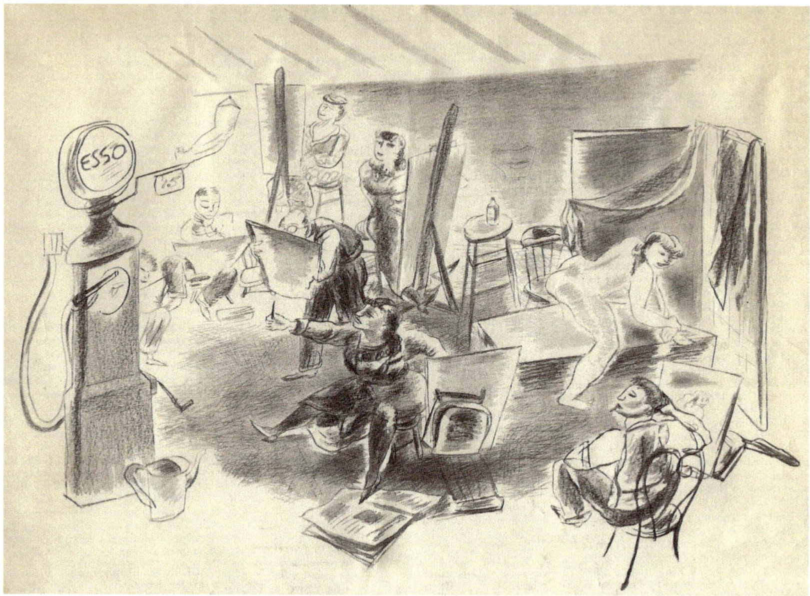

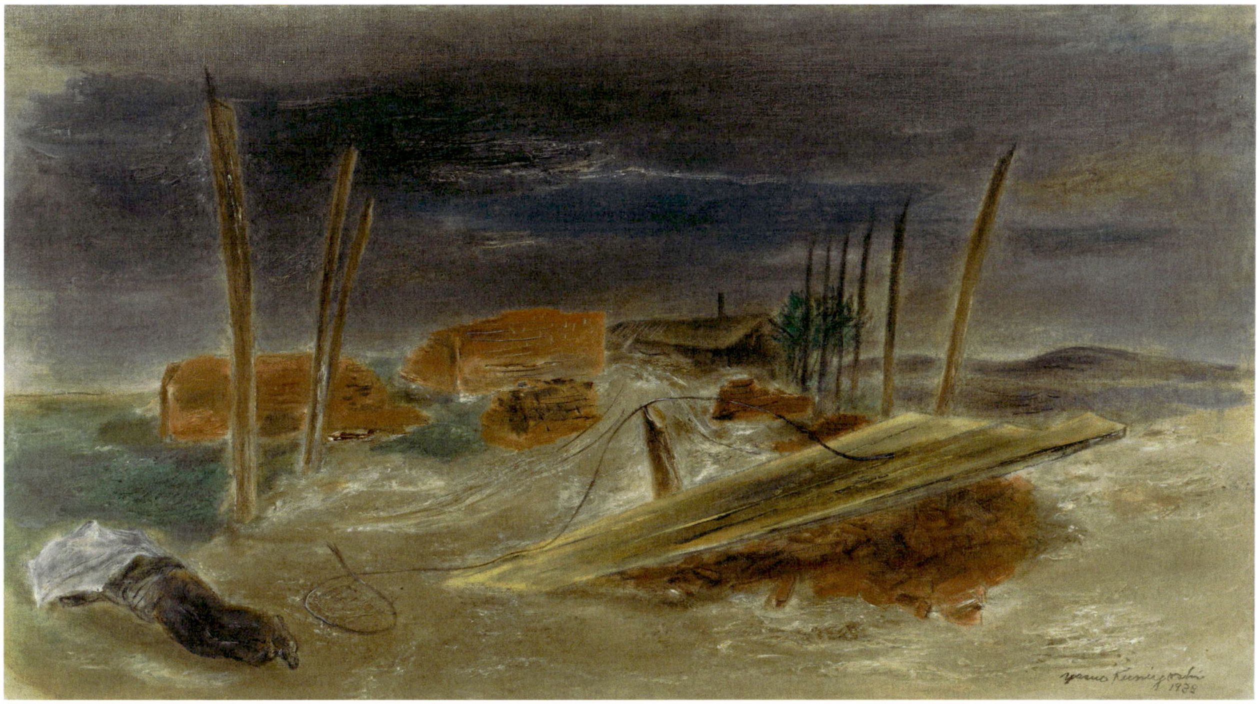

FIG. 48
Yasuo Kuniyoshi, *Deserted Brickyard*, 1938, oil on canvas, 20 ⅛ × 35 ¼ in. Honolulu Museum of Art, Gift of Philip E. Spalding, 1949

WOMAN PAINTINGS OF THE 1930S

During this period of political ferment many of Kuniyoshi's works were oblique in their reflection of the times, and he developed what would become one of his most celebrated subjects: the single woman, scantily dressed and seated in a simple interior. He painted these from models, although at some point in the process he would stop using them and develop the painting on his own. This new working method allied him with many of his American contemporaries, who have been called "studio painters" as they habitually painted from models or still-life setups in their studios. Many of his Penguin Club friends, like Kuhn and Pascin, worked like this, as did some younger painters who were beginning to emerge, like Raphael Soyer—but in Kuniyoshi's case the change was directly inspired by what he had seen in France, after which he "stopped working from the imagination and started working from reality."[102] His friend Pascin was repeatedly cited by contemporary critics as an influence on Kuniyoshi. Although Kuniyoshi here aligned himself more with common practice than was the case with the eccentric subjects he invented in the 1920s, his paintings are still clearly his, easily distinguishable from those of his contemporaries. Comparing a painting like *Daily News* (1935) with a typical Pascin such as *Reclining Model*, Kuniyoshi's is more solid and substantial (pl. 34; see fig. 30). The paint is thicker and more sensuous, and in the background he used the oil paint abstractly, swirling around thick passages in a way that suggests an inner mental agitation projected out from the pensive woman. His tactile application of the paint looks forward to the abstract expressionists of the next generation, and if we were to apply the dualities here Kuniyoshi, with his physical, expressive use of the European medium of oil paint, seems more Western than Pascin, who thinned his paint down so it worked almost like watercolor.

Daily News gets its title from the newspaper the woman holds, and newspapers would accompany most of the women Kuniyoshi painted in this series. I have previously argued that these moody, partly disrobed women can be seen as sex objects, subject to the male gaze, as in conventional feminist analysis, but that there is another dimension to them: they also serve as alter egos for the artist.[103] Because of his origins, and the fact that he regularly was in the company of fellow Japanese, Kuniyoshi was keenly aware of the rise of Japanese militarism and he took an explicit public stand against the policies of his native country. In the early 1920s his paintings had been animated by curiously cheerful figures, and later in the decade seductive reclining women tended to take their place. His women of the 1930s are thinking; accompanied by newspapers and set against backgrounds of swirling, agitated passages of thick oil paint, they are sensuous sex objects, but also projections of the artist's mental state, figures of empathy.

Although they are simply models posed in the studio, the political implications of the passive women featured with newspapers that bring word of the world outside the studio were not lost on Kuniyoshi's contemporaries. Critic Forbes Watson, in a rousing editorial titled "Slackers Under the Skin" from 1939 chose to juxtapose his text with a full-page reproduction of Kuniyoshi's *I'm Tired*, an image of a dark-eyed young woman in a slip resting her elbows on an issue of the *Daily News* and staring gloomily at it. Watson raised an emotional issue, one often voiced in artists' circles in these years: "Good God, how can you go on chattering about sculpture and painting when the children of Poland lie slaughtered by Hitler's bombs?" His vehement answer was, "Every good sculpture, painting, book, poem, composition that we now produce is a direct shot against barbarism, a direct help to civilization." In this context, Kuniyoshi's painting was one of those shots, while its meditating woman served as an illustration of those who "would rather 'sob at the radio' than do our jobs."[104] Similarly, the sultry woman in *Waiting* (1938) holding a cigarette with a glass of red wine before her, lost in thought while her elbow rests on a newspaper, embodies both sensuality and melancholy (pl. 37).

Critics repeatedly praised Kuniyoshi's painterly sensibility, and felt this quality was essential to the success of his art. His small painting *Café* (1937) can serve as an example (pl. 35). The lithograph he made of the same image is his most popular print, perhaps because the chic young woman sits next to a suggestively empty chair and looks directly out at the viewer, unlike most of Kuniyoshi's women. Kuniyoshi painted her using his distinctive palette of earth tones, with a restrictedness that encourages highly refined distinctions of color. The brown of her hat is slightly redder than that of the fur shawl that encircles her, and the brown of the table is more orange than either of them. Her red lips are the most intense color in the painting, and they are a muted red. Much of her face is thinly painted, if it is painted at all—in part it is just the gray charcoal under drawing, which then is articulated by patches of thicker cream color at her jaw, cheek, and nose. The tactility of the paint rises to a crescendo in the excited textures that communicate the furriness of her shawl, and a single stroke of impasto black paint snakes across her hat, defining the hatband, establishing a sinuous counterpoint to the busy activity of the fur. She sits calmly before a creamy gold and gray background, which evolves into a passage of thickly textured paint strokes to the left of her head, like an emanation of the mental activity that is going on behind her impassive face. The partially full glass on the table indicates her bohemian lifestyle, while the open newspaper suggests the world beyond the café, adding a lone note of white to the sophisticated browns that warm the rest of the painting.

The woman in *Girl Thinking* (1935) sits lost in thought, her legs open toward us, her slip falling down to expose one breast (pl. 33). But she is suggestive rather than explicit: her slip just covers her crotch, and her exposed breast, as is the case with all the women in this series, is not realistically delineated—it is a mound, and while it faces us directly, it only suggests a breast. In addition, a subtle color scheme also sends a message: her slip is pink, making it clear that her skin is not. This is consistent with the tawny skin color we have seen in Kuniyoshi's figures, including his self-portraits.

Jacqueline Francis, in her book *Making Race*, a study of three artists working in the United States before World War II (Malvin Gray Johnson, an African American; Max Weber, a Jew; and Kuniyoshi), writes of skin color in Kuniyoshi's art: "There is no question that he repeatedly represented a darkened whiteness, moving whiteness as a category away from ideals and absolutes, and throwing the certainty of race altogether into doubt."[105] In the early 1940s his friend Harry Sternberg made a silk-screened portrait of Kuniyoshi, seated, surrounded by the white-stemmed bowl, the grapes, the pitcher that repeatedly appear in his still-life paintings of the period (fig. 49). The inverted table refers to Kuniyoshi's 1940 still life, *Upside Down Table and Mask* (pl. 39). Sternberg also depicted three partly dressed women swirling around the table, and he colored the lower one bright pink, while the other two are a kind of warm yellow-brown, which echoes the skin of Kuniyoshi, seated in the foreground—and makes explicit the element of self-identification invested in Kuniyoshi's painting of skin. In 1941, Jacob Lawrence would become Kuniyoshi's gallery mate at the Downtown Gallery; skin color and the issues of race that attend it were regular themes in his art. Kuniyoshi said that he wanted to paint not one woman, but "universal woman"—not a portrait, but a general type. If a universal woman could be conjured by mixing all the women in the world together, her skin would not be pink, but she would correspond to the American

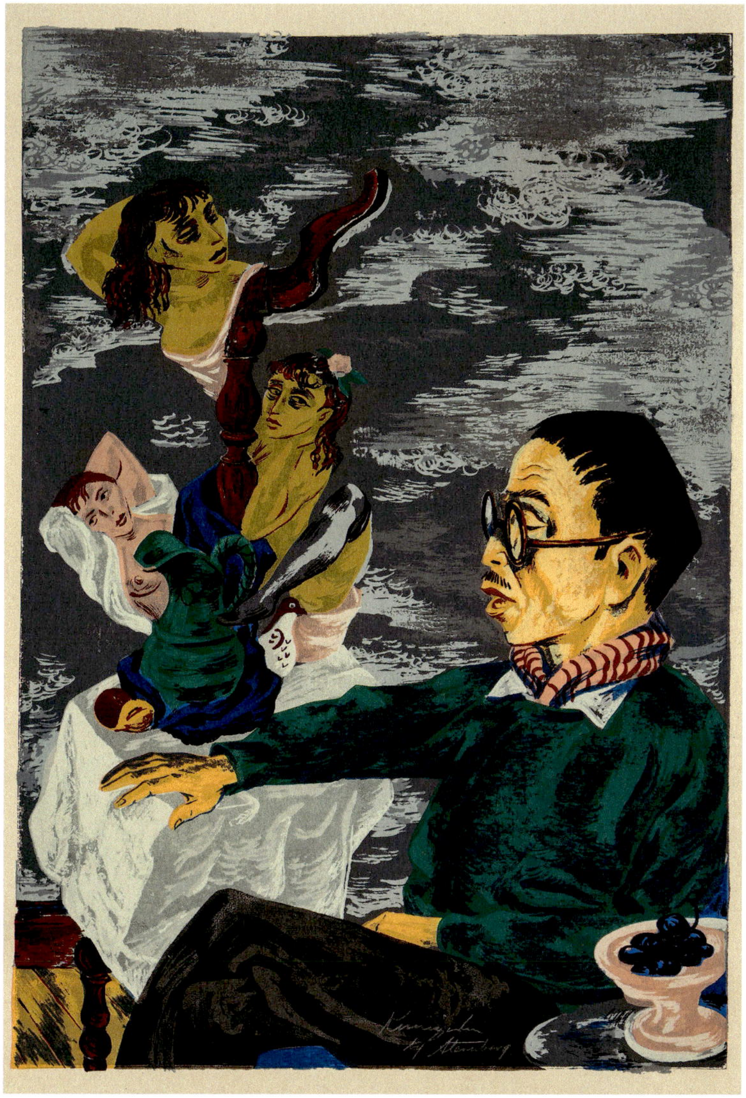

FIG. 49
Harry Sternberg, *Portrait of Yasuo Kuniyoshi*, 1943–44, screenprint on paper; sheet: 26 5/8 × 18 5/8 in., image: 24 3/8 × 16 3/8 in. Hirshhorn Museum and Sculpture Garden, Smithsonian Institution, Washington, DC; The Joseph H. Hirshhorn Bequest, 1981

idea of the "melting pot"—the idea of the United States that Kuniyoshi believed in and exemplified.[106]

In the year of his second marriage, 1935, Kuniyoshi received a Guggenheim grant that enabled him and his bride to travel to the Southwest and Mexico. The trip was not a success—he got ill with stomach flu and it was uncomfortably hot much of the time. But he did get to study frescoes by the Mexican muralists, and visited Tamiji Kitagawa, the main Japanese artist living in Mexico. He was impressed by the vast empty spaces of the United States that would influence his paintings over the coming years, like *Between Two Worlds* (1939) with an iconography that stressed not only the openness of the land, but the American practice of throwing things away rather than repairing them—landscapes littered with ruined objects would appear increasingly in his works as the war approached (pl. 38). This one is another of his unusual paintings, with the three women, lushly proportioned and, for the 1930s, skimpily dressed in shorts and halter tops, enjoying one another's camaraderie at the far right of the canvas. Painted with his typically rich, warm palette and creamy paint strokes, the rest of the scene is devoted to some discarded wood, a broken wheel, a barren tree, and an ominous building set against the sooty sky. Kuniyoshi told an interviewer that this impregnable-looking structure on a bluff was an "insane asylum," which presents a somber contrast to the robust female trio turning their backs on it.[107]

PHOTOGRAPHY AND THE LATER 1930S

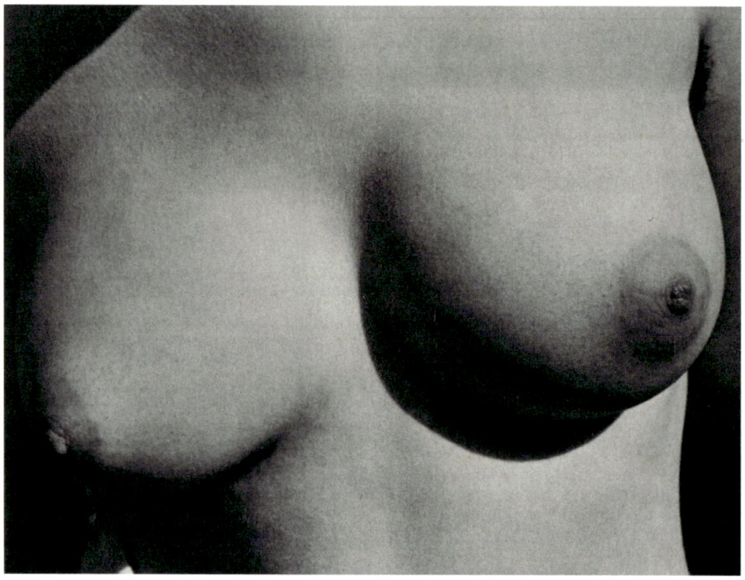

In the second half of the 1930s, Kuniyoshi started taking photographs and printing them for his own pleasure. His enthusiasm for the new, lightweight Leica 35mm camera was shared by many of his painter friends, including Reginald Marsh, Woodstock artists Konrad Cramer and Emil Ganso, and Kuniyoshi's gallery mates at the Downtown Gallery, Ben Shahn and Charles Sheeler. He set up a darkroom in his Woodstock studio in 1937, and art writer Harry Salpeter reported that his camera was "the almost constant companion of his leisure hours."[108] His photography was generally seen as a "hobby," but he had a trained artist's eye and an acute sense of visual form and composition—today his photographs are treated as works of art and are in museums and art collections. He took and printed around four hundred photographs, and three-quarters of them are owned by two collections: the Fukutake Collection in Okayama, Japan, and the J. Paul Getty Museum in Malibu, California. Many of the pictures are casual: a group was taken when one of Kuniyoshi's art classes went on a picnic, another when he and his wife hosted a party in the backyard of their house in Woodstock. Like his friend Reginald Marsh, he photographed a series of bathers on the beach at Coney Island, and made snapshot portraits of fellow artists. One series is of a statuesque nude model; in several prints he cropped the image to focus on her ample breasts, with the earthiness that characterizes some of his work in other media. He won a prize from Leica in 1936 for a photograph from this series (fig. 50). With its overt sexuality it was by far the most explicit photograph in the Leica annual book of 148 images, many of which featured children and animals. The eroticism underlying much of Kuniyoshi's art, encouraged by Parisian practices, sometimes provoked censorious reactions in the United States, for example at the University of Wyoming in 1936, when the president of the school ordered five paintings of nudes removed from an exhibition, including one by Kuniyoshi.[109] In a similar vein, Charles Alan, who worked as an assistant to Kuniyoshi's dealer, Edith Halpert, told about an evening with several artists and their wives where Kuniyoshi showed pornographic Japanese prints he had been recently given by a friend, generating a lively discussion until Halpert reacted with disapproval and he hastily put them away.[110]

While many of his photographs were taken head-on, he also often positioned himself above or below a scene, resulting in uptilted compositions with strong diagonal axes that echo tendencies in his paintings and drawings. *Bathers, Coney Island* (1938) is one example, where the large man's foot protruding under the railing at the right, and the subsequent jump to the woman directly below the boardwalk, creates a spatial leap (fig. 51). Other of his photographs suggest the mood of rising anxiety found in his paintings of the later 1930s. *May Day Parade* (1937) records costumed demonstrators during a political march down Fourteenth Street, where Kuniyoshi had his studio (fig. 52). Two marchers, wearing huge grotesque masks caricaturing Hitler and Mussolini, confront an anonymous spectator cropped at the left, forebodings of the war to come. On a more elegiac note, Kuniyoshi took a series of photographs of an abandoned shed, sensitive studies of the texture of the wood but also images of the shattered destruction of a man-made structure (fig. 53). Their ragged geometries evoke feelings similar to those summoned up by his paintings and drawings of ruined buildings in the western United States. Kuniyoshi's photographic activity produced a richly varied body of work in the late 1930s, but it was abruptly curtailed after the Japanese bombing of Pearl Harbor on December 7, 1941. As a Japanese citizen, he was classified an "enemy alien" by the U.S. government and was not permitted to possess a camera.

Kuniyoshi had gotten over his shyness with women, and as he was charming, an elegant dresser, and a successful artist many women were attracted to him and he to them, as Sternberg's portrait, with women swirling around, suggests (see fig. 49). Sternberg explained, "Yas was small, not good

FIG. 50
Yasuo Kuniyoshi, *Nude*, about 1936, from *Leica 1937 Photo Annual*, Kuniyoshi Library, Woodstock Artists Association and Museum Archives, Woodstock, New York

FIG. 51
Yasuo Kuniyoshi, *Bathers, Coney Island*, 1938, gelatin silver print, $7\frac{9}{16} \times 9\frac{9}{16}$ in. J. Paul Getty Museum, Los Angeles

FIG. 52
Yasuo Kuniyoshi, *May Day Parade*, 1937, gelatin silver print, $7\frac{7}{16} \times 9\frac{1}{2}$ in. Joy of Giving Something/ Forward Thinking Museum, www.jgsinc.org

FIG. 53
Yasuo Kuniyoshi, *Judson Smith's Barn 5*, 1938, photograph, $7\frac{1}{2} \times 9\frac{1}{2}$ in. Fukutake Collection, Okayama, Japan

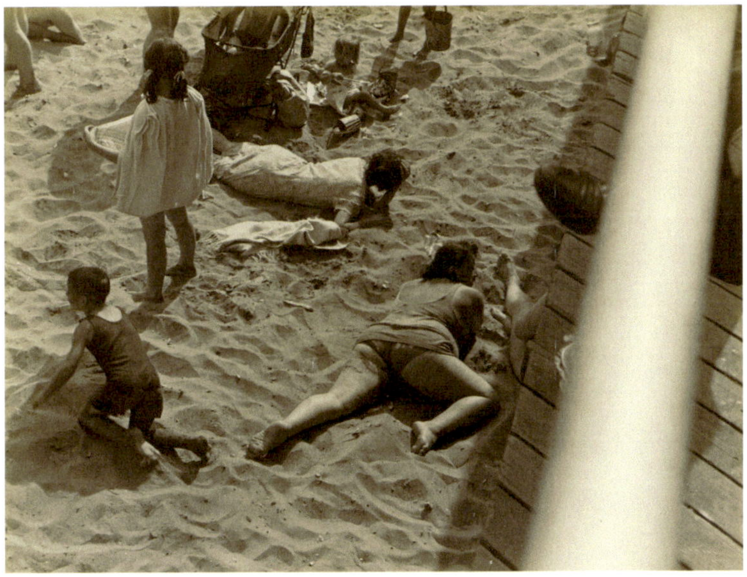

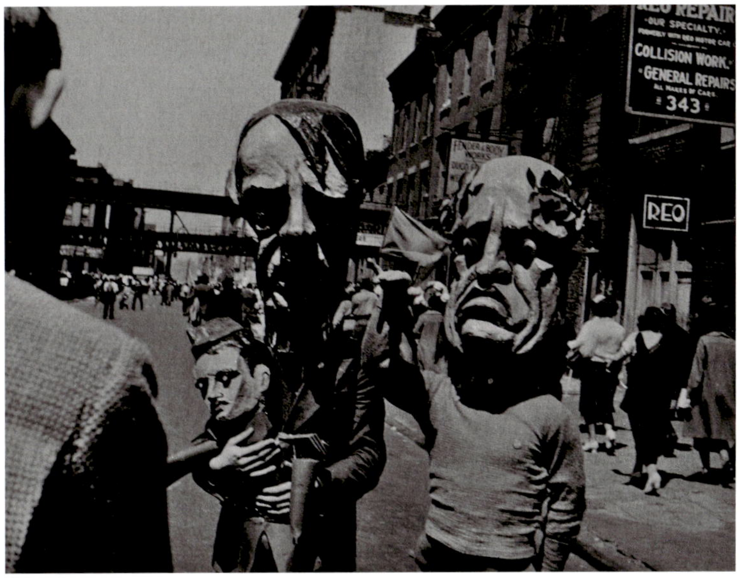

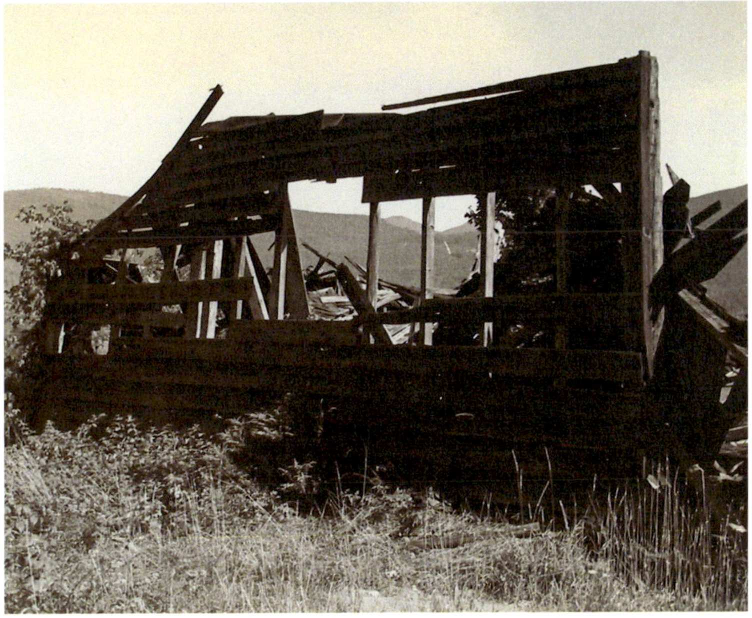

looking, almost like the caricature Japanese, with protruding buck teeth—but the girls were crazy about him."[111] Lily Harmon wrote about her affair with Kuniyoshi in her autobiography, *Freehand* (1981). An aspiring artist, she rented a studio next to his at Thirty East Fourteenth Street and was seduced by him. Harmon, who would later be married to art collector Joseph Hirshhorn for eight years, commented on Kuniyoshi's accent in reference to his 1946 painting, *Look, It Flies!*: "'Rook, it fries!' Why does he choose titles with all those r's? He can't pronounce them." But she also observed, "Kuniyoshi's way of talking serves him well. He is the most popular of artists, for speeches, for committees. He has wonderful humor." When she told her husband Sidney about their affair he responded, "How could you?...A Jap!" which encouraged Harmon to divorce him. But Kuniyoshi was not divorcing Sara, so Harmon moved on, recording for posterity in her memoir, "He is as delicate and adroit in his lovemaking as in his paintings."[112]

In 1941, Kuniyoshi left his wife for a woman named Myra, and set out on a tour of the Southwest (he would reunite with Sara in 1944). The landscapes that resulted push further his imagery of vast spaces filled with broken and decaying objects, including scenes of deserted, crumbling cemeteries and weed-strewn vistas, like *Nevadaville* (1942) with its rotting, abandoned cigar billboard (fig. 54). In the South and Midwest he admired "that something vastness and primitiveness which is different from Maine ruggedness, I thought it is more of a beginning of creation of earth," and wrote that he hoped he would be able to return someday to do it justice in his painting.[113] With these sentiments about true American beauty residing in rural midwestern landscapes he approached the ideals of the Regionalist painters of the 1930s, Thomas Hart Benton, Grant Wood, and John Steuart Curry. But he disagreed with their nationalistic arguments, and he expressed his melting-pot ideals in a lecture at the Museum of Modern Art in 1940:

> Mr. Benton forgets that whatever is American today is the product of a conglomeration of customs and traditions of many peoples. If we are to further the growth of American art it must spring from many sources, and needless to say, that which has been attained up to date has been a culmination of not only native but foreign forces.[114]

He spent most of his career in New York City and associated with urban realist painters, and did much of his painting

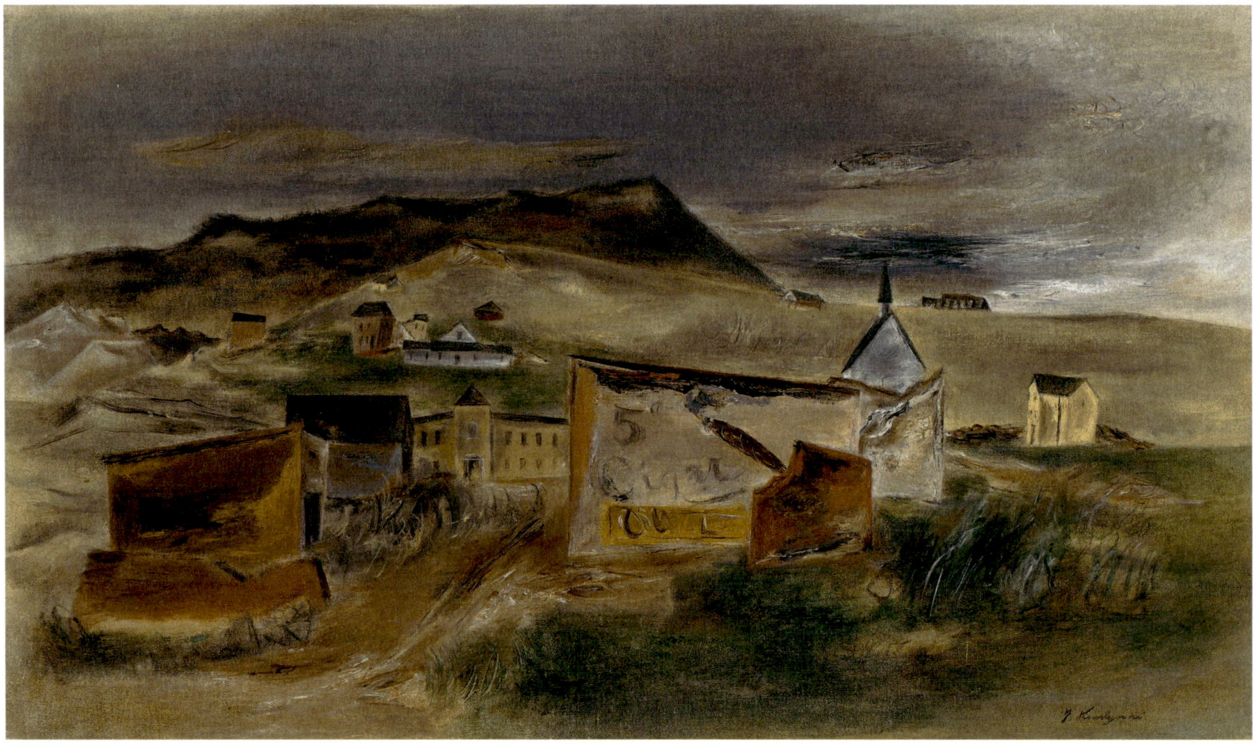

FIG. 54
Yasuo Kuniyoshi, *Nevadaville*, 1942, oil on canvas, 24 3/8 × 40 1/8 in. Virginia Museum of Fine Arts, Richmond; John Barton Payne Fund, 44.8.1

FIG. 55
Yasuo Kuniyoshi, *Lay Figure*, 1937–38, oil on canvas, 38 3/16 × 58 3/16 in. Collection Walker Art Center, Minneapolis; Gift of the T. B. Walker Foundation, Gilbert M. Walker Fund, 1948

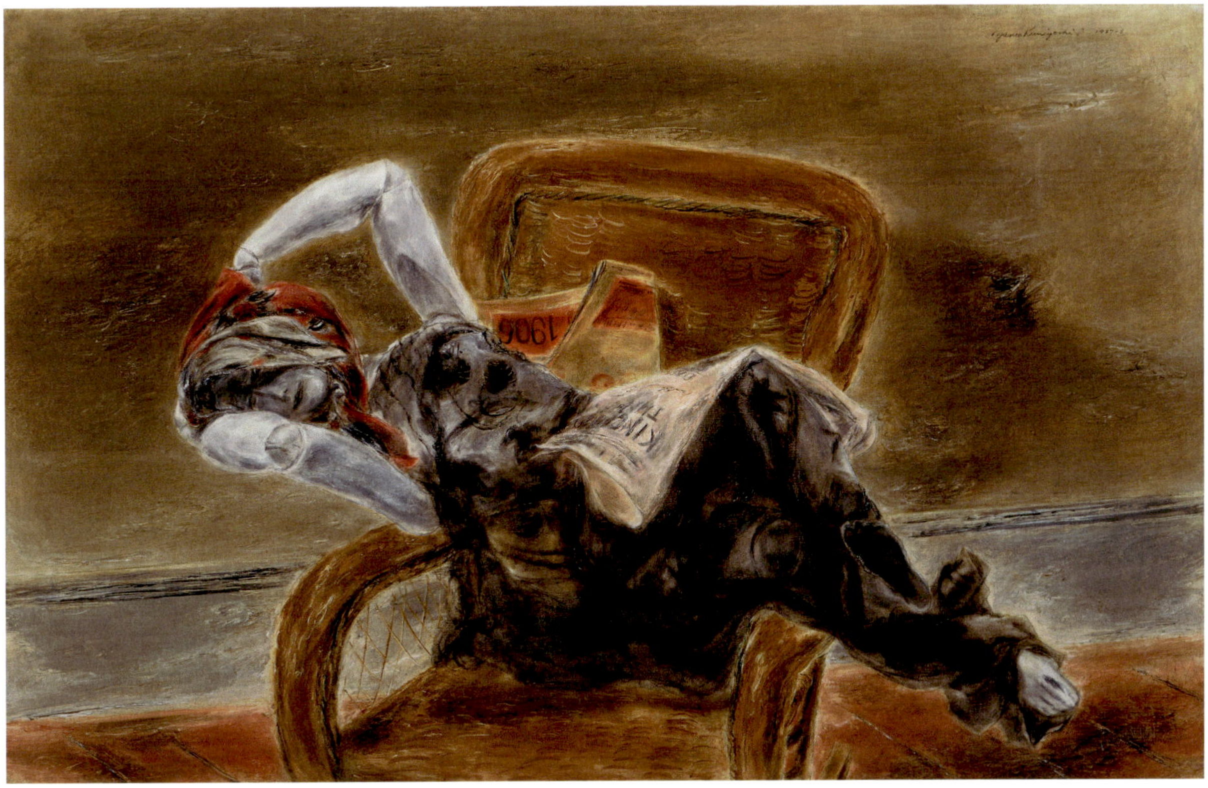

there, but unlike many of his contemporaries he rarely painted urban scenes.

His still-life paintings, like his landscapes, became more monumental and more brooding in the later 1930s, as international tensions were on the rise. He developed his fascination with still-life painting into new directions, novel fusions of figure and landscape painting. In *Lay Figure* (1937–38) a wooden mannequin sprawls diagonally across the wicker chair where sensual models previously posed; she wears delicate, lacy fabrics, and a newspaper is draped over her thighs (fig. 55). She smiles slightly as her arms are raised seductively above her head, but she is inanimate, creating an uneasy tension between the human and the inhuman already seen in European art with De Chirico's influential mannequins and the statues of Magritte. Kuniyoshi as usual made the words on the newspaper frustratingly illegible—but the magazine squeezed between the figure and the back of the chair clearly reads "1906"—the year the artist came to the United States. In *Upside Down Table and Mask* the mask plays a role similar to the mannequin: it is a face, but not human (see pl. 39). It perches near the top of an unsteady, irrational assemblage of objects—a blue vase that seems to levitate, a folding ruler that is bent so it cannot measure, a table missing a leg and turned over so it cannot function, and a copy of the *Daily News*—suggesting that current events are behind this precarious instability.

THE WAR YEARS

The Japanese military bombed Pearl Harbor in Hawaii in a surprise attack on December 7, 1941. Four days later Kuniyoshi wrote his artist friend George Biddle, who was a friend of President Franklin Roosevelt and whose brother, Francis, was U.S. attorney general, "A few short days has changed my status in this country, although I myself have not changed at all."[115] Legally a Japanese citizen, he immediately became an "enemy alien," under suspicion from the government. He was fortunate compared to his fellow Japanese immigrants on the West Coast, who were rounded up and evacuated to internment camps, but it still was a period of terrible stress and anxiety for him. Not only did he surrender his camera, but his binoculars were confiscated. He could not go from his New York apartment to Woodstock without permission; he could not fly; his bank account was frozen; and he had to observe a curfew. He felt uncomfortable and under suspicion, particularly when he was in public. In the months immediately after Pearl Harbor he could not leave his building, and his teaching assistant, Anne Helioff, would bring his students and their artworks down from the Art Students League on Fifty-Seventh Street to his studio on Fourteenth Street.[116] Friends and supporters sent letters to government officials assuring them of his loyalty to the United States and the cause of democracy. One was from his fellow artists in An American Group, an organization of figurative artists that Kuniyoshi served as president, and another was from a group of his students. It was on record that for years he had opposed Japanese military aggression in China.[117] He quickly volunteered to work for the American propaganda effort, and wrote two speeches that were translated into Japanese and broadcast to Japan over Voice of America, the official broadcasting arm of the U.S. government. He also made a series of drawings for the Office of War Information (OWI) for the American propaganda effort. With their depictions of explicit violence these constitute a dramatic departure from his previous work. Intended as propaganda, they also express a cathartic release from the tensions he felt, while manifesting a painful ambivalence: fierce opposition to Japanese policies from an artist who was himself Japanese. Working for the government was a complicated process, as the OWI propaganda poster project itself was controversial: conservatives opposed it, and there was a debate between officials who felt commercial illustrators were best suited to create effective images and those who wanted fine artists involved. The former won in the end, and consequently none of Kuniyoshi's works were actually made into posters that were circulated, though many of his drawings still exist as documents of his artistic and political commitments. Some might think that his activities on behalf of the Allies were self-serving, since as an enemy alien he was suspect and therefore he asserted his loyalty, but his actions were consistent with his earlier sympathies: he had long believed in the virtues of democracy and opposed Japan's militaristic impulses.

In April 1942 he made huge caricatures of the Axis leaders with two fellow Art Students League instructors. Jon Corbino, who was Italian, satirized Mussolini; George Grosz, a radical leftist who had fled Germany, drew Hitler; and Kuniyoshi lampooned Hirohito; photographs of the artists with their satiric creations were featured in newspapers and *Time* magazine.[118] Meanwhile, Kuniyoshi was working with representatives of the OWI who gave him guidance concerning his propaganda drawings. He was asked to illustrate "the Japanese enemy," and made several drawings of a seated warrior in traditional samurai armor. After Thomas Mabry, a representative of the OWI, respectfully suggested that these were a little remote, and wrote, "I should appreciate very much your trying your hand at a poster on the recent Japanese atrocities," Kuniyoshi erupted into the most violent images of his career.[119] These charcoal drawings included brutal scenes such as *Hanged* (1943), where a woman, identifiable as Chinese by her face and her dress, has been lynched next to the suspended, bleeding body of a trussed up infant (pl. 44). In the rear a Japanese soldier, identifiable by his samurai sword, stands with his back turned from the gruesome scene. The bare tree that had suggested new life in Kuniyoshi's 1920s works like *Boy Stealing Fruit* has become a mechanism of murder. The brutality of the image harks back to scenes from Goya's famous *The Disasters of War* series, such as *Tampoco* (after 1810; fig. 56). World War II artists in the United States who were striving to represent the cruelties of the war often evoked Goya, along with Daumier and Callot. Unlike Goya, who usually indicated a hint of a horizon to create a sense of a landscape where these atrocities took place, Kuniyoshi floated his figures in an undefined, nightmarish space. Often the victims were identifiably Chinese. In Kuniyoshi's *Killer, or Chinese woman praying* (1942), women and children are menaced by an aggressive soldier who is identified as Japanese by the flag that hangs from the rifle he is swinging like a baseball bat (pl. 42). In statements Kuniyoshi made during the war he often cited the Chinese resistance: "It is not a racial war. Look at the Chinese. They are an Oriental people, yet they are fighting the Japanese along with the other United Nations."[120] This argument lay behind the emphasis on Chinese victims in his propaganda drawings.

While working on this assignment Kuniyoshi invented an image that he drew in several variations, titled *Clean Up This Mess* (1942): a giant hand holds a bag of garbage ready to drop it (pl. 41). The sack is filled with symbols of Japan: the flag, broken samurai swords dripping with blood, an octopus, bombs, and in the example illustrated here, a little Japanese soldier struggling to climb out of the bag. The artist threw himself into the poster assignment, making scores of violent drawings that helped exorcise some of his emotions during this troubled time. But virtually none of them were produced as posters; according to the records, he was paid for two.[121] One was the *Water Cure* (1942), for which he made several

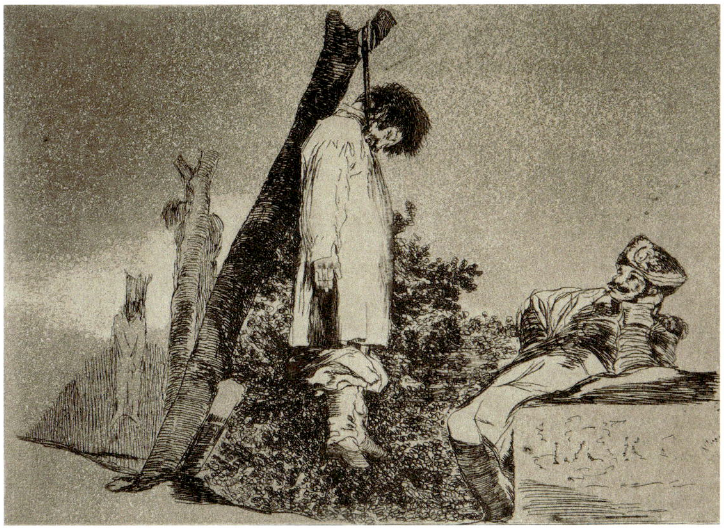

FIG. 56
Francisco de Goya, *Tampoco (Not [in this case] either)*, plate 36 from *Los Desastres de la Guerra*, published 1863, etching; burnished aquatint, drypoint, burin, and burnisher; plate: 6 ⅛ × 8 ¹⁄₁₆ in., sheet: 9 ⅜ × 13 ¹⁄₁₆ in. Yale University Art Gallery, New Haven; University Purchase

FIG. 57
Yasuo Kuniyoshi, *Water Cure*, 1943, lithograph in black, handcoloring with ink and watercolor on paper, 40 × 28 in. Gallery Nii, Osaka, Japan

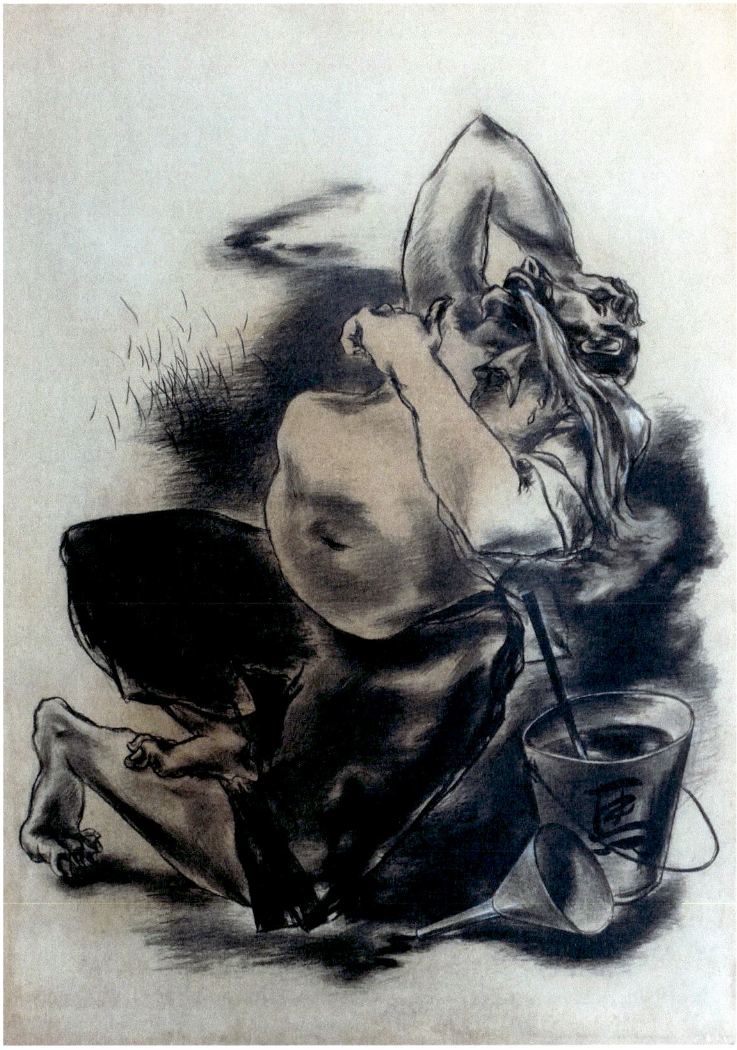

studies and a large finished drawing of a subject that is still relevant in the days of waterboarding (pl. 43; fig. 57). The drawings focus on a single bound figure, writhing in agony as he is tortured by being nearly drowned with water from a bucket that is labelled "Horse" in Japanese—he is being treated like an animal. The large, finished drawing shows the "horse" bucket and a siphon next to the victim as liquid pours from his gaping mouth. The body language of the figure gives the image its power, from the head, thrown back in agony, to the painfully twisted foot at the left. This drawing was in the collection of Ben Shahn, Kuniyoshi's friend who was also making drawings for the OWI and whose career repeatedly overlaps with the artist's.

The only Kuniyoshi drawing that was actually printed as a poster was *Torture* (1943), derived from a magnificent study of a muscular man's torso from the back, scarred with slashing wounds as he struggles against handcuffs (pl. 47; fig. 58). It harks back to Michelangelo's bound slaves: the pathos of the figure is heightened due to the contrast between his powerful body and his helplessness. As ShiPu Wang has pointed out, here the artist dropped his signifiers of Japanese identify to create an image of universal suffering due to war.[122] The image was printed a few times with different slogans, but never published as an edition, thanks to the dictates of Price Gilbert, a former executive from the Coca-Cola Company, who was hired by the OWI and who favored posters designed by commercial artists over those made by fine artists.[123] The poster appeared again in a painting by Ben Shahn, *We Fight for a Free World!* (about 1942), where Shahn paid tribute to his fellow artists by depicting a

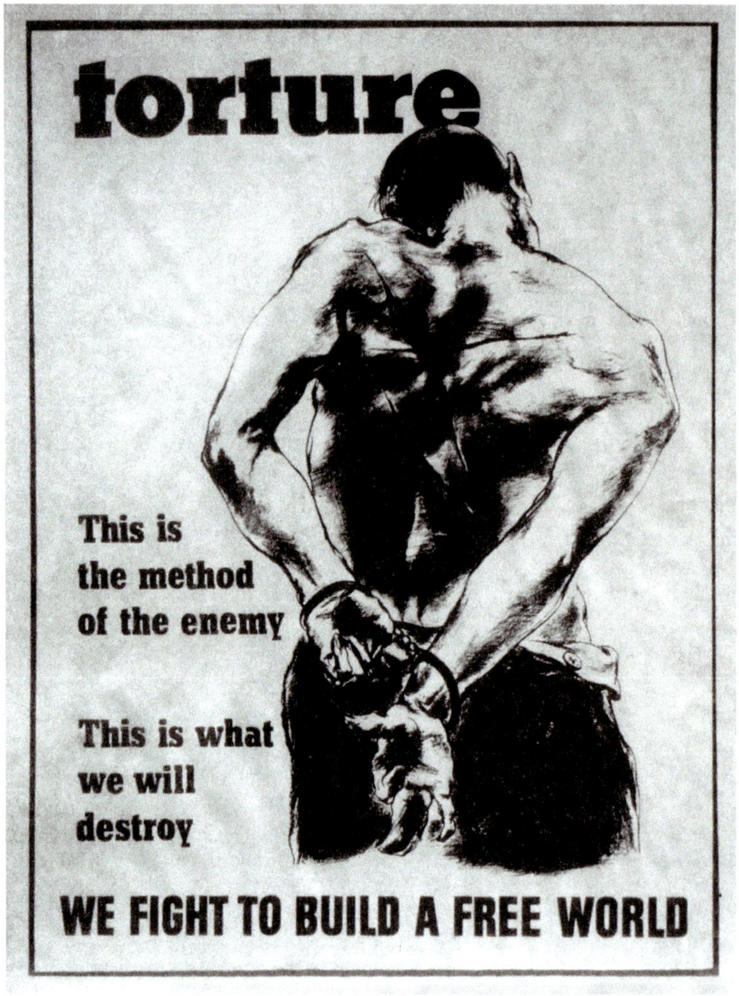

FIG. 58
Yasuo Kuniyoshi, *Torture (1)*, 1943, poster, 20 × 14 3⁄16 in.

FIG. 59
Ben Shahn, *We Fight for a Free World!*, about 1942, tempera on board, 13 × 30 in. Courtesy of Michael Rosenfeld Gallery LLC, New York

group of five posters, by Charles White, Käthe Kollwitz, himself, Kuniyoshi and Bernard Perlin, hanging on a brick wall (fig. 59).

WARTIME SPEECHES

As the most famous Japanese artist in the United States, Kuniyoshi took an active public role in this period, serving in pro-democracy organizations, making many speeches and appearances. His two talks for radio broadcast to Japan were both titled "Japan Against Japan," and in each he was introduced as sharing the name of Utagawa Kuniyoshi, to connect him to nineteenth-century Japanese artistic traditions. In his February 1942 speech he addressed people in the cultural fields, and argued that the freedoms afforded by the democratic system are essential for creativity. He cited a long list of European artists and intellectuals who had recently fled Europe to attain the freedoms available in the United States. As an example of democracy in action he recounted how, shortly after Pearl Harbor, he resigned from a jury for the Pennsylvania Academy of the Fine Arts because of his new status as an enemy alien, only to have his resignation firmly refused. This was especially meaningful because he had previously agreed to judge a show of student work for China Relief, but after the Pearl Harbor attack he was asked to switch to being just a sponsor. In his second speech, in mid-March, he emphasized antimilitarism. He recounted his experiences as a child with militarism in Japan, and argued that he was not a traitor, but "loyal to the democratic way of living... which I hope will some day be extended to Japan."[124] He also stated that the war was a race war only on the Axis side, but for the Allies it was a war of ideas: "Our democratic idea against the idea of totalitarianism.... Your leaders tell you that the white people regard the colored peoples as an inferior race but your Nazi partner is the only country who so regards you." He concluded by predicting that recent Allied losses would be turned around: "Your warlords have started this war; it is we who shall finish it." Throughout this period he was resolute in his opposition to Japan: in a newspaper interview he urged that Tokyo be bombed, and he made some startling propaganda drawings of bombs dropping on the Japanese capital.[125] But he was always on the side of the Japanese people, against their militaristic rulers, and in New York he was active with several Japanese American groups that shared his beliefs.

When he addressed the Japanese American Committee for Democracy (JACD) in April 1942, along with his usual points about the virtues of the democratic system he mentioned "narrow-mindedness and prejudice towards us." He suggested that this could be partly remedied if the Japanese in the United States were less shy and self-segregating. He also condemned contemporary painting in the Axis countries: "The painting

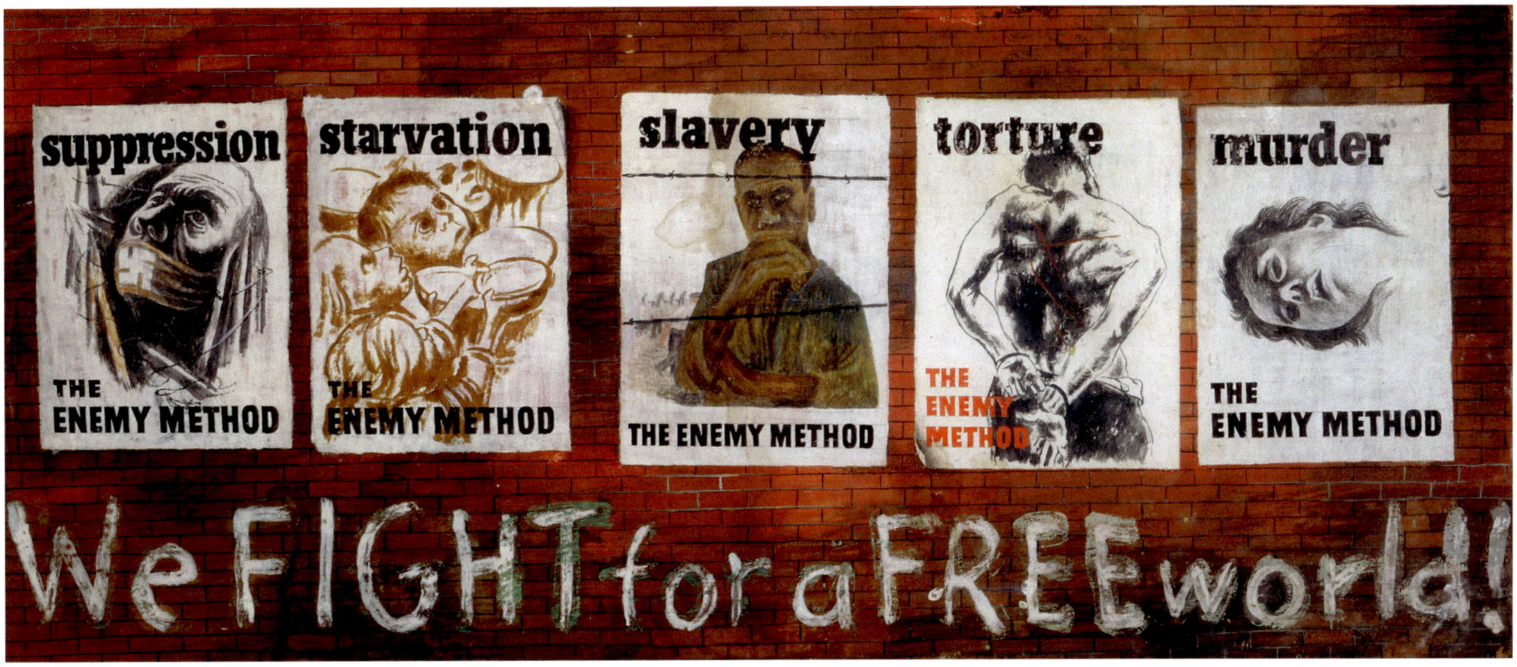

of Nazi-Germany and Japan today is barbaric and oppressive and reflects the false precepts under which it exists."[126] He was an active member of the JACD, and the chair of its Arts Committee, which included artists such as Isamu Noguchi and Chuzo Tamotzu.[127] The JACD opposed the internment camps, seeing them as manifestations of racism, but it actively supported Franklin Roosevelt in his bid for re-election in 1944, believing that he was the best choice to combat fascism, which was the JACD's highest priority. Although today many Japanese Americans hold Roosevelt responsible for the internment camps, the JACD defended him, arguing that Roosevelt supported the creation of a Japanese American army troop, and the internment camps were the responsibility of General DeWitt "under pressure . . . from the race haters of the West Coast."[128] Kuniyoshi also spoke under the auspices of the JACD at a "Nisei-For-Roosevelt Rally" where he said, "How envious I am of you fellow Japanese Americans who are citizens and therefore are privileged to vote in this vital election."[129] Meanwhile, Kuniyoshi's friend from the Art Students League, Toshi Shimizu, who had welcomed him when he returned to Japan in 1931, was painting battle scenes for the Japanese government, as was Kuniyoshi's former supporter, Foujita.

Kuniyoshi organized a retrospective exhibition of his work, in May 1942 at the Downtown Gallery, for the benefit of China Relief. One painting of his for each year from 1921 to 1941 was borrowed back from museums and collectors. Admission was charged and his painting, *Girl with Flowered Hat*, was raffled off, all the proceeds going to China Relief. But later that year when a number of artists' groups, including An American Group of which he was president, persuaded the Metropolitan Museum of Art to hold an exhibition titled *Artists For Victory*, Kuniyoshi was not permitted to exhibit, because he was not a citizen of the United States.

Addressing a Japanese American audience at a "Rally For Victory in the Far East" near the end of the war, in December 1944, Kuniyoshi was candid about some of his experiences in the years since Pearl Harbor:

> I too felt the shock of the war, as you did, even though I had the insulation of friends and advisors. The blow struck by Japan upon this nation became a very personal one, as if I had stretched out my hand and committed the act myself. I know the sting of segregation and the look that condemns one as an enemy.[130]

Kuniyoshi's statement is typical of his generosity of spirit: he acknowledged to his Japanese American audience that during these trying years he had support that they may not have had, and he admitted feeling some level of complicity with the Japanese attack. His remark about the looks condemning him was borne out by sculptor Robert Laurent, Kuniyoshi's friend since the Ogunquit colony years, who described going to Gertrude Vanderbilt Whitney's funeral in Manhattan in April 1942: "[A]s Yas and I walked down the Avenue together, it seemed to me that the crowds along the sidewalks were all staring at Yas, as if an enemy were in their midst."[131] During this period he was still an enemy alien, subject to a curfew. Japanese American journalist Ayako Ishigaki, who also made antimilitaristic broadcasts to Japan (under her assumed name, Matsui, so as not to endanger her family there) recalled that Kuniyoshi and her husband, painter Eitaro Ishigaki, were neighbors and would go up to the roofs of their adjacent studio buildings to visit each other at night.[132]

In his "Rally for Victory" speech Kuniyoshi recounted that recently he was awarded a major honor, first prize at the Carnegie International exhibition: "To have received the prize at this crucial stage of the war seemed almost beyond belief." This was an example of American democracy, and he added, "It was also heartening to have a fellow Negro artist [Horace Pippin] singled out for a prize in the same exhibition." He praised the Japanese American troops fighting on the Allied side, but at the same time admitted he was "aware of other problems and injustices that have become so paramount these last few years."[133] *PM* magazine in 1944 reported that Kuniyoshi "considers the evacuation of Japanese Americans from the West Coast one of the undemocratic tragedies of the war."[134]

WORLD WAR II PAINTINGS

Given his time-consuming, patriotic activism and his slow painting process, Kuniyoshi was not prolific during these years, but he did make some striking paintings. *At Work* (1943) is the last of his painted self-portraits (pl. 46). Less assertive than his *Self-Portrait as a Golf Player*, it is small and he is impassive, reflecting the stresses of the war years. It is based directly on a photograph of him painting, to which he added the half-nude model behind him. *At Work* serves as a statement of the artist's working method. The model, his muse, represents the earthy sensuality of the real world, the source of his imagery. After working directly from her he would turn away and focus exclusively on the painting itself, transforming reality into a work of art.

My Man was also painted in 1943 and also is small in size (fig. 60). Again focused on a man and a woman, it is another one-of-a-kind Kuniyoshi painting. A young sailor and his lady friend overlook a beach with bathers inspired by Kuniyoshi's Coney Island photographs. Unlike the murky brown and gray skies of his previous landscapes, here the sky is pale blue and the sand is gold and orange, part of Kuniyoshi's move toward brighter color in his later works. The sailor leans confidently on the railing, looking jauntily over his shoulder, but the girl clutches him anxiously, distress on her face. Her emotions encapsulate the feelings of many who sent loved ones off to fight in the war. As Kuniyoshi told a reporter "you don't have to paint war scenes to reflect the war."[135] This was the sentiment behind a series of monumental allegorical paintings he executed during the war years, when he was not occupied making propaganda drawings for the government.[136]

Somebody Tore My Poster (1943) is an early example of these mysterious, evocative paintings Kuniyoshi made during the war and a few years after (pl. 45).[137] An elegant woman dominates the painting, partially turning toward the viewer but looking down, lost in thought. A weathered wall behind her supports the figure of a woman circus performer who at first glance seems to float in space, but is a paper doll tacked in place. Behind the central woman is the poster that gives the painting its title. Nearly illegible because of the destruction that has been wreaked upon it, it is a propaganda poster by Ben Shahn. Its ragged edge suggests an act of vandalism, and lends an air of desolation that will reappear in many of the artist's works in this period. Titled *We French Workers Warn You . . .*, it depicts a group of French laborers raising their arms in surrender to the Nazi-dominated Vichy government (fig. 61). One of their thick hands seems to threaten the woman's head from behind; its bluntness contrasts with her slender right hand elegantly poised with her cigarette. Her left hand rests sensitively on a railing in the foreground, and together they make clear how much Kuniyoshi's art has changed in comparison with the 1920s, when his figures featured comically stubby hands with tiny fingers. The woman turns away from the surrendering workers, while the acrobat seems to emerge from her head, suggesting an alternate state of mind, but there is no clear narrative behind this scene; it is deliberately ambiguous and evocative.

In 1946 he made two more powerful paintings of isolated women that combine with *Somebody Tore My Poster* to form a trilogy. *She Walks Among the Ruins* is aptly titled, as a somber woman, eyes downcast, tightens her red scarf as she moves away from a ruined landscape that contains a blasted walled city and another torn poster, this one an ad for cigarettes (pl. 52). It is painted with the rich, muted color and tactile

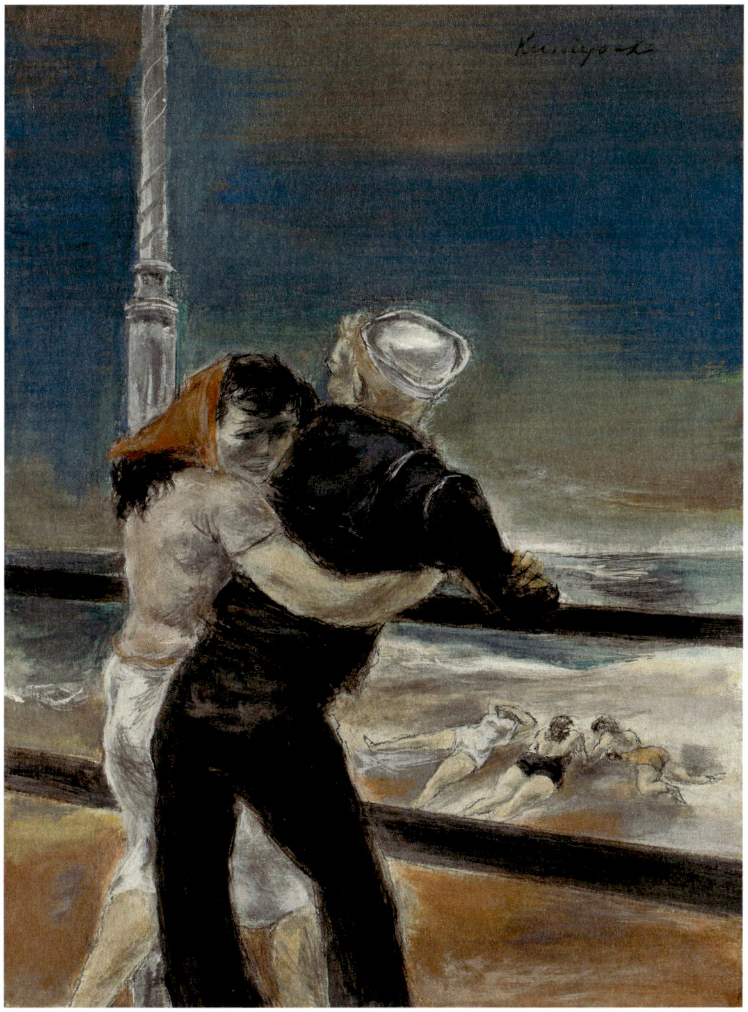

FIG. 60
Yasuo Kuniyoshi, *My Man*, 1943, casein on board, 14 ¾ × 10 ½ in. Art Institute of Chicago, Olivia Shaler Swan Memorial Collection

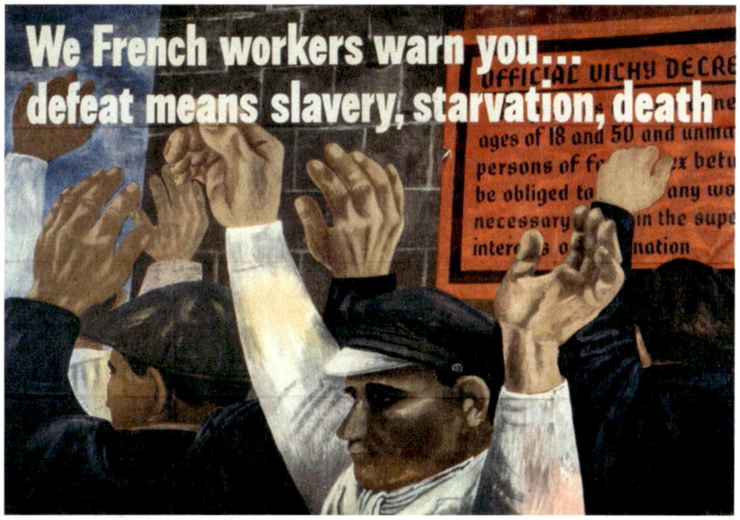

FIG. 61
Ben Shahn, *We French Workers Warn You . . . Defeat Means Slavery, Starvation, Death*, about 1942–43, print, 28 ½ × 39 ⅞ in. Office for Emergency Management, War Production Board, NARA Still Picture Branch, National Archives, Washington, DC

brushwork typical of Kuniyoshi's paintings, but this exquisite suavity is put at the service of a melancholy message. The same goes for *Look, It Flies!*, though here at least the woman is amusing herself with a toy bird that moves when its string is pulled (pl. 53). But she is somber, and the taut string presents a literal image of tension, as she stands before a crumbling cemetery of the sort that appeared in Kuniyoshi's scenes of the Southwest in the early 1940s. The torn posters are replaced by a half-buried billboard advertising an optician, a reference to sight that recalls the haunting optician's billboard in F. Scott Fitzgerald's 1925 novel, *The Great Gatsby*, as well as several works from 1946 by Kuniyoshi's friend Reginald Marsh, such as *Eyes Examined*, where an alluring young woman strides by two men who ignore her while above them the multiple signs of eyes with spectacles rebuke their inattention.[138] The optician's sign is a rich and loaded subject: it refers to sight, the crucial sense for a visual artist; it is also a disturbing image of a part of a person detached from the body, an uncanny effect beloved by the surrealists. Found in a rural setting such a sign is an example of the folk art that Edith Halpert showed in her gallery; in an urban setting, as Marsh depicted, it becomes a pre-pop manifestation of twentieth-century advertising culture. Kuniyoshi's partially buried billboard is both the latter and an image of the ephemerality of such commercial pursuits. It is balanced by crumbling cemetery ruins on the other side of the woman, who somberly concentrates on animating a bird that cannot fly.

The withdrawn character of these women explodes into raw emotion in one painting from this period, another unprecedented work, *Mother and Daughter* (pl. 51). Painted in 1945, the last year of the war and the year of the atomic bombing of Hiroshima and Nagasaki, Kuniyoshi reverted to his former palette of browns and lacquer red to represent an older woman embracing a younger one with an expression that mixes relief with grief. The girl's face is obscured by her mother's, but her emotion is indicated by the detail of her hand pulling the curtain at the right until it is rigid. The following year Ben Shahn continued his artistic dialogue with Kuniyoshi, painting the masculine equivalent of *Mother and Daughter* with his *Brothers* (1946), where most of the painting is taken up by two tightly embracing siblings.

In the mid-1940s, Kuniyoshi was developing other ambitious compositions that complemented his woman series. His friend Stuart Davis invented the term "stillscape" for works that fused the traditional genres of still life and landscape painting, a term that applies to several of Kuniyoshi's paintings as well, including *Rotting on the Shore*, a despairing painting from 1945 (pl. 49). A wall at the left separates us from the view of the gray ocean beyond, the two spaces linked by a barren tree. The shore is littered with rubble and bugs, and dominated by a chalice-like white bowl that holds a grisly plaque: it is an oval fisherman's trophy, but the catch proudly mounted there is a half-eaten, rotting carcass. I have previously suggested that Kuniyoshi's repeated depictions of marine life resonate with Japanese artistic traditions, and in this case one precursor to this grim scene is Takahashi Yuichi's *Salmon* (1877), a painting celebrated in Japan as a masterpiece of nineteenth-century Yōga (fig. 62). It would be reproduced in a book surveying modern Japanese art published in Japan in 1951 that also included works by Kuniyoshi and Foujita, the only nonresidents among the Yōga painters.[139]

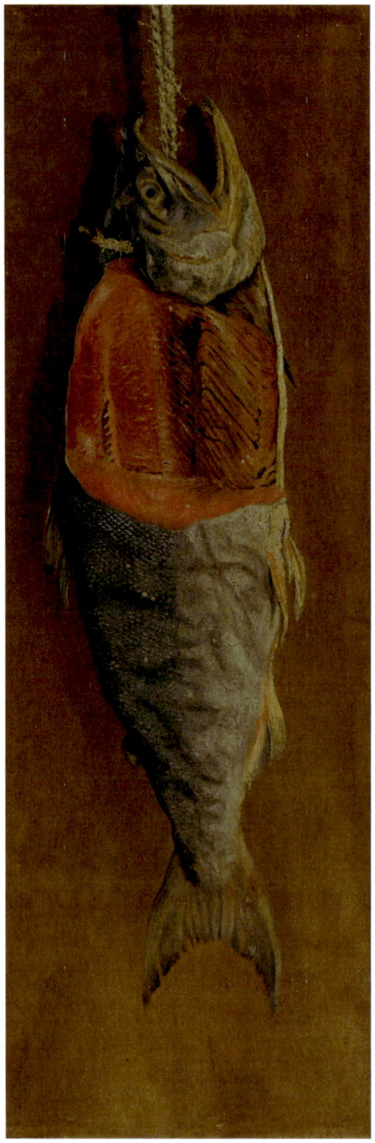

FIG. 62
Takahashi Yuichi, *Salmon*, 1877, oil on paper, 55 × 18 in. Tokyo University of the Arts

The titles of two major paintings dominated by carousel horses, *Headless Horse Who Wants to Jump* (1945) and *Festivities Ended* (1947), suggest their somber moods (fig. 63; pl. 55). Here Kuniyoshi continued the surrealist technique of depicting living creatures as lifeless replicas. The headless horse is missing most of its legs as it leans upright on a support that also anchors a tattered print of Kuniyoshi's *Torture* poster. A small house in the background of the rocky landscape gives a lonely hint of domestic contentment in this tableau of decay. Kuniyoshi owned a carousel horse, and in happier days he photographed it in his backyard, the figure seeming to soar across the distant Woodstock mountains (fig. 64). The subject was not unique to him: his friend Reginald Marsh repeatedly represented carousels as manifestations of the exuberant, often sexual energy of the city (fig. 65); Mervin Jules, a participant in Kuniyoshi's liberal artists political groups, portrayed helpless envoys riding endlessly around a carousel in *Diplomats*, a work from 1938. The wooden horse again dominates the landscape in Kuniyoshi's *Festivities Ended*, this time more intact but painfully inverted in front of the remains of a circus, where a couple of listless figures sprawl among collapsed tents at the left. At the right a billboard looms, advertising some health service that involves, again, seeing, as its main image is a monstrously large eyeball.

Kuniyoshi ironically titled a major painting featuring a lone girl swinging precariously in the window frame of a

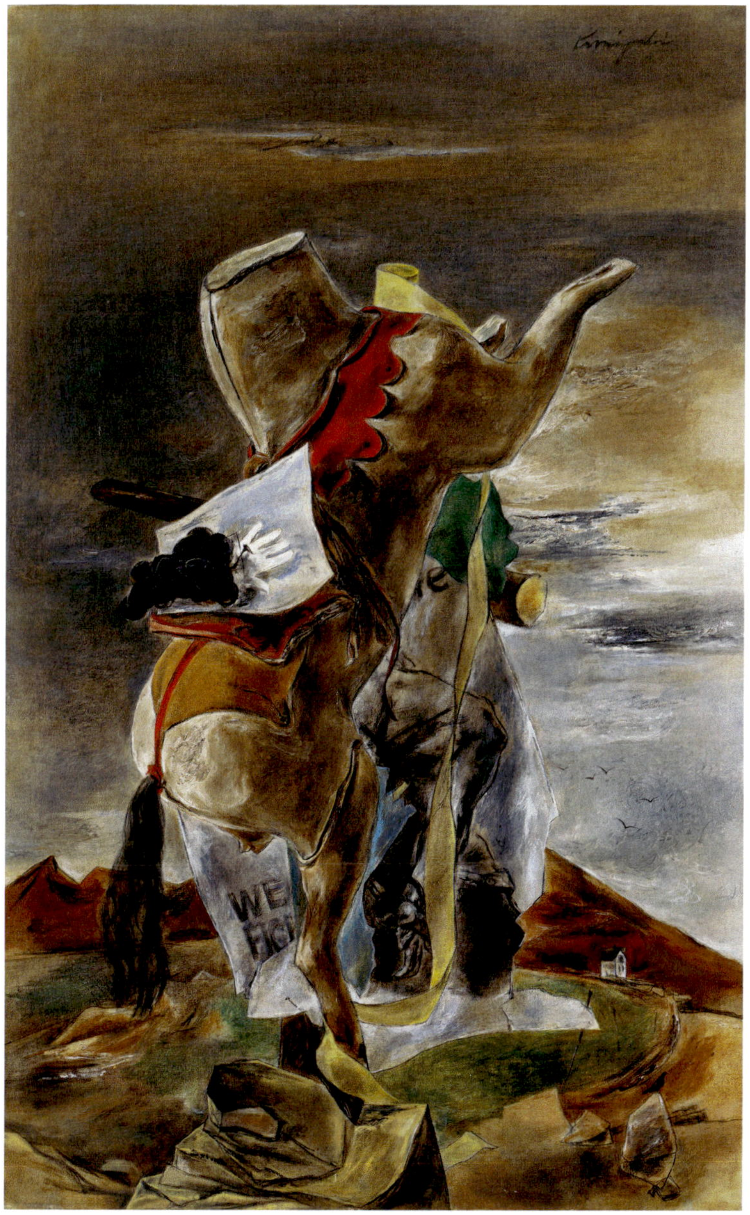

FIG. 63
Yasuo Kuniyoshi, *Headless Horse Who Wants to Jump*, 1945, oil on canvas, 57 1/16 × 35 7/16 in. Ohara Museum, Kurashiki, Japan

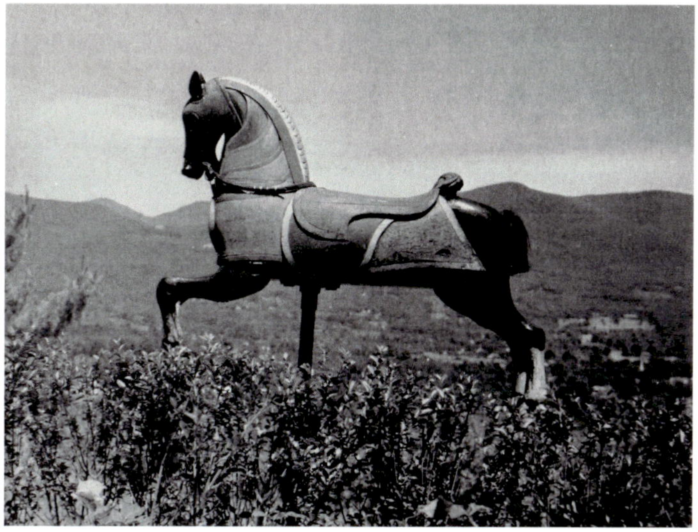

FIG. 64
Yasuo Kuniyoshi, *Carousel Horse*, n.d., photograph, 7 ½ × 9 ½ in. Collection of Jim and Marie Sullivan

destroyed building *This Is My Playground* (1947; pl. 58). The tattered poster at the left, pinned to a dead tree, could be a target, or the red sun of the Japanese flag gone black, and most of the text on the building, although blurred, can be deciphered. A hand with a pointing finger, a commonplace in graphic design of the period, directs us to the word *rodeo*, faded, as the festivities ended long ago. Below it is the fragmented indication of "July 4," a patriotic, if battered, reference to Independence Day, and, on a more private level, to the birthday of the artist's wife, Sara, with whom he was now reunited. Ravaged, ruined landscapes like these appear frequently in American art of the later 1940s, as artists responded to the trauma of the war. The affinities with Ben Shahn continue, as Kuniyoshi's young girl, fragile but happy as she plays among the devastation, could be swinging with the girls in Shahn's *Liberation* (1945; fig. 66).

While Kuniyoshi had a difficult time during the war, there were upsides as well. His first prize at the 1944 Carnegie International meant so much to him, coming as it did while the war still raged. In 1940 he had published his major autobiographical statement, "East to West," in the *Magazine of Art*, and it was republished, with slight additions, as a small, hardcover book in a series of monographs about prominent American artists by An American Group in 1945; it is a basic source for those interested in the artist. During the summer of 1944 in Woodstock he worked on additional autobiographical writings, though they were never published. They tend to be informal and fragmentary. In one he wrote about his morbid state of mind, but the rest are meditations about a variety of

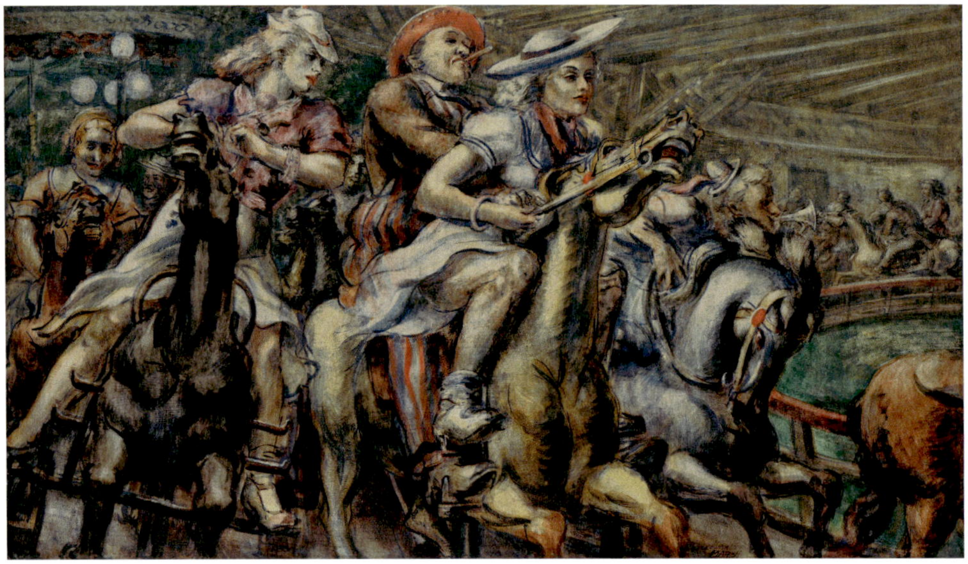

FIG. 65
Reginald Marsh, *Wooden Horses*, 1936, tempera on board, 24 × 40 in. Wadsworth Atheneum Museum of Art, Hartford, CT; The Dorothy Clark Archibald and Thomas L. Archibald Fund, The Krieble Family Fund for American Art, The American Paintings Purchase Fund, and the Ella Gallup Sumner and Mary Catlin Sumner Collection fund

FIG. 66
Ben Shahn, *Liberation*, 1945, gouache on board, 29 ¾ × 40 in. Museum of Modern Art, New York; James Thrall Soby Bequest

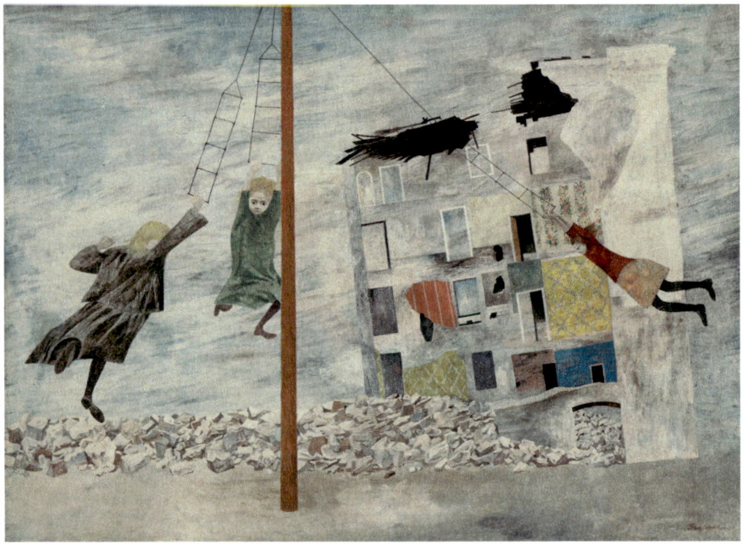

topics, including his working process, the various genres of painting, different regions of the United States, and his fellow artists. Some are substantial statements about art, while others are personal: "I'm glad that people never asked me anything about Myra because I think they know and never took seriously. Instead they ask me about Sara."[140]

In his drawing *Hot Day* (before 1948) with swift strokes of ink he beautifully evoked a scene of sensuous relaxation before a fan (pl. 57). It could be seen as an expression of relief at the end of the war, again with a woman as the artist's alter ego. But it is exceptional, as most of his works from the late 1940s communicate a sense of violence and horror. In *Disturbing Dream* from 1948 he took the subject of his lyrical painting *Dream* from 1922 (see fig. 14) and his imagery of proud circus performers and transmuted them into a nightmarish tableau. One trapeze artist has lost hold of her swing in midair and reaches desperately, but unsuccessfully, toward the rescuing hands of her partner (pl. 59). The cheerful pastel colors of his new palette cannot mitigate the feeling of disaster in this small, emotion-packed canvas.

In this period Kuniyoshi continued his practice of making highly finished black ink drawings that were worked out

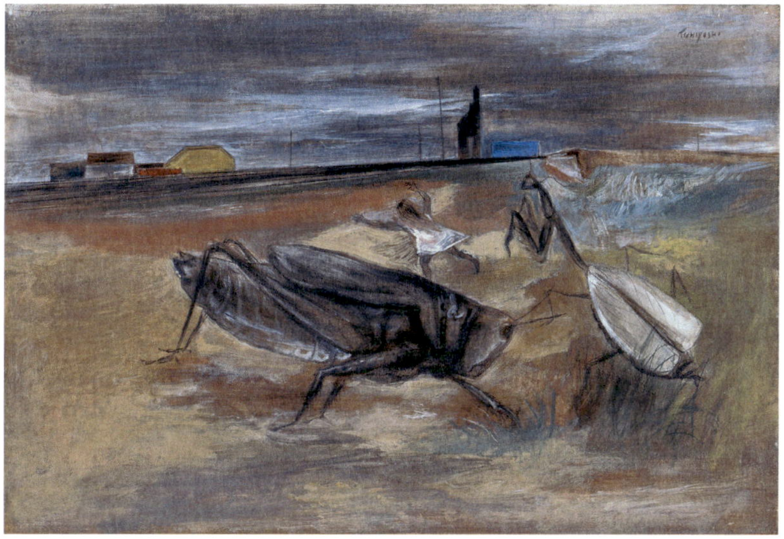

FIG. 67
Yasuo Kuniyoshi, *Little Girl Run for Your Life,* 1946, casein on gesso panel, 14 × 20 in. Fukutake Collection, Okayama, Japan

FIG. 68
Yasuo Kuniyoshi, *She Mourns*, 1946, gouache, ink, and graphite on paper, 26 × 20 ¼ in. Georgia Museum of Art, University of Georgia, Athens; Eva Underhill Holbrook Memorial Collection of American Art, Gift of Alfred H. Holbrook

in a series of preliminary studies. *Murdered* (1944) is another violent scene, of a disheveled woman lying on her back with her clothes partially torn off, next to a garbage can overflowing with litter (pl. 48). The contrast between her disarray and the precisely ruled lines of the background, the eloquently empty foreground, and the delicately rendered little plants growing next to her heightens the sense of her violation. In a second version of this subject he cropped her body and introduced two scrawny dogs circling around her. The dogs appear again, without the dead woman, in a small painting of a desolate landscape in which the scavenging animals regard each other hungrily (pl. 50). *Little Girl Run for Your Life* (1946) presents a bug's-eye view of the world as a huge grasshopper and praying mantis battle each other in the foreground while a small girl in the middle ground flees (fig. 67). The irrational scale of the insects recalls the surrealists, who were fascinated by praying mantises, and Max Ernst's *Two Children Frightened by a Nightingale* (1924) comes to mind, as Kuniyoshi used his insect imagery and radically low point of view to communicate a sense of anxiety. In *Flesh Fly* (about 1947) the artist executed an obsessively realistic rendering of a monstrously enlarged, parasitic creature, again transforming his earlier, cheerful fascination with the insect world into a disturbing vision (pl. 56). As was his common practice, a series of studies preceded this highly finished charcoal drawing. He also painted two canvases with lone mourning women, handkerchiefs to their eyes, expressing a sense of despair similar to the weeping women Picasso painted during the war with a more cubist vocabulary (fig. 68).

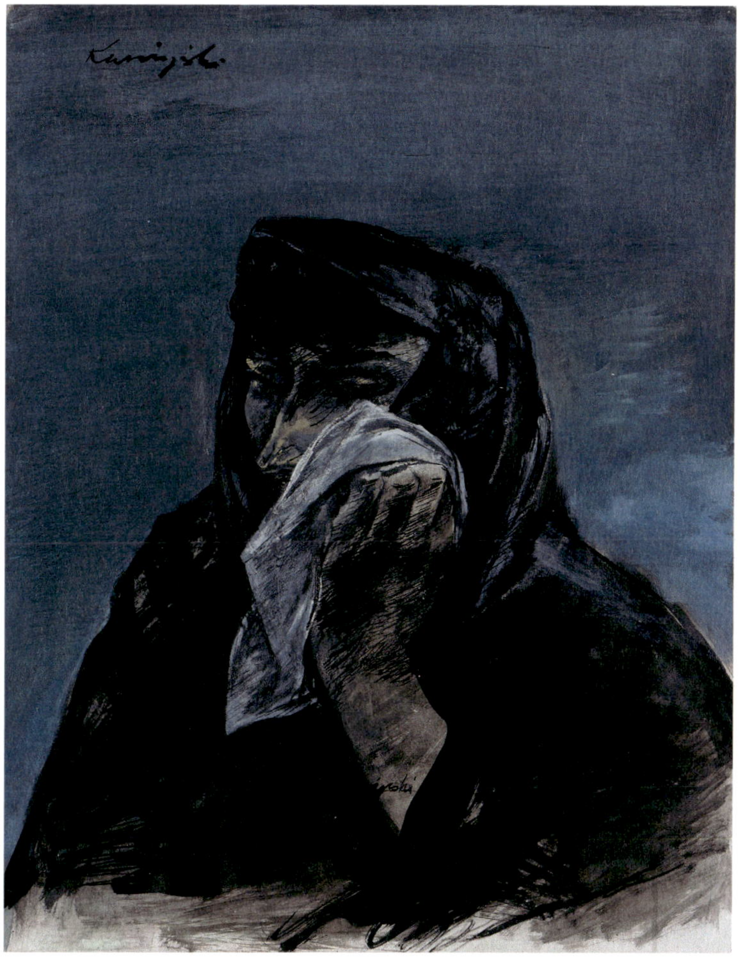

At the end of the war, after being outspokenly opposed to Japanese militarism Kuniyoshi immediately started efforts to help the Japanese victims of the two atomic bombs, and of the internment camps in the United States. He tried to enlist in the U.S. Army, requesting that he be sent to work in Japan, but his application was turned down due to his age. He then organized benefits in Woodstock to aid the Japanese who were in internment camps, donating big paintings on paper he made on the spot to auctions whose proceeds went into a fund he established to help the internees.

POSTWAR ISSUES

The year after the war ended Kuniyoshi, through no will of his own, was again plunged into an artistic controversy, though for once it had little to do with his nationality. In 1946 the State Department organized *Advancing American Art*, an exhibition of recent American art to tour internationally, to establish that American society was not just materialistic, as its reputation was abroad. The exhibition grew out of the debates about art during the war, when it was frequently argued that the artistic freedom afforded artists in a democracy proved the value of the American system of government. The government, however, had little experience organizing art exhibitions, and two strategic mistakes were made: for the sake of expediency it was decided that the government would purchase the works, and would use just one curator/juror, without a panel of advisors.[141] The exhibition, which included works by Kuniyoshi and forty-one of his contemporaries, was successfully shown at the Metropolitan Museum of Art, and it then traveled to Paris and several sites in Czechoslovakia without incident. But conservative American politicians and the Hearst newspapers mounted a vehement attack on it. They did not like art that was not realistic, they were upset that some of the artists selected had leftist political involvements, and they were outraged that the government had paid for the paintings. Of the eighty-four works in the show that traveled to Europe, Kuniyoshi's *Circus Girl Resting* (1925), painted twenty years before the exhibition, became the symbol of the exhibition and the target of ridicule (see pl. 25). The painting was the closest thing to a nude in the show, and the girl was rendered in Kuniyoshi's exaggerated figurative style of the 1920s. The right-wing critics had no appreciation for her unrealistic proportions, nor for her sly cheerfulness. She was featured in the article that started the attack, *Look* magazine's "Your Money Bought These Paintings," and philistine insults were flung at her. Representative John Jennings Jr. (R-TN) told the House that the show's organizers in the State Department were a "motley crew" who

> say they want the people of foreign countries to know what American women look like, and they get up a caricature, a squat creature of the muck and mire and hold this misshapen thing up to the world as an American circus performer taking a rest.[142]

One congressman said she was "better equipped to move a piano than to play one," and the president of the United States, Harry Truman, famously claimed when shown a picture of *Circus Girl Resting*: "If that's art, then I'm a Hottentot."[143] The negative outcry proved too much, and despite the positive reception of the exhibition abroad the tour was cancelled. The paintings were auctioned off to nonprofit institutions with big discounts, the bulk of them going to the University of Oklahoma and to Alabama's Auburn University, which got *Circus Girl Resting*, and subsequently resisted several attempts to purchase it out of its collection.

Kuniyoshi's prominence was fortified in 1948 when *Look* magazine polled sixty-eight art critics, museum directors, and curators across the United States as to who were the best painters in the country, and he was voted third, after John Marin and Max Weber, and before Stuart Davis and Edward Hopper.[144] This was the same magazine whose article a year before, "Your Money Bought These Paintings," led to the demise of the *Advancing American Art* exhibition—and all eleven painters who won its recent poll had been in that show.[145] Later that year Kuniyoshi was profiled in *Look*, "one of America's most honored artists fuses East and West," in the December 7 issue, the anniversary of Pearl Harbor. More significantly, he was honored with the first retrospective exhibition given to a living artist by the Whitney Museum of American Art. It was organized by his old friend, Lloyd Goodrich, who had been a student with him at the Art Students League. Goodrich wrote an excellent short catalog that for decades has been the standard text about Kuniyoshi. The show featured 131 paintings, drawings, and prints by the artist, and its opening was followed by a dinner party at Café Montparnasse on Bleecker Street that was attended by three hundred people. Kuniyoshi was understandably nervous about these events, and got drunk to get through them. He visited the exhibition as it was about to open with critic Aline Louchheim, who described him:

> He is always in motion, making small, springy gestures as his eyes dart busily behind large horn-rimmed glasses. His clowning is deliberate and he is usually the butt of his own humor. His speech is brisk and staccato, and, in the Japanese way, he substitutes "r" for the unpronounceable "l."[146]

The exhibition was very positively received, with the significant exception of the critic, Clement Greenberg, who slammed the artist in his review in *The Nation*: "Kuniyoshi hardly matters to serious painting in America." With the absolute faith in his opinions that would bring him power, Greenberg wrote that "the sole substance of his claim to be remembered" was that he was "one of the most prominent of the American assimilators of French post-impressionist art," paying no attention to Kuniyoshi's accomplishment in bridging Asian and American artistic traditions. Going against the many critics over the years who admired the artist's individuality, Greenberg wrote that he "never struck one as an independent force." He felt the drawings were "academically facile," and mystically declared that what "we see" in the paintings is "the vivid semblance but not the genuine reality of paint quality, sensibility, lyricism."[147] More typical of critics' responses to Kuniyoshi's painting was Henry McBride's from 1942: "He has a richness of texture in his pigments that no other painter among us approximates. He has a reserved palette that puts added distinction to the vitality of his colors, and his line is always nervous and sensitively alive."[148] Greenberg ended his review by urging that instead of Kuniyoshi, readers should look at paintings by the late Arnold Friedman, a painter whose work he would promote for his entire career, without much success. But the antagonism of this critic, who would become the authoritative critical voice of the next generation, foreshadowed what was to come in the last years of Kuniyoshi's life.

As a well-known and highly esteemed artist Kuniyoshi was asked to teach and lecture all over the country, and did stints in Oakland and Denver. Sculptor Sidney Simon, one of the founders of the Skowhegan School of Painting and Sculpture in Maine, wrote an account of a talk Kuniyoshi gave there soon after the school was founded in 1947. The talk was recorded, which made Kuniyoshi nervous, so he wrote it out and read it, resulting in an uncharacteristically boring presentation. But Simon's account of its aftermath gives a good sense of Kuniyoshi's charm and humor, and also of how his Japanese origins were integral to his self-presentation:

> He had a terrible time with pronouncing some of the words—and his voice droned in a monotone. The students—a bright earnest group in their mid 20's—a lot of G.I.'s etc. had stock questions for such speeches—Either "is art a weapon?" or "What is the difference between Realism and Reality." He got the latter and he had a terrible time with the "L's." He told the story of arriving at that dock in Seattle and his need to go to the bathroom—with no English—he made a gesture with both bent knees clenched together and pointing at his groin—made himself understood and was pointed to a nearby water closet, which he entered. He described visually the stance or gesture he had made, getting a huge roar of laughter after the dry speech, and said, "We Japanese love beautiful pottery"—and he described the toilet bowl he found in the WC. With his hands he traced its shape and curves—its whiteness. Then he said, "Large, ugly rusty pipe comes down and enters beautiful pot—must be very important for such a combination." So he mounted bowl and held on to pipe. He then added—"Going to bathroom in America is very private. Married two times—always go to bathroom by self—always hold on to pipe. Everything come out all right. Difference between Realism and Reality!"[149]

For four years, from 1947 to 1951, Kuniyoshi dedicated a tremendous amount of his time and his talents to the Artists Equity Association, an idealistic organization devoted to improving the lot of artists in the United States, based on the model of Actors' Equity and the American Society of Composers, Authors, and Publishers (ASCAP). A popular and respected personality who over the years had won significant prizes for his art, he became increasingly involved with artists' organizations, often as an officer. Consequently when a group of four hundred artists met at the Museum of Modern Art in 1946 to create Artists Equity, he was elected its first president, and in the coming years he would pour a great amount of his time and energy into the organization. Following the termination of the federal arts' projects of the Depression years, and in face of the antagonism toward contemporary art from red-baiting members of Congress, many artists felt isolated and unprotected. In an essay about Artists Equity, David Sokol has articulated some of the concepts behind the organization:

> Artists Equity did . . . everything possible to avoid identification with any political ideology. Fully aware that they had learned something during both the Great Depression and the war about both generating public support and the need to band together,

> the founding artists developed the structure of an organization that also scrupulously avoided any aesthetic allegiance and tried never to take public stands other than on matters of financial importance to its member artists.[150]

Equity was concerned with practical issues, including health insurance for artists, copyrights for artworks, and encouraging museums in the United States to exhibit contemporary American art. The organization was determined to be national, to represent artists from all over the country. In his essay, Sokol makes it clear that Kuniyoshi, who was elected to two consecutive terms as president, serving four years, the maximum allowed, was a charismatic and effective leader, and the driving force behind the organization during its formative years. Artist Harry Sternberg described how he conducted meetings:

> When Kuniyoshi was President of the artists' organization he knew nothing about Robert's Rules, and cared less. He ran the meetings by his own ideas of who should speak—where and when votes were to be taken.
>
> Only Yas could have gotten away with this! For some reason when he banged the gavel and said "Enough talk," we stopped talking. If a meeting went on too long he simply announced that the meeting was over and walked away. Rarely was a committee elected—mostly he just appointed them! We all loved it—and let him get away with it. For under that fine Japanese grin lay a fine temper... a dedicated and honest man.[151]

Artists Equity campaigned to have contemporary American art shown at the Metropolitan Museum of Art, whose director, Francis Henry Taylor, shared the conservatives' antipathy toward it. They did make progress on that front, as the museum consented to host an exhibition of works by living American artists. This was a victory for Kuniyoshi and Equity, but the results were mixed, as the project inspired the famous "Irascibles" photograph that helped launch the abstract expressionist artists to dominance over Kuniyoshi's generation. The photograph marks a turning point in American art history and is often seen as a heroic episode in that history, but it is rarely considered from the point of view of Kuniyoshi and his allies, who were trying to help their fellow artists. They campaigned for the exhibition and once it was approved they did their best to select a jury that spanned the country, and that included artists of many aesthetic persuasions. But they were met with a widely publicized letter of protest from eighteen painters and ten sculptors who would become known as the abstract expressionists. Subverting the process before it began, these artists refused to submit their works on the grounds that the jury (which included Kuniyoshi) was "notoriously hostile to advanced art."[152] As a writer in the *New York Herald Tribune*, probably art critic Emily Genauer, responded, "the fairness or wisdom of condemning a jury before it has even started to consider the evidence may be questioned."[153] She also pointed out that eleven of the twenty-eight protesters had already had their works shown at the museum that they claimed was antagonistic to "advanced art." Her article was titled "The Irascible Eighteen," which gave its title to the famous photograph of fifteen of the signers, including future luminaries such as Willem de Kooning, Jackson Pollock, and Mark Rothko; it was published in *Life* magazine on January 15, 1951. The full-page photograph came before three pages of smaller reproductions of works from the Metropolitan's exhibition, including Kuniyoshi's 1950 *Fish Kite*, which was grouped with works by several other artists who have disappeared from art history (see pl. 61). This issue of the magazine marks a changing of the guard in American art, and there is no doubt that the artists among the Irascibles have fared much better historically than the Metropolitan prizewinners like Karl Knaths and Rico Lebrun, though the future will tell when it comes to Irascibles like James Brooks and Jimmy Ernst. As Bradford R. Collins stated in his enlightening essay, "*Life* Magazine and the Abstract Expressionists,"

> The seamless screen of bohemian oratory maintained by artists of the New York School in the 1950s masked the fact that with them originated today's model of art as a career to be manufactured, in opposition to the older model of it as a vocation to be followed.[154]

And there was Kuniyoshi, emerging from his harrowing World War II years as an "enemy alien" with, on one hand, congressmen ridiculing his art and suggesting he had communist sympathies, while on the other, some of his fellow artists, whose status he had labored to improve, dismissed him as a reactionary. No wonder much of the art he made in his last few years was shot through with pessimism and despair.

LATE WORKS

In the period before his death from stomach cancer in 1953, Kuniyoshi continued to develop his art in new directions, while at the same time he revisited and reinterpreted themes that had occupied him in earlier years. Although he was on the other side of the generational divide from the abstract expressionists, his work evolved in ways that paralleled their innovations. He never gave up representation, but for the most part he abandoned working from the model. His paintings became larger, their space more shallow, and their color more hot and high key, thanks in part to the new Shiva Ponsol, a non-water-soluble polymer paint he was experimenting with. The lively colors created a dissonant contrast with the grotesque and disillusioned subjects they illustrated. At the very end of his career he turned to painting with sumi ink, making large, finished drawings in black and white, anticipating or contemporary with the black-and-white works of Pollock, de Kooning, Barnett Newman, Robert Motherwell, and Franz Kline.

Forbidden Fruit (1950) shows the artist reinterpreting themes from his earlier years, as it recapitulates *Boy Stealing Fruit* of 1923 (pl. 60; see pl. 13). Now the color is raised to an intense pitch, with much of the composition arranged into flat rectangles so the bright reds can express themselves directly, as in the paintings of Mark Rothko. But Kuniyoshi remained dedicated to the figure, and here a small boy eyes a table laden with fruit—however now he does not slyly grab it, like his triumphant predecessor from 1923—the fruit is forbidden, and he can only look at it longingly. The detached table leg that arbitrarily lies on the table before him, and the precarious tower of watermelon slices, skewered by a yellow stick, add to the suppressed emotions that erupt with the vivid color.

The moods of dislocation and disillusionment in Kuniyoshi's late works were at odds with his presence in the art world, where he was a public figure. He spoke often, and he had a winning personality—idealistic, funny, and unpretentious. When he retired as president of Artists Equity in 1951, Hudson Walker, the director of Equity, wrote to him: "Your very hard work and the long hours you put in on behalf of Equity, were only matched by your good judgment in handling people and difficult situations."[155] But with his repeated representation of masked figures in his late works, his art came to be dominated by images of duplicity, literally two-facedness. He also revisited his old theme, circus performers, with a new, despairing vision. Unlike his earlier images, many of these figures are clearly male, when their faces are not covered by masks, and they can be read alternately as self-portraits, or as comments on the artists and politicians who were part of Kuniyoshi's world. *I Wear a Mask Today* (1946–47) is one of the earlier and gentler of these paintings, a small canvas dominated by the figure of a performer who is in the process of lifting a mask from his face with a sensitive hand, and it has been convincingly interpreted as autobiographical (pl. 54).[156] We can see only the mask, not the face it hides, and, with its half-opened mouth and upturned eyebrows, it conveys a sense of sorrow and vulnerability. A circus tent appears at the left, and at the right fragments of a circus poster, including a stout woman with a snake, and the letters *ow* that suggest words like *show*—or an expression of pain. Such overlapped and partial images are typical of Kuniyoshi's works in this period, and they intimate a fragmented and frustrating world.

As mentioned above, following precedents from the School of Paris, circus imagery appeared in the works of many other American figurative painters, particularly Walt Kuhn. Among others in Kuniyoshi's artistic circle, Karl Zerbe showed a clown painting in the *Advancing American Art* exhibition, and Andrée Ruellan, Kuniyoshi's Woodstock friend, also depicted masked carnival figures in these years, in a more cheerful mood. Although Kuniyoshi was estranged from the abstract expressionist group, Philip Guston was a regular visitor to Woodstock and a friend of Kuniyoshi's, one who did not sign the Irascibles letter. Guston bought a house in Woodstock in 1947, and casual photographs document his rapport with Kuniyoshi. They were good friends until the younger artist's move into abstract painting at the end of the decade, which Kuniyoshi did not approve of.[157] Guston's paintings of the mid-1940s, like *If This Be Not I* (1945) with its masked figures in a decrepit landscape, occupy the same artistic territory as Kuniyoshi's works from the same years (fig. 69). When Kuniyoshi first showed one of his new paintings at the Art Students League it created controversy in the school, and one can imagine that the example of Kuniyoshi courageously moving away from the established style that had brought him acclaim might have been in the back of Guston's mind when he made his radical move from abstraction back to figuration in 1970.[158]

From another perspective, one could cite affinities between Kuniyoshi's circus works and Japanese prints of performers, like the eighteenth-century actor portraits by Tōshūsai Sharaku. But a major precursor was Daumier, one of Kuniyoshi's favorite artists, who made traveling performers part of his repertoire in works like *Sideshow/Parade* (about 1865–66), with its weary, jaded

FIG. 69
Philip Guston, *If This Be Not I*, 1945, oil on canvas, 42 ¼ × 55 ¼ in. Mildred Lane Kemper Art Museum, Washington University in St. Louis; University purchase, Kende Sale Fund, 1945

FIG. 70
Honoré Daumier, *Sideshow/Parade*, about 1865–66, charcoal, pen and ink, gray wash, watercolor, gouache, and Conté crayon on woven paper, 17 ¼ × 13 ¼ in. Private collection

FIG. 71
Yasuo Kuniyoshi, *Revelation*, 1949, oil on canvas, 70 ⅛ × 46 ⅜ in. Wichita Art Museum, Kansas; The Roland P. Murdock Collection

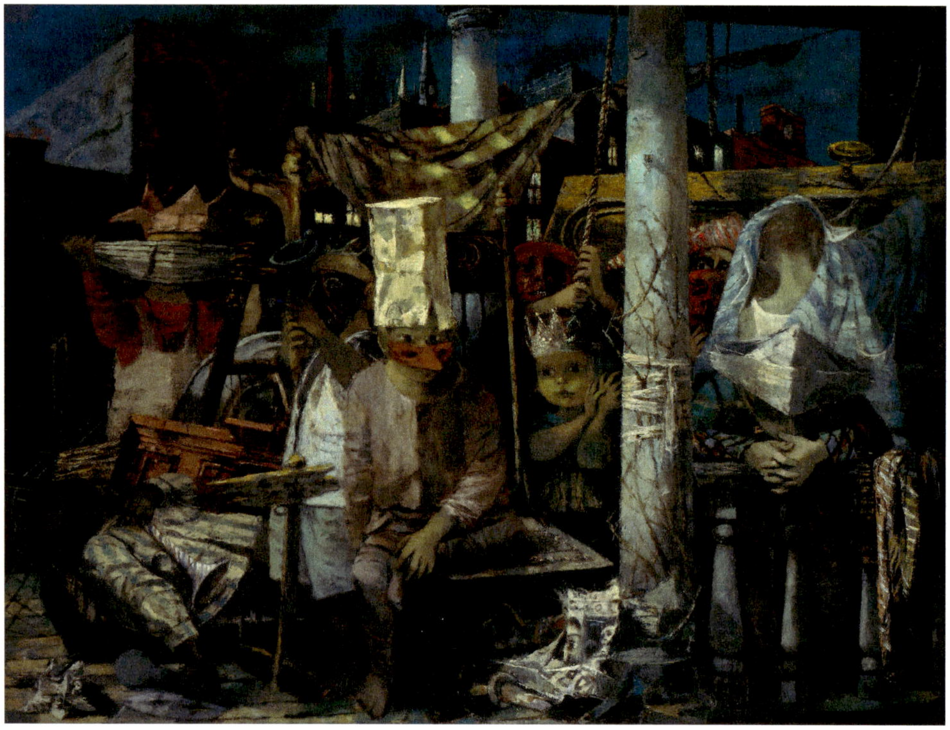

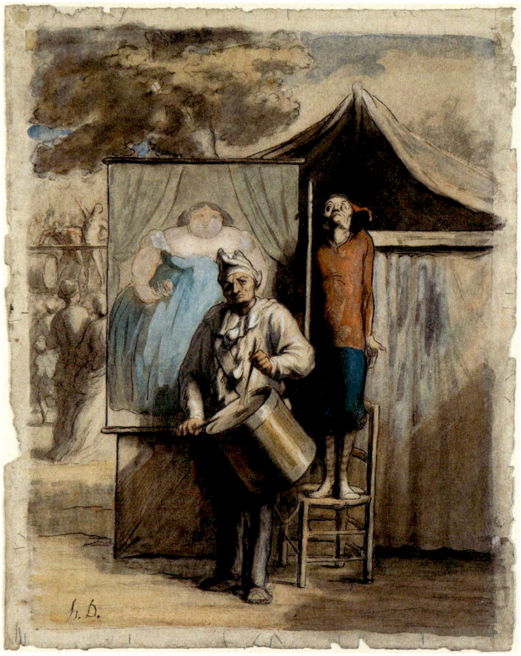

drummer who stands before a circus poster of a fat woman, as does Kuniyoshi's clown (fig. 70).[159]

In *Revelation* (1949), one of the largest paintings in his career, Kuniyoshi continued his vocabulary of fragmentation and melancholy, expressed in paradoxically bright orange and blue contrasts (fig. 71). Here a mutilated mannequin dominates the foreground, arms spread out as if crucified, face covered with a sadly smiling mask. She stands before a torn poster of a muscular man seen from the back, taken from the famous sixteenth-century Renaissance anatomy book by Andreas Vesalius. To the left the upper body of a woman irrationally emerges from the background as she hides her face in her hand in an expression of grief. *Fakirs* (1951) presents another conglomeration of grotesques in a luridly colored landscape, with a circus tent in the background (pl. 62). Kuniyoshi once more depicted tension literally, as the boy at left tugs at the cloth that shrouds the horn being tooted by the grim masked figure in the center, while the dwarfish boy on the right hangs from the horn blower's upheld arm. At the lower right an upside-down acrobat, cropped by the edge of the painting, adds to the mood of inversion and incompleteness. The figures perform their joyless concert in an environment electrified by contrasting bright oranges and blues, animated by sharp-edged, aggressively pointed forms. The title suggests that they are beggars or swindlers, but

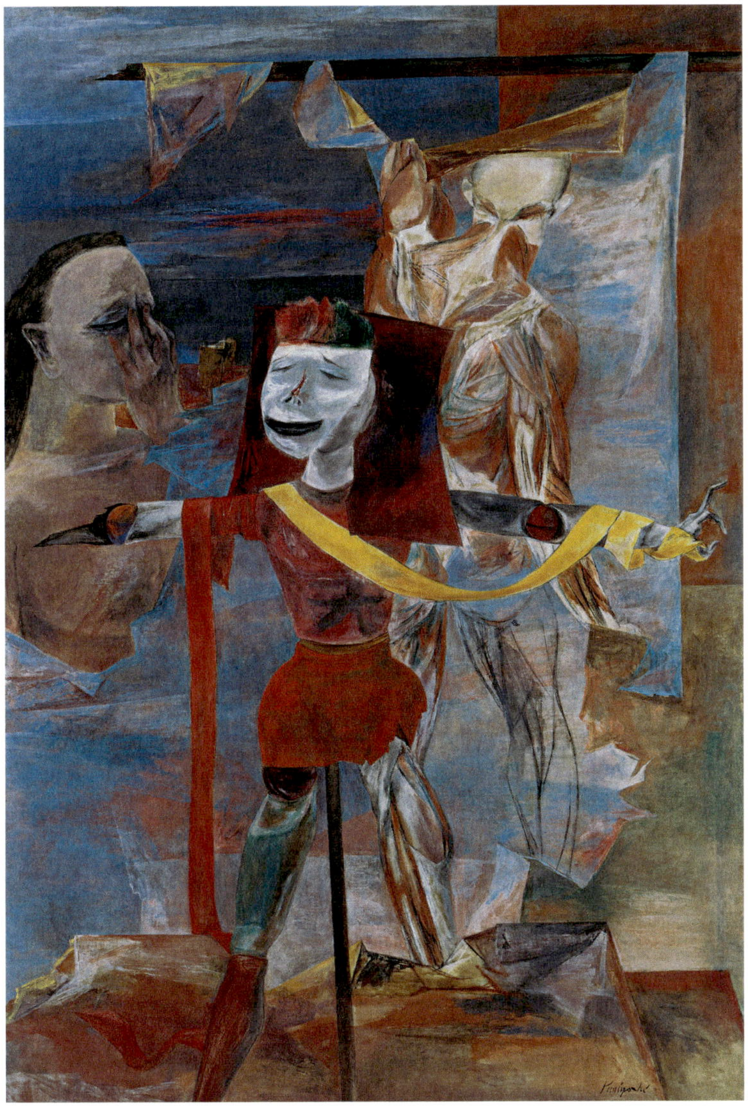

it has a second meaning: between 1891 and 1914, and occasionally later, students at the Art Students League put on annual exhibitions that they called Fakir shows, displaying their comic parodies of esteemed academic paintings, as Kuniyoshi may have made an insider's reference to the traditions of the art school that sustained him for much of his career.[160]

The dominant painting of this late group is *Mr. Ace* (1952) presided over by the title character who lifts a ludicrous, red-nosed mask to reveal a face made cruel from experience (pl. 63). The figure looks directly out to confront us with a cynical smile. He could be interpreted as a world-weary self-portrait of the artist, but he is also the image of those who opposed Kuniyoshi from the right and from the left as he worked to realize his deep faith in the democratic system. As the painter Julian Levi described him: "His constant interest has been to advance professional standards, a task to which he freely lends his excellent judgment, tact, and above all his emphatic use of the word, 'democracy.'"[161] The person Levi described would seem to inhabit a different world from the gray-faced Mr. Ace, who looks down at us with distain.

Fish Kite (1950; pl. 61) is a remarkable late painting in which Kuniyoshi adopted an explicitly Japanese theme, as he would again in his last painting, *Oriental Presents* of 1952. Dominated by the shrill reds, oranges, and pinks the artist favored in his late works, it is ostensibly a cheerful subject, the annual Boys' Day in Japan that was observed by parading banners and colorful kites in the shape of carp fish through the streets. But despite its bright colors and celebratory subject, the figures in the painting are troubled: the boy who holds the kite has his eyes downcast, and the girl acrobat, who raises her hands to support her upside-down partner, is frowning. The date, "July 4," is again legible: is it a tribute to Sara Kuniyoshi's birthday, or an evocation of the holiday celebrating "independence" in the United States, or both? In this essay I have often cited prototypes for Kuniyoshi's works from both European/American sources and Asian ones, images he may have drawn upon consciously or unconsciously. In *Fish Kite* he selected a specifically Japanese subject, one with precursors in the work of, among others, Utagawa Kuniyoshi, whose 1849 print of a fish kite and an actor's portrait look forward to the flattened space of the younger Kuniyoshi's image.

In 1952, Kuniyoshi had the honor of being one of four artists representing the United States at the Venice Biennale, along with Alexander Calder, Stuart Davis, and Edward Hopper. But while he continued to be celebrated in the West, he also remained involved with his native country, where his art was often featured in publications in the context of Yōga painting. The Japanese art magazine *Atelier* reproduced his paintings not only in 1931, when he exhibited them in Japan, but in several subsequent issues, and as mentioned above, a 1951 book surveying modern Japanese art reproduced works by both Kuniyoshi and Foujita in the Yōga section, claiming the two artists for their native country.[162] Meanwhile, Kuniyoshi was helping Japanese artists exhibit in the United States. Using the prestige he won from being awarded first prize at the Carnegie International exhibition in 1944, he initiated the idea of having Japan represented at the 1952 International. He then acted as liaison between the Pittsburgh museum and Japanese officials as fifteen Japanese painters showed their works, including Jiro Yoshihara, who would soon create the avant-garde Gutai movement in Japan.[163] This was the first time such a group had exhibited in the United States since the war, and Kuniyoshi continued to work assiduously to help Japanese artists, graciously writing short essays for two, Tatsuo Arai and Kakuzo Inoue, when they showed their works in New York, and introducing Kenzo Okada, an important painter of the next generation, to dealers and the art world in New York.[164]

The situation with Foujita, however, was not so pleasant. Kuniyoshi knew Foujita when he lived in Paris, and Foujita wrote him a supportive letter of introduction for his trip to Japan and met him at the boat when he arrived at Yokohama.[165] But later their politics diverged seriously as Foujita returned to his native country and became a military painter, putting his talents to work supporting the Japanese war effort. A flamboyant personality, he was the leading artist-advocate of militarism, and after the war, when Japanese attitudes reversed dramatically, he was ostracized and left Japan searching for a new place to live. He gained admission to the United States and arranged to show his works in a gallery in New York in 1949. To his dismay, his exhibition inspired a letter of opposition signed by fifty-three artists, organized by Kuniyoshi's friend Ben Shahn.[166] The letter defined Foujita as "a war criminal artist," and no works were sold out of his show. In his letters Foujita bitterly blamed Kuniyoshi for fomenting resistance to him, which makes sense given Kuniyoshi's heartfelt opposition to Japanese militarism, plus the suffering it had caused him.[167] But there is no mention of this episode in Kuniyoshi's papers, and he was not one of the signers of the anti-Foujita letter. In any case, Foujita seems to have prepared for the American market by adopting a Kuniyoshi subject, the lone woman in a café, for one his most popular paintings, *Café* (1949), rephrasing it with his precisely linear, heavily detailed realism.

Kuniyoshi began a late lecture with a quote from Alan Watts, the popularizer of Eastern philosophy in the United States in the 1950s: "Walk on! For we can only understand life by keeping pace with it, by a complete affirmation and acceptance of its magic-like transformations and unending changes."[168] He was never very concerned with religion (I asked Sara Kuniyoshi if they were married in a religious ceremony and she emphatically replied "No!!"). But as he got older he turned with Sara to the study of Zen Buddhism, by way of Alan Watts. This late enthusiasm typifies his hybrid identity—he came to a belief system from his native country through a writer from his adopted country.

LATE INK DRAWINGS

In his last years Kuniyoshi produced a series of sumi ink drawings, returning to a Japanese medium and technique that brought him much praise in the 1920s, but to much different effect.[169] Now his piling up the ink and scratching into it for highlights had an urgency that was not present earlier. He completed around twenty of these late drawings; they are powerful and emotional, and bring his career to a resounding close. A group of them were made at Woodstock in the summer of 1952, when he was beginning to feel the effects of the cancer that had not yet been diagnosed. His dealer, Edith Halpert, showed ten of them in the October after he died, and called them "ink paintings." In the words of the artist and critic Fairfield Porter, "To me they are the most moving things Kuniyoshi ever made."[170] Kuniyoshi focused on a few themes, including a demented juggler who wears a pathetic mask and the cockaded hat of a nineteenth-century military commander—an image of militarism gone mad (fig. 72). Kuniyoshi's growing interest in abstraction is clear in the intricate composition of geometric lines in the background. The juggler helplessly tries to keep three balls aloft in a scene that prophesizes disaster. Kuniyoshi had previously depicted a grotesquely masked military man wearing a cockaded hat, a clown's nose, and a coat with epaulets in a late painting, *Exit*, from 1948–50 (fig. 73). The image of an evil emissary of militarism wearing a nineteenth-century hat was featured in Sakari Suzuki's earlier antiwar painting and appeared again in leftist artist Philip Evergood's *Fascist Leader* (1946; fig. 74) in the *Advancing American Art* show. Kuniyoshi's art, while personal, was aligned with that of his progressive, humanist, figurative colleagues. He joined Raphael Soyer and other artists in 1953 to found an art magazine, *Reality: A Journal of Artists' Opinions*, aimed at defending representational art in face of the increasing popularity of abstraction.

In several of his last drawings Kuniyoshi returned to the insect life that had fascinated him from his early days. But now the world of the insects is one of predators and victims, as in *Work at Dawn* (1952), where an ant carries a dead praying mantis, much larger than itself, across a dark landscape (pl. 65).

With his majestic *Fish Head* (1952), Kuniyoshi crafted a savage finale to the fish imagery that occupied him through his career (pl. 64). The decapitated head of a fish sits upright; its gaping mouth displays spiky teeth silhouetted against the pale gray background. Ironically, this brutal trophy rests on a stylish platter in the shape of a whole fish. The cloth that is

FIG. 72
Yasuo Kuniyoshi, *Juggler*, 1952, casein on gessoed panel, 15 ⅛ × 20 in. Museum of Fine Arts, Boston; Gift of the William H. Lane Foundation

FIG. 73
Yasuo Kuniyoshi, *Exit*, 1948–50, oil on canvas, 50 × 30 in. Metropolitan Museum of Art, New York; Morris K. Jesup Fund, 1950

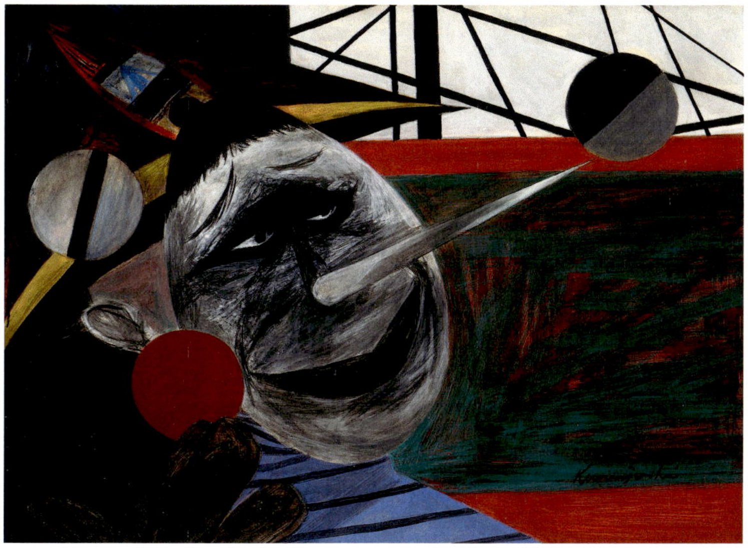

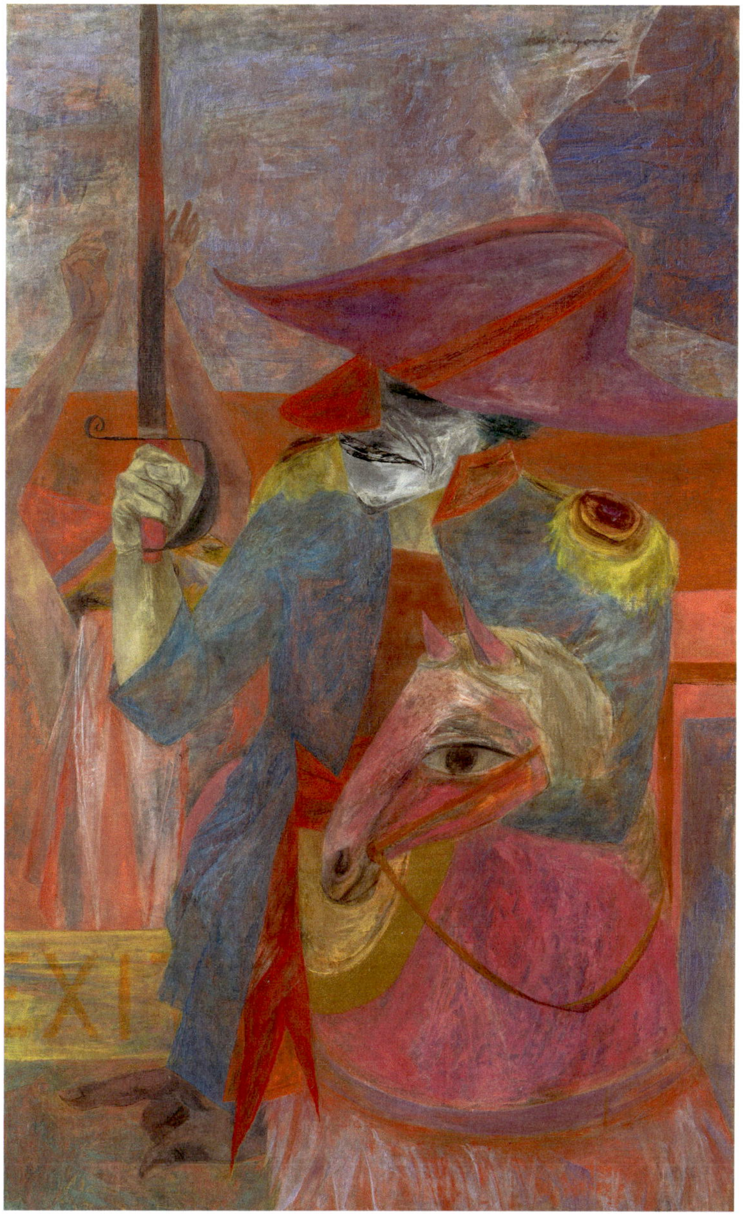

wrapped around the severed base of the head is literally torn, as Kuniyoshi established its white highlights by scraping through the thick ink into the paper. The drawing evokes the pathos of a crucifixion, and the cloth is reminiscent of the loincloth crucified Christ wears in many traditional religious works, including the first painting Kuniyoshi ever exhibited (see fig. 8). Images of dead fish appear frequently in Western art, including the works of William Merritt Chase, an early teacher of Kuniyoshi's. Chase's still lifes of fish were well known; they descended from those by Edouard Manet, and like them are about the prelude to a nice meal, incidentally involving death. The subject also appeared in paintings by Kuniyoshi's contemporaries in New York, for example paintings exhibited by Philip Evergood and Nahum Tschacbasov in the *Advancing American Art* show. But for images that share Kuniyoshi's sense of the implacable savagery of death one has to look back to Goya, or to some of Kuniyoshi's Japanese precursors, such as Takahashi Yuichi or the great Hokusai, whose sayings Kuniyoshi was fond of quoting and who made

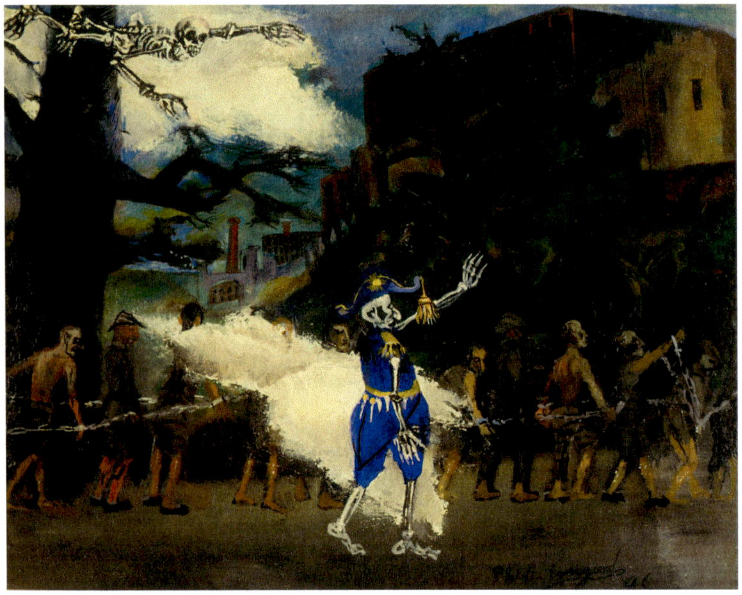

FIG. 74
Philip Evergood, *Fascist Leader*, 1946, oil on canvas, 20 × 25 in. Jule Collins Smith Museum of Fine Art, Auburn University, Alabama; Advancing American Art Collection

FIG. 75
Katsushika Hokusai, *Handscroll with Miscellaneous Subjects* (detail), 1839, handscroll; ink and color on paper, image 15 ¼ × 3 ⅛ in. Freer Gallery of Art, Smithsonian Institution, Washington, DC; Gift of Charles Lang Freer

FIG. 76
Adrian Siegel, *Yasuo Kuniyoshi*, n.d., gelatin silver print, 10 × 8 in. Woodstock Artists Association and Museum Archives, Woodstock, New York

several watercolors of fish heads, with varying degrees of dark humor (fig. 75; see fig. 62).[171]

The largest work in the late series is *Old Tree* (about 1953; pl. 66). It is far from the slender young trees that ornamented Kuniyoshi's earlier paintings, like the one out the window of *Boy Stealing Fruit*, or the one being photographed by the artist in *Self-Portrait as a Photographer* (see pls. 13, 23). Now the tree is dense and complex, its many branches spreading over the entire page and beyond. The darkest portion of this very dark work is the center, where the black trunk rises from the bottom of the page and extends past the top. From that central axis a web of branches extends, rendered in black ink on white paper, with white slashes torn in. A barely perceptible horizon indicates the landscape behind the tree, and spots of white or gray portray the light seeping through. But the drawing is dominated by darkness, and it takes a while to notice the black bird in profile sitting on a branch at the lower right. Kuniyoshi piled up the black ink and then tore into it with sharp tools—a photograph by Adrian Siegel shows him, now white haired, working on the drawing with a razor blade (fig. 76). The scarred and physical surface gives a sense of the bark of the tree, a tree that has lived a long time and has seen a lot of life pass before it. The tactility of the piece—its worked and textured surface, the play of opposites, of black and white, and many shades of gray—parallel the monochrome works of the abstract expressionists, like Franz Kline, while also evoking the brush and ink traditions of Asian art. The tree is upright and weathered, complicated and powerful, and scarred by experience: it stands in for Kuniyoshi himself, a fitting finale to the artist's rich and accomplished career.

POSTSCRIPT

A recurrent question during Kuniyoshi's life and after is whether he was an "American" artist. As we have seen, he could not become a citizen of the United States because of restrictive immigration laws, an issue that kept coming up over the course of his career. ShiPu Wang titled his book about Kuniyoshi *Becoming American?*, and sees this as the central issue in evaluating the artist's career. At the margins what makes an artist "American" is mutable and contestable, echoed in the debates about immigration that are very much with us today. To consider Feininger and Pascin, or James McNeill Whistler and Mary Cassatt, who spent most of their careers abroad, American artists is a bit like considering Kuniyoshi a Japanese artist—but that happens to be the case in Japan, where his works are exhibited and sought after more avidly than in the United States. In fact he is a transnational artist, bridging two countries with two great artistic traditions, one reason he is so relevant today. At the same time, his complex art is scarcely known in France, the country whose modern art was one of his inspirations, nor in the rest of Europe.

In 1972, after the death of Edith Halpert, much of her collection was sold at an auction at Sotheby-Parke-Bernet. The

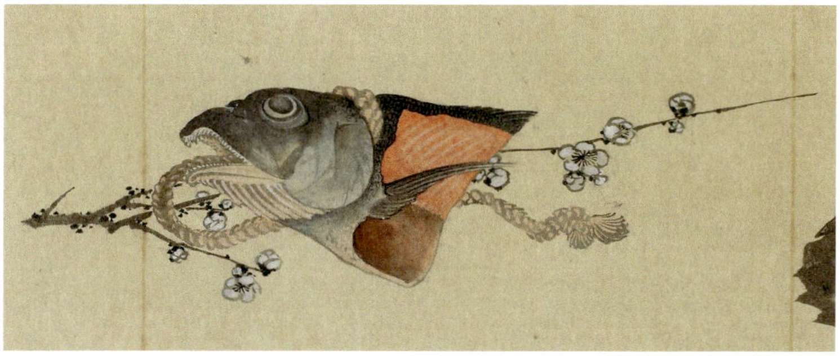

surprise of the sale was the high prices that Kuniyoshi's works brought: *Little Joe with Cow* sold for $220,000, far more than works by Stuart Davis, Ben Shahn or Georgia O'Keeffe, and over six times its estimate of $35,000. The Japanese economy was starting to surge, and the painting was bought by a Japanese dealer, a trend that would continue through the 1980s. Japanese collectors, led by Tetsuhiko Fukutake, whose publishing business was based in Kuniyoshi's hometown of Okayama, were offering many times the market value for Kuniyoshi's paintings, and several American museums, as well as collectors, were willing to sell.[172] The flow of works by Kuniyoshi increased interest in the artist in Japan, and as I have pointed out, his artistic production was limited: he worked slowly, and made many works that were one-of-a-kind. As mentioned earlier, the catalogue raisonné of his paintings lists only 353 works, and that includes some black ink drawings. Soichiro Fukutake, son of Tetsuhiko, has continued his father's activity, building his Kuniyoshi collection while also creating spectacular contemporary art museums on Naoshima island, near Okayama. Today the Fukutake collection in Okayama is the largest collection of Kuniyoshi's art in the world, and his works are proudly displayed in many Japanese museums.

The many American writers who claimed there was something "Oriental" about his art were right: he incorporated elements from Asian artistic traditions, in terms of technique, composition, and subject matter, into his art in many inventive ways. And he was right when he said, "Except for my physical appearance and my name I am just as much an American in my approach and thinking as the next fellow. I'm as American as the next fellow."[173] But the fact he felt he had to exclude his physical appearance and his name acknowledged the dominant stereotype and suggests the pressures Kuniyoshi faced. Had he lived a year longer he would have been an American citizen: as he was dying immigration law was changing to permit Asians to become citizens. He asked his wife and his lawyer to please get him the necessary papers, but they were too late. At the same time, during his illness he was planning for his second trip back to Japan, where a major retrospective exhibition of his work, which would turn out to be posthumous, was being planned. To the end he was a product of both cultures, and his bicultural identity enriched his art and makes it resonate with us today. It resonates also thanks to his talent as a visual artist: from his early works with their cheerful mixture of innocence and sophistication, to the grim and powerful works that conclude his career, Kuniyoshi made art that communicates a range of emotions and enriches the lives of sensitive viewers in the present.

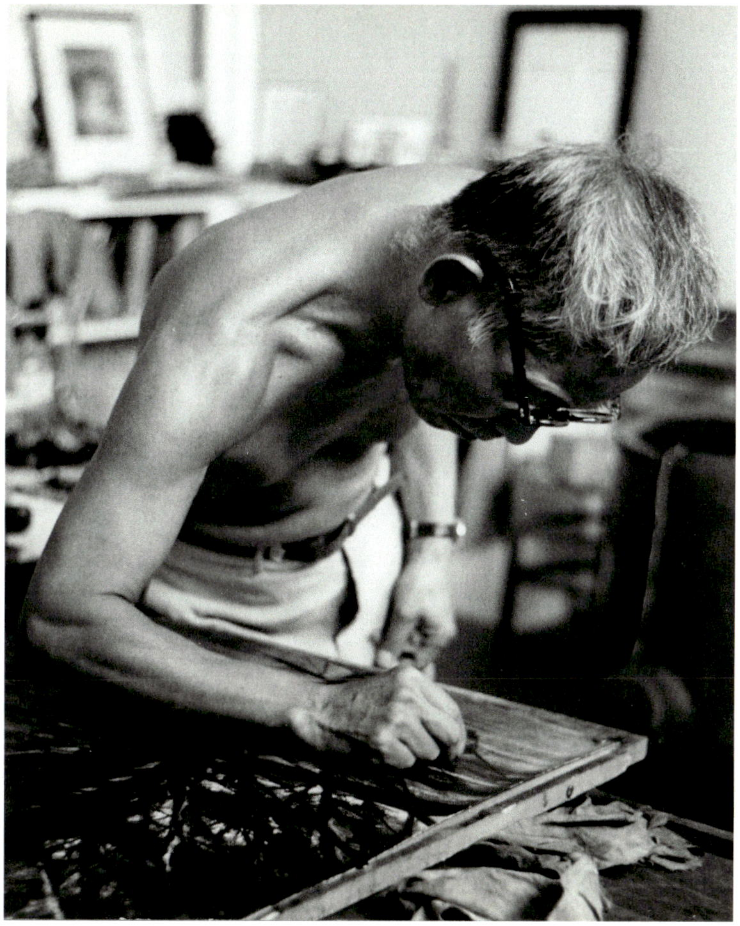

Notes

p. 12: "People think . . . babies": Yasuo Kuniyoshi, "East to West," *Magazine of Art* 33 (February 1940): 77.

THE ARTISTIC JOURNEY OF YASUO KUNIYOSHI

1 Yasuo Kuniyoshi, *Yasuo Kuniyoshi* (New York: American Artists Group, 1945), n.p. This is the artist's most important autobiographical statement, originally published as "East to West," *Magazine of Art* 33 (February 1940): 72–83.

2 Ritsuko Ozawa and Kazuma Suzuki, eds., *Yasuo Kuniyoshi* (Okayama: Fukutake Publishing, 1991). The catalogue raisonné of the artist's paintings lists 353 works but includes several ink drawings.

3 For examples, see the comparisons of works by two of Kuniyoshi's friends: Chuzo Tamotzu's lithograph *East 13th Street* (1937) with his linocut of a horse in a landscape (ca. 1957), and Eitaro Ishigaki's oil painting *Man with the Whip* with his ink brush drawing illustrating his wife's memoir of her life in Japan, in Tom Wolf, "The Tip of the Iceberg: Early Asian American Artists in New York," in *Asian American Art: A History, 1850–1970*, ed. Gordon H. Chang, Mark Dean Johnson, and Paul J. Karlstrom (Stanford, CA: Stanford University Press, 2008), 84–85, 92–93.

4 Kuniyoshi, *Yasuo Kuniyoshi*, n.p.

5 There are several opinions about Kuniyoshi senior's profession; most convincing is the account by Katsumi Senoo, curator emeritus at the Okayama Prefectural Museum. Senoo's knowledge about Kuniyoshi's father comes in part from interviewing people who knew him in Okayama. He has been very generous in sharing his research with me.

6 Kuniyoshi, *Yasuo Kuniyoshi*, n.p. Mr. Senoo suggests that the painting was by Kanokogi Takeshiro (1874–1941), a depiction of a battle scene between Chinese and Japanese forces.

7 Lloyd Goodrich, Interviews with Yasuo Kuniyoshi, January 6, 1948, artists' files, Whitney Museum of American Art, New York.

8 Will South, Marian Yoshiki-Kovinick, and Julia Armstrong-Totten, *A Seed of Modernism: The Art Students League of Los Angeles, 1906–1953* (Pasadena: Pasadena Museum of California Art, 2008).

9 Kuniyoshi, *Yasuo Kuniyoshi*, n.p.

10 Ibid.

11 For examples of Kuniyoshi's early dark landscapes, see Ozawa and Suzuki, *Yasuo Kuniyoshi*, nos. 1, 5, 7, 15.

12 Kenneth Hayes Miller, "The Third Dimension in Painting," a lecture given several times in the 1920s, in Lincoln Rothschild, *To Keep Art Alive: The Effort of Kenneth Hayes Miller, American Painter, 1876–1952* (Philadelphia: Art Alliance Press, 1974), 80.

13 Lloyd Goodrich, *Kenneth Hayes Miller* (New York: Arts Publishing, 1930), 6.

14 Lloyd Goodrich, Notes on interviews with Kuniyoshi, January 6, 1948, Whitney Museum of American Art.

15 Richard Lahey Papers, Archives of American Art, Smithsonian Institution (hereafter cited as AAA), microfilm reel 378, frame 20.

16 Harry Salpeter, "Kenneth Hayes Miller: Intellectual," *Esquire*, October 1937, 69.

17 Kenneth E. Silver, *Chaos and Classicism: Art in France, Italy, and Germany, 1918–1936* (New York: Guggenheim Museum, 2010).

18 Yasuo Kuniyoshi, "Autobiography," August 24, Yasuo Kuniyoshi Papers, AAA, box 1, folder 15. In the early 1940s, Kuniyoshi wrote statements for an autobiography that he never completed. They have been frequently quoted in the literature about the artist. The Archives of American Art has two crucial holdings of Kuniyoshi material that are repeatedly cited here: the Yasuo Kuniyoshi Papers, which have been scanned and are available on the Archives' website, and Kuniyoshi's two scrapbooks, which are available at the Archives.

19 Paul Cummings, "Oral history interview with Katherine Schmidt," 8–15 December 1969, AAA, 10.

20 Sara Mazo Kuniyoshi, interview by the author, January 7, 1992, New York. Marian L. Smith, "'Any woman who is now or may hereafter be married . . .': Women and Naturalization, ca. 1802–1940," *Prologue* 30 (Summer 1998): "Under the act of March 2, 1907, all women acquired their husband's nationality upon any marriage occurring after that date. This changed nothing for immigrant women, but U.S.-born citizen women could now lose their citizenship by any marriage to any alien. Most of these women subsequently regained their U.S. citizenship when their husbands naturalized. However, those who married Chinese, Japanese, Filipino, or other men racially ineligible to naturalize forfeited their U.S. citizenship." http://www.archives.gov/publications/prologue/1998/summer/women-and-naturalization-1.html.

21 "No Fake Bohemian Can Join Penguins," *The Sun*, January 8, 1917, Walt Kuhn Papers, AAA, microfilm reel D240, frame 838.

22 Schmidt, interview. Sidney Geist, "The Firemen's Ball for Brancusi," *Archives of American Art Journal* 16, no. 1 (1976): 9. For the Penguins, see also Christine I. Oaklander, "Walt Kuhn and the Penguin: High Jinks and Experimental Art," *Archives of American Art Journal* 49, nos. 3–4 (2010): 51–59.

23 Kuniyoshi, *Yasuo Kuniyoshi*, n.p.

24 Horace Brodzky, "'A Temporary Group' At the Penguin," *Playboy: A Portfolio of Art and Satire* (1919): 22.

25 Mary Meixner, "Yasuo Kuniyoshi Talks with Students," *College Art Journal* 13 (Fall 1953): 14.

26 See Geist, "Firemen's Ball for Brancusi," 8–11.

27 Siegfried Wichmann, *Japonisme, The Japanese Influence on Western Art Since 1858* (New York: Thames and Hudson, 1999), 415n10, "Interiors and modules": "The expression Japonisme was probably first formulated by Philippe Burty in 1872. Burty wrote a series of articles under the title 'Japonisme' in *La Renaissance Littéraire et Artistique* from May 1872 to February 1873."

28 For Field's commission of a mural from Picasso, which was never completed, see William Rubin, "Appendix: The Library of

Hamilton Easter Field," *Picasso and Braque, Pioneering Cubism* (New York: Museum of Modern Art, 1989), 63–69. For Field, see Doreen Bolger, "Hamilton Easter Field and His Contribution to American Modernism," *American Art* 20, no. 2 (1988): 79–107, and Wendy Jeffers, "Hamilton Easter Field: The Benefactor from Brooklyn," *Archives of American Art Journal* 50, nos. 1–2 (2011): 26–37.

29 Halpert, quoted in Jeffers, "Hamilton Easter Field," 26.

30 Hamilton Easter Field, "George Santayana and Others," *Arts* 1 (February–March 1921): 20. The portrait of Catalina Schuyler (ca. 1720–25) is in the collection of the New-York Historical Society.

31 Hamilton Easter Field, foreword to *Catalogue of an Exhibition of the Paintings of Hamilton Easter Field* (New York: Berlin Photographic, 1912), 4.

32 Hamilton Easter Field, "Comment on the Arts" (reviewing December 1921) *Arts* 2, no. 3 (1922): 172.

33 Hidemichi Tanaka, "Cézanne and Japonisme," *Artibus et Historiae*, no. 44 (2001): 219n43.

34 The reviews quoted here can all be found in Kuniyoshi's scrapbook, available through microfilm, Kuniyoshi Papers, AAA, reel D176. Anonymous, "Exhibitions That Forecast an Epidemic of Modernism," *The World*, January 15, 1922, Kuniyoshi Papers, AAA, microfilm reel D176, frame 87.

35 Henry McBride, "Art News and Reviews," *New York Herald*, January 8, 1922, 3.

36 Anonymous, *Evening Sun*, January 14, 1922, Kuniyoshi Papers, AAA, microfilm reel D176, frame 86.

37 Both quotes are from Kuniyoshi, *Yasuo Kuniyoshi*, n.p.

38 For an informative discussion of the role of Japanese folk art in Kuniyoshi's work, see Gail Levin, "Between Two Worlds: Folk Culture, Identity, and the American Art of Yasuo Kuniyoshi," *Archives of American Art Journal* 43, nos. 3–4 (2003): 2–17.

39 The women in the show were Elizabeth Burroughs, Isabella Howland, Molly Luce, Eloisa Schwab, Henrietta Shore, Ivy Troutman, and Marguerite Zorach.

40 Kuniyoshi, quoted in Aline B. Louchheim, "Kuniyoshi: Look, My Past," *ARTNews* 47 (April 1948): 47.

41 Henry McBride, "Kuniyoshi's Debut in the Daniel Gallery," *New York Herald*, January 8, 1922, Kuniyoshi Papers, AAA, microfilm reel D176, frame 78.

42 Forbes Watson, "The Art of Kuniyoshi Combines Qualities of East and West," January 21, 1925, Kuniyoshi Papers, AAA, microfilm reel D176, frame 167.

43 Kuniyoshi's *The Shore* is reproduced in Guy Pène duBois, "Art By the Way," *International Studio* 77 (July 1923): 352.

44 Forbes Watson, "Art Notes," 1926, Kuniyoshi Papers, AAA, microfilm reel D176, frame 182.

45 Alexander Brook, "Yasuo Kuniyoshi," *Arts* 5 (January 1924): 26.

46 *Evening Post*, March 26, 1926, and "Kuniyoshi Shows Paintings Done Abroad," *Brooklyn Eagle*, 1926, Kuniyoshi Papers, AAA, microfilm reel D176, frames 180–81.

47 *Sunday World*, 1924, in ibid., frame 144.

48 *Arts*, February 25, 1925, in ibid., frame 177.

49 *Tribune*, January 4, 1925, in ibid., frame 169.

50 William Murrell, *Yasuo Kuniyoshi*, Younger Artists Series No. 4 (Woodstock, NY: W. M. Fisher, 1922), n.p.

51 Another, more violent, precedent is Jean-François Millet's *The Pig Killers* (ca. 1867–70, National Gallery of Canada, Ottawa).

52 The two watercolors by Homer that Field owned were *The Turtle Pound* (1898, Brooklyn Museum), and *The Coming Storm* (1901, National Gallery of Art, Washington, DC).

53 In recent years this imagery has been adopted by artist Masami Teraoka (b. 1936). Hokusai's *Girl Diver and Octopi* (1814) is in the British Museum, London.

54 Kuniyoshi to Carl Zigrosser, [n.d.], Carl Zigrosser Collection, Special Collections, Van Pelt Library, University of Pennsylvania. Because this letter is undated, it could be from the Kuniyoshis' second trip to Paris, in 1928.

55 *Exhibition of American Art*, Chambre Syndicale de la Curiosité et des Beaux-Arts, Paris, June 9–July 5, 1924. Organized by the Art Patrons of America, the exhibition featured 309 works by contemporary American artists of all persuasions.

56 Forbes Watson, "American Art in Paris," *Arts* 6 (August 1924): 103.

57 Alexander Brook, "Yasuo Kuniyoshi–A Tribute," in *Yasuo Kuniyoshi, 1889–1953*, (Austin: University Art Museum, University of Texas at Austin, 1975): 51. He sometimes performed at the famous Palace Theater. Mazo, interview.

58 Avis Berman, *Rebels on Eighth Street: Juliana Force and the Whitney Museum of American Art* (New York: Atheneum, 1990), 256.

59 Transcript of Skowhegan School of Painting and Sculpture lecture, 1951, Kuniyoshi Papers, AAA, box 1, folder 40.

60 Catherine M. Lewis, Richard Anthony Lewis, and Rand Jerris, "A Game of Considerable Passion: Golf in American Art," in *The Art of Golf* (Atlanta: High Museum of Art, 2012), 75.

61 Mazo, interview.

62 Duncan Phillips, "The Washington Independent," *Arts* 13 (April 1928): 243.

63 Schmidt, interview.

64 M. P. [Murdock Pemberton], "The Art Galleries," *New Yorker*, December 1, 1928, 102; *American*, November 25, 1928, Kuniyoshi Papers, AAA, microfilm reel D176.

65 Julius Meier-Graefe, "A Few Conclusions on American Art," November 1928, 83, Kuniyoshi Papers, AAA, microfilm reel D176, frame 276.

66 Audrey McMahon, "A Perspective View of the New York Season," *Parnassus* 5 (May 1930): 5.

67 Forbes Watson, "The All American Nineteen," *Arts* 16 (January 1930): 303, 305.

68 Kuniyoshi, quoted in Samuel M. Kootz, *Modern American Painters* (New York: Brewer & Warren, 1930), 43.

69 I thank Michael Gotkin for his insights about the house and garden.

70 Yasuo Kuniyoshi to Katherine Schmidt, 1931, Yasuo Kuniyoshi Papers, Philadelphia Museum of Art (hereafter cited as Kuniyoshi Papers, PMA).

71 Ibid., before September 29, 1931.

72 Ibid., December 5, 1931.

73 Ibid., November 20, 1931.

74 "Kuniyoshi, Noted Artist Developed in U.S., Visiting Fatherland For Exhibition," Osaka paper, October 16, 1931, Kuniyoshi Papers, AAA, microfilm reel D176, frame 342.

75 Yasuo Kuniyoshi, "Art and Artists in Japan," *Arts Weekly*, April 23, 1932, 150.

76 Kuniyoshi to Schmidt, January 15, 1931, Kuniyoshi Papers, PMA.

77 "An Accumulation of Sadness," *PM*, November 27, 1944, 17.

78 Kuniyoshi, *Yasuo Kuniyoshi*, n.p.

79 Benita Eisler, *O'Keeffe and Stieglitz: An American Romance* (New York: Doubleday, 1991), 346; Laurie Lisle, *Portrait of an Artist: A Biography of Georgia O'Keeffe* (New York: Washington Square Press, 1981), 258–61; Roxana Robinson, *Georgia O'Keeffe: A Life* (New York: Harper Perennial, 1999), 378f.

80 Philippa Gerry Whiting, "Rockefeller Center Début," *American Magazine of Art* 26 (February 1933): 84.

81 Edward Alden Jewell, "Kuniyoshi, in New One-Man Exhibit at Downtown Gallery, Shows Considerable Progress," *New York Times*, February 8, 1933.

82 The main scholarly examination of Kuniyoshi's still-life paintings, which has been very helpful to what I write here, is Bruce Weber's "Yasuo Kuniyoshi's Symbolic Still Lifes: Mind at Work," in *Yasuo Kuniyoshi: Artist as Photographer* (Annandale-on-Hudson, NY: Edith C. Blum Art Institute, 1983), 25.

83 Kuniyoshi, "Universality in Art," typescript, April 17, 1943, Kuniyoshi Papers, AAA, box 1, folder 9.

84 Sara Mazo Kuniyoshi recalled, "He loved Goya"; Mazo, interview.

85 Paul Fiene would be a witness at Kuniyoshi's second wedding, in 1935.

86 Weber makes the parallel between Kuniyoshi's still lifes and those of the magic realists and the Pittura Metafisica artists around Giorgio De Chirico. Weber, "Yasuo Kuniyoshi's Symbolic Still Lifes," 25. A similar horse weather vane can be seen in a photograph of a folk art exhibition at Edith Halpert's Downtown Gallery reproduced in Graham Shearing, review of *The Girl with the Gallery: Edith Gregor Halpert and the Making of the Modern Art Market*, by Lindsay Pollock, *Archives of American Art Journal* 46, nos. 1–2 (2006): 49.

87 Weber also suggests that another still life, *Broken Objects*, which the artist painted in 1944 when his relationship with his other lady friend ended, reflects his personal, romantic life. Weber, "Yasuo Kuniyoshi's Symbolic Still Lifes," 25, 46n33.

88 Elizabeth McCausland, "A Good American Alien: Kuniyoshi's Art in Retrospective Show," *Springfield (Mass.) Sunday Union and Republican*, May 3, 1942, Elizabeth McCausland Papers, AAA, box 30, folder 14.

89 Kuniyoshi, quoted in Louchheim, "Kuniyoshi: Look, My Past," 47.

90 Kuniyoshi, "Autobiography," December 23, 1944, Kuniyoshi Papers, AAA, box 1, folder 14.

91 Kuniyoshi, "Miscellaneous Subject Files," Kuniyoshi Papers, AAA, box 1, folder 27.

92 Kuniyoshi to Schmidt, December 27, 1931, and January 10, 1932, Kuniyoshi Papers, PMA.

93 Goodrich interview with Kuniyoshi.

94 Morris Gilbert, "Portrait of an Artist," *New York World-Telegram*, February 23, 1940.

95 Warren Dennis, "My Summer with Kuniyoshi," manuscript sent to the author, January 18, 1995.

96 Kuniyoshi's illustrations accompanied two short stories in *Harper's Bazaar*: Richard Sherman, "Casanova in the Morning," July 1935; and Colette, "Nonoche," March 1937.

97 Several of Kuniyoshi's textiles designs can be found in the library of the Museum of Modern Art, New York, and in the Fukutake Collection, Okayama, Japan.

98 Ruth L. Benjamin, "Japanese Painters in America," *Parnassus* 7 (October 1935): 13. Other than Kuniyoshi the artists Benjamin mentions in this article are Isami Doi, Roy Kadowaki, Kaname Miyamoto, Thomas Nagai, Kikuta Nakagawa, Fuji Nakamizo, Soichi Sunami, Chuzo Tamotzu, and Bumpei Usui.

99 Melville Upton of the *New York Sun*, quoted in "The Twain Meet," *Art Digest* 9 (March 1, 1935): 15.

100 "Japanese Artists Portray Horrors of War Machine," *New York Post*, [n.d.], Elizabeth McCausland Papers, AAA, box 27, folder 29–31.

101 Tamotzu apparently made several versions of this image, and the one reproduced here may not be the exact one he showed in 1937.

102 Kuniyoshi, *Yasuo Kuniyoshi*, n.p.

103 See Tom Wolf, *Yasuo Kuniyoshi's Women* (San Francisco, CA: Pomegranate, 1993).

104 Forbes Watson, "Slackers Under the Skin," *Magazine of Art* 32 (October 1939): 557.

105 Jacqueline Francis, *Making Race: Modernism and "Racial Art" in America* (Seattle: University of Washington Press, 2012), 101.

106 In Junichiro Tanizaki's famous meditation on Japanese aesthetics, *In Praise of Shadows*, published in 1933, the author writes extensively

about Asian versus white skin color, which also is an issue in many of his novels. See Tanizaki, *In Praise of Shadows*, trans. Thomas J. Harper and Edward G. Seidensticker (New Haven, CT: Leete's Island Books, 1977). Kuniyoshi, "I paint universal woman, as I think woman should be," Kuniyoshi "Autobiography," November 8, 1944.

107 Gilbert, "Portrait of an Artist."

108 Harry Salpeter, "Yasuo Kuniyoshi: Artists' Artist," *Esquire*, April 1937, 73.

109 "The Fig-leaf Comes to Campus," *The Nation*, March 18, 1936. The other paintings were by Emil Ganso, Bernard Karfiol, David Morrison, and Jules Pascin.

110 Alan, quoted in Lindsay Pollock, *The Girl with the Gallery: Edith Gregor Halpert and the Making of the Modern Art Market* (New York: Public Affairs, 2006), 218.

111 Harry Sternberg, interview by the author, summer 1998, Escondido, CA.

112 Lily Harmon, *Freehand* (New York: Simon and Schuster, 1981), 98. Harmon divorced her husband in 1940; her remark about Kuniyoshi's *Look, It Flies!* comes from knowing him later, as she was active in some of the artists' organizations he was involved with after the war. For Harmon, see Howard E. Wooden, *Lily Harmon, Fifty Years of Painting: A Retrospective Exhibition* (Wichita, KS: Wichita Art Museum, 1982).

113 Kuniyoshi, "Autobiography," August 26 (see note 18, above).

114 Kuniyoshi, "What Is American Art?" draft transcript of a talk at the Museum of Modern Art, February 1940, Kuniyoshi Papers, AAA, box 1, folder 9.

115 Kuniyoshi to George Biddle, December 11, 1941, Kuniyoshi Papers, AAA. For a detailed discussion of Kuniyoshi's art and experiences during World War II, see ShiPu Wang, *Becoming American? The Art and Identity Crisis of Yasuo Kuniyoshi* (Honolulu: University of Hawaii Press, 2011), and for a shorter study, Tom Wolf, "The War Years," in *Yasuo Kuniyoshi: Whitney Museum of American Art at Philip Morris* (New York: The Museum, 1986), n.p.

116 Anne Helioff, interview by the author, May 30, 1983, Woodstock, NY.

117 Gilbert, "Portrait of an Artist." This article reported that one of Kuniyoshi's paintings had been bought by the Japanese ambassador, and observed: "Imagine the chagrin at the embassy when it became known recently that K was a contributor to funds for Chinese relief and had publicly condemned the Japanese invasion of China. Curious inquirer humbly asks to know sad fate of honorable painting."

118 "Three Good Hates," *Time*, April 20, 1942, 41.

119 Thomas Mabry, quoted in Wolf, "War Years," *Yasuo Kuniyoshi*, n.p.; see also Wang, *Becoming American?*, 75.

120 Yasuo Kuniyoshi, "The Artist and the War," *Common Ground* 4 (Spring 1944): 34.

121 In addition an OWI receipt dated April 17, 1943 exists for "Finished sketches, Sketches for a booklet, *This is Japan*" by Kuniyoshi, but the sketches have not been located.

122 Wang, *Becoming American?*, 88–89.

123 ShiPu Wang, "Japan against Japan: U.S. Propaganda and Yasuo Kuniyoshi's Identity Crisis," *American Art* 22 (Spring 2008): 47.

124 Yasuo Kuniyoshi, "Japan to Japan," March 12, 1942, Kuniyoshi Papers, AAA, box 1, folder 28.

125 "Japanese Artist Urges Intensive Raids on Tokio," *New York Herald Tribune*, May 2, 1942. The Fukutake Collection has several examples of these bomb drawings.

126 Kuniyoshi speech to JACD, April 15, 1942, Kuniyoshi Papers, AAA, box 1, folder 22.

127 For the Japanese American Committee on Democracy, see Greg Robinson, "Nisei in Gotham: The JACD and Japanese Americans in 1940s New York," *Prospects: An Annual of American Cultural Studies* 30 (October 2005): 581–95.

128 Japanese American Committee for Democracy Newsletter, Election Extra to Support Franklin Delano Roosevelt, Kuniyoshi Papers, AAA, box 1, folder 29.

129 Yasuo Kuniyoshi, "Nisei-For-Roosevelt Rally," Kuniyoshi Papers, AAA, box 1, folder 29.

130 Yasuo Kuniyoshi, "Rally for Victory in the Far East," speech, December 1944, Kuniyoshi Papers, AAA, box 1, folder 29.

131 Robert Laurent, "Memories of Yas," *College Art Journal* 13 (Autumn 1953): 9.

132 Ayako Ishigaki, "Fashizumu no arashi no nakade" [In a storm of fascism], in *Umi o watatta ai no gaka: Ishigaki Eitarō no shōgai* [A painter of love who went overseas, a biography of Eitaro Ishigaki] (Tokyo: Ochanomizu shobō, 1988), 182, kindly translated for me by Midori Yamamura.

133 Kuniyoshi, "Rally for Victory."

134 "An Accumulation of Sadness," 17.

135 Ibid.

136 I use the term "allegory" here in the sense that Cécile Whiting does in her book, *Antifascism in American Art* (Yale, 1989): to define paintings with imagery that is ambiguous and evocative, as opposed to propaganda images with literal political messages, produced by some of Kuniyoshi's contemporaries in this period.

137 For an extensive discussion of this work, see Wang, *Becoming American?*, chap. 4.

138 I am following Marilyn Cohen's interpretation of the work: *Reginald Marsh's New York: Paintings, Drawings, Prints, and Photographs* (New York: Whitney Museum of American Art, 1983), 27.

139 *The Complete Works of World Art*, vol. 25, Japan 4, *Japanese Modern* (Tokyo: Heibonsha, 1951).

140 Kuniyoshi, "Autobiography."

141 For information about the exhibition, see Hugo Weisgall, *Advancing American Art* (Prague: U.S. Information Service, 1947); Margaret Lynne Ausfeld and Virginia M. Mecklenburg, *Advancing American Art: Politics and Aesthetics in the State Department Exhibition, 1946–48* (Montgomery, AL: Museum of Fine Arts, 1984), 19–20; and Scott Bishop et al., *Art*

Interrupted: Advancing American Art and the Politics of Cultural Diplomacy (Athens: Georgia Museum of Art, 2012).

142 Jennings, quoted in Susan Sivard, "The State Department 'Advancing American Art' Exhibition of 1946 and the Advance of American Art," *Arts Magazine* 58 (April 1984): 96.

143 Truman, quoted in Margaret Lynne Ausfeld, "Circus Girl Arrested: A History of the *Advancing American Art* Collection, 1946–1948," in Ausfeld and Mecklenburg, *Advancing American Art*, 19–20.

144 *Look*, February 3, 1948, 44–48. The painters, in order, were John Marin, Max Weber, Kuniyoshi, Stuart Davis, Ben Shahn, Edward Hopper, Charles Burchfield, George Grosz, Franklin Watkins, Lyonel Feininger, and Jack Levine; the last two tied for tenth place.

145 This was pointed out by Sivard, "State Department 'Advancing American Art,'" 98.

146 Louchheim, "Kuniyoshi: Look, My Past," 47.

147 Clement Greenberg, "Art," *The Nation* 166 (May 15, 1948): 594.

148 Henry McBride, "Attractions in the Galleries," *New York Sun*, May 8, 1942.

149 Sidney Simon, letter to the author, January 11, 1992.

150 David Sokol, "The Founding of Artists Equity Association after World War II," *Archives of American Art Journal* 39, nos. 1–2 (1999): 21.

151 Harry Sternberg to Arthur Secunda, forwarded to the author by Secunda, April 1988.

152 Open letter to Roland L. Redmond, President of the Metropolitan Museum of Art, 1950 May 20, Hedda Sterne Papers, AAA.

153 "The Irascible Eighteen," *New York Herald Tribune*, May 23, 1950.

154 Bradford R. Collins, "*Life* Magazine and the Abstract Expressionists, 1948–51: A Historiographic Study of a Late Bohemian Enterprise," *Art Bulletin* 73 (June 1991): 295.

155 Hudson Walker to Kuniyoshi, May 15, 1951, quoted in Sokol, "Founding of Artists Equity," 27.

156 Wang, *Becoming American?*, 123.

157 Mike (Matsumi) Kanemitsu, interview by the author, January 21, 1991, Los Angeles.

158 Artist and former Kuniyoshi student Arthur Secunda remembered the controversy about Kuniyoshi's new style at the League. Secunda, interview by the author, summer 1998, Los Angeles.

159 In his Woodstock house, Kuniyoshi arranged a group of photographs of artists he admired on a window ledge on the second floor, overlooking his garden. These were photographs he had cut out and simply framed with glass and tape. The artists were Delacroix, Corot, Courbet, Daumier, Renoir, Cézanne, Toulouse-Lautrec, Matisse, Picasso, and two Americans: Ryder and Eakins.

160 Ronald G. Pisano and Bruce Weber, *Parodies of the American Masters: Rediscovering the Society of American Fakirs, 1891–1914* (Stony Brook, NY: Museums at Stony Brook, 1993).

161 Julian Levi, "Yasuo Kuniyoshi," *Living American Art Bulletin*, April 1939.

162 See note 139, above.

163 In the foreword to the catalog, Gordon B. Washburn, the director of the exhibition, wrote, "The suggestion to include Japanese paintings . . . came from Mr. Yasuo Kuniyoshi, who sent us photographs for our selections and put us in touch with the Japanese authorities." The Japanese artists who exhibited were Nobuya Abe, Usaburo Ihara, Genichiro Inokuma, Yasuo Kazuki, Zenzaburo Kojima, Setsuko Migishi, Saburo Miyamoto, Masanari Murai, Taro Okamoto, Key Sato, Kunitaro Suda, Kazuo Tamura, Kazu Wakita, Sotaro Yasui, Jiro Yoshihara. *The 1952 Pittsburgh International Exhibition of Contemporary Painting* (Pittsburgh: Carnegie Institute, 1952), n.p. Bert Winther-Tamaki describes the inclusion of nineteen Japanese painters in the 1952 Salon de Mai exhibition in Paris as "in effect, the postwar debut of Japanese art on the world stage." The Carnegie show was the equivalent in the United States. Winther-Tamaki discusses the controversial negative review given to the Japanese paintings shown in Paris by critic Atsuo Imaizumi. At the time Imaizumi was already working on Kuniyoshi's 1954 exhibition in Japan that would be posthumous for the artist. Bert Winther-Tamaki, *Maximum Embodiment* (Honolulu: University of Hawaii Press, 2012), 154.

164 Atsuo Imaizumi, "Yasuo Kuniyoshi in His Later Years," in *Yasuo Kuniyoshi* (Tokyo: Tokyo Shimbun, 1975), 26.

165 This is according to Ayako Ishigaki, "Fashizumu no arashi no nakade."

166 Kawashima Kazuho, "The Life and Art of Foujita Tsuguharu, and Ben Shahn's Condemnation," *Journal of Naniwa College*, no. 22 (1998): 352.

167 Phyllis Birnbaum, *Glory in a Line: A Life of Foujita, the Artist Caught Between East and West* (New York: Faber and Faber, 2006), 276, 286.

168 Yasuo Kuniyoshi, undated artist's statement, Kuniyoshi Papers, AAA, box 1, folder 10.

169 I discuss this group in greater detail in "The Late Drawings of Yasuo Kuniyoshi," *Drawing, The International Review published by the Drawing Society* (January–February 1992): 100–104.

170 Fairfield Porter, "Yasuo Kuniyoshi," *ARTNews* 52 (November 1953): 42.

171 Another such image by Hokusai is *Salted Salmon and Mice* (ca. 1836), an independent work from a painting album *(nikuhitsu gajō)* in the collection of the Katsushika Hokusai Museum of Art, Tsuwano, Japan.

172 Jo Ann Lewis, "The Disappearing Art of Yasuo Kuniyoshi," *Washington Post*, June 19, 1990, C3. Brian Wallis, "Let's Make a Deal: MOMA Sells Kuniyoshi to Buy Picasso Sketch," *Art in America* 80 (March 1992): 29–30.

173 Kuniyoshi, "What Is American Art?"

PLATES

All plates represent works in the exhibition *The Artistic Journey of Yasuo Kuniyoshi*.

Artworks are oil on canvas, unless otherwise noted.

Dimensions are in inches, with height preceding width.

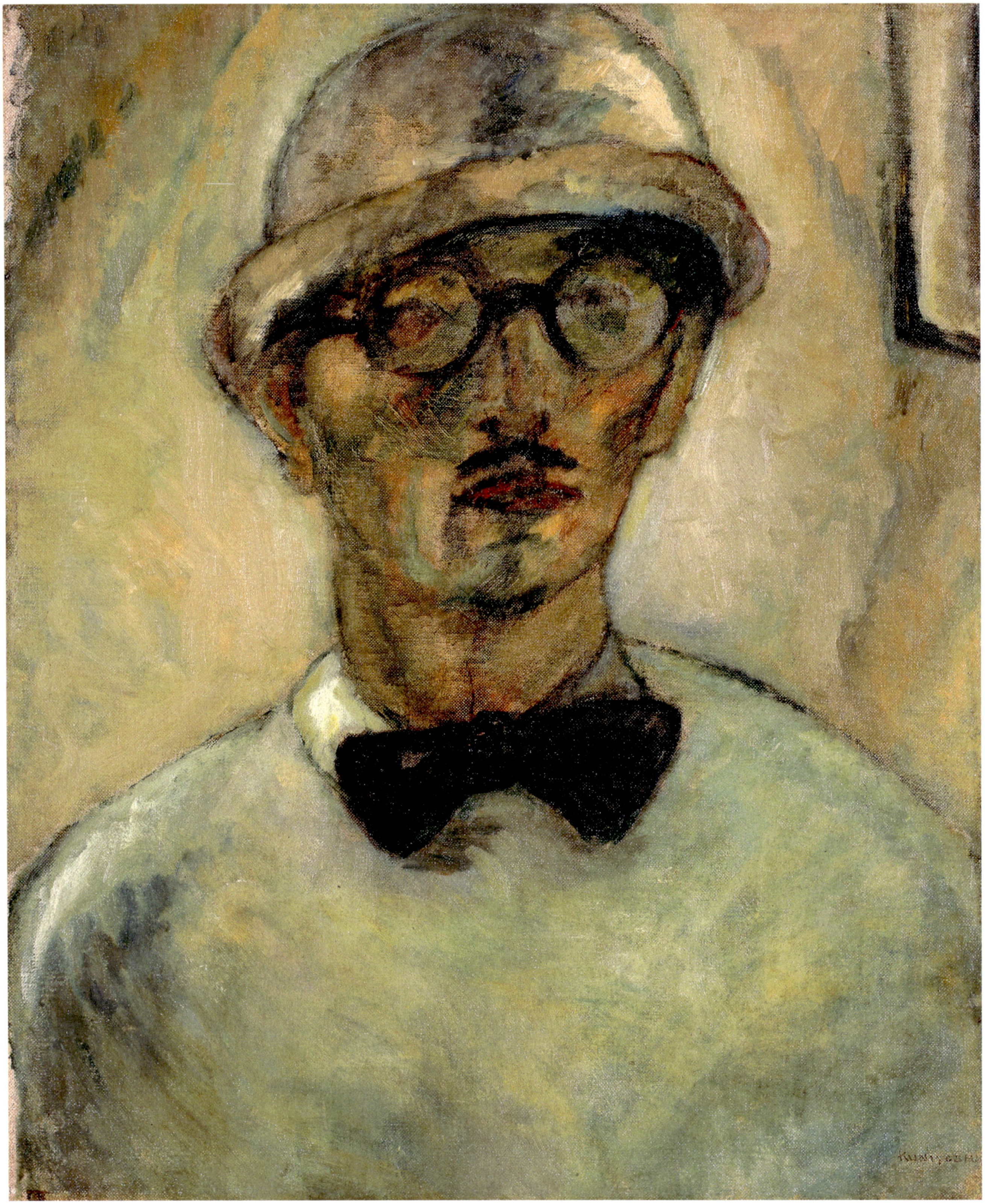

1
Self-Portrait
1918
20 × 16 in.
Fukutake Collection,
Okayama, Japan

2
Landscape
1920
16 ⅛ × 20 ⅛ in.
Smithsonian American
Art Museum, Museum
purchase, 1965.38

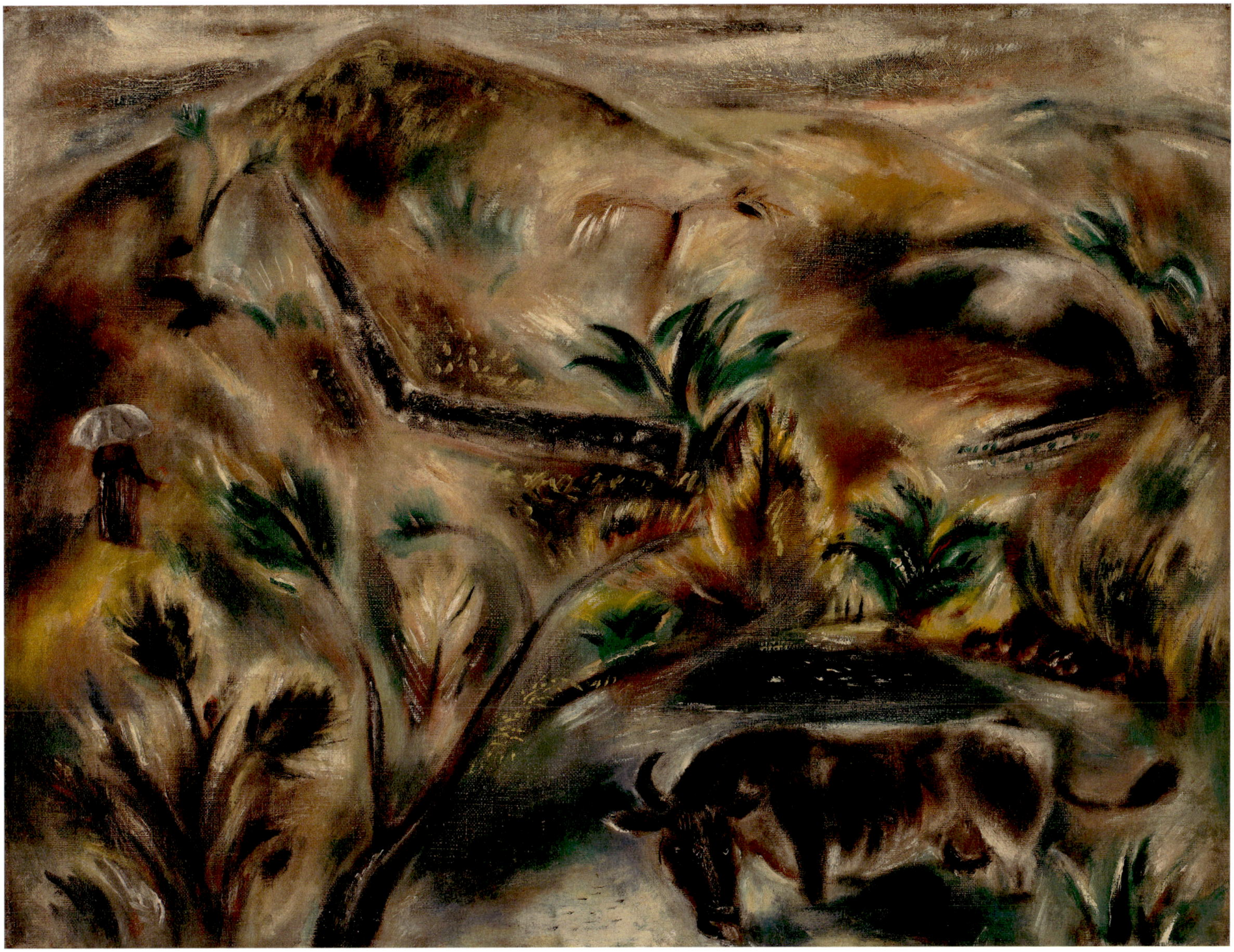

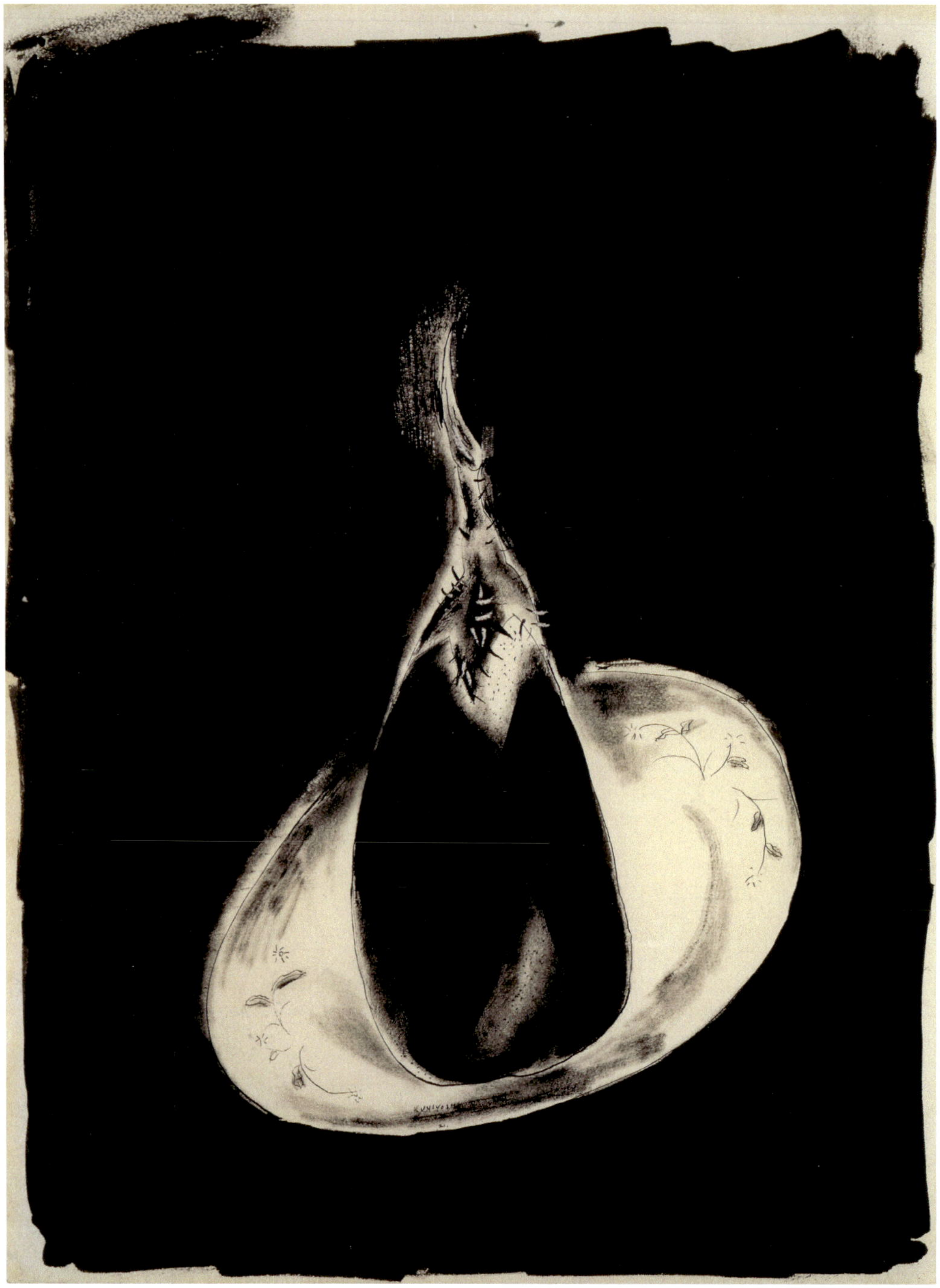

3
Eggplant
1921
ink on paper
image: 15 ½ × 10 ¾ in.
sheet: 24 ½ × 19 ¾ in.
University of Iowa Museum of Art, Iowa City; Museum purchase

4
The Widow
1921
pen and black ink and wash
15 ½ × 11 ³⁄₁₀ in.
The Fine Arts Museums of San Francisco, Gift of George Hopper Fitch, 1986.2.80

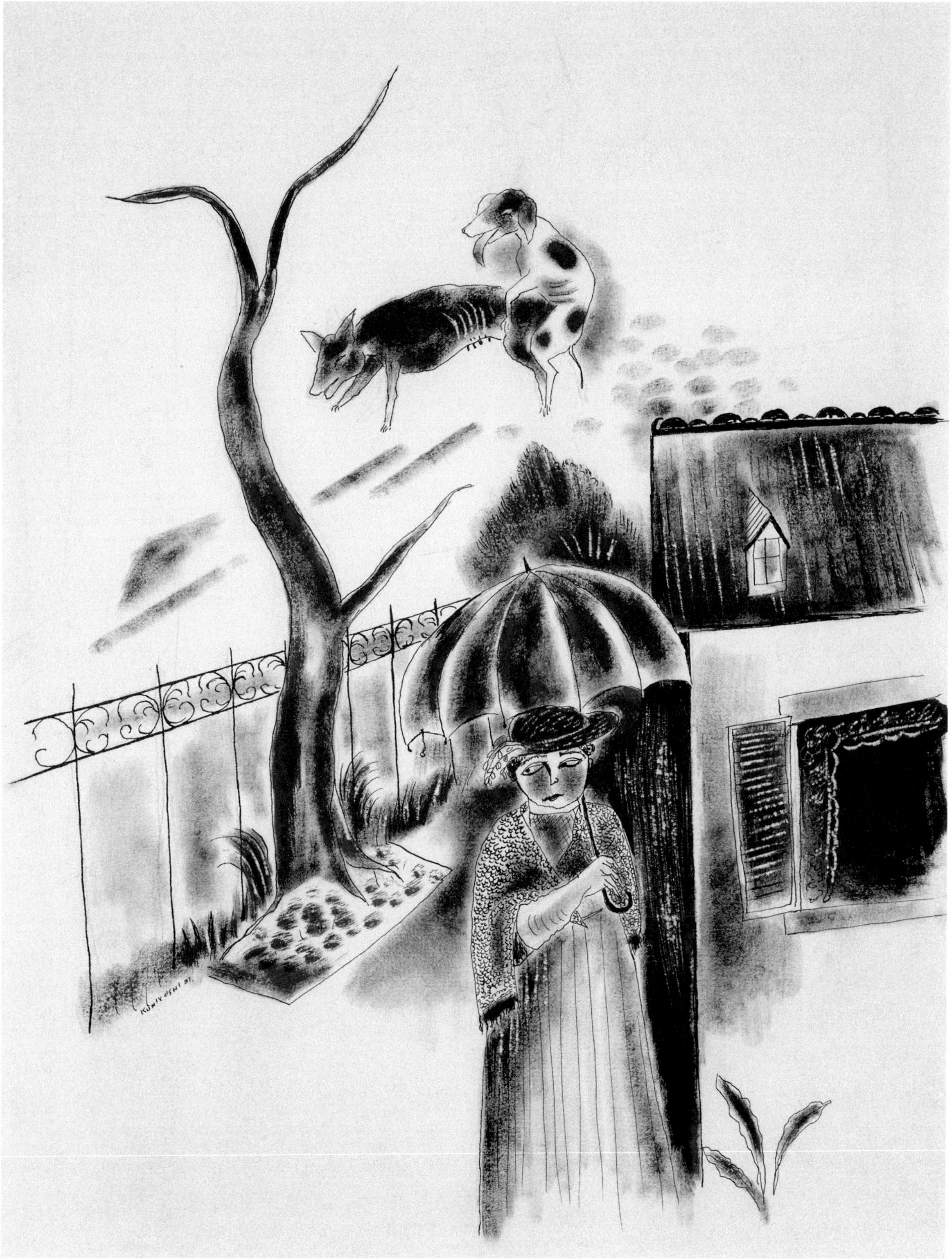

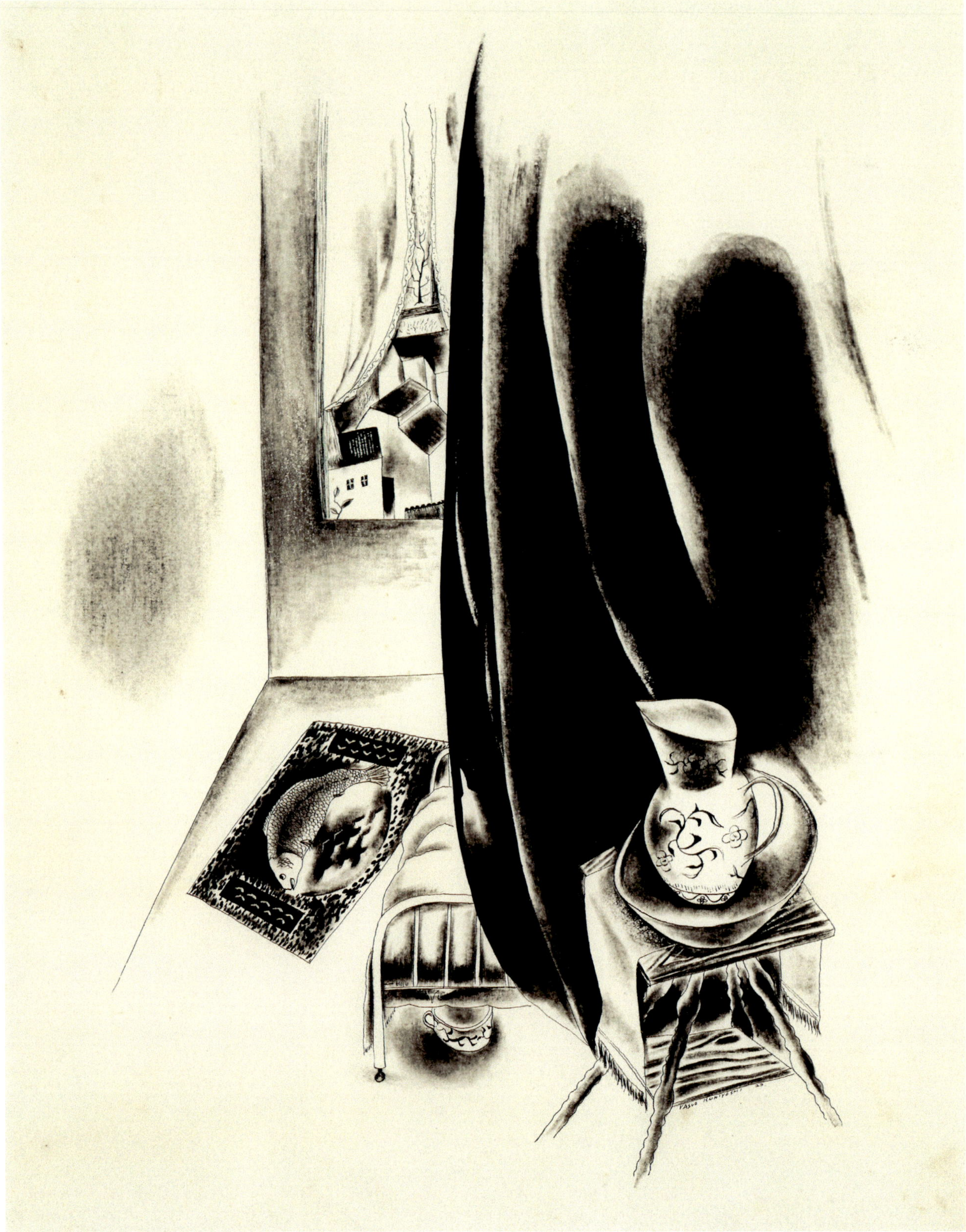

5
Bedroom
1922
pen, brush, black ink, and charcoal
19¾ × 15¼ in.
St. Louis Art Museum, Missouri; Museum purchase, 151:1966

6
Remains of Lunch
1922
pen and ink, brush and ink on paper
13⅞ × 10½ in.
Smithsonian American Art Museum, Museum purchase through the Luisita L. and Franz H. Denghausen Endowment, 2003.18

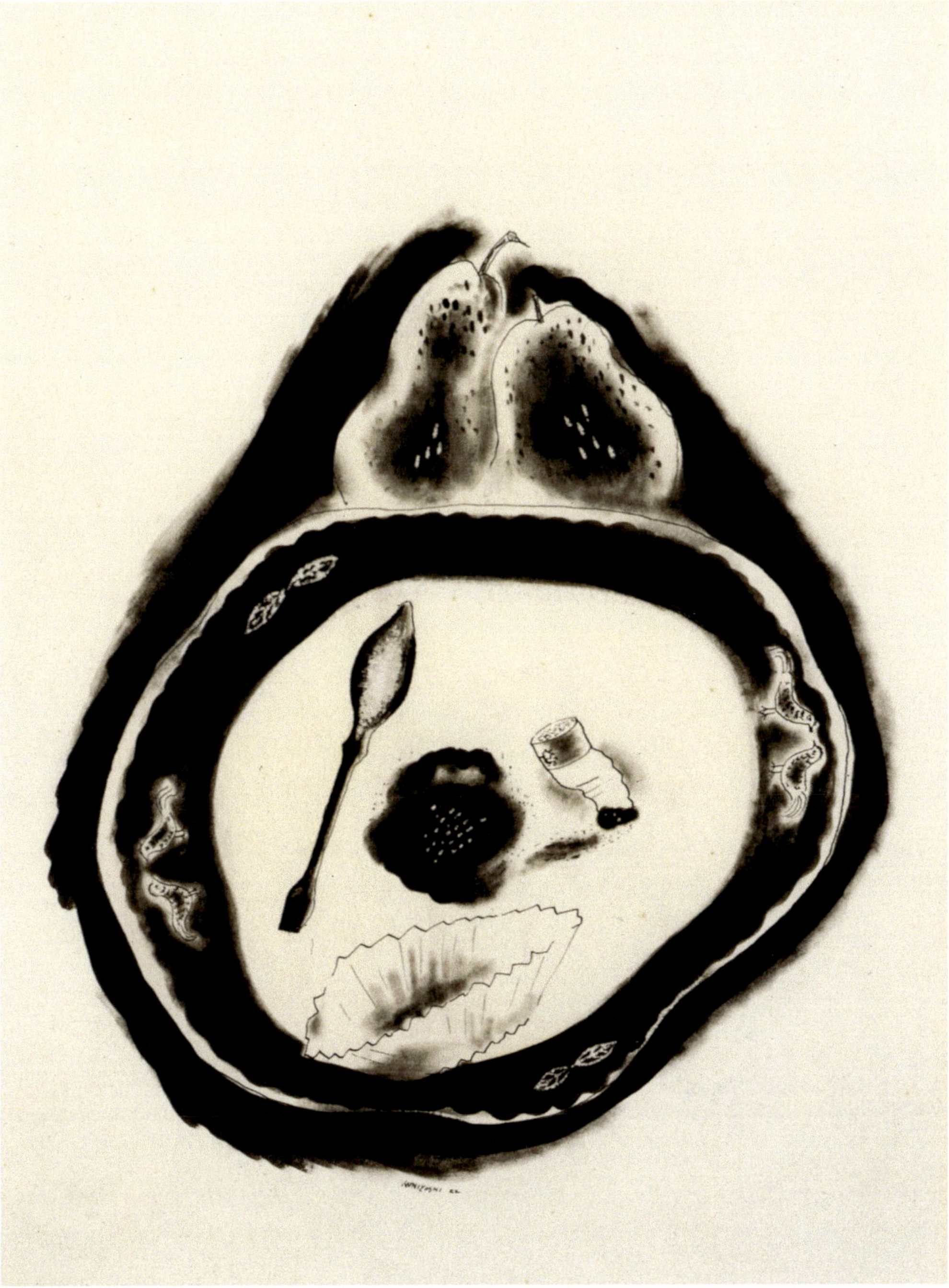

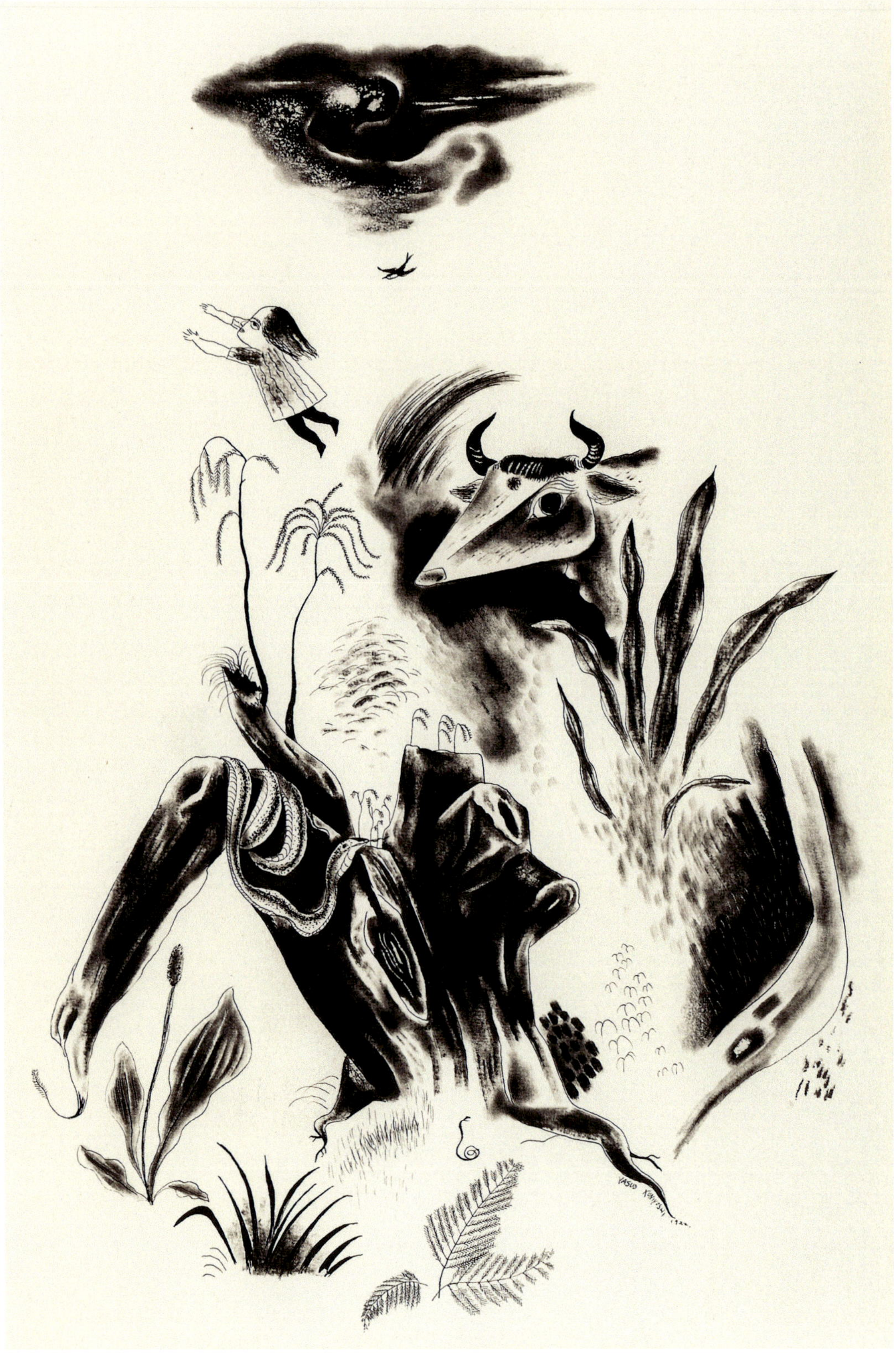

7
The Dream
1922
ink and ink wash
on paper
22 ⅜ × 15 ⅜ in.
Amon Carter Museum,
Fort Worth, Texas

8
*The Calf Doesn't Want
To Go*
1922
ink on paper
15 ⅜ × 22 ⅝ in.
Museum of Modern
Art, New York;
Katherine S. Dreier
Bequest

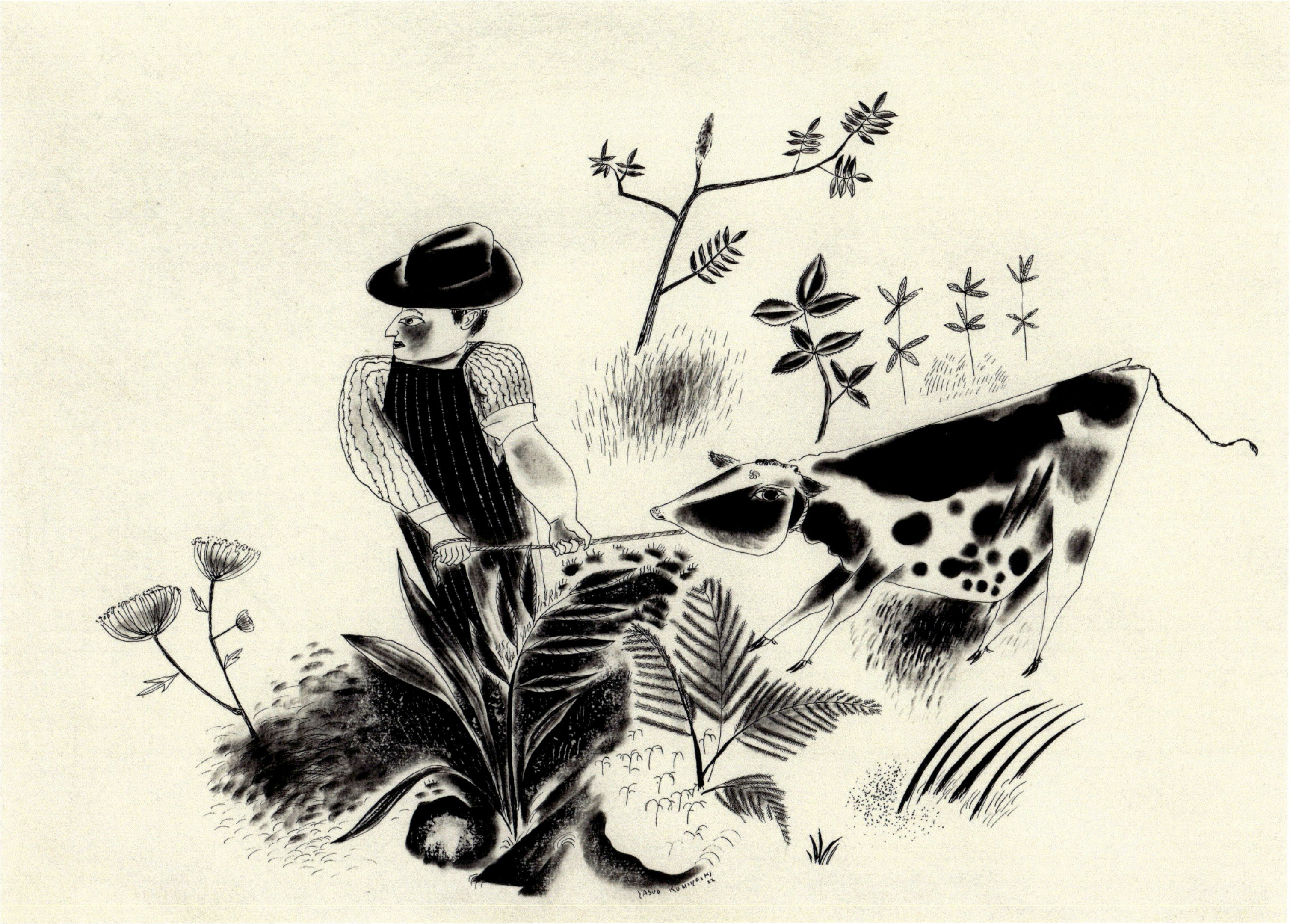

9
Adam and Eve
(The Fall of Man)
1922
20 × 30 in.
Private collection

10
Upstream
1922
29 ¼ × 23 ¼ in.
Denver Art Museum,
Bequest of Marion
Hendrie, 1973.56

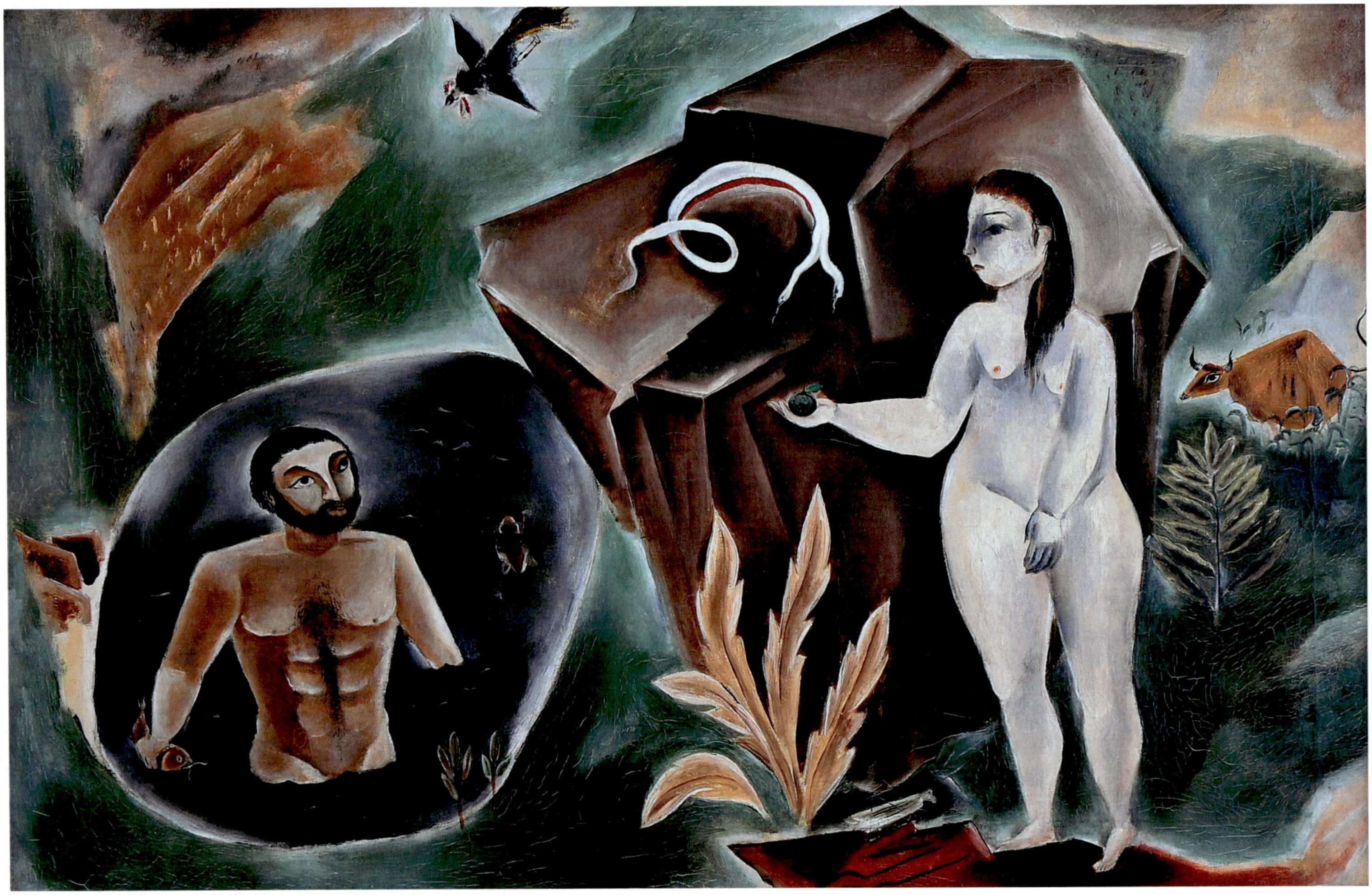

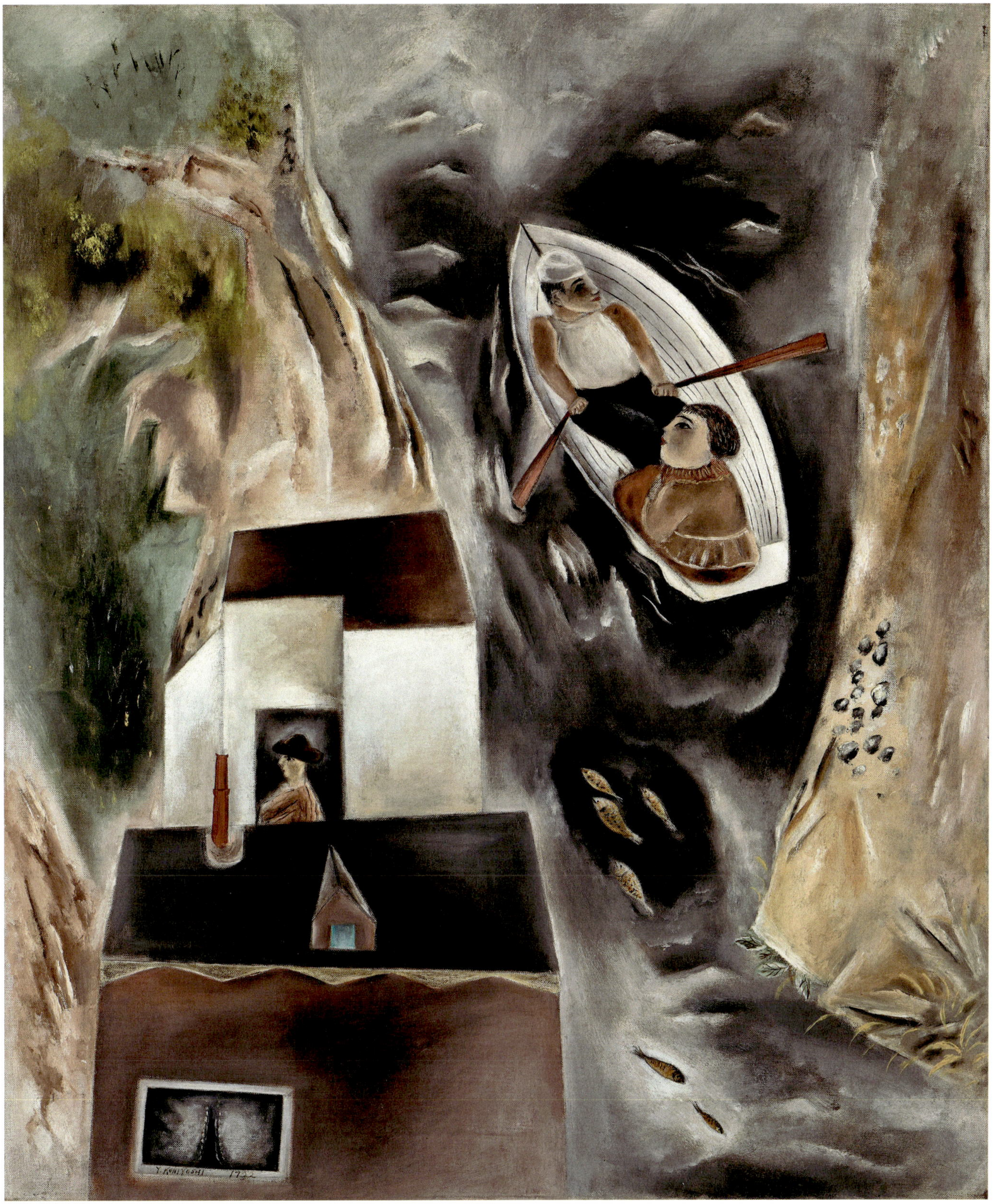

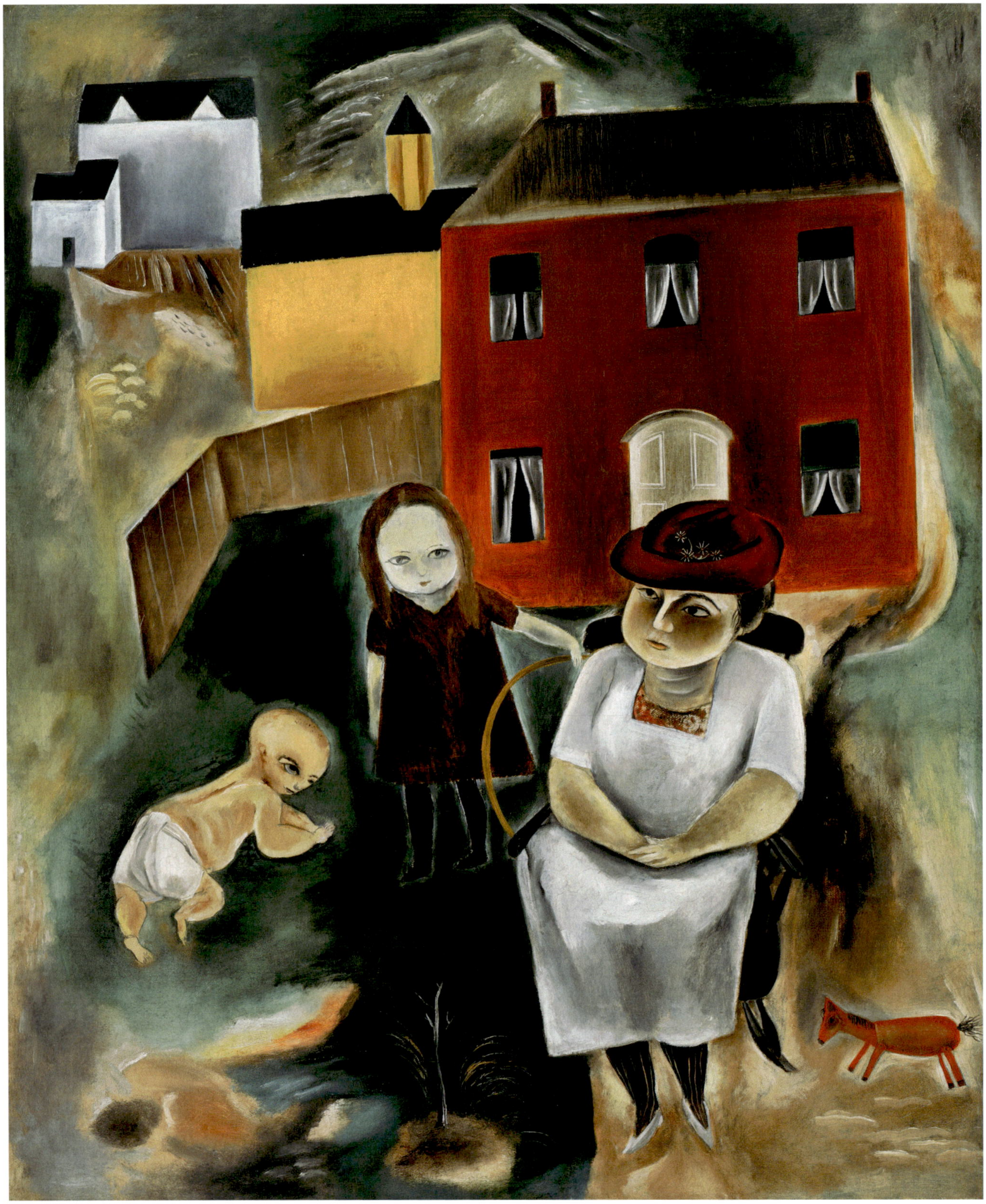

11
Maine Family
about 1922–23
30 ¼ × 24 ⅛ in.
The Phillips Collection,
Washington, DC;
Acquired 1940

12
Little Joe with Cow
1923
28 × 42 in.
Crystal Bridges
Museum of American
Art, Bentonville,
Arkansas

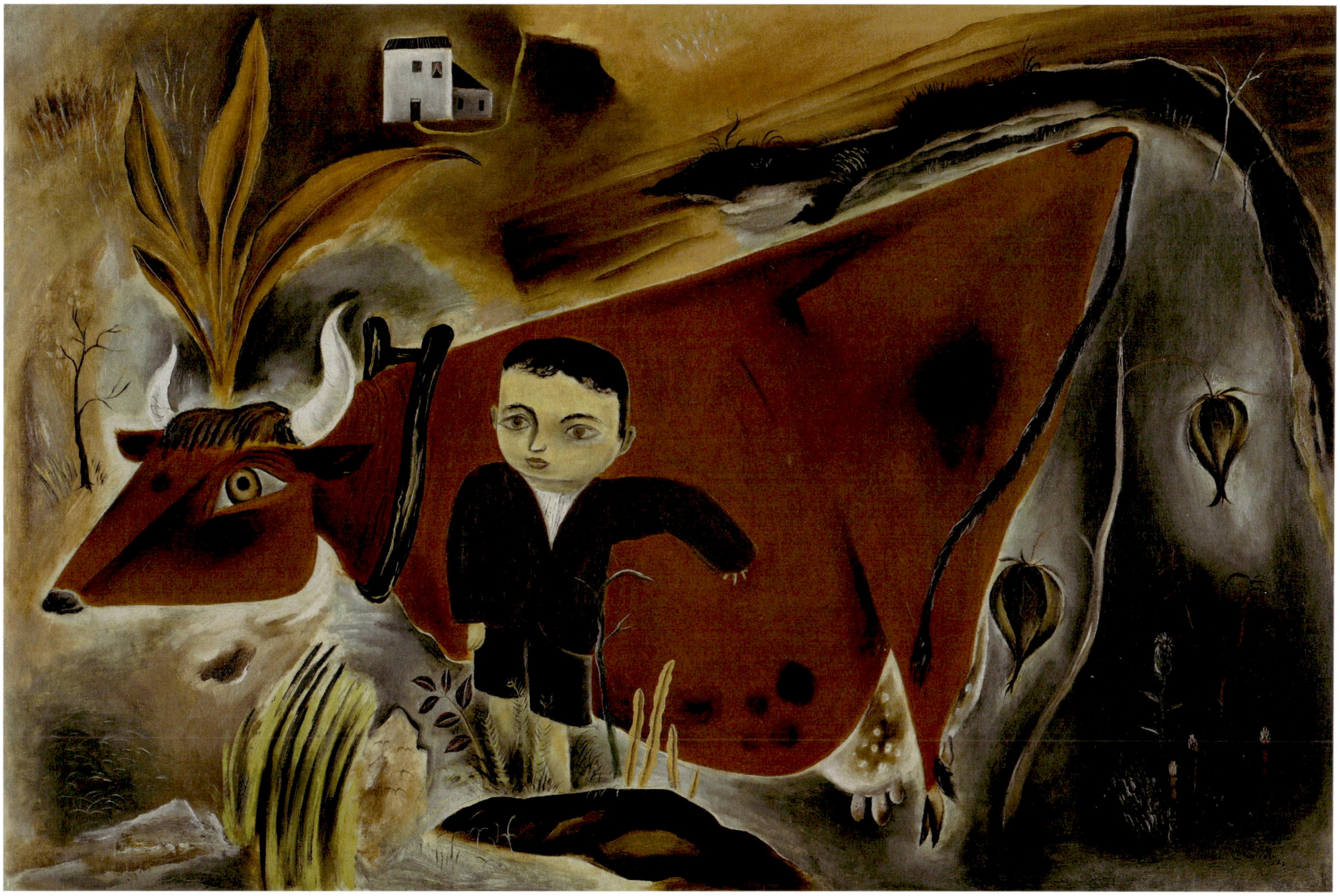

13
Boy Stealing Fruit
1923
20 × 30 in.
Columbus Museum of Art, Ohio; Gift of Ferdinand Howald, 1931.194

14
Grapes in White Bowl
1923
pen, ink, colored ink, and graphite on paper
22 ⅛ × 15 ¼ in.
Wadsworth Atheneum Museum of Art, Hartford, Connecticut; Gift of William E. Hill

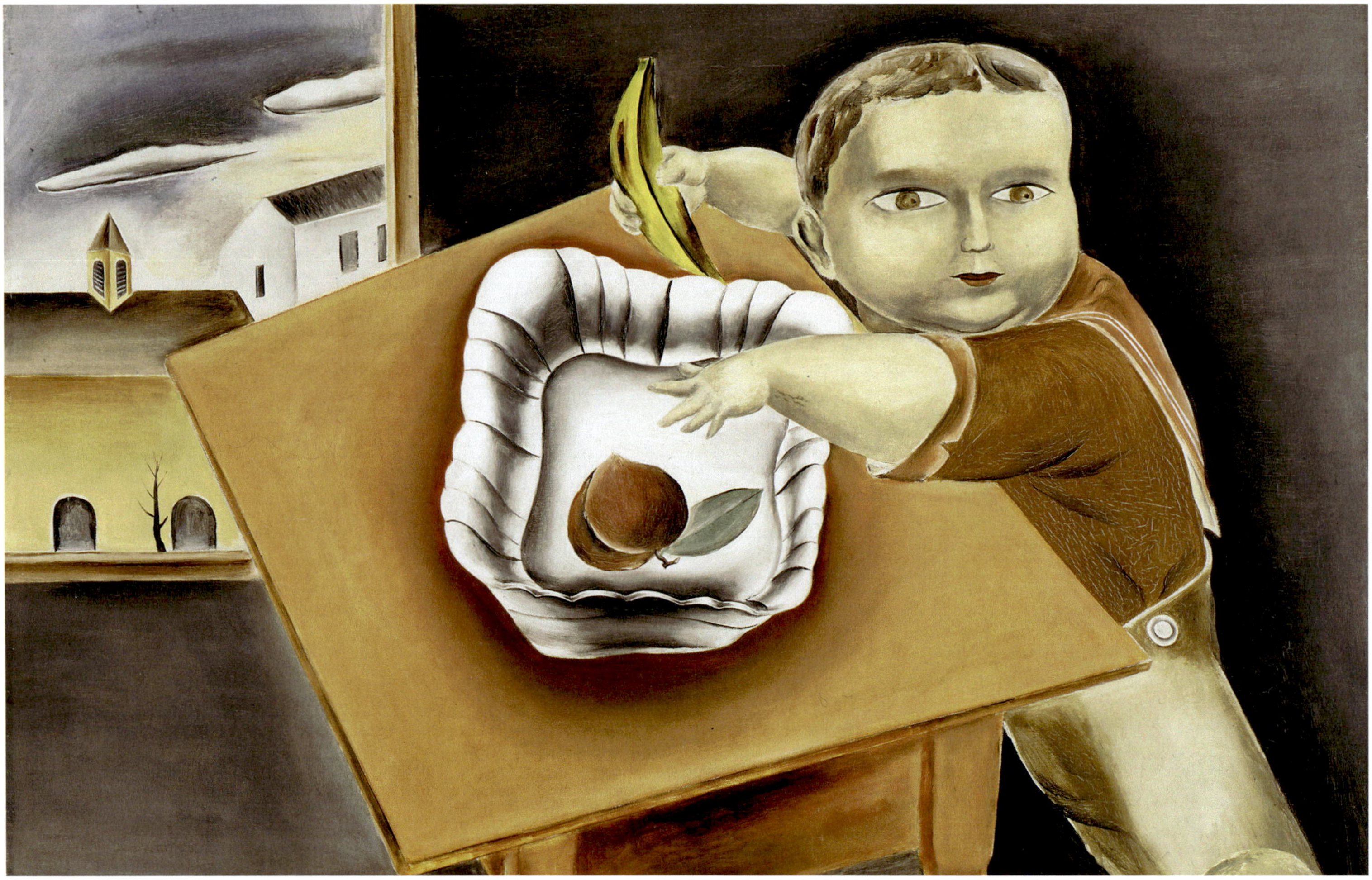

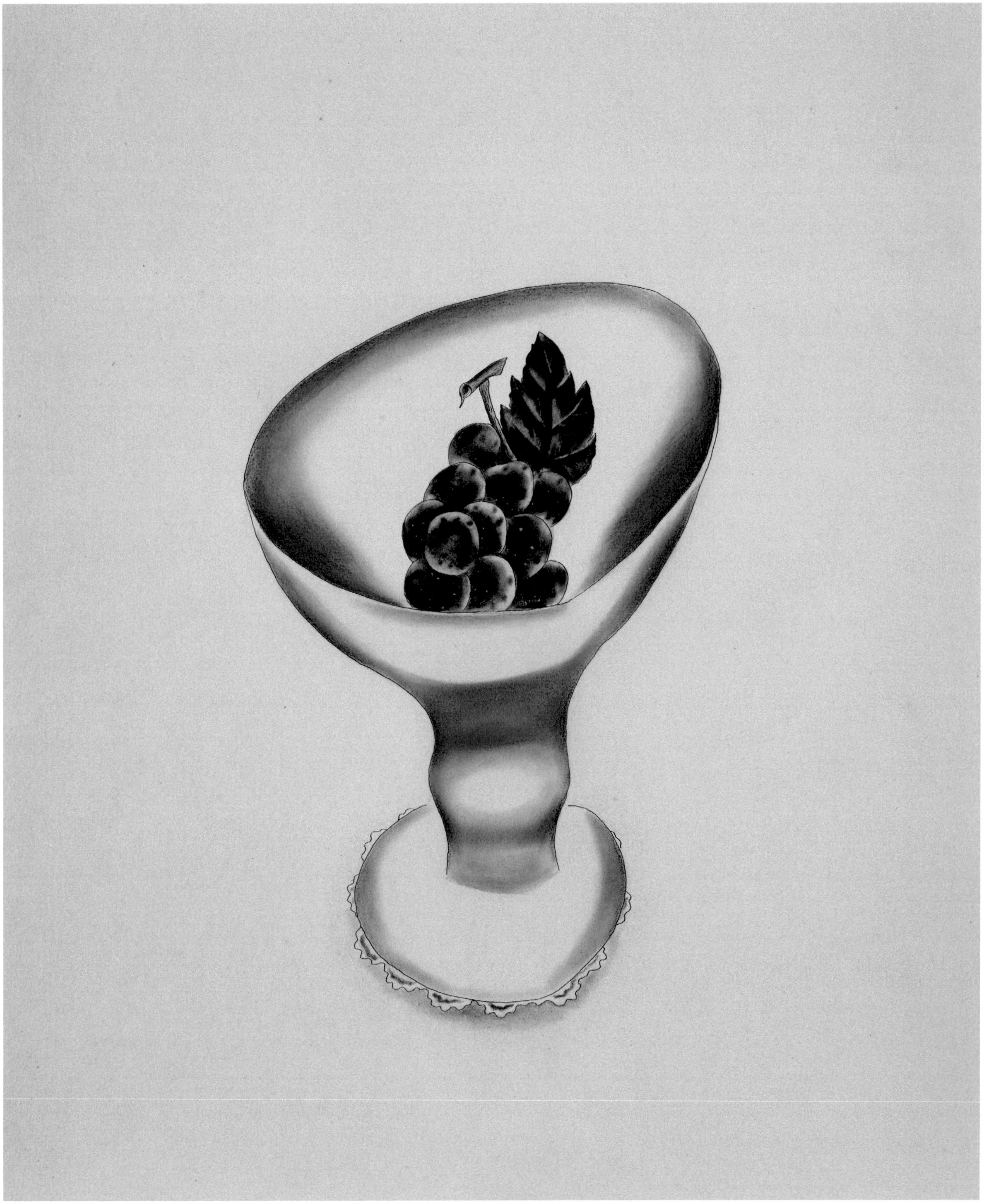

15
Sisters Frightened by a Whale
1923
15 ⅛ × 22 3/16 in.
University of Tsukuba, Ibaraki, Japan; The Ishii Collection

16
Squash
1924
pencil, pen, ink, and watercolor on paper
15 ¼ × 22 ¼ in.
Indianapolis Museum of Art, Indiana; The Robert and Traude Hensel Collection

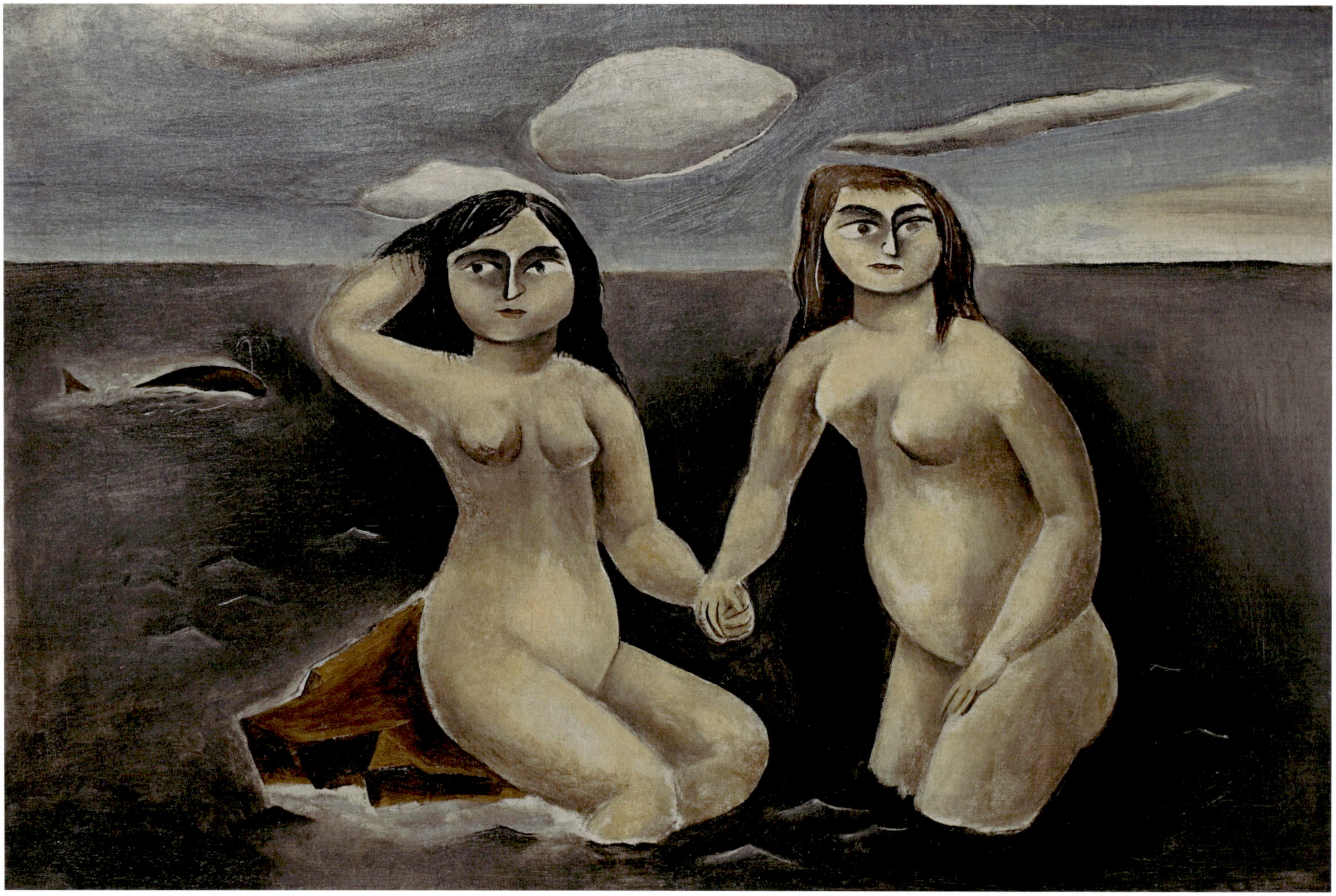

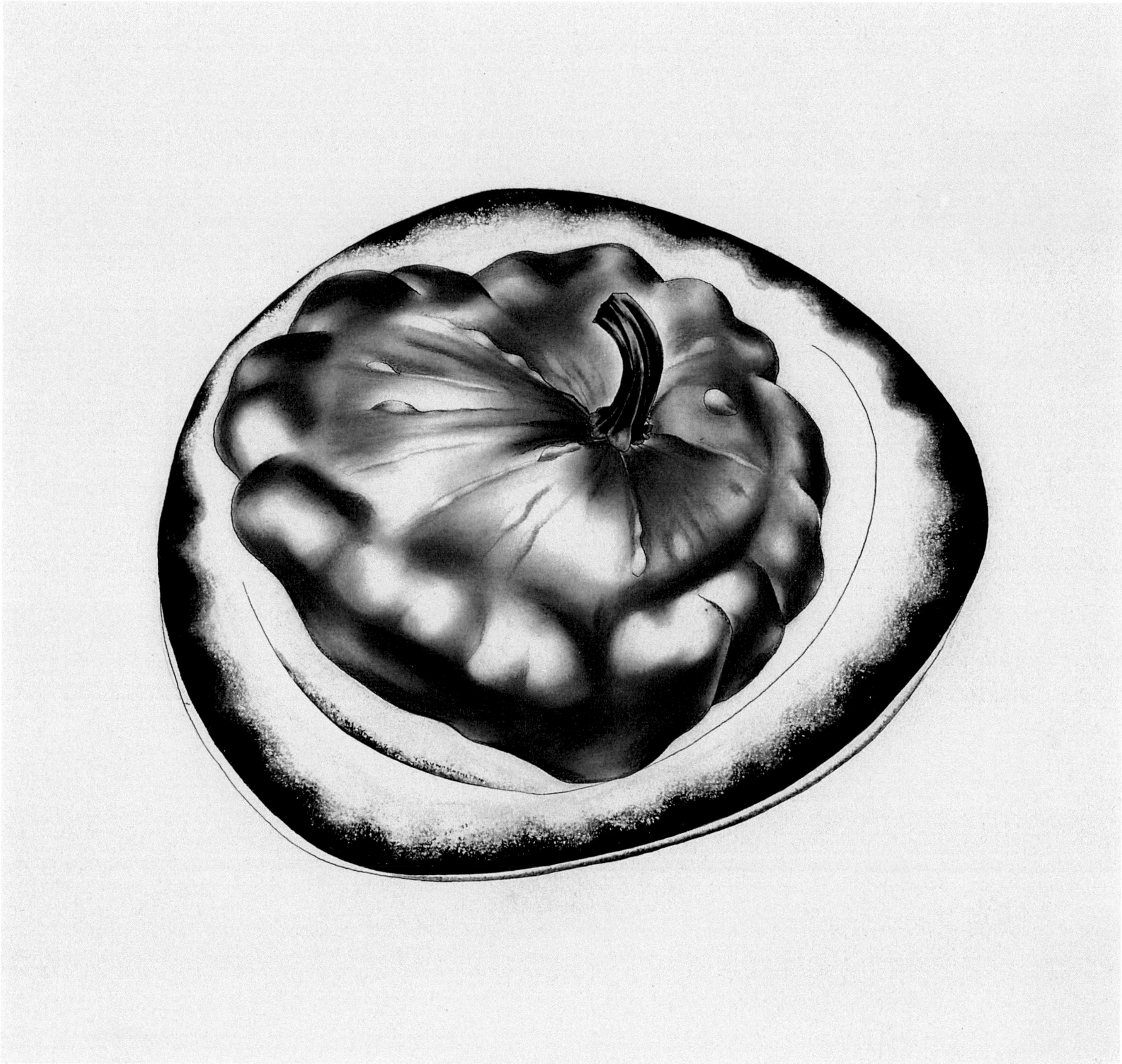

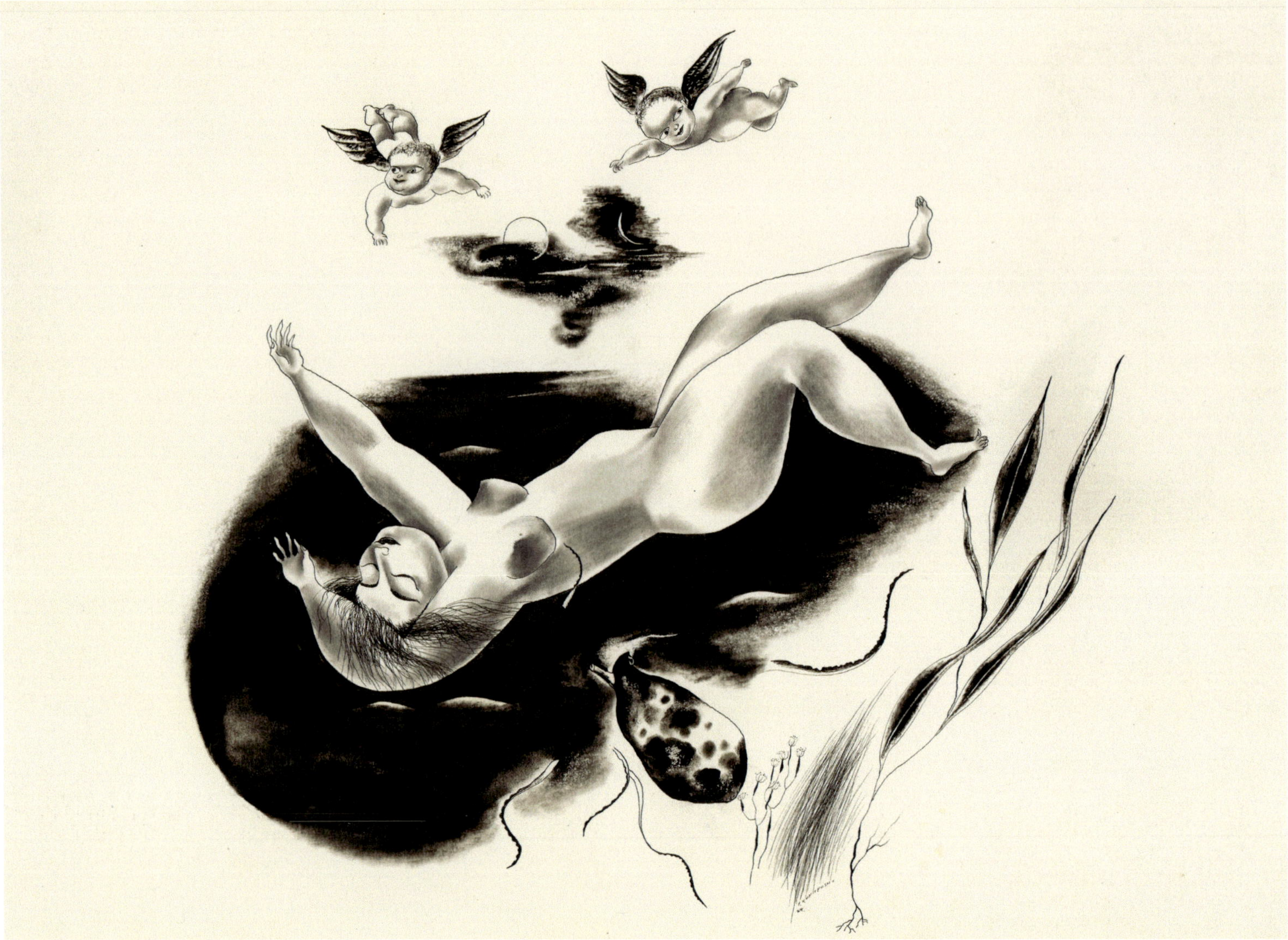

17
Sleeping Beauty
1924
pen and ink, brush and ink, and graphite pencil on paper
sheet (irregular): 15 ½ × 22 ½ in.
Whitney Museum of American Art, New York; Gift of Mrs. Edith Gregor Halpert

18
Bad Dream
1924
ink on paper
24 × 30 in.
Collection Ogunquit Museum of American Art, Maine; Gift of Henry Strater, 1953.12

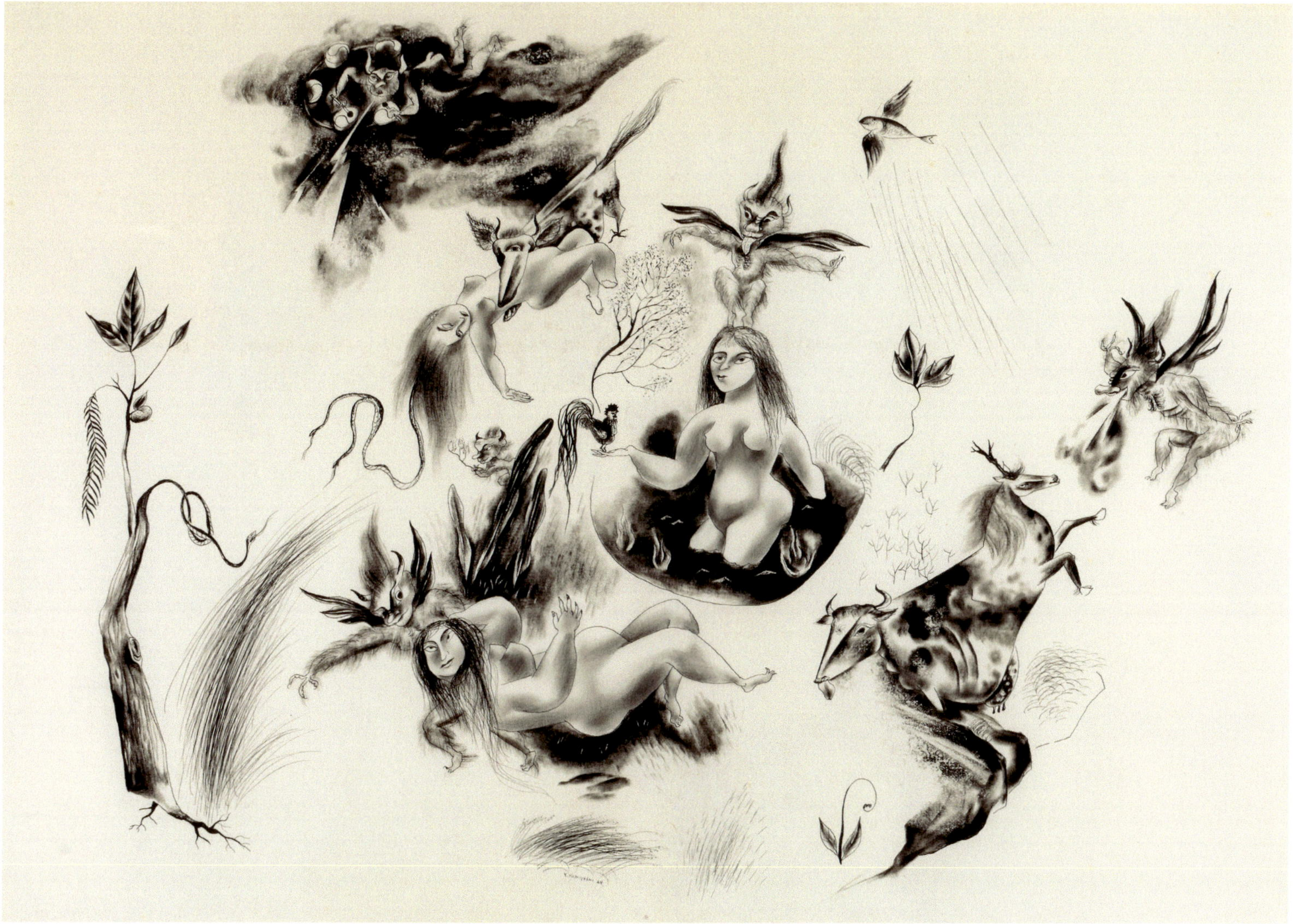

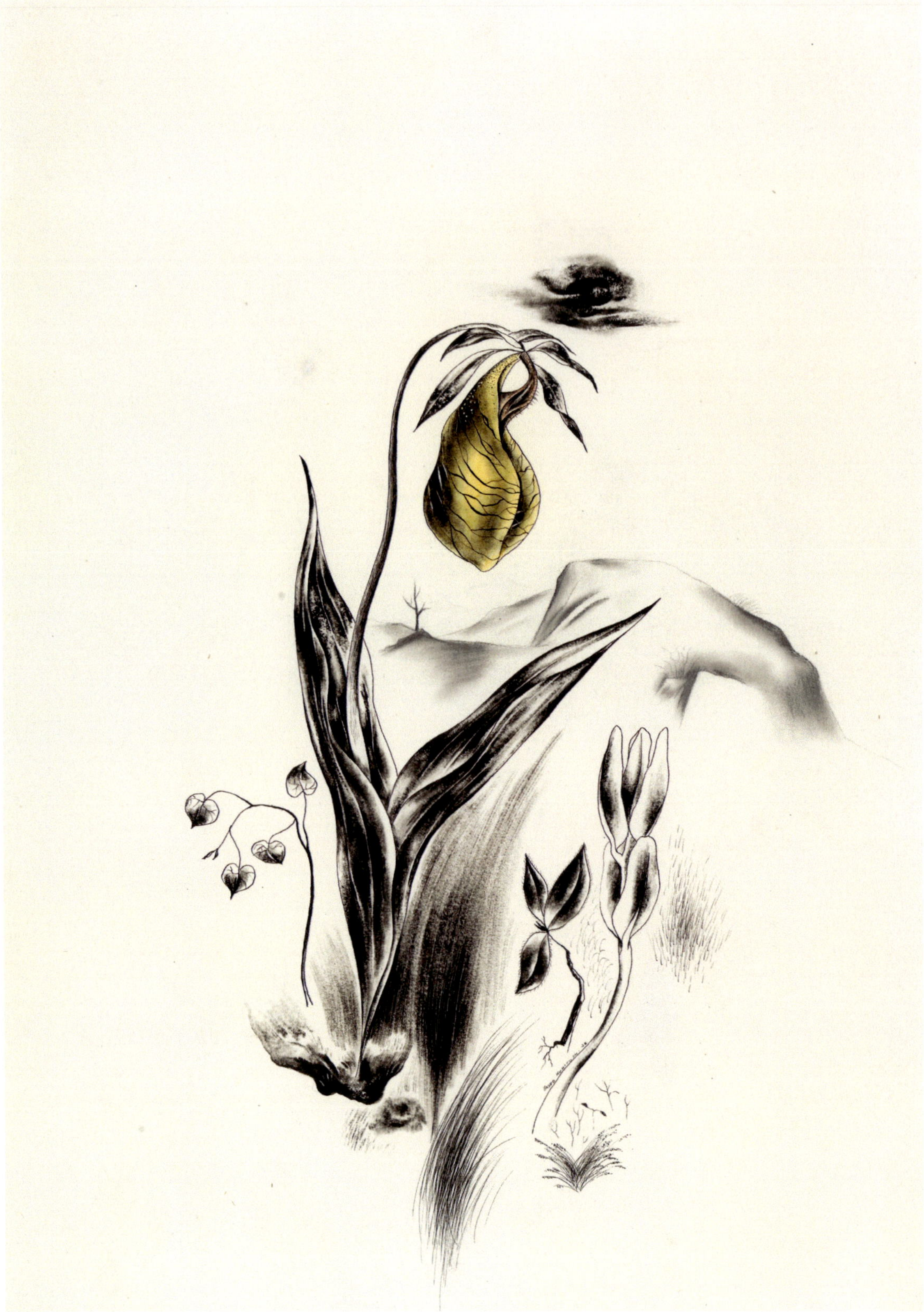

19
Lady Slipper
1924
pen, brush and colored ink on paper
sheet: 22 ¼ × 15 ¼ in.
Whitney Museum of American Art, New York; Gift of Gertrude Vanderbilt Whitney

20
Fisherman
1924
ink on paper
22 × 28 ⅜ in.
Museum of Modern Art, New York; Given anonymously (by exchange)

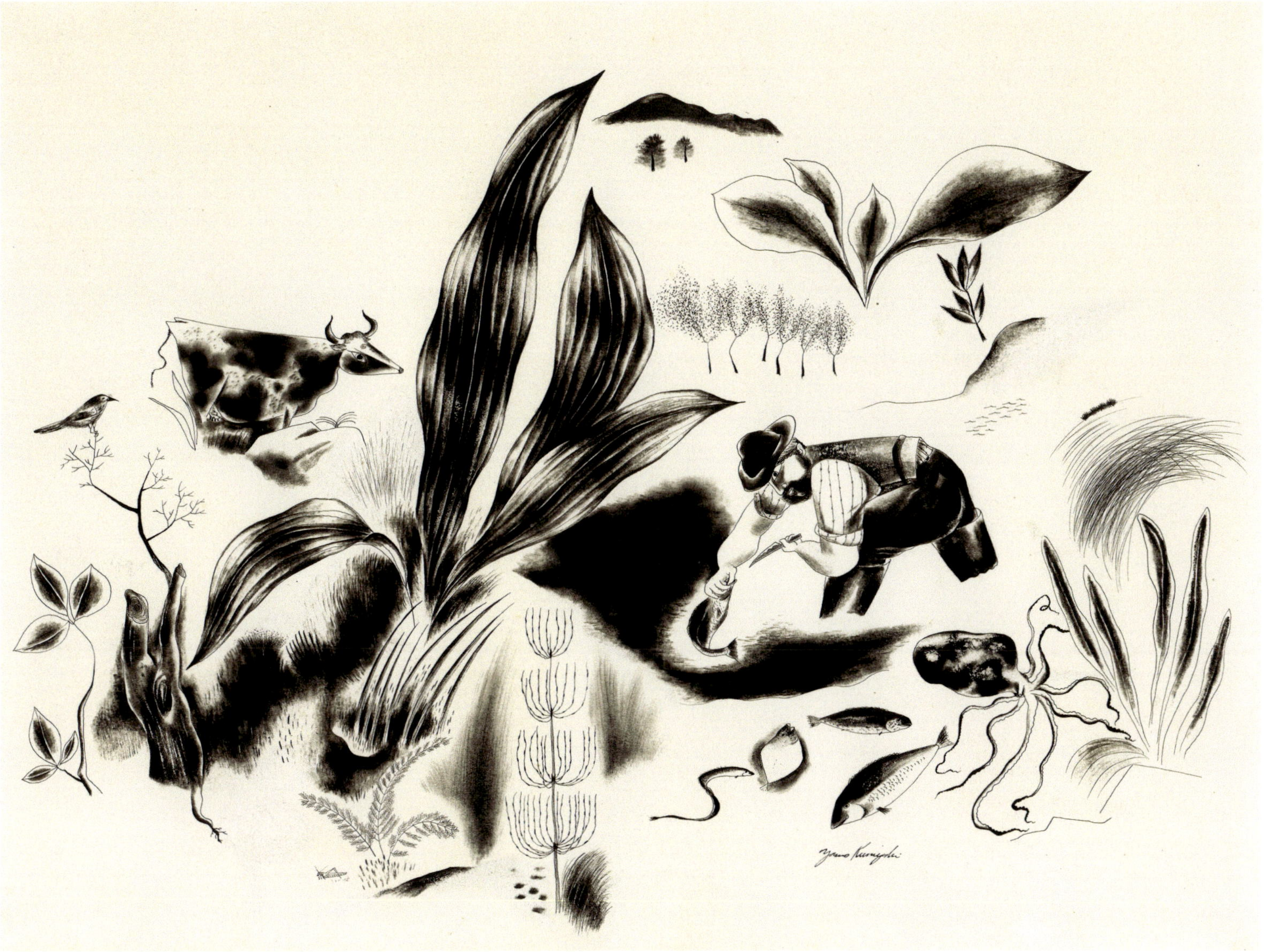

21
The Swimmer
1924
20 ½ × 30 ½ in.
Columbus Museum of Art, Ohio; Gift of Ferdinand Howald, 1931.196

22
Child Frightened by Water
1924
30 ⅛ × 24 1/16 in.
Hirshhorn Museum and Sculpture Garden, Smithsonian Institution, Washington, DC; Gift of Joseph H. Hirshhorn, 1966

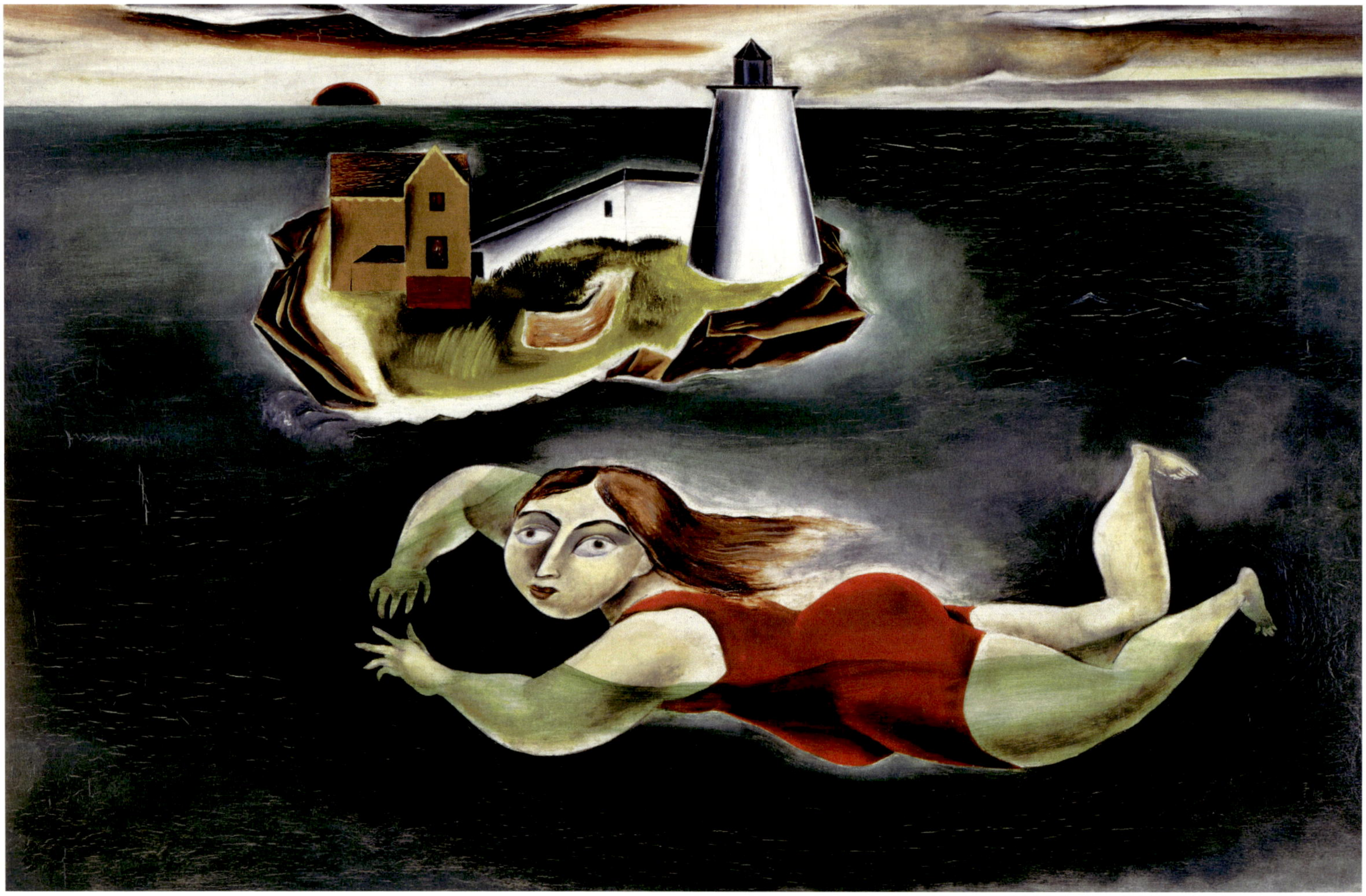

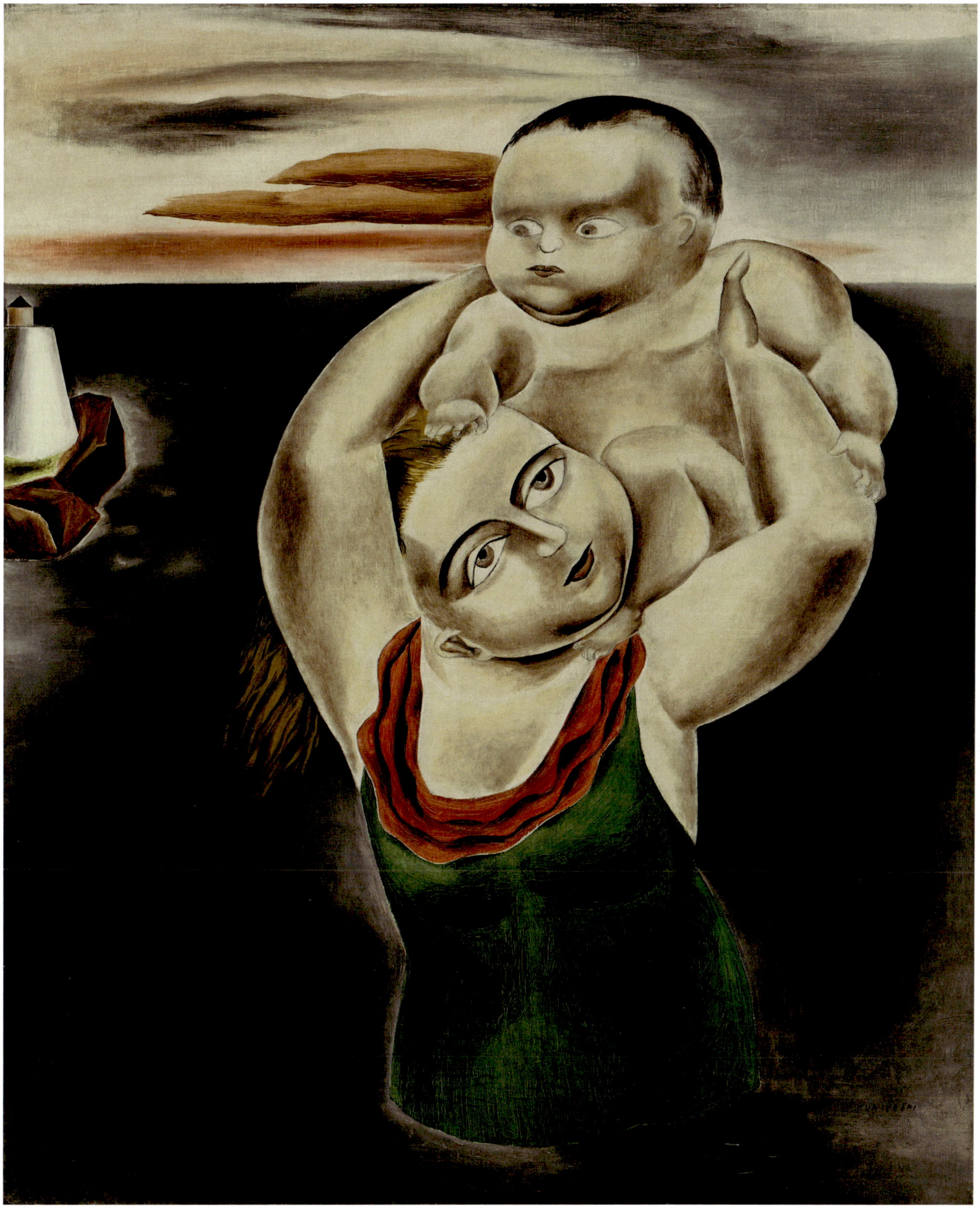

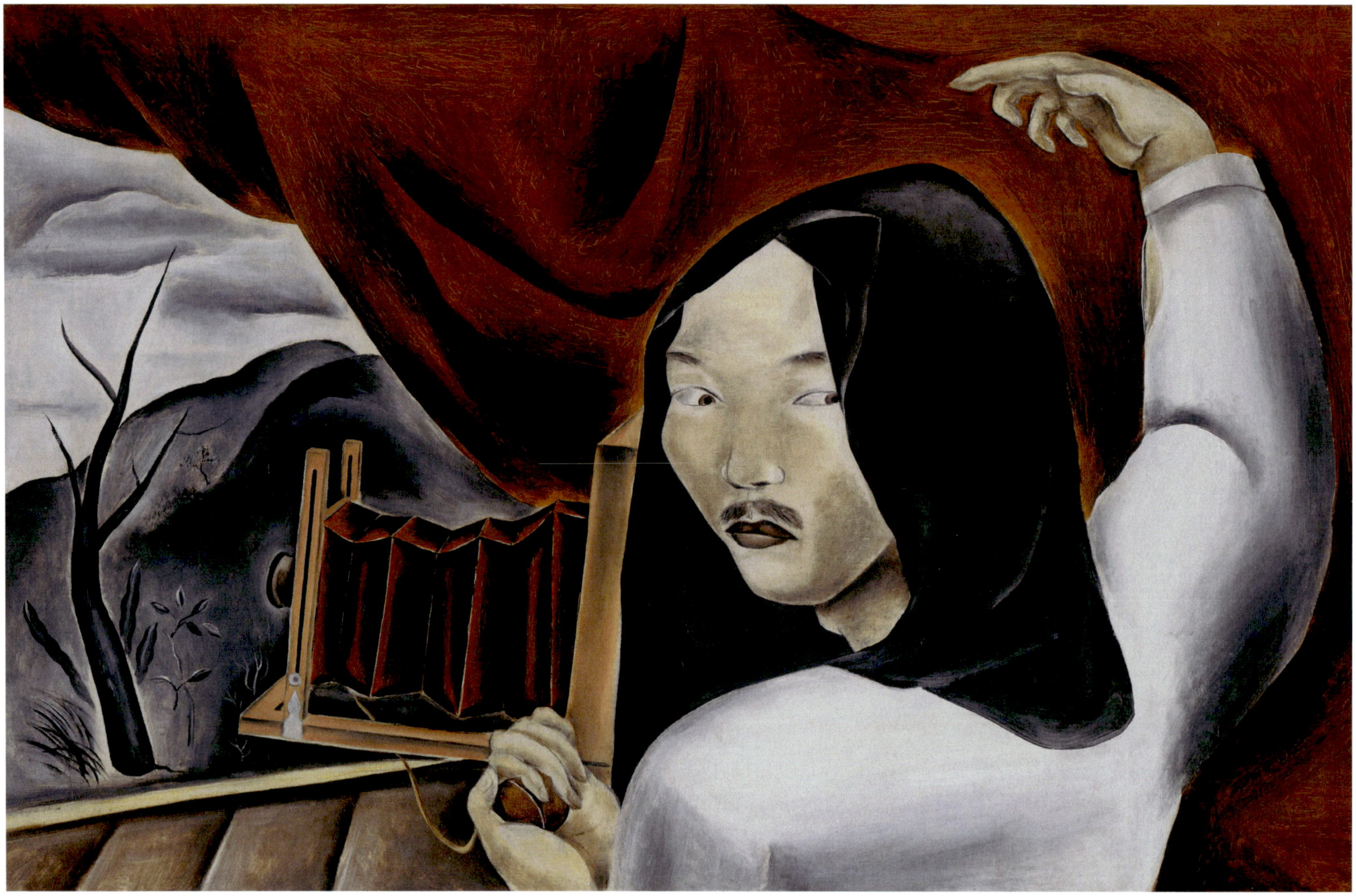

23
Self-Portrait as a Photographer
1924
20 ½ × 30 ¼ in.
Metropolitan Museum of Art, New York; Bequest of Scofield Thayer, 1982

24
Island of Happiness
1924
24 × 30 in.
Museum of Contemporary Art, Tokyo

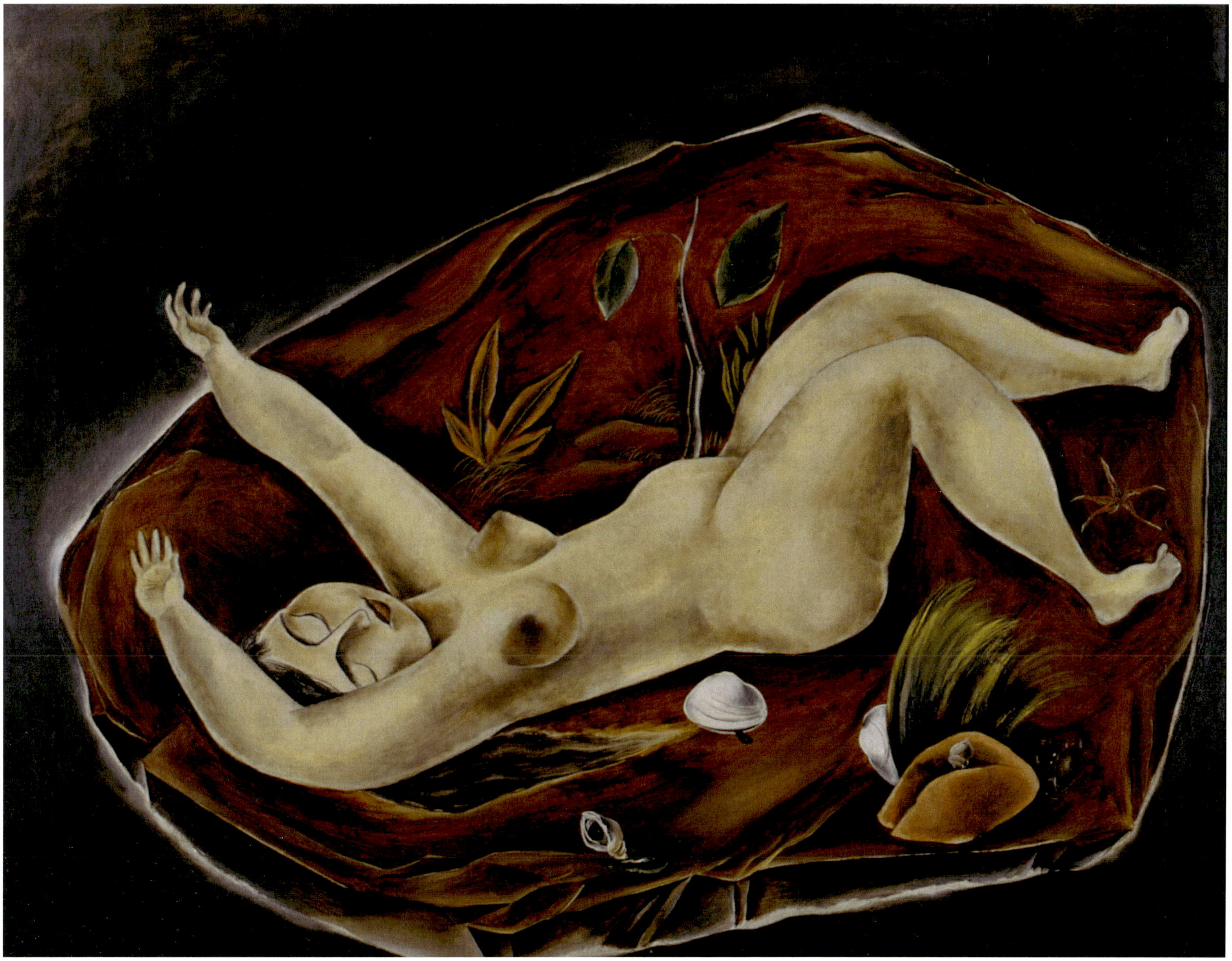

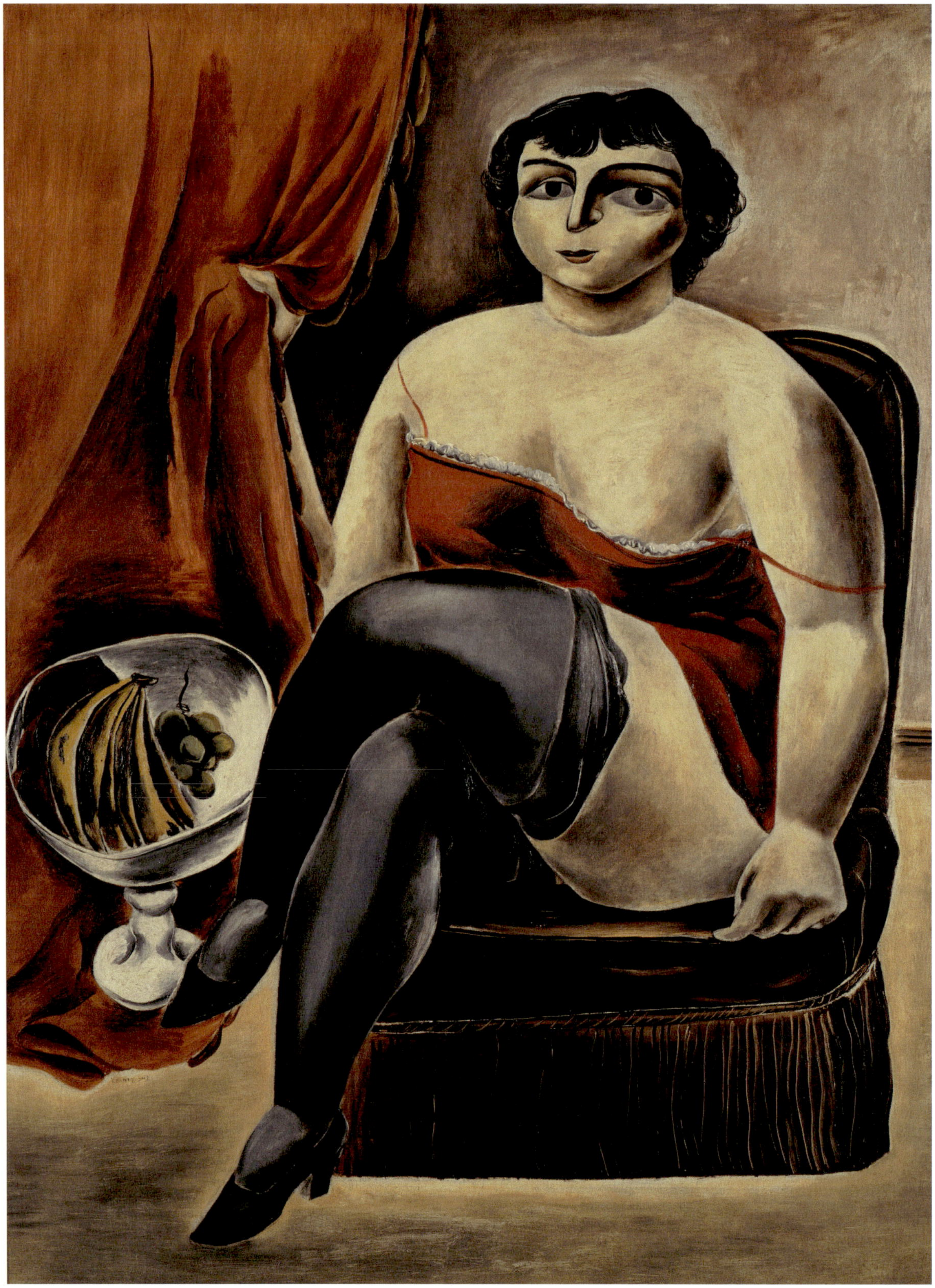

25
Circus Girl Resting
1925
38 ⅖ × 28 ½ in.
Jule Collins Smith Museum of Fine Art, Auburn University, Alabama; Advancing American Art Collection

26
Orange
1925
watercolor and ink on paper
14 ¼ × 18 ⅞ in.
Currier Museum of Art, Manchester, New Hampshire; Gift of Warren S. Hallamore in memory of his sister, Alma G. Hallamore

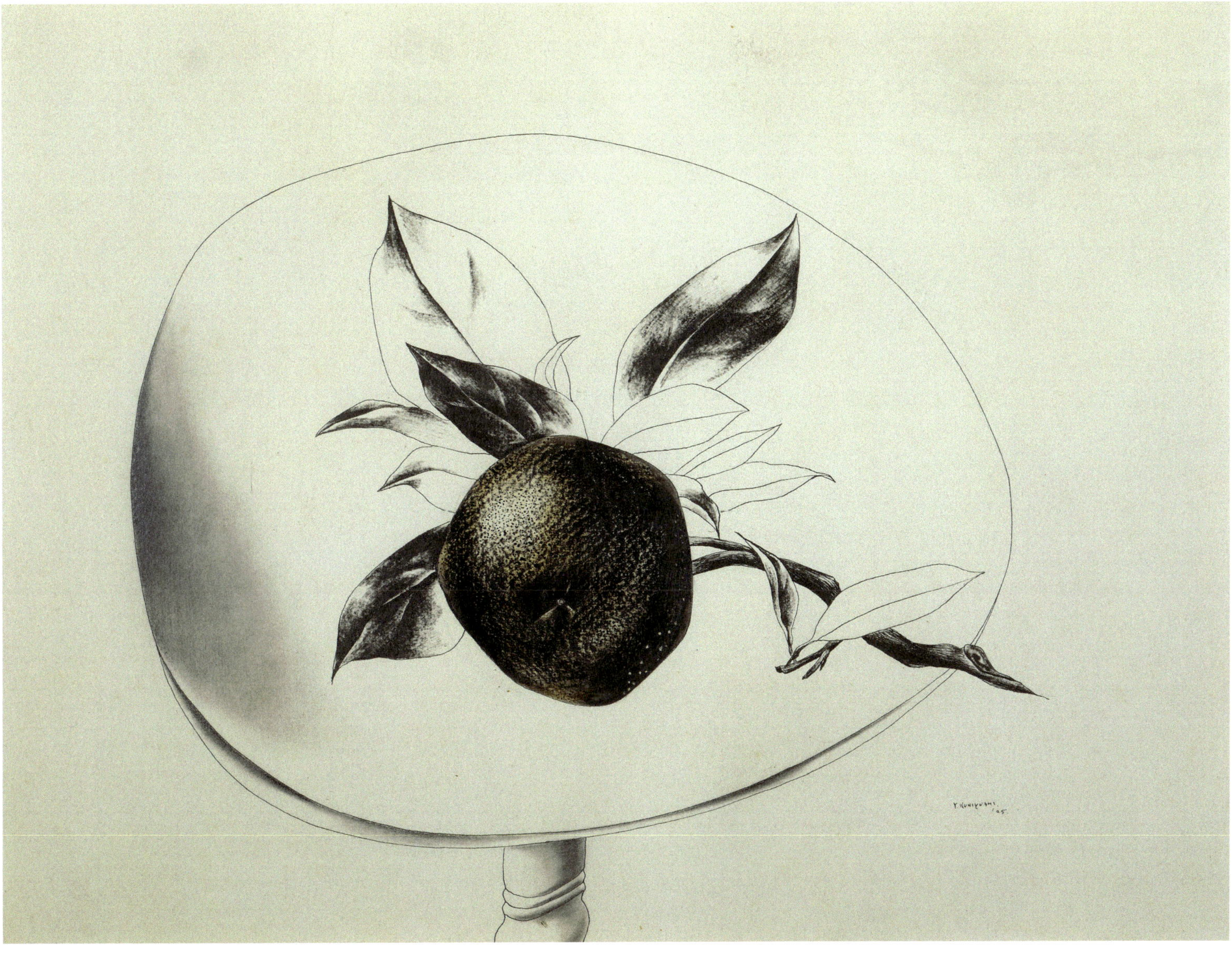

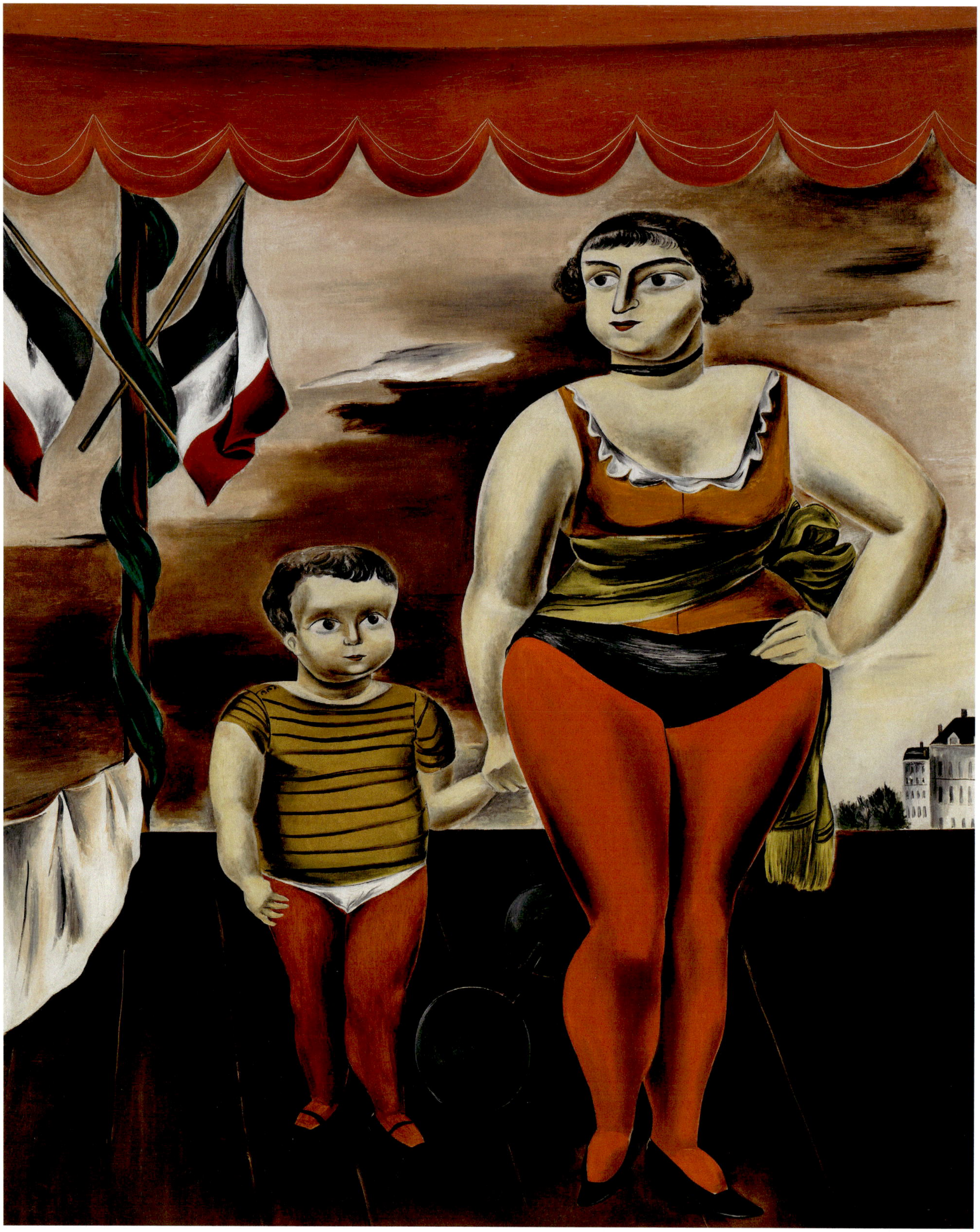

27
Strong Woman with Child
1925
57 ¼ × 44 ⅞ in.
Smithsonian American Art Museum, Gift of the Sara Roby Foundation, 1986.6.50

28
Girl on a Sofa
1925
36 ¾ × 43 in.
Collection of the ASU Art Museum, Tempe, Arizona; Gift of Oliver B. James

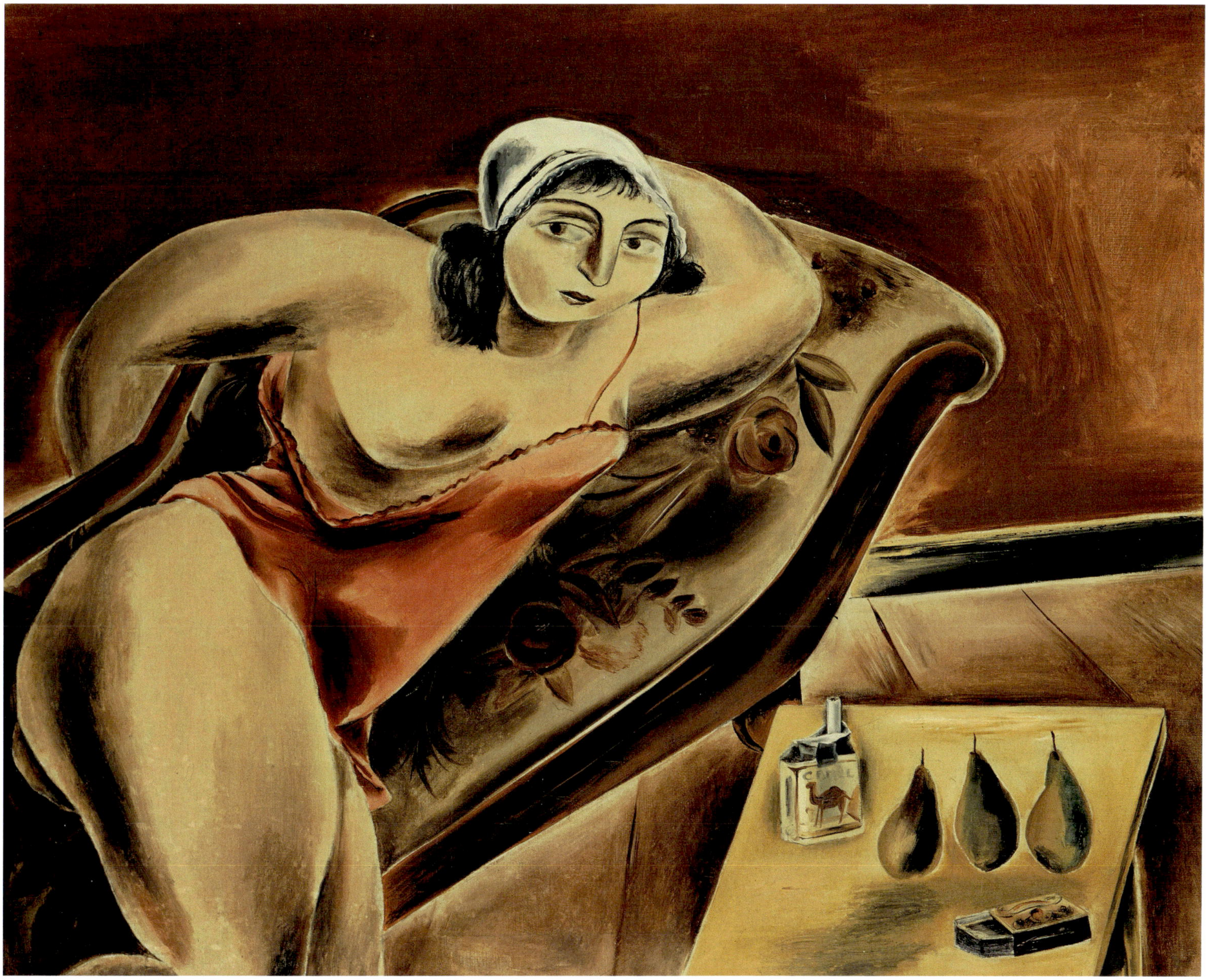

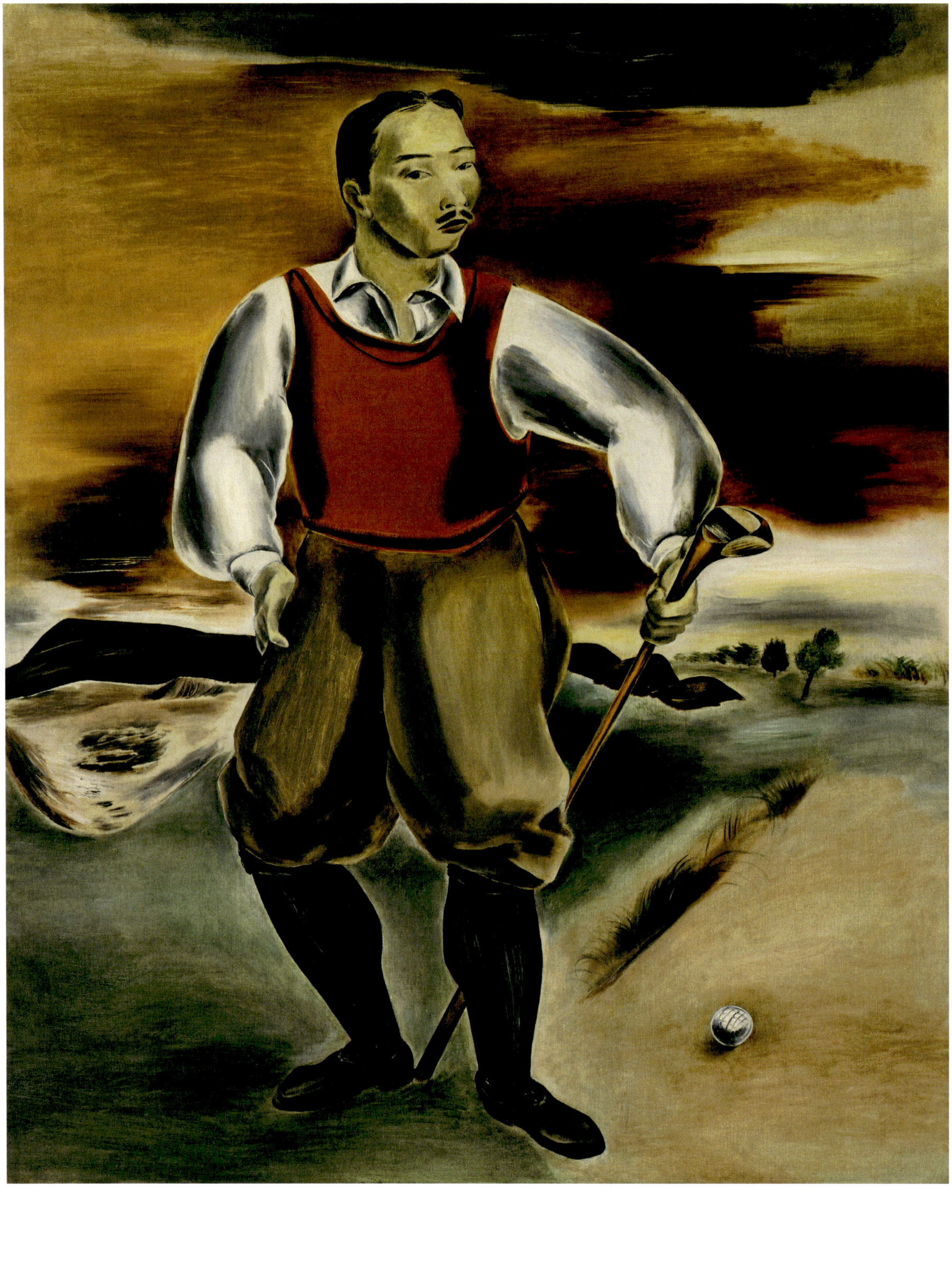

29
Self-Portrait as a Golf Player
1927
50 ¼ × 40 ¼ in.
Museum of Modern Art, New York; Abby Aldrich Rockefeller Fund

30
The Twist Loaf
1930
oil on linen
30 ¼ × 42 ¼ in.
Whitney Museum of American Art, New York; Purchase

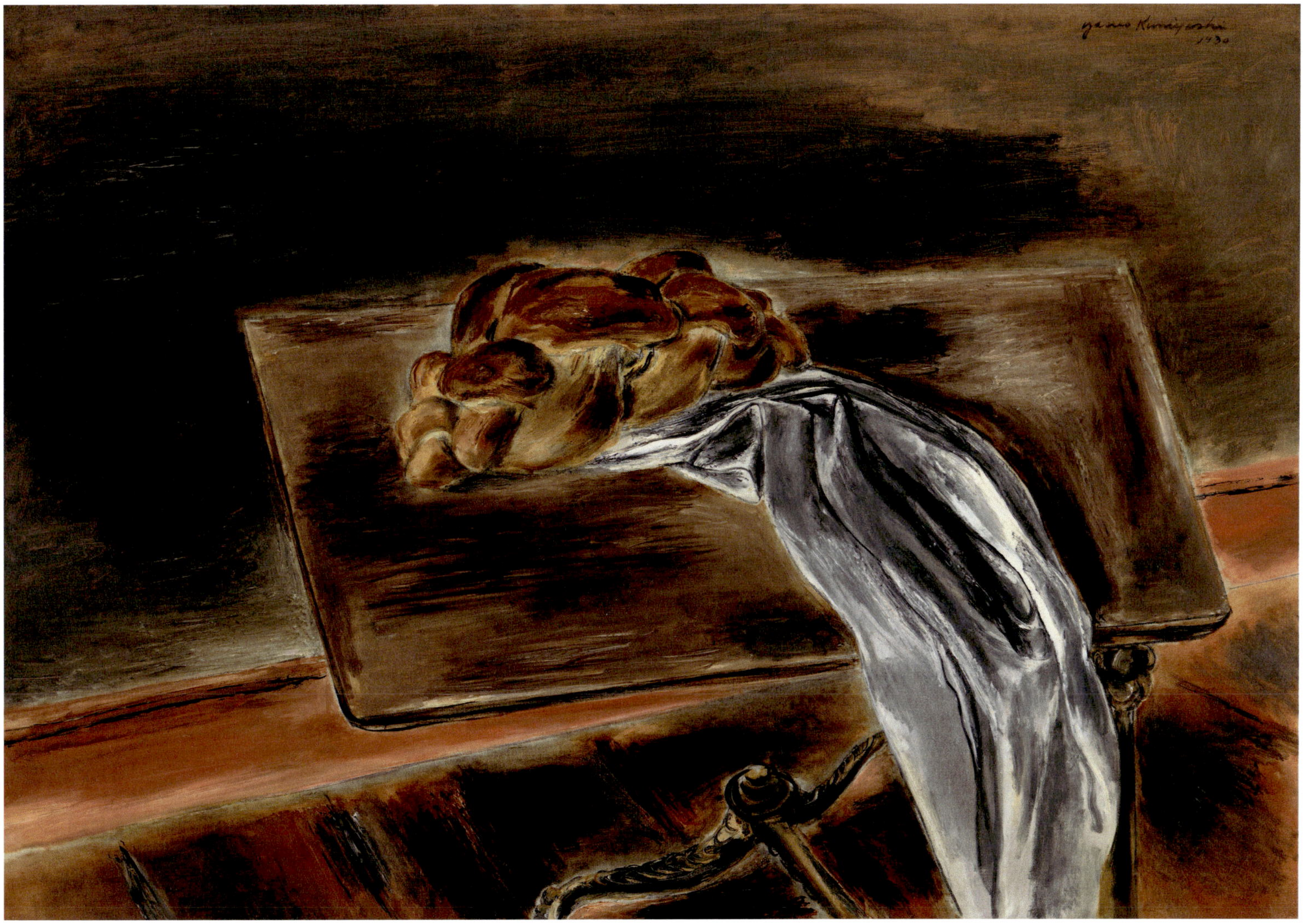

31
Weathervane and Objects on a Sofa
1933
34 × 60 in.
Santa Barbara Museum of Art, California; Gift of Wright S. Ludington

32
Untitled (Boat Deck)
1930s
ink on paper
21 × 15 in.
Private collection

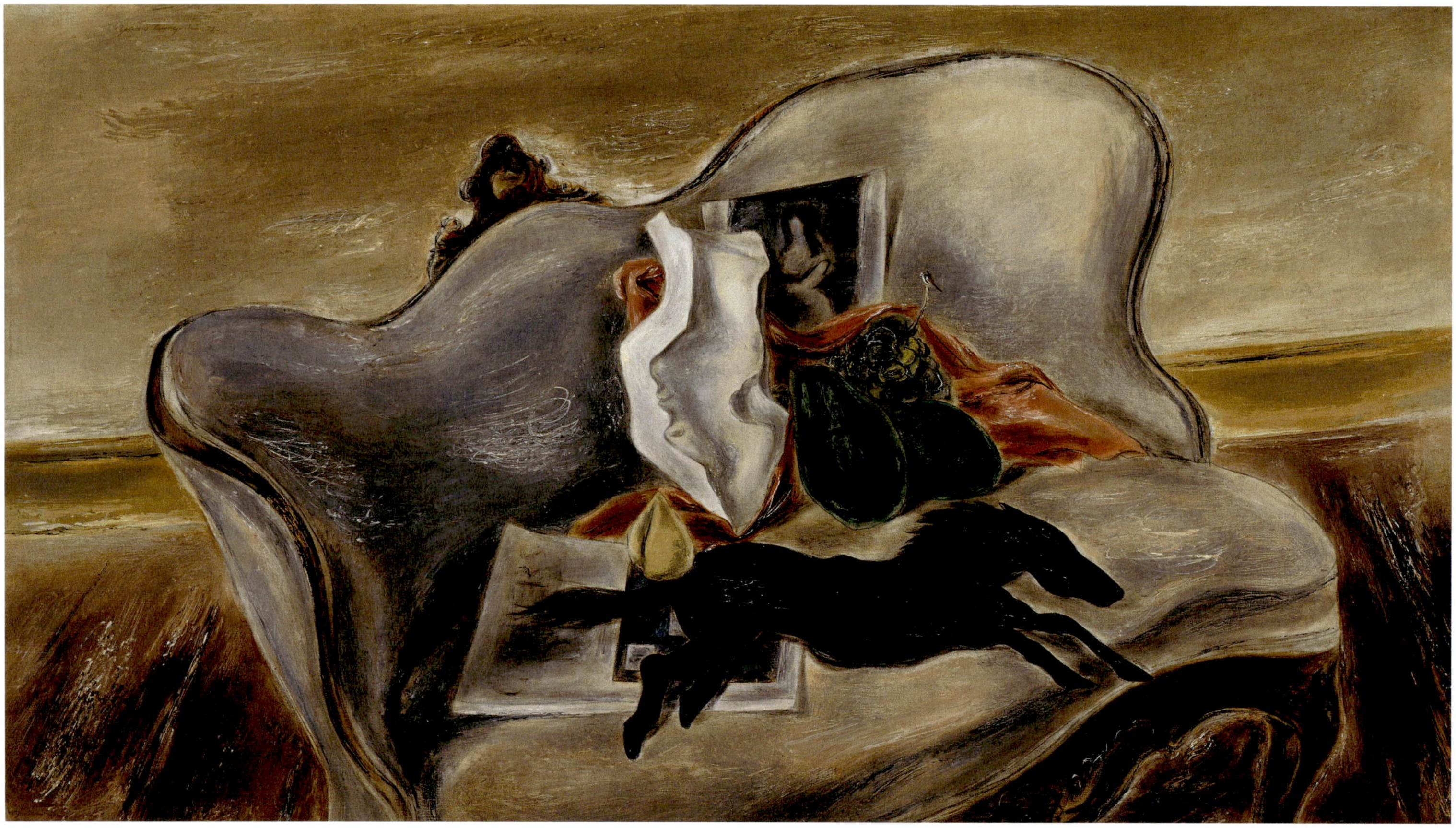

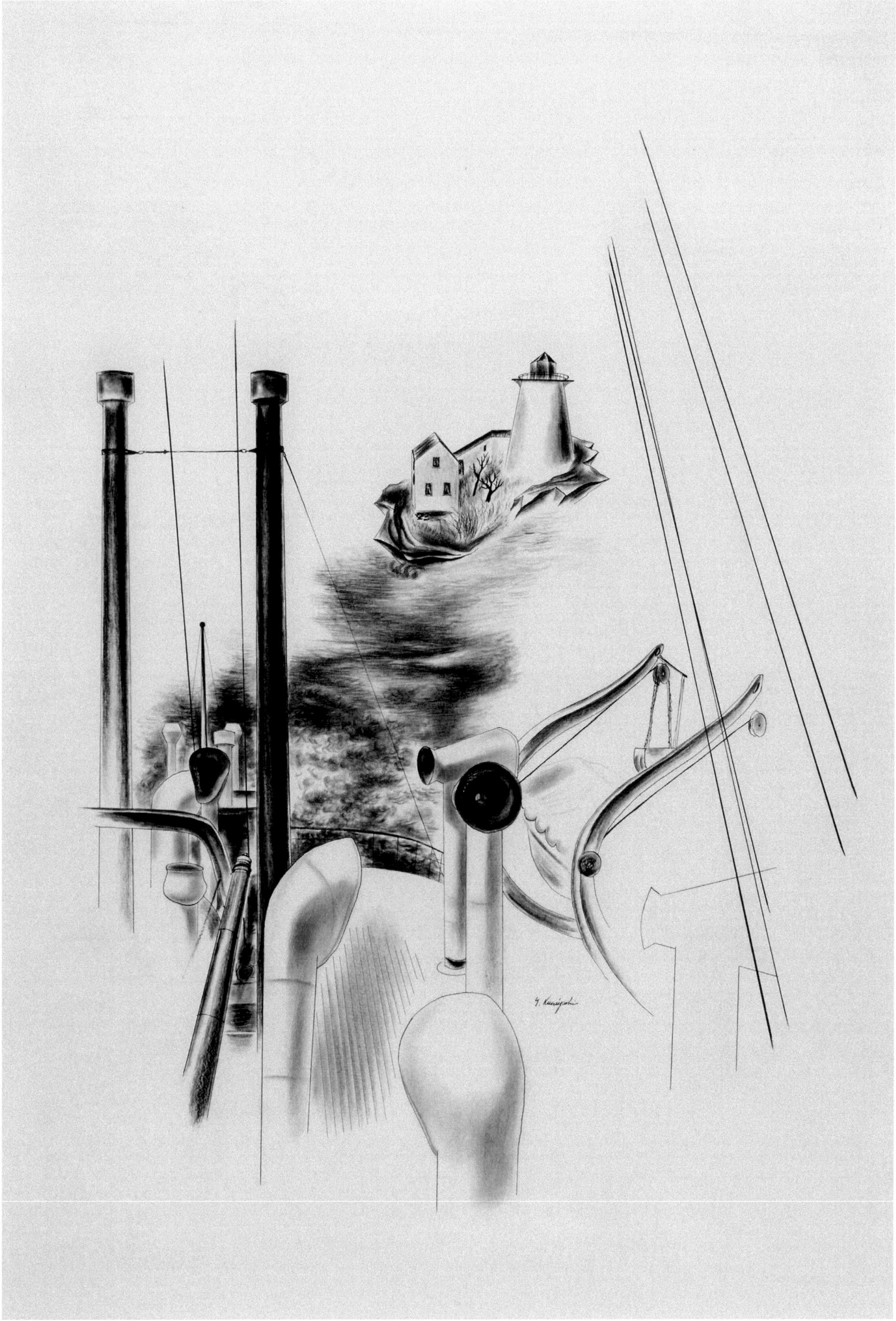

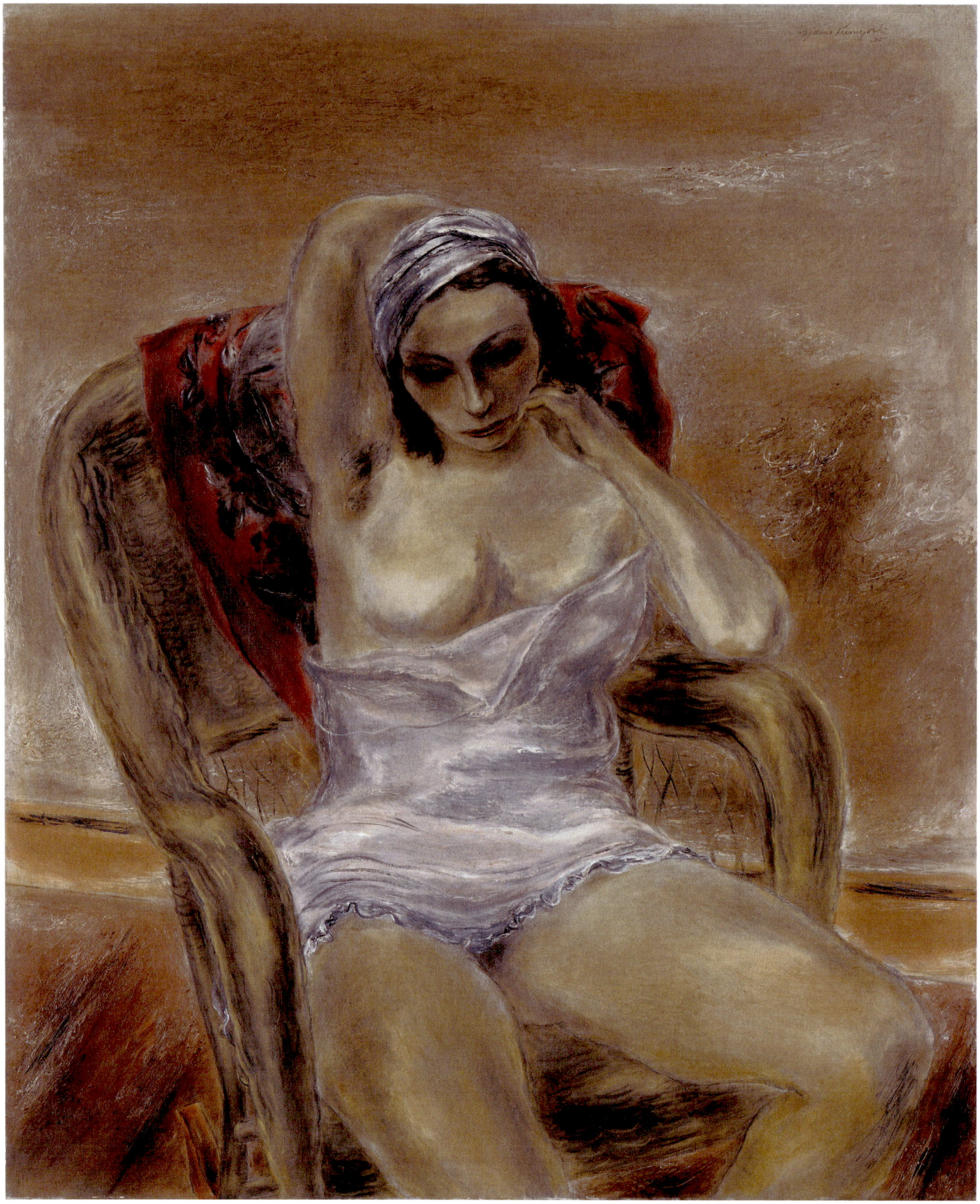

33
Girl Thinking
1935
50 × 40 in.
Fukutake Collection, Okayama, Japan

34
Daily News
1935
50 × 33 3/16 in.
Cincinnati Art Museum, Ohio; The Edwin and Virginia Irwin Memorial, 1959.48

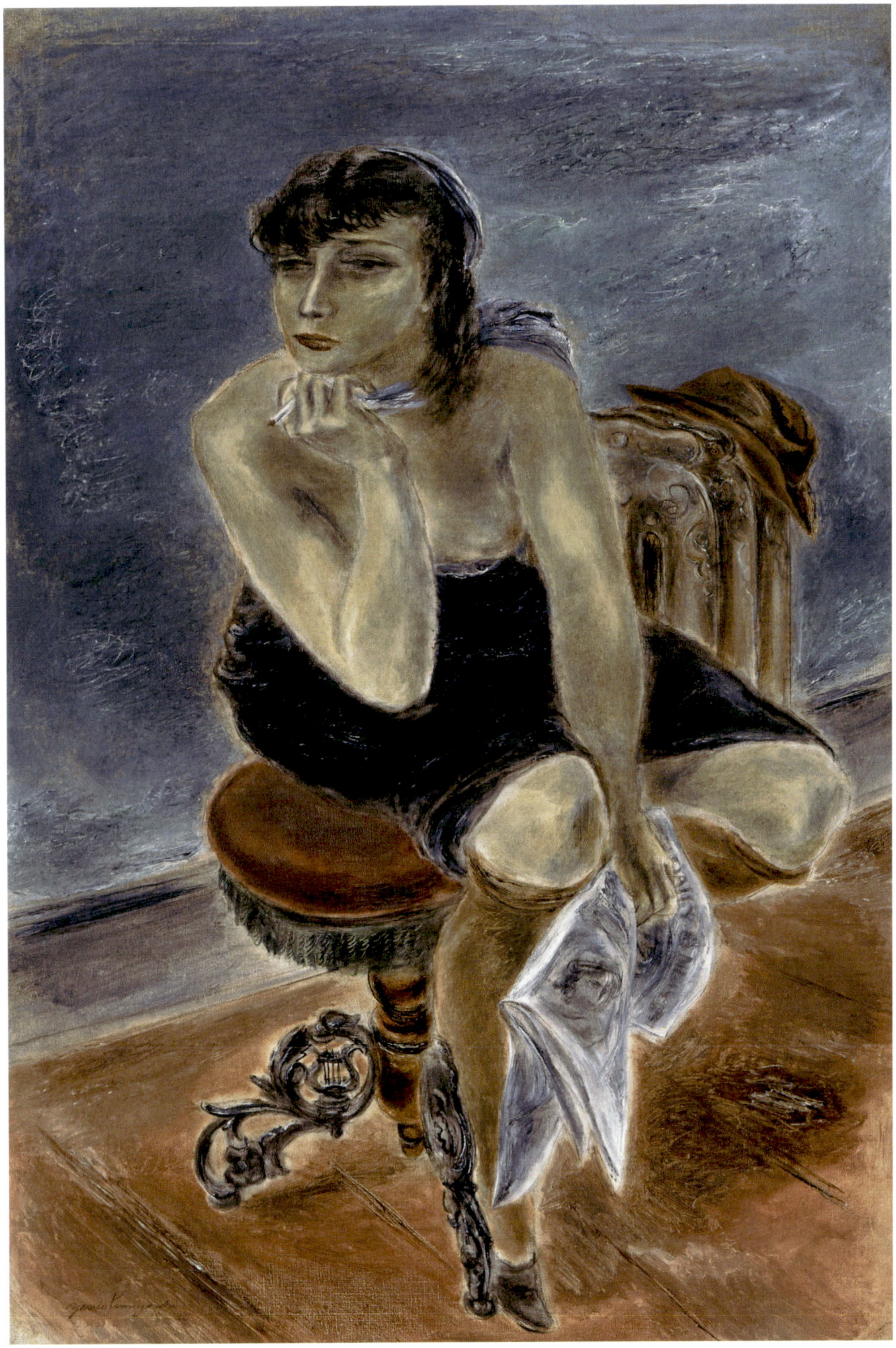

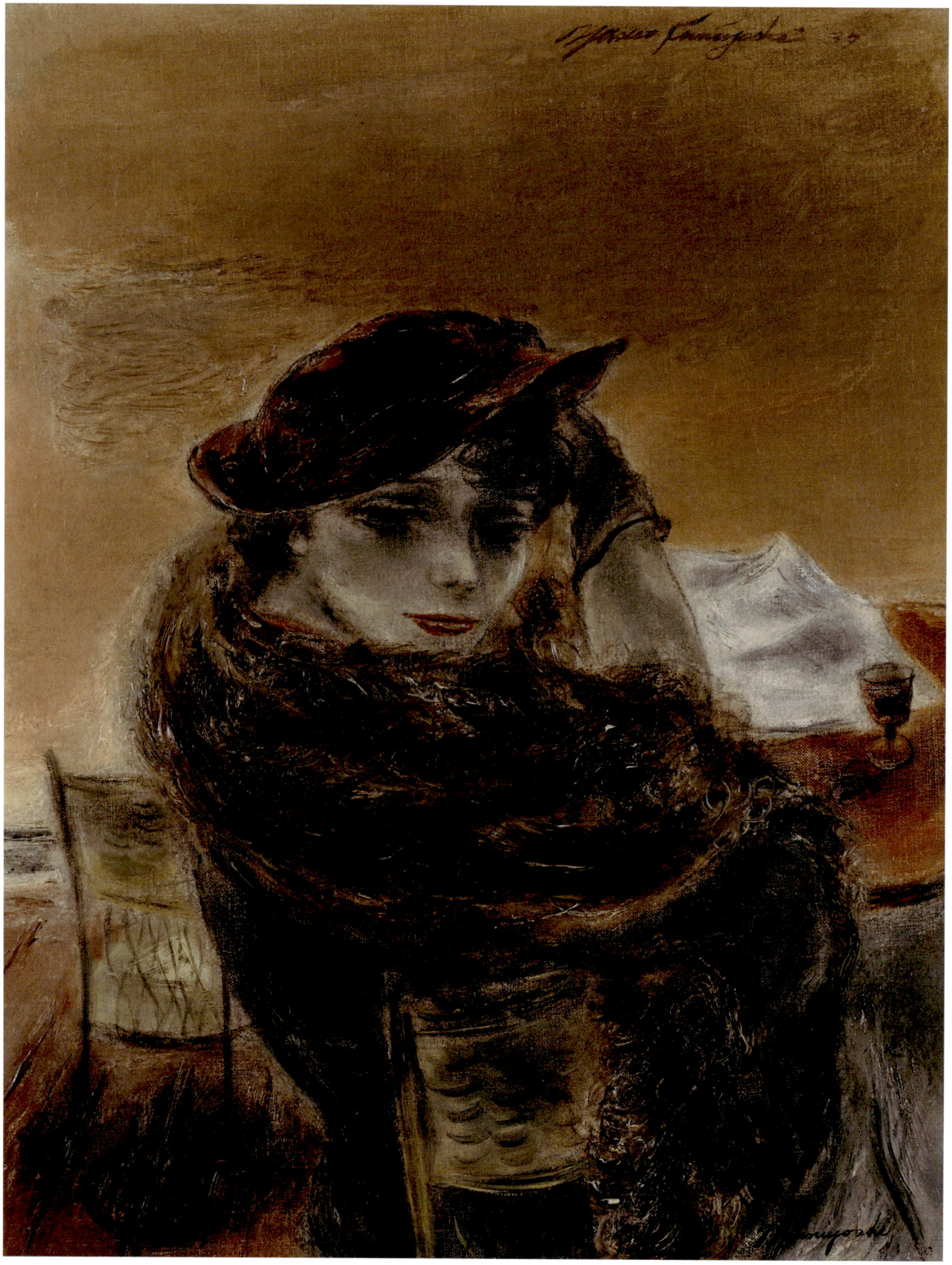

35
Café
1937
oil on linen
16 ¼ × 12 ⅜ in.
Whitney Museum of American Art, New York; Museum purchase

36
Watermelon
1938
40 × 56 in.
Fukutake Collection, Okayama, Japan

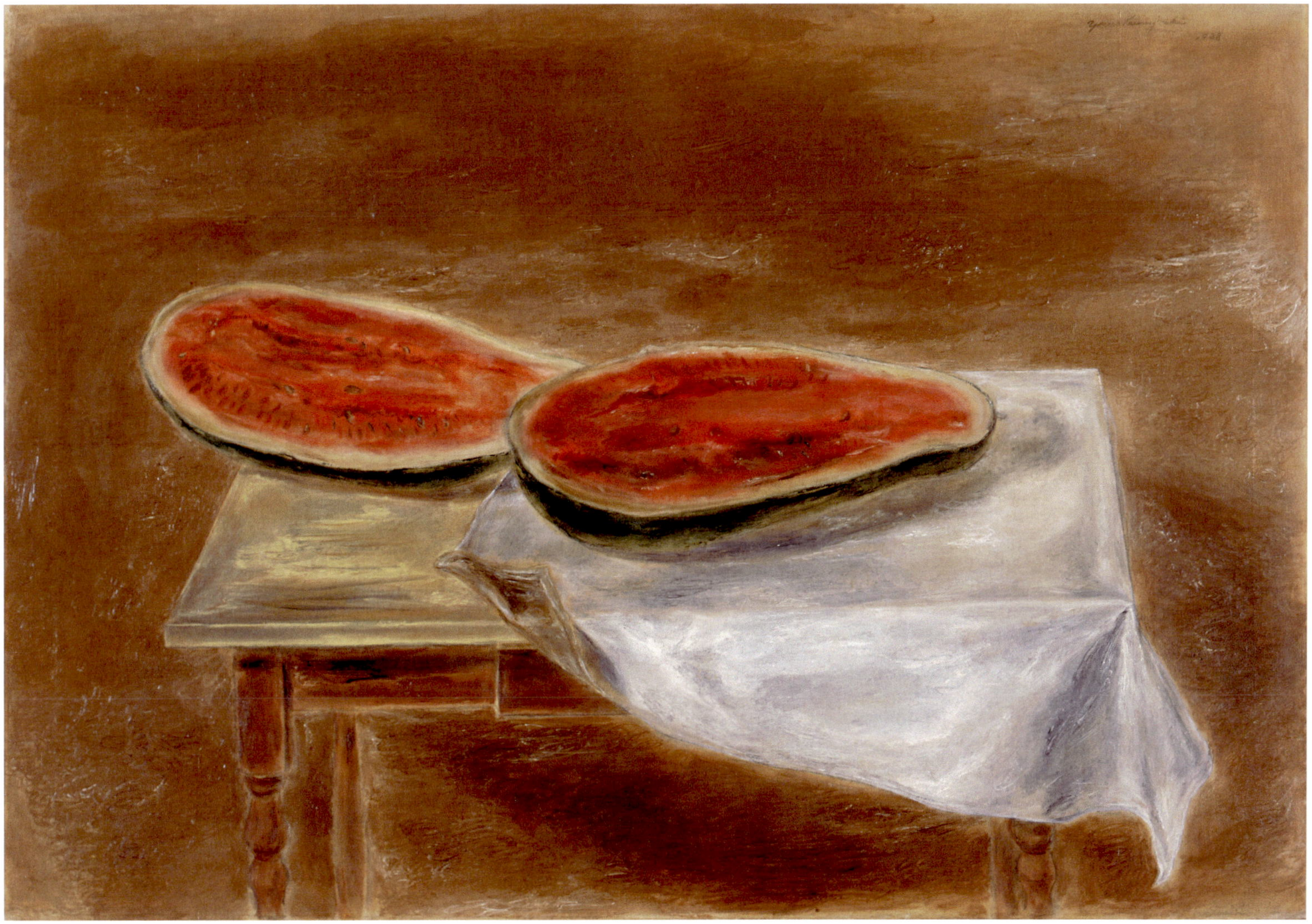

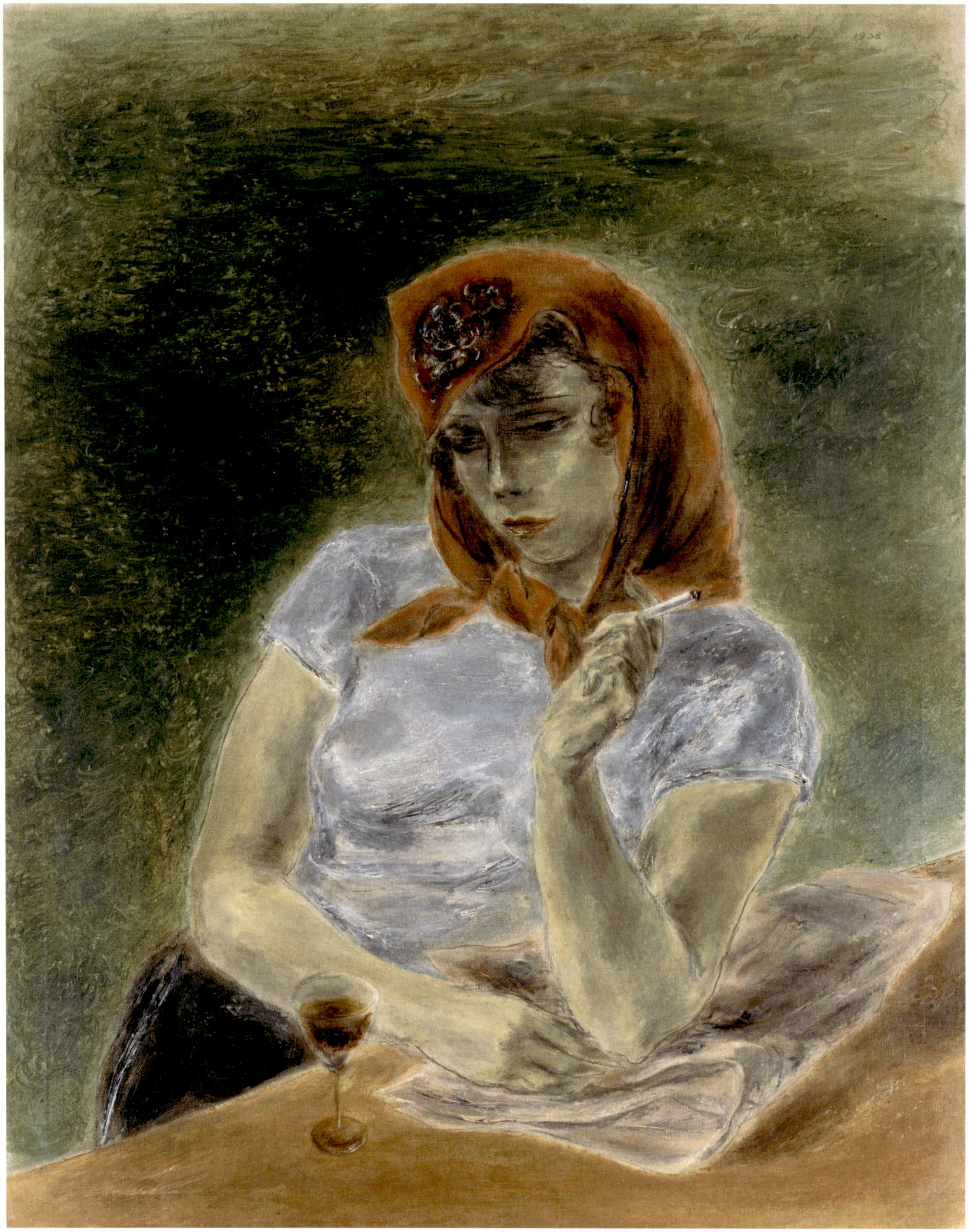

37
Waiting
1938
40 × 31 in.
Collection of Gallery Nii, Osaka, Japan

38
Between Two Worlds
1939
24 × 40 3/16 in.
Collection of Gallery Nii, Osaka, Japan

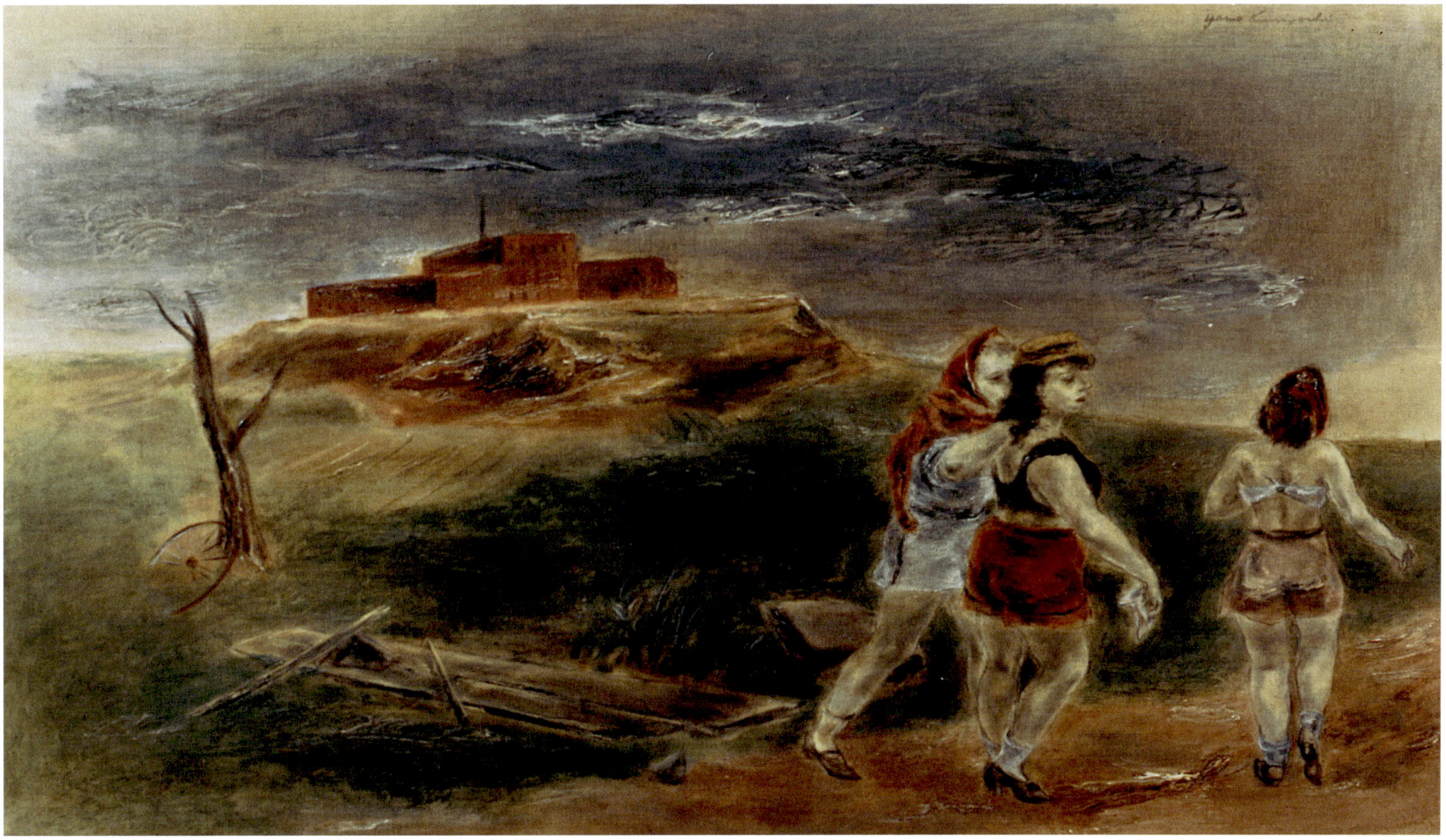

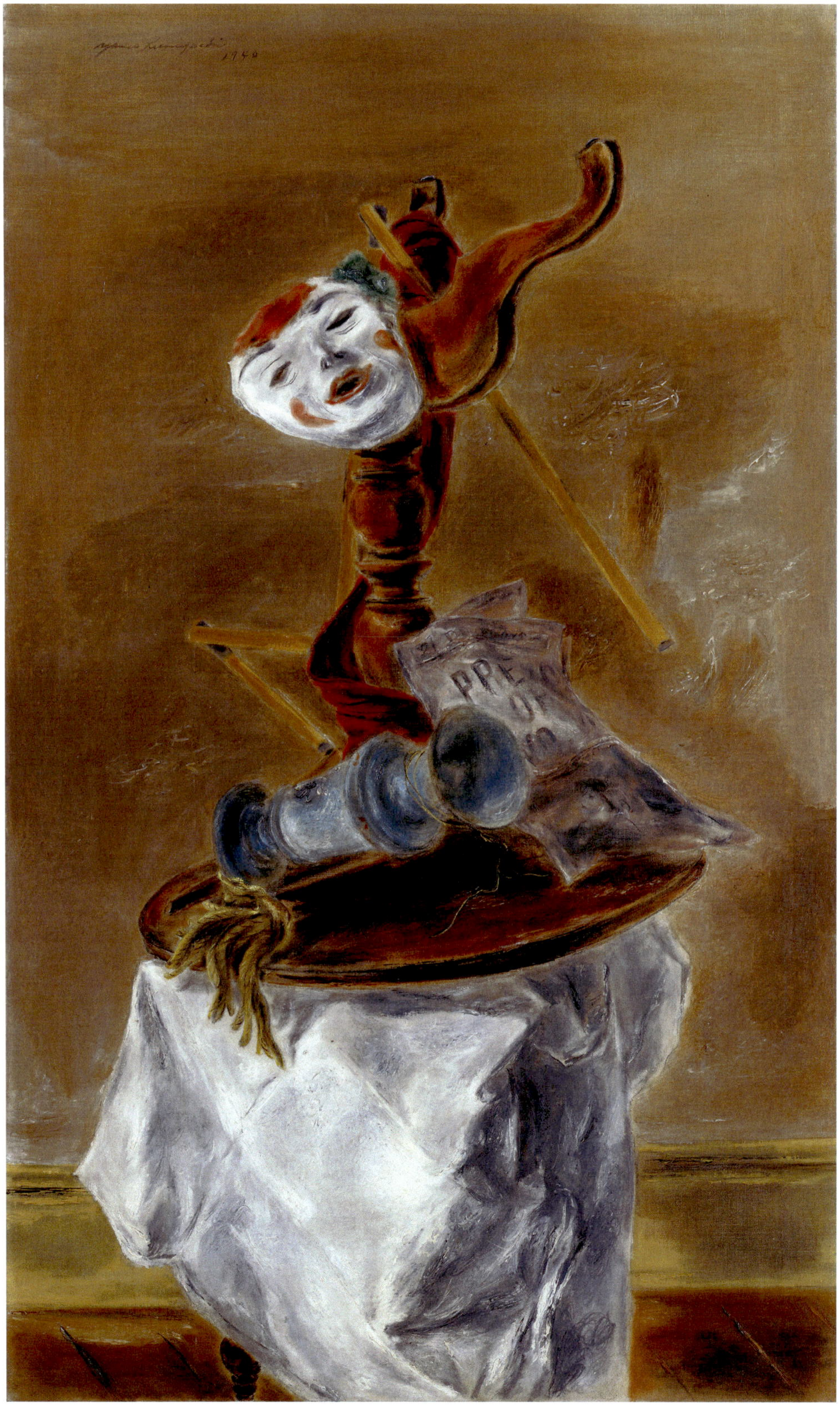

39
Upside Down Table and Mask
1940
60 ⅕ × 35 ⅕ in.
Fukutake Collection, Okayama, Japan

40
End of Juanita
1942
44 ¼ × 34 ¼ in.
Brooklyn Museum, New York; Bequest of Edith and Milton Lowenthal

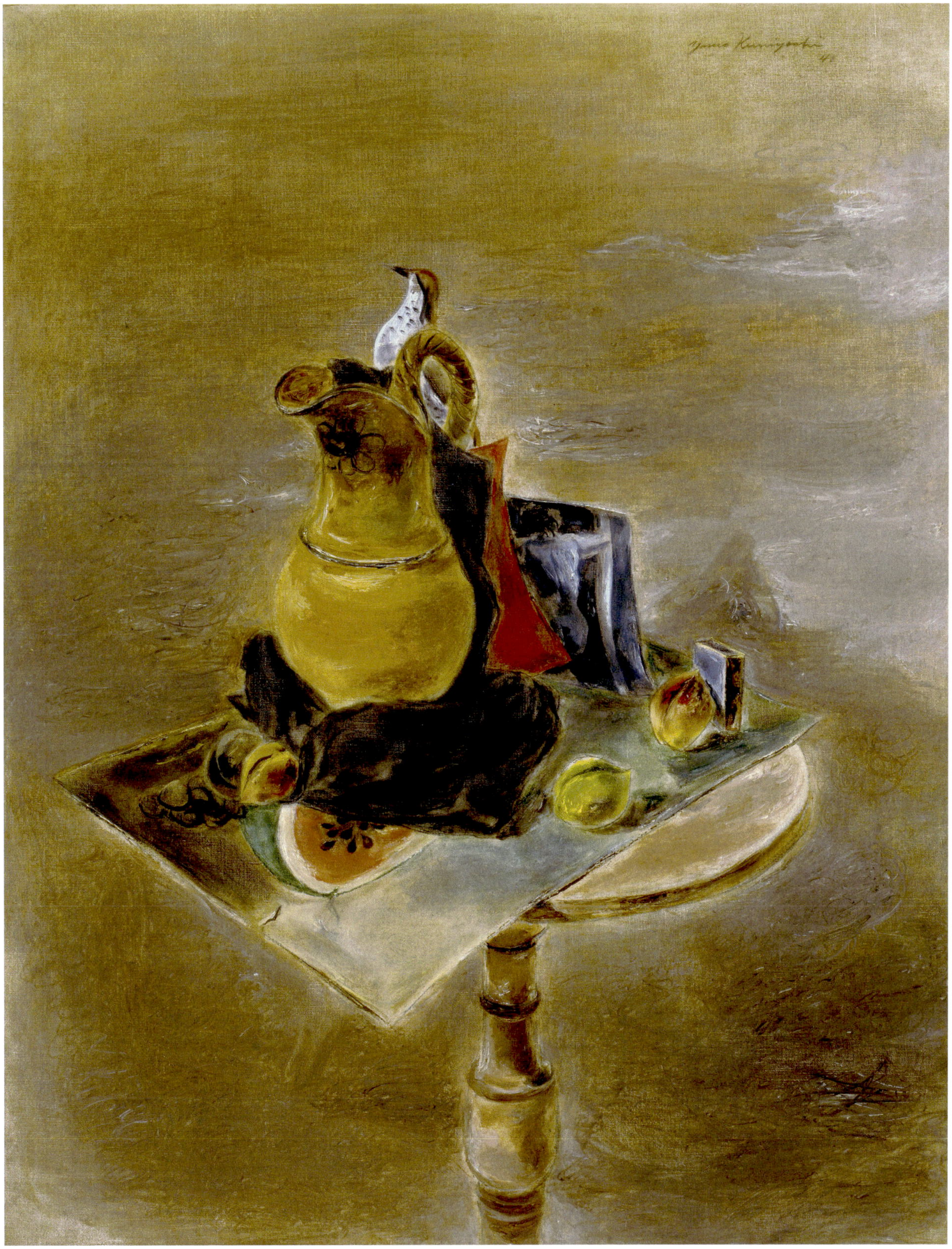

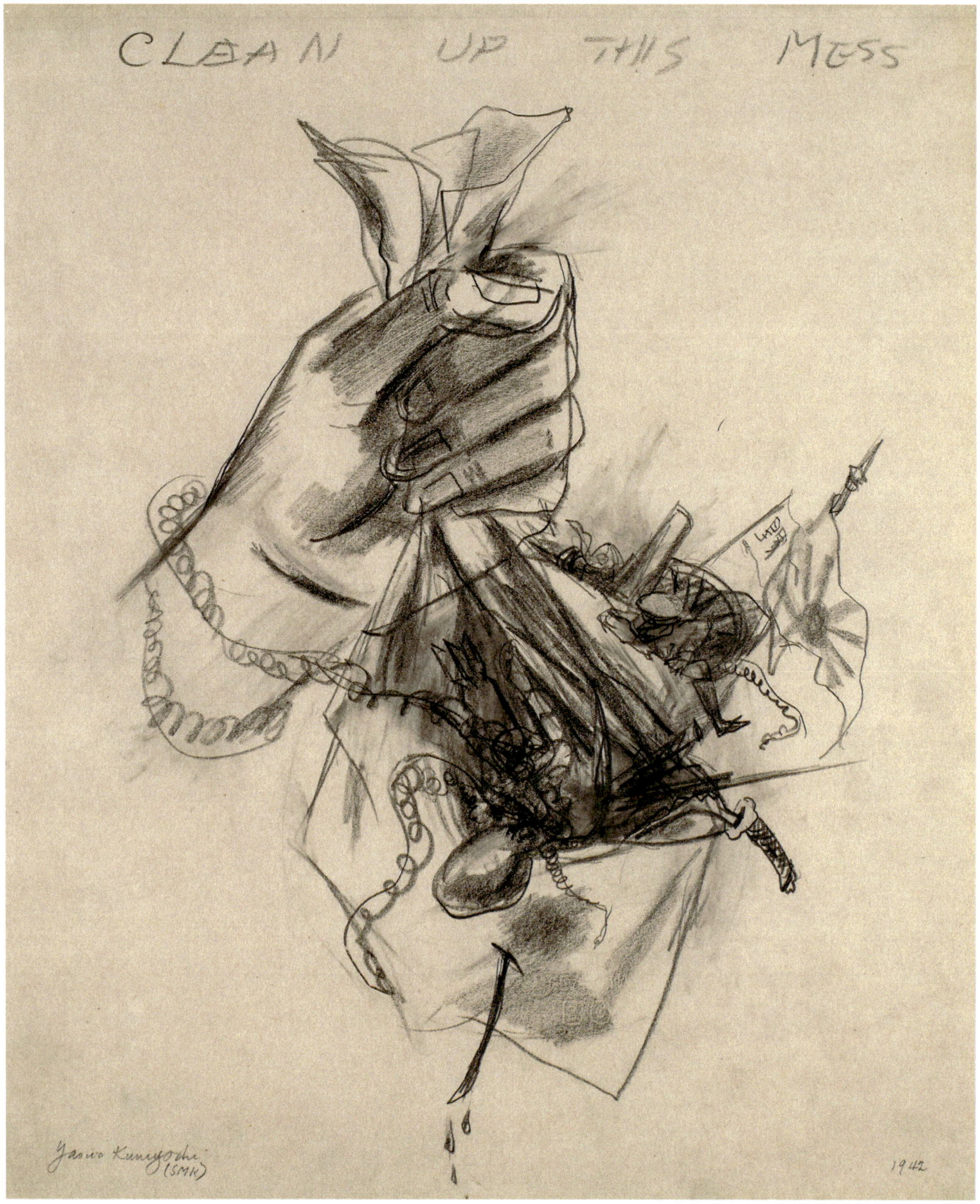

41
Clean Up This Mess No. 2
(Study for War Poster)
1942
pencil on paper
16 4/5 × 13 7/10 in.
Fukutake Collection,
Okayama, Japan

42
Killer, or Chinese
woman praying (Study
for War Poster)
1942
pencil on paper
16 4/5 × 13 7/10 in.
Fukutake Collection,
Okayama, Japan

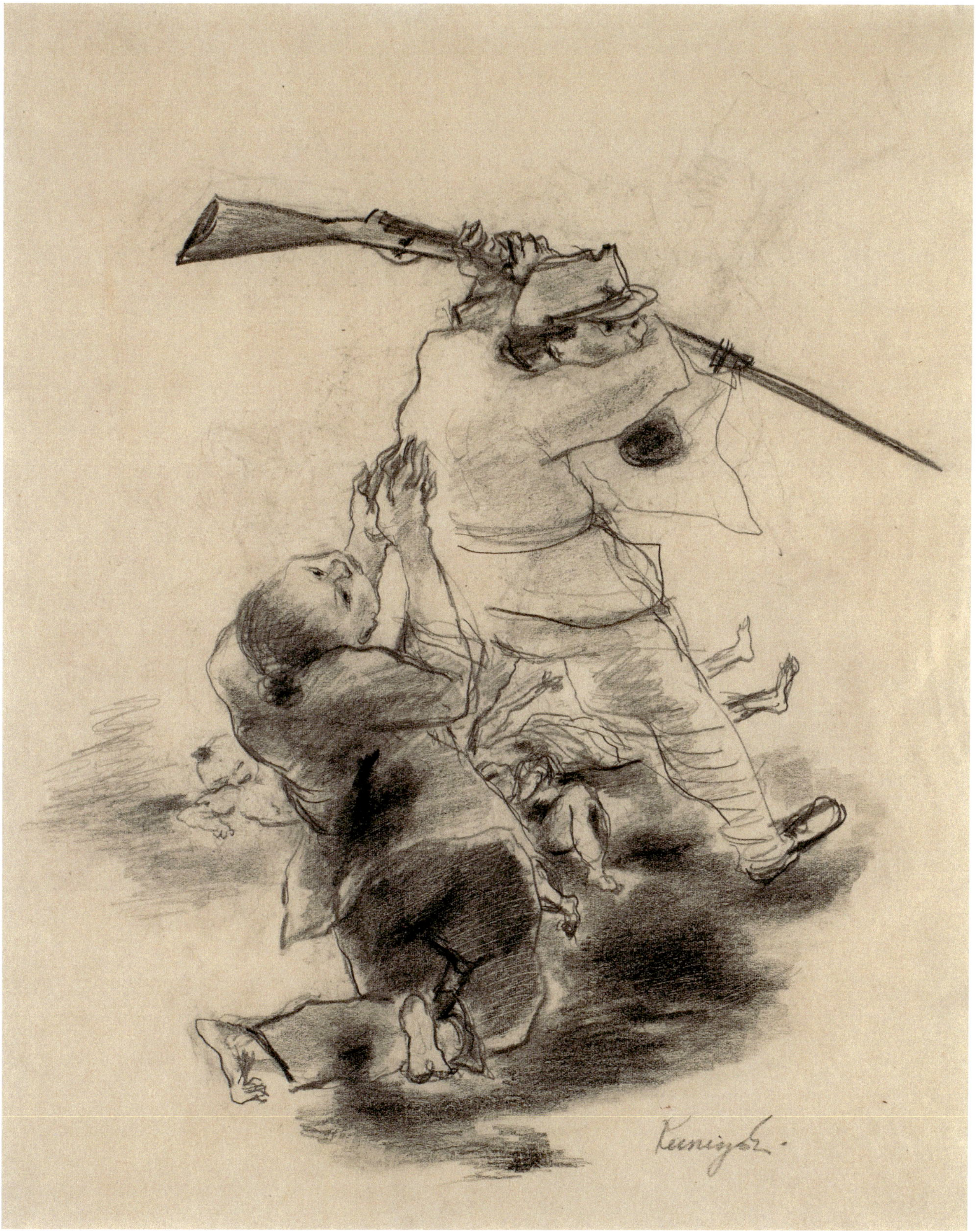

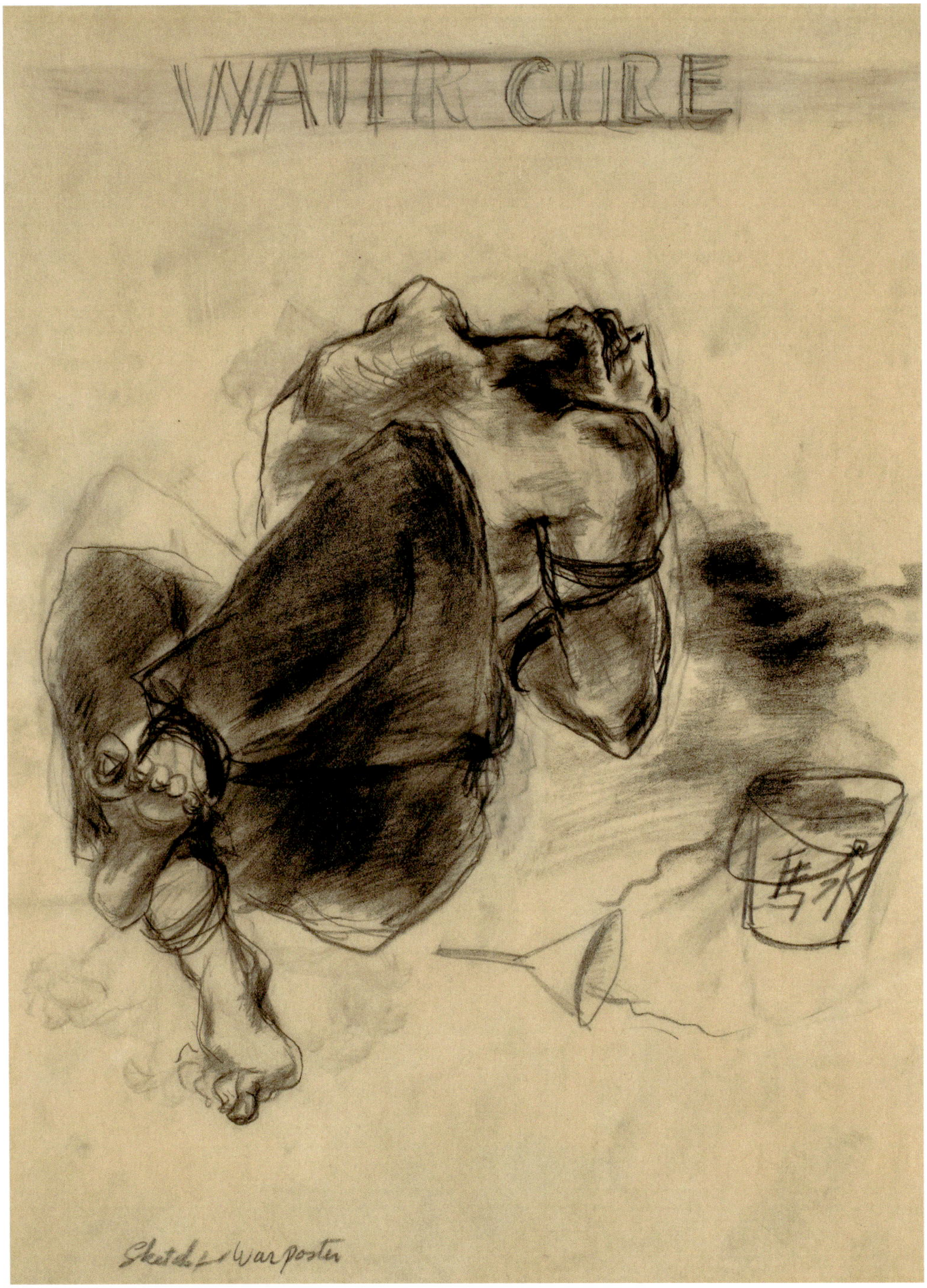

43
Water Cure No. 1 (Study for War Poster)
1942
pencil on paper
16 4/5 × 13 7/10 in.
Fukutake Collection, Okayama, Japan

44
Hanged (Study for War Poster)
1943
pencil on paper
16 3/5 × 13 7/10 in.
Fukutake Collection, Okayama, Japan

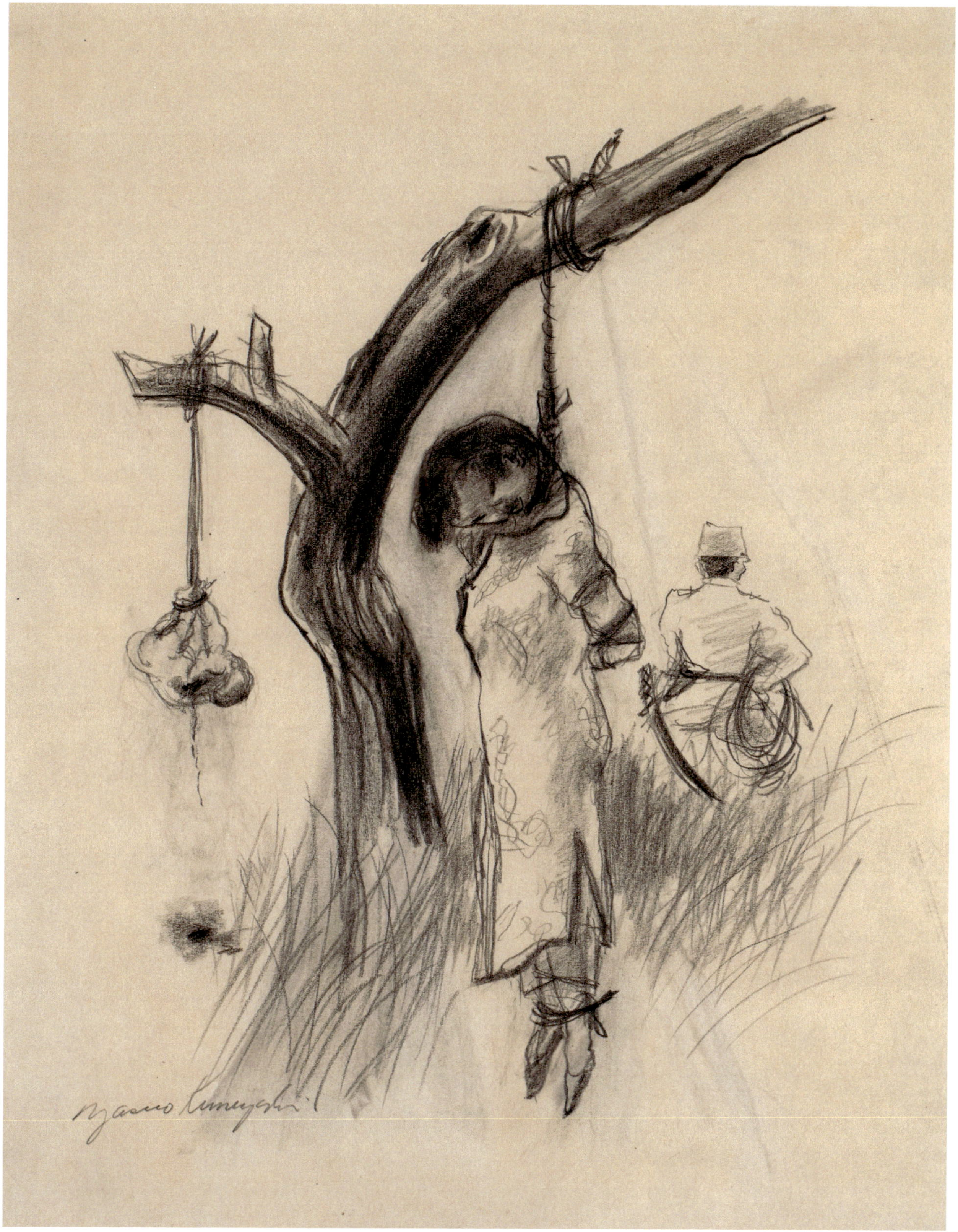

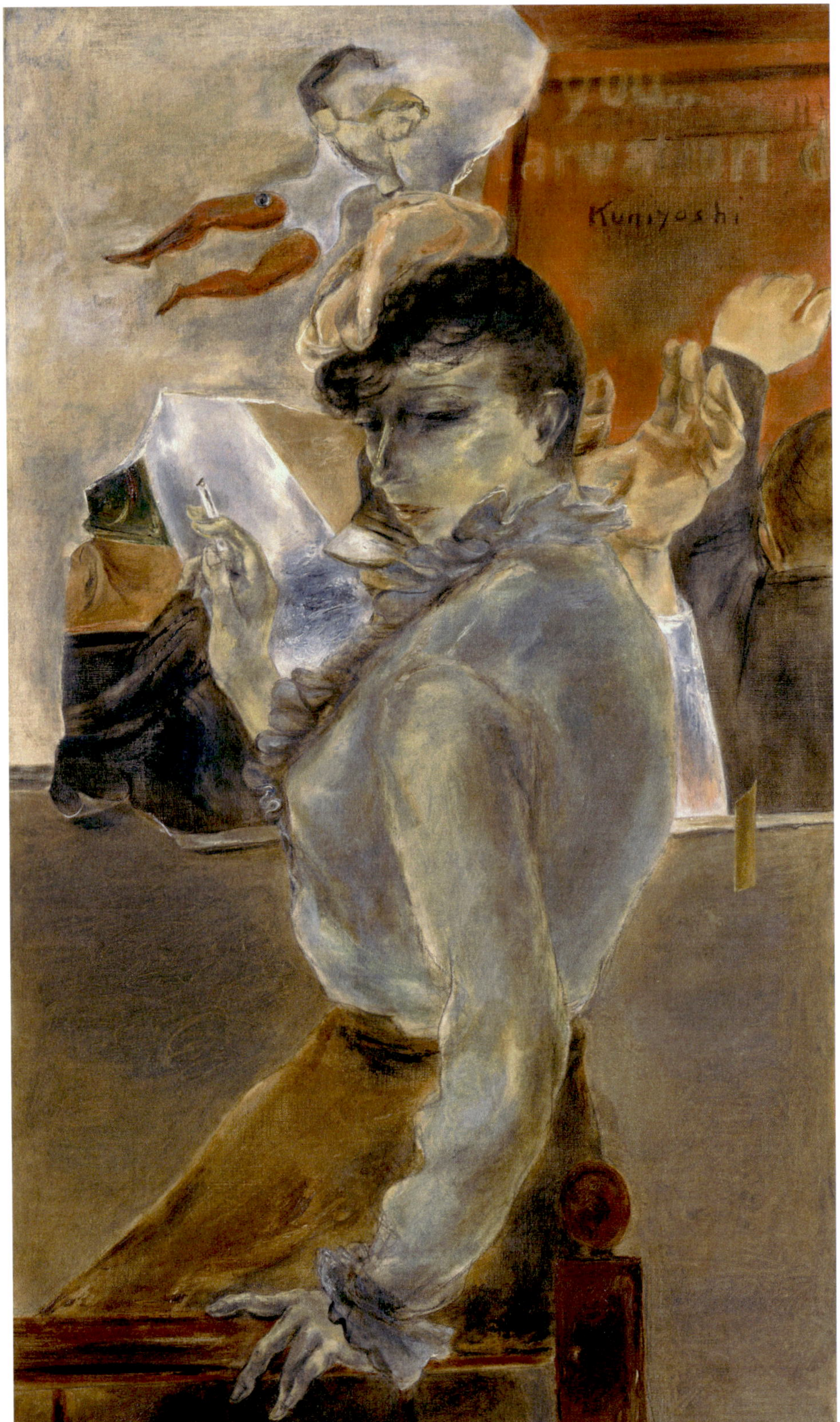
Kuniyoshi

45
Somebody Tore My Poster
1943
46 1/16 × 26 3/16 in.
Collection of Gallery Nii, Osaka, Japan

46
At Work
1943
casein on gesso panel
19 × 14 in.
Fukutake Collection, Okayama, Japan

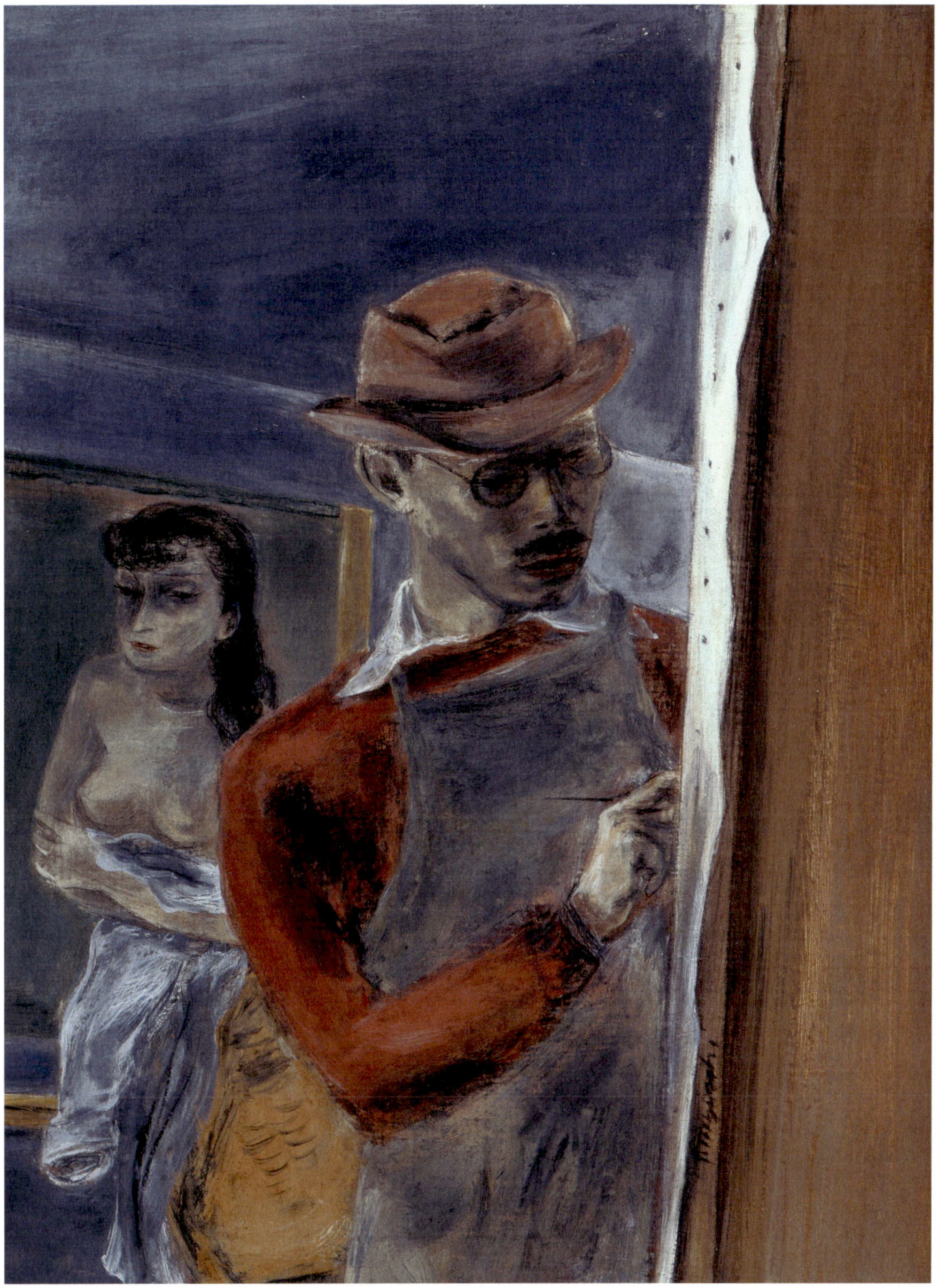

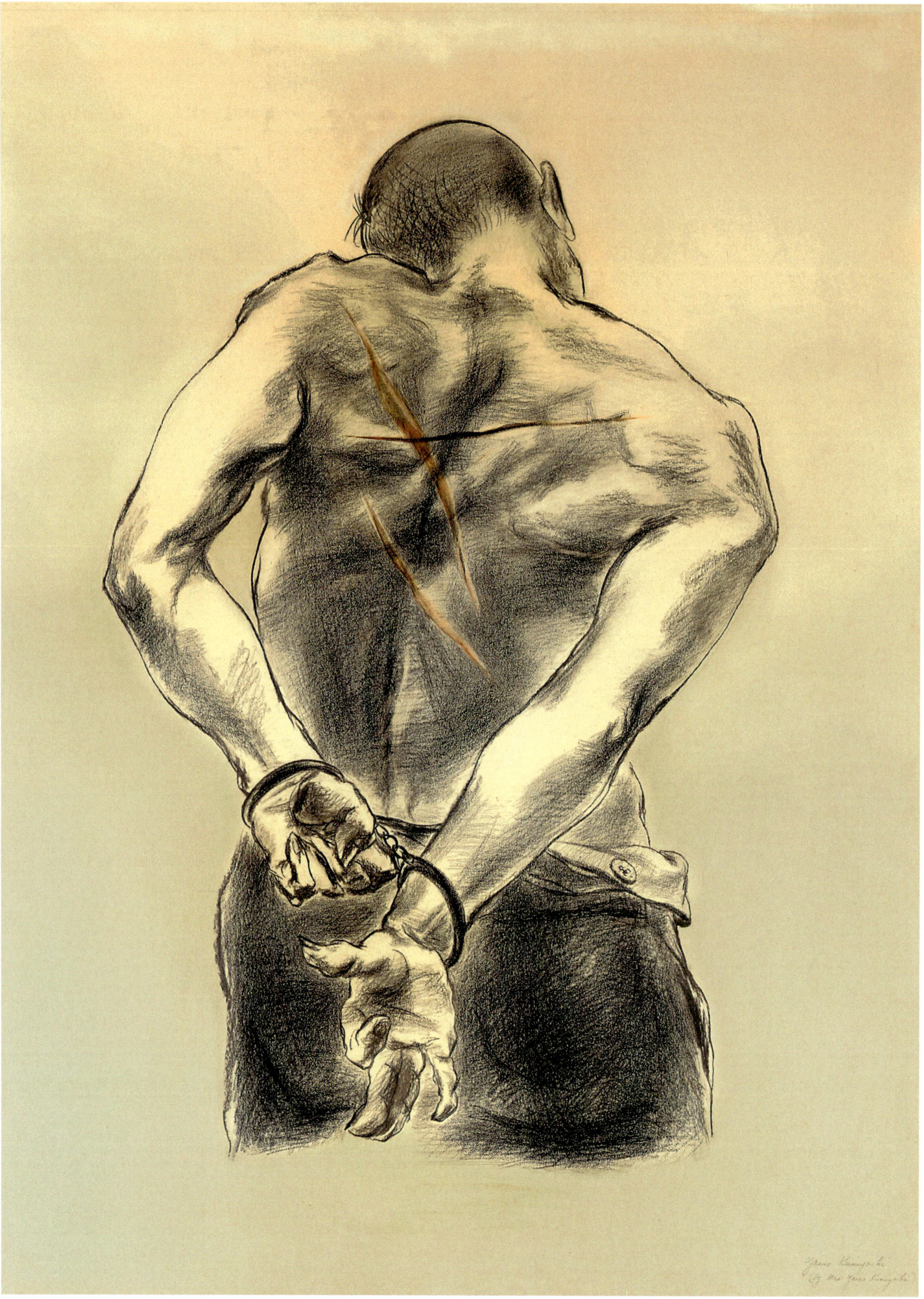

47
Torture
1943
pencil on paper
40 × 28 ½ in.
Collection of John Cassara

48
Murdered
1944
ink with pen and dry brush on paper
sheet: 22 ⁹⁄₁₆ × 28 ⅝ in.
Brooklyn Museum, New York; Gift of Mrs. Milton Lowenthal

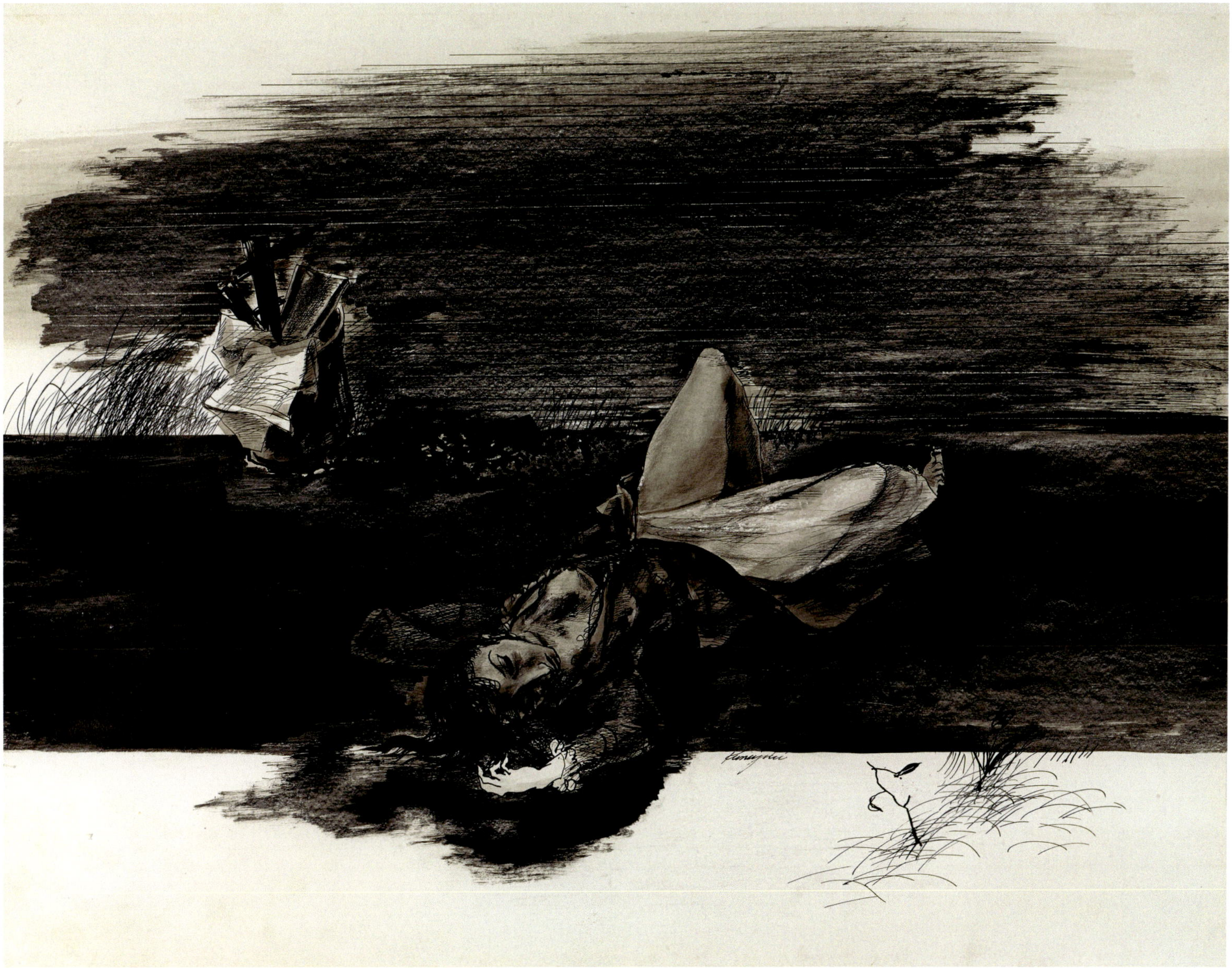

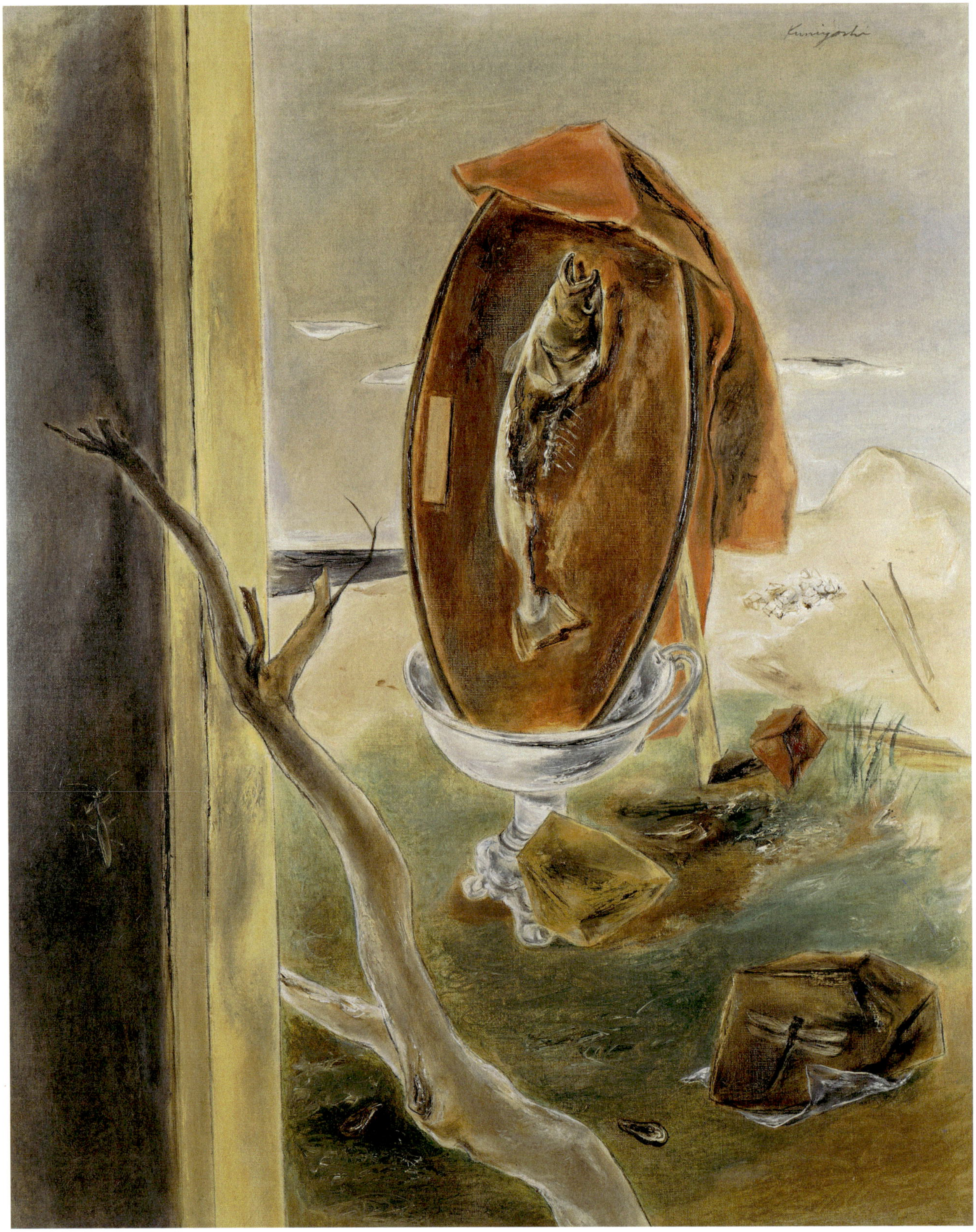
Kuniyoshi

49
Rotting on the Shore
1945
46 × 36 in.
Norton Museum of Art, West Palm Beach, Florida; Bequest of R. H. Norton

50
Landscape with Two Dogs
1945
10 ⅝ × 18 ½ in.
Fukutake Collection, Okayama, Japan

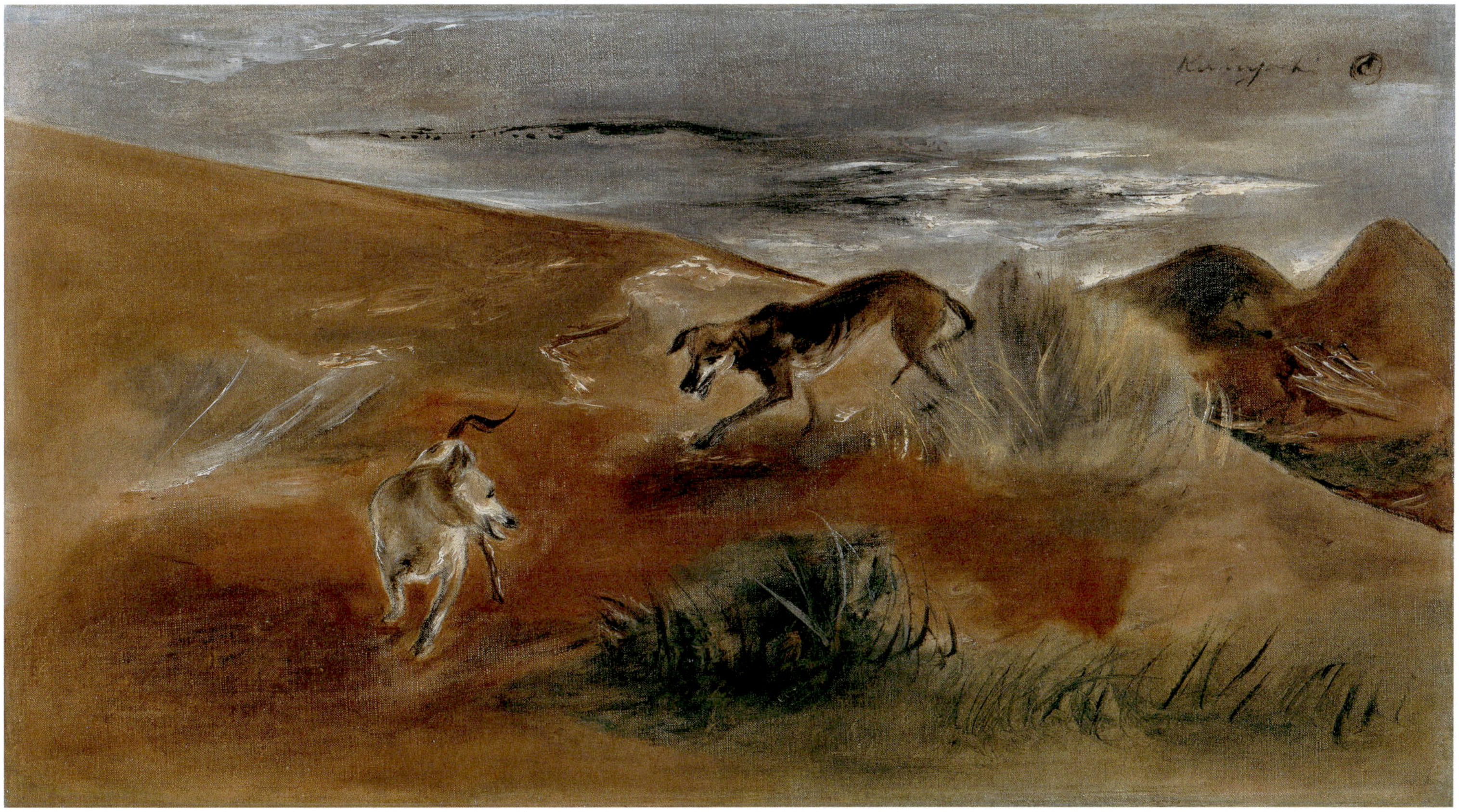

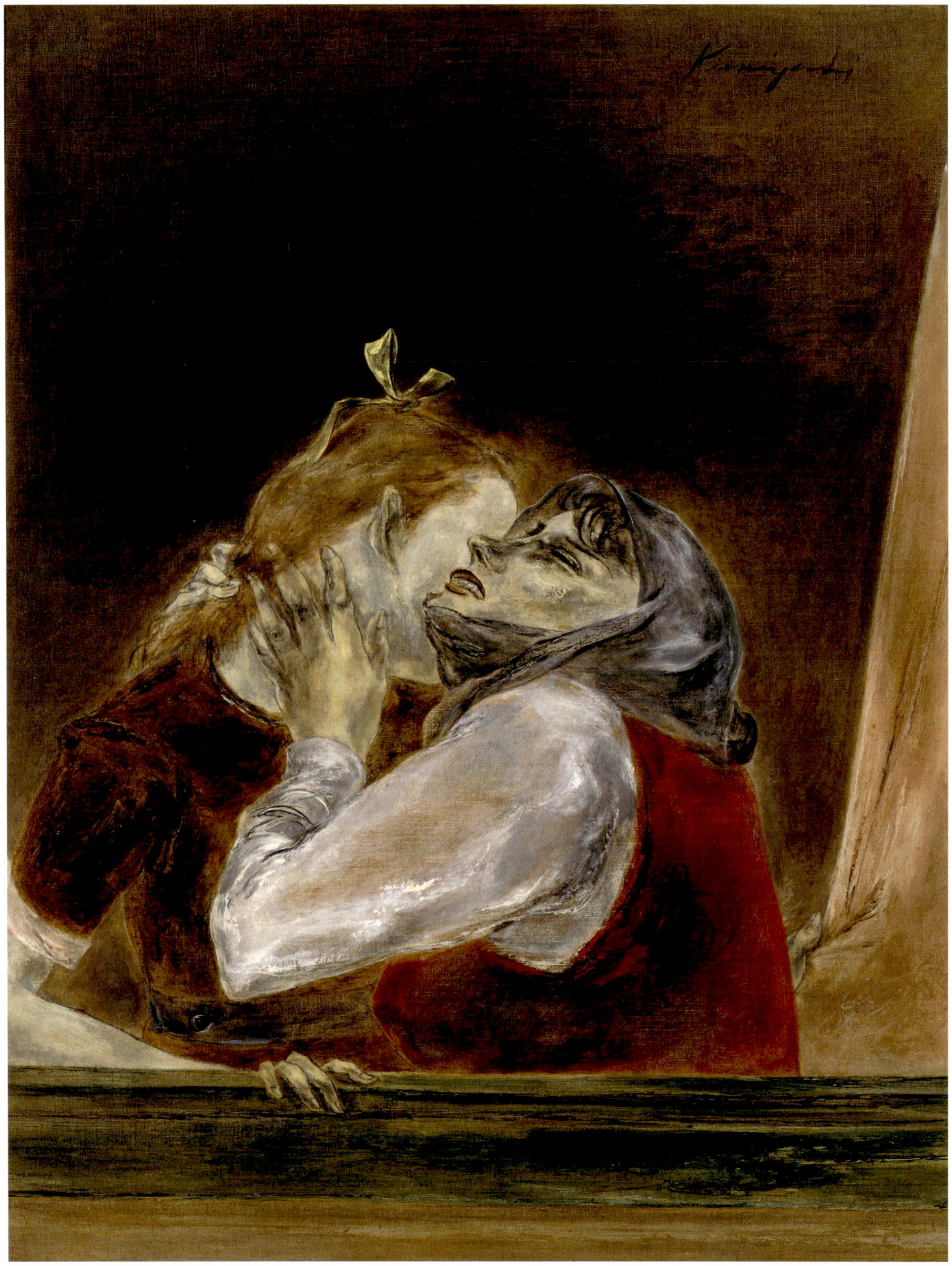

51
Mother and Daughter
1945
40 ¼ × 30 ¼ in.
Carnegie Museum of Art, Pittsburgh; Patrons Art Fund

52
She Walks Among the Ruins
1945–46
43 × 34 in.
Menard Art Museum, Komaki, Aichi, Japan

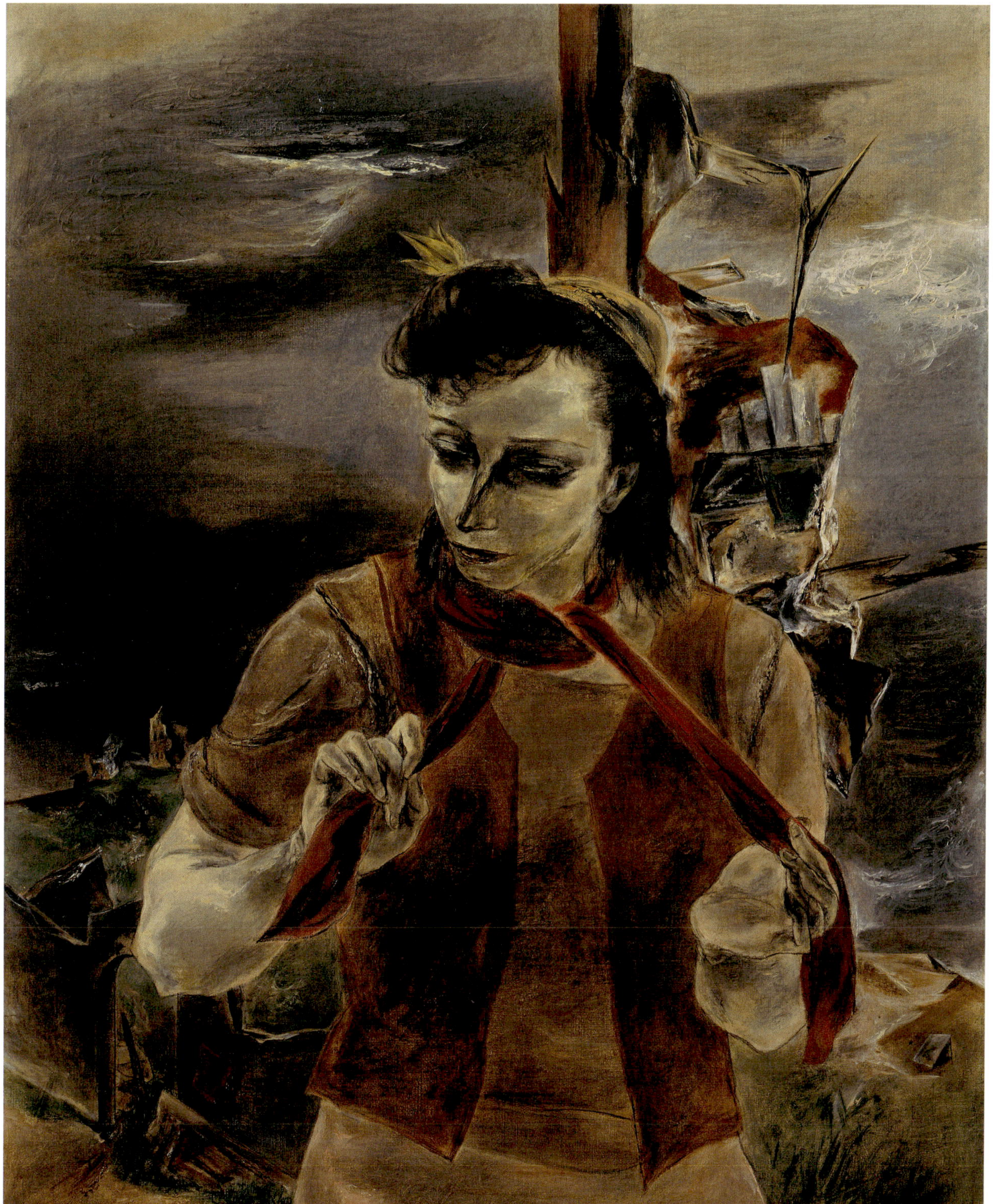

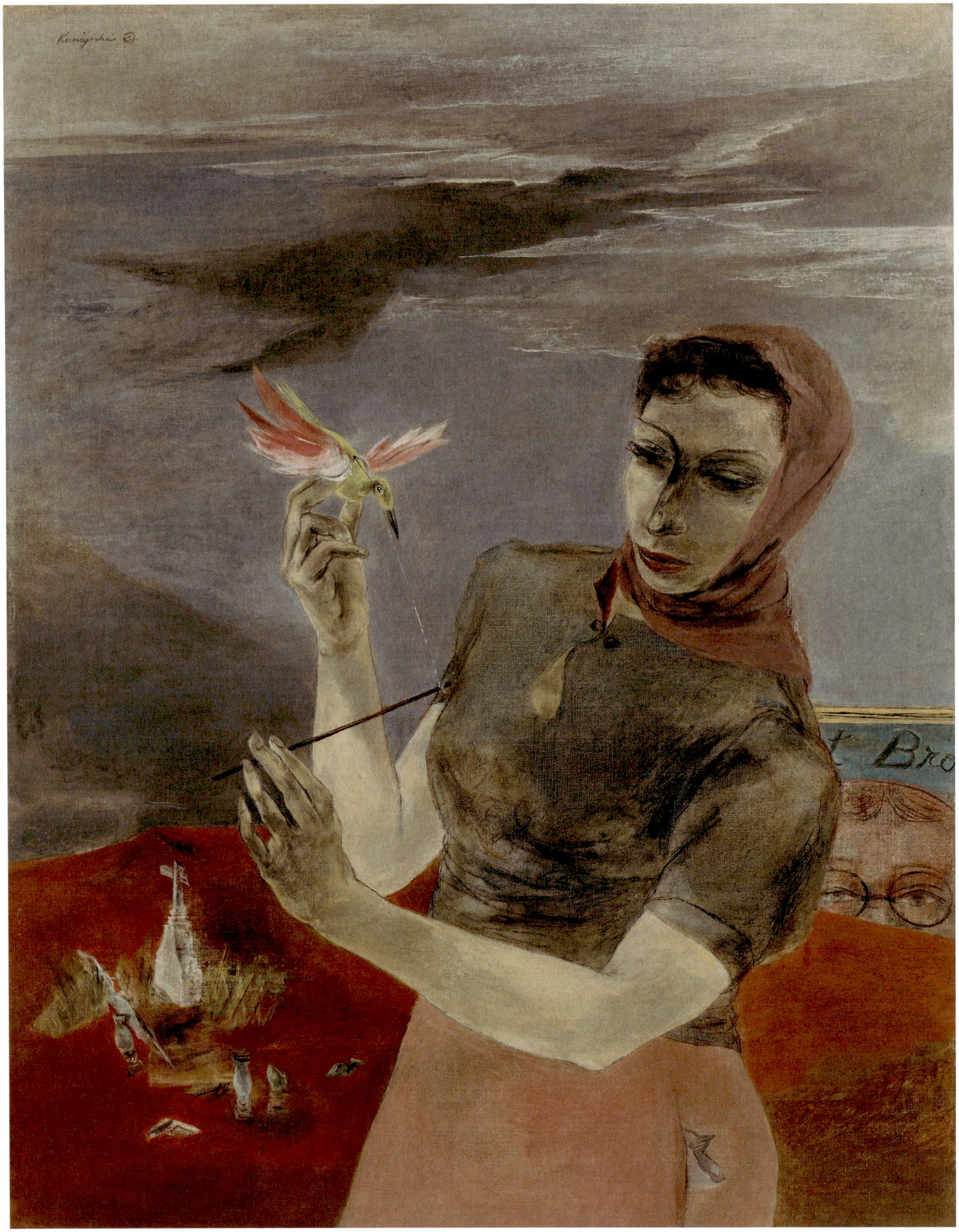

53
Look, It Flies!
1946
39 ¾ × 30 ⅜ in.
Hirshhorn Museum and Sculpture Garden, Smithsonian Institution, Washington, DC;
Gift of the Joseph H. Hirshhorn Foundation, 1966

54
I Wear a Mask Today
1946–47
wax on canvas
12 ⅕ × 9 in.
Fukutake Collection, Okayama, Japan

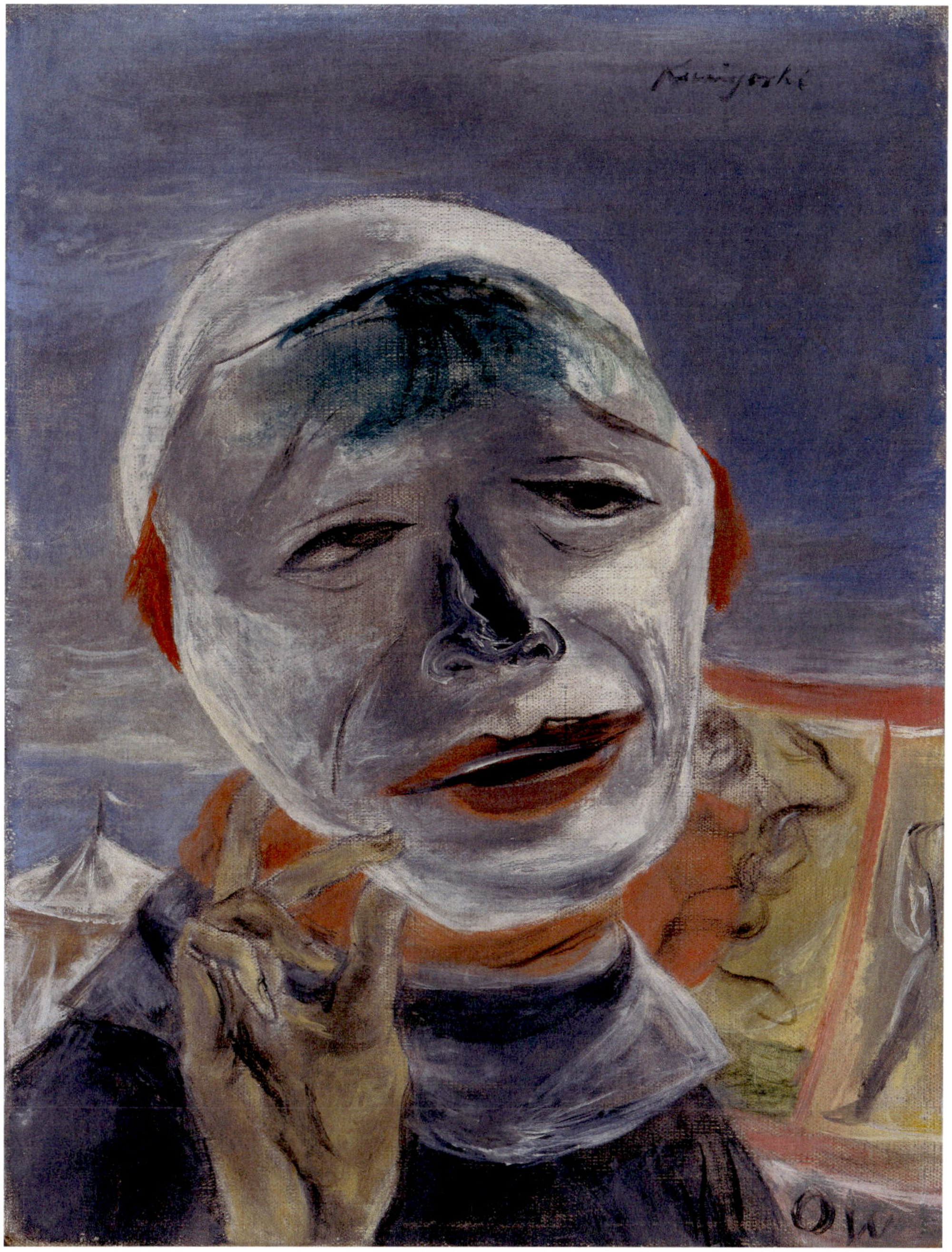

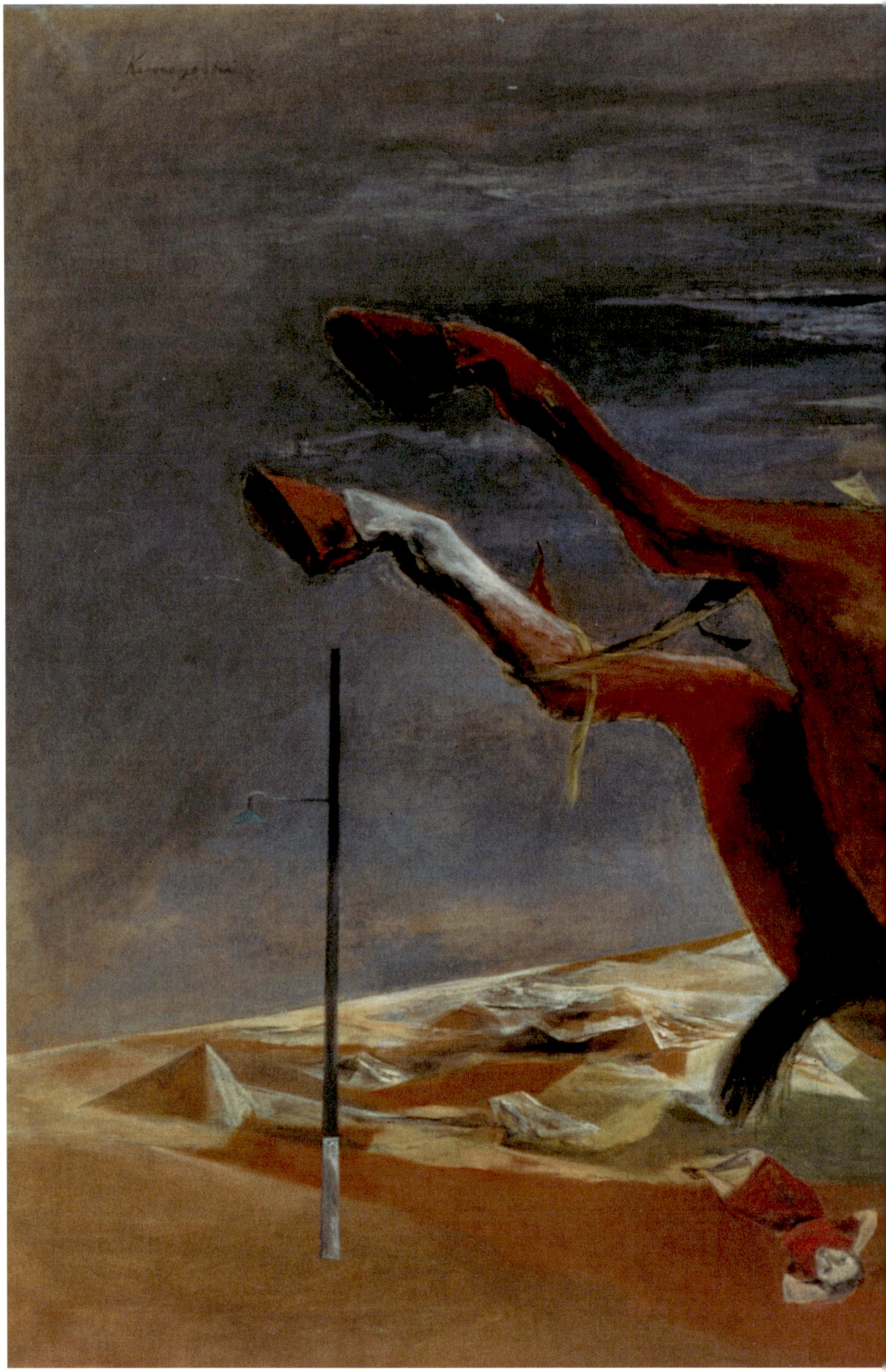

55
Festivities Ended
1947
39 3/10 × 69 1/5 in.
Okayama Prefectural
Museum of Art, Japan

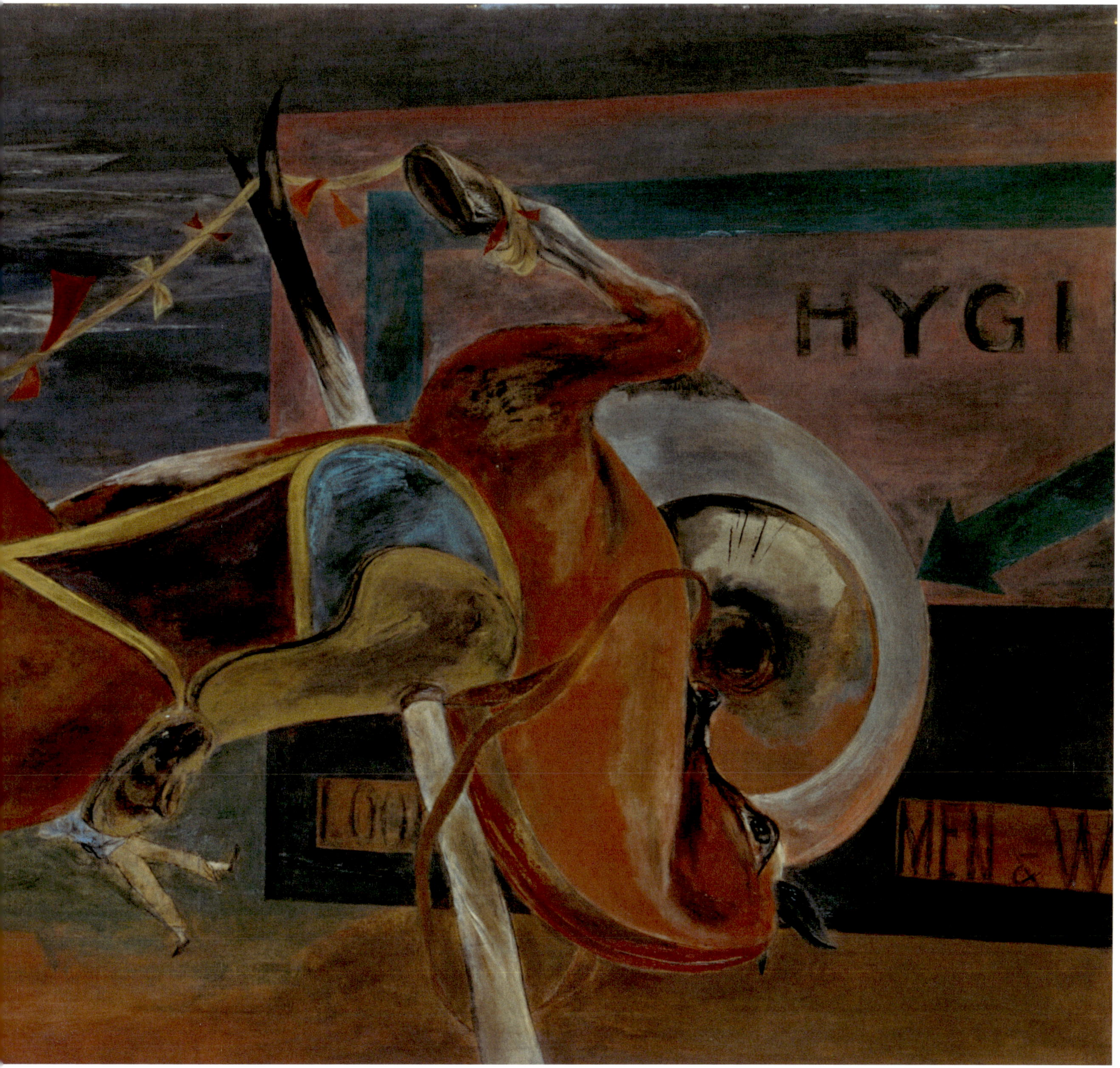
HYGI
MEN & W

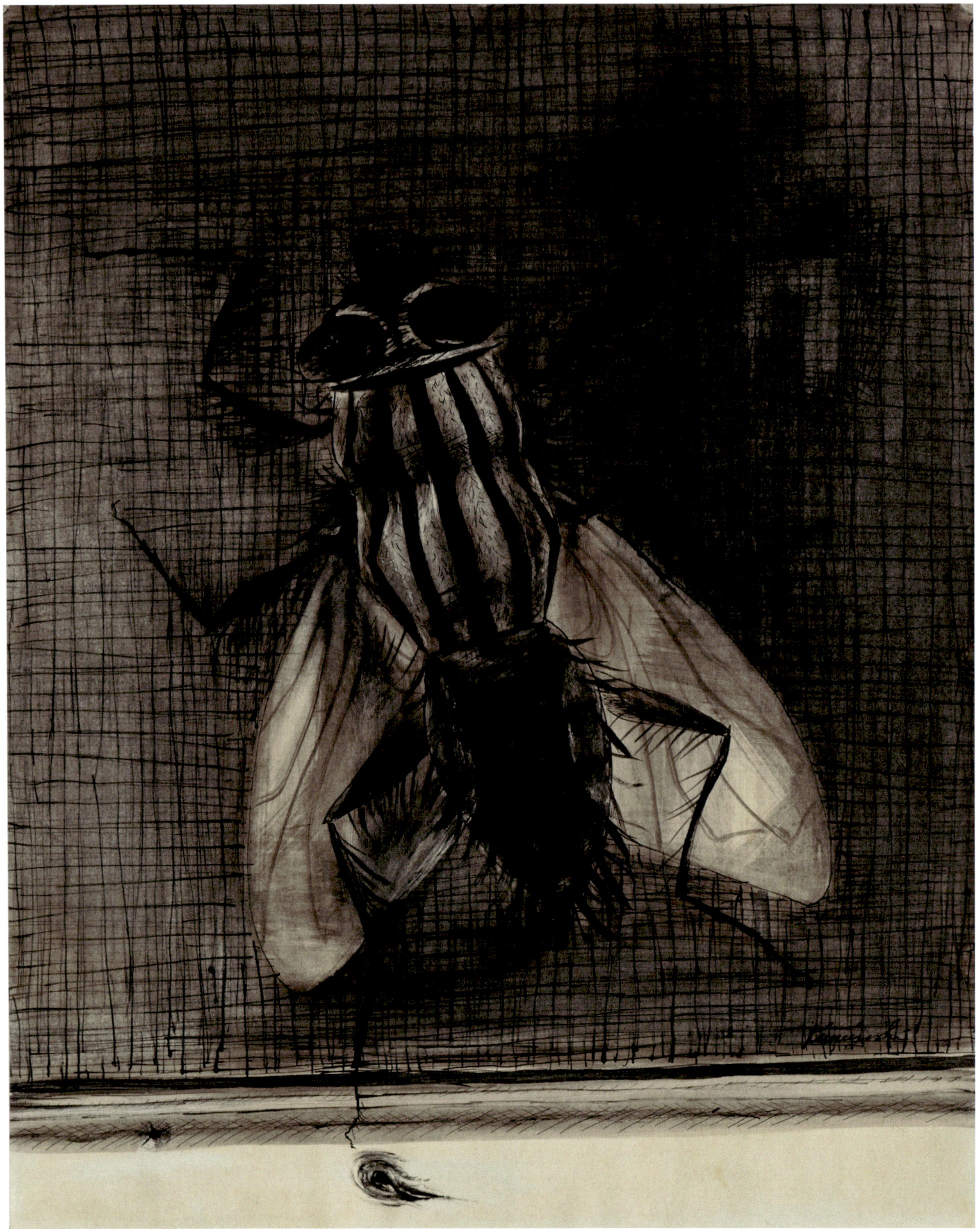

56
Flesh Fly
about 1947
ink and gouache on paper
sheet: 28 × 22 in.
Modern Art Museum of Fort Worth, Texas; Gift of Mrs. Sam B. Cantey III, 1980.10.G.Dr

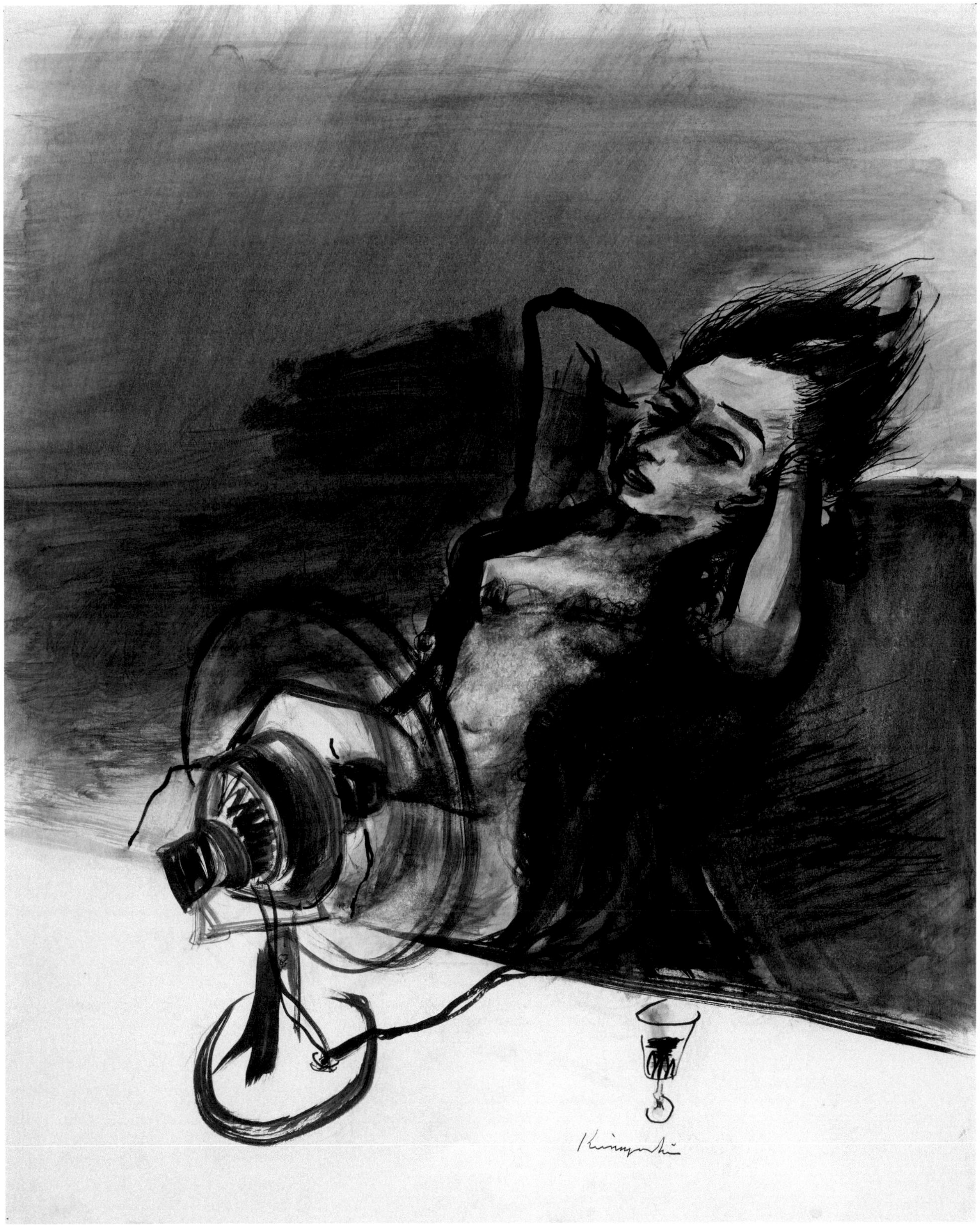

57
Hot Day
before 1948
brush and gray and black ink, with black chalk, abrasion and traces of graphite and white chalk
sheet: 28 ½ × 22 ½ in.
The Cleveland Museum of Art, Ohio; Hinman B. Hurlbut Collection, 1919.1948

58
This Is My Playground
1947
27 × 44 in.
Fukutake Collection,
Okayama, Japan

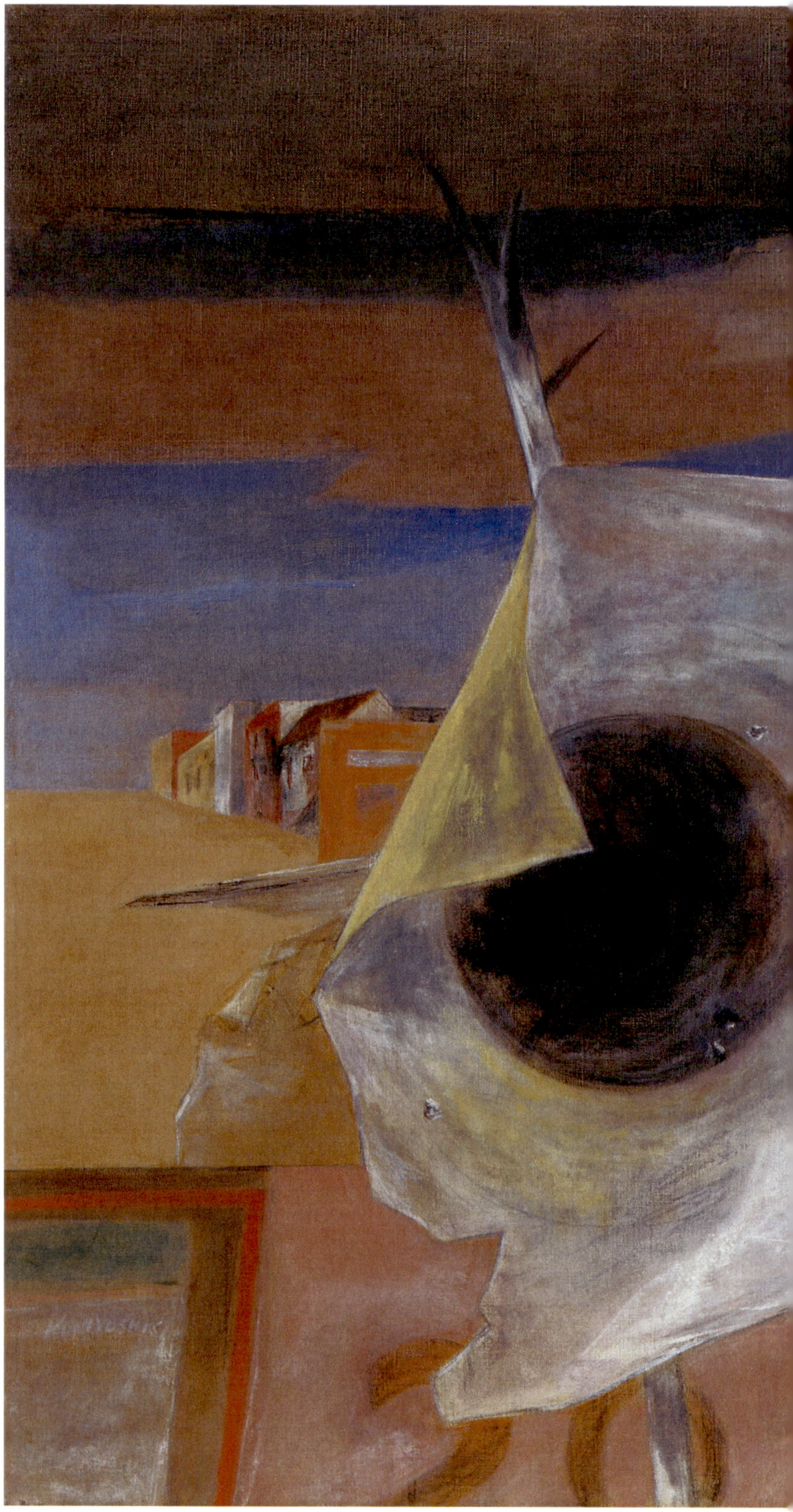

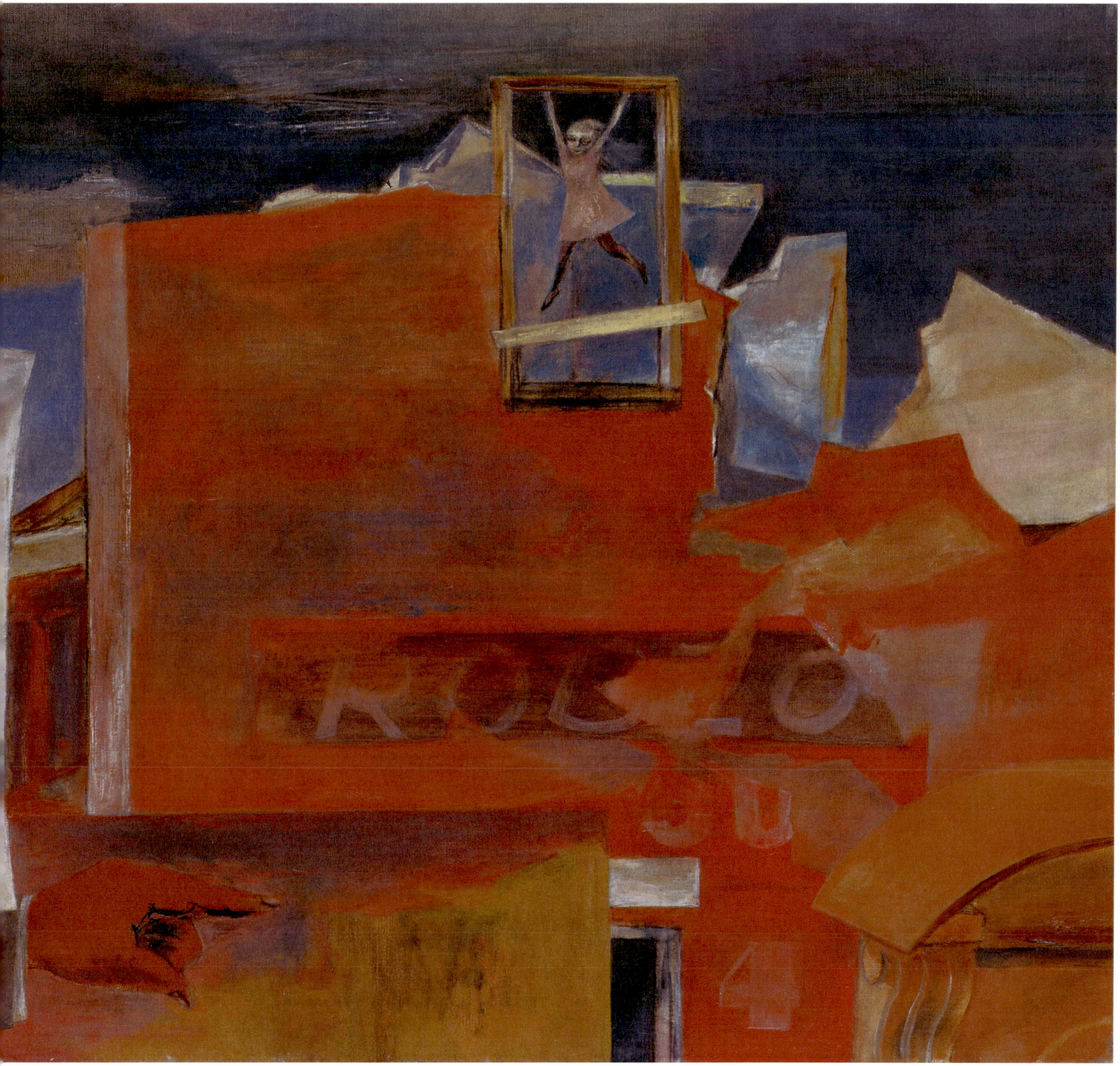

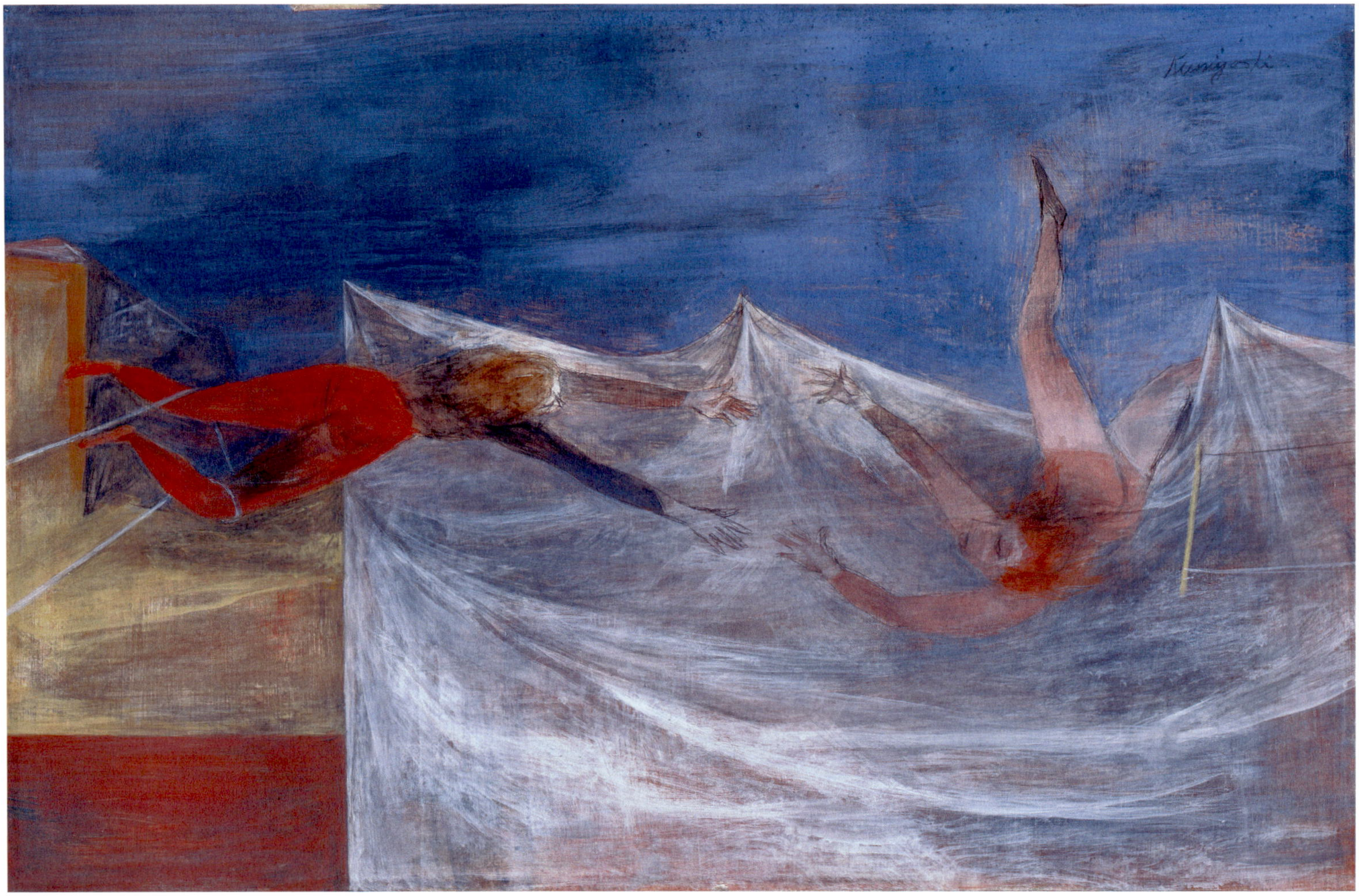
Kuniyoshi

59
Disturbing Dream
1948
casein on gesso panel
20 × 30 in.
Fukutake Collection,
Okayama, Japan

60
Forbidden Fruit
1950
32 2/3 × 50 1/5 in.
Syracuse University
Art Collection

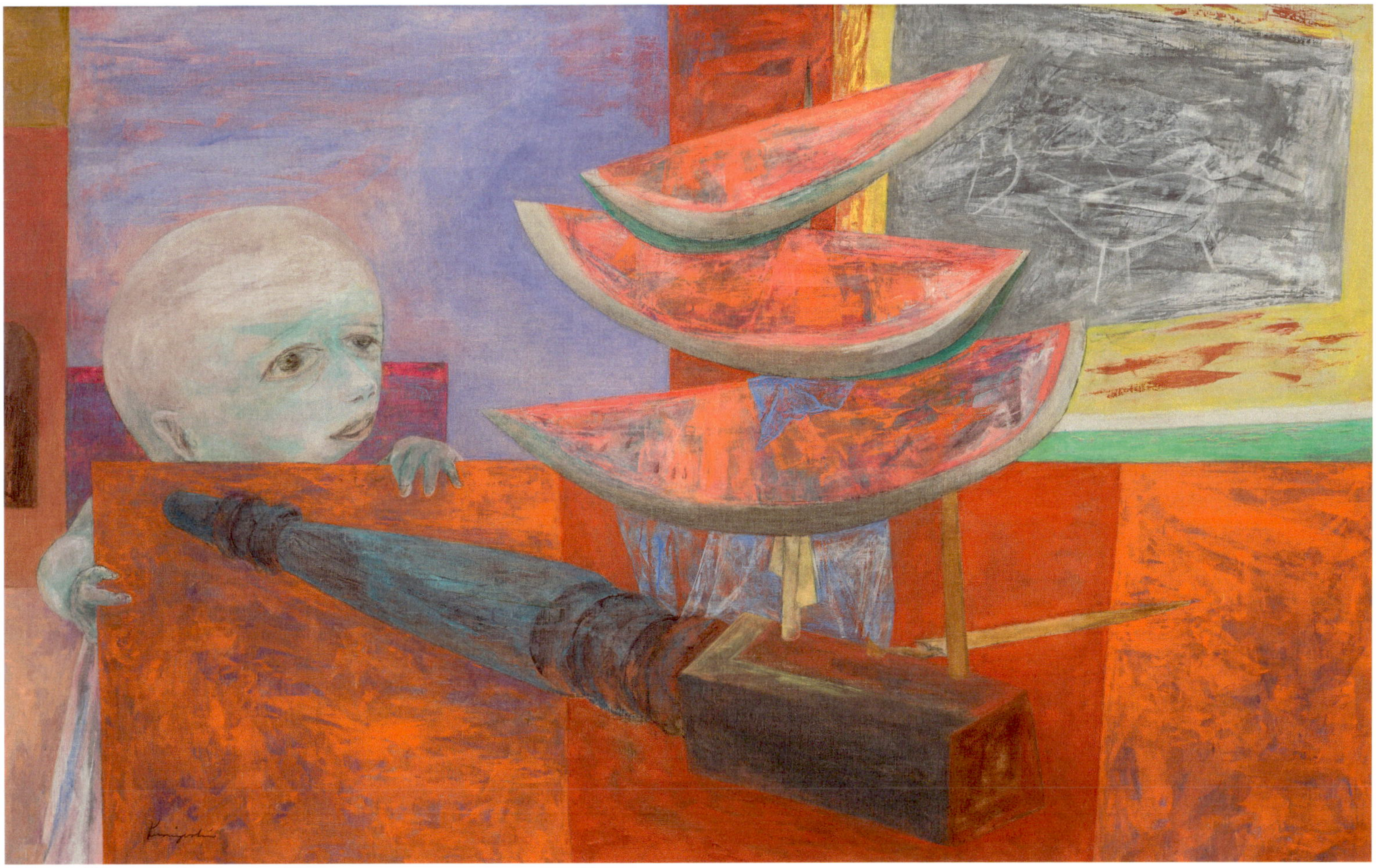

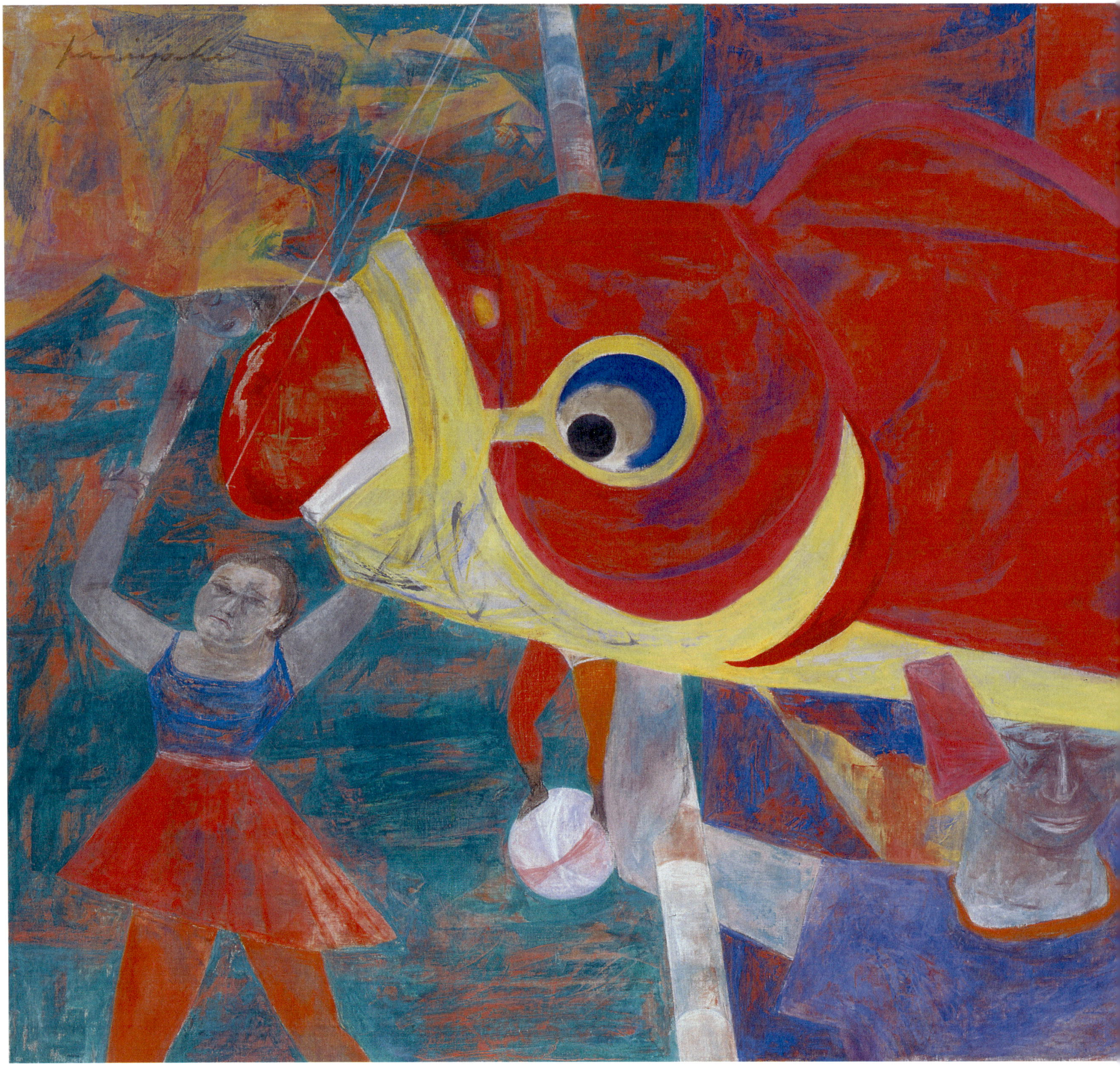
Kuniyoshi

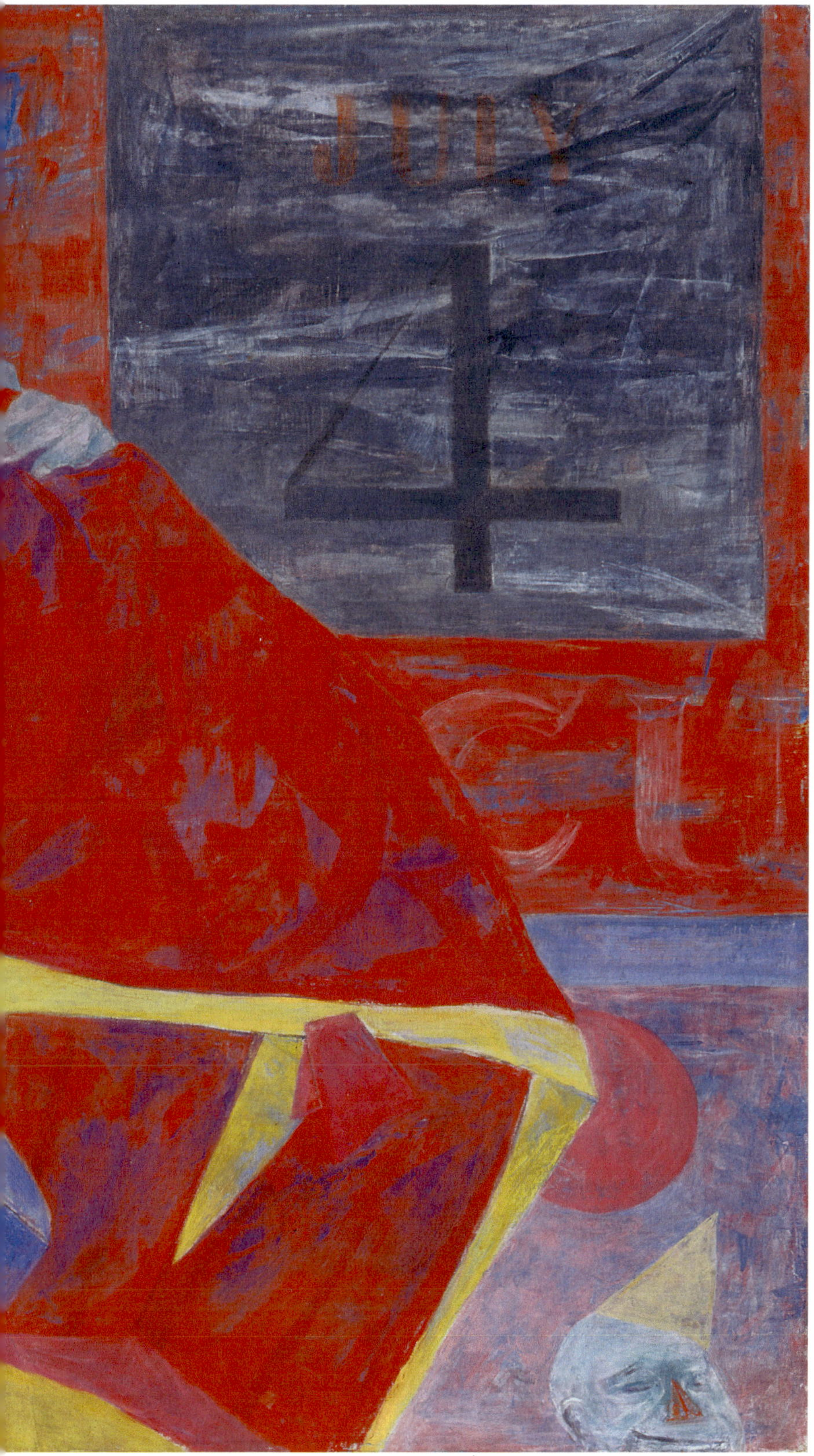

61
Fish Kite
1950
30 × 49⅖ in.
Fukutake Collection,
Okayama, Japan

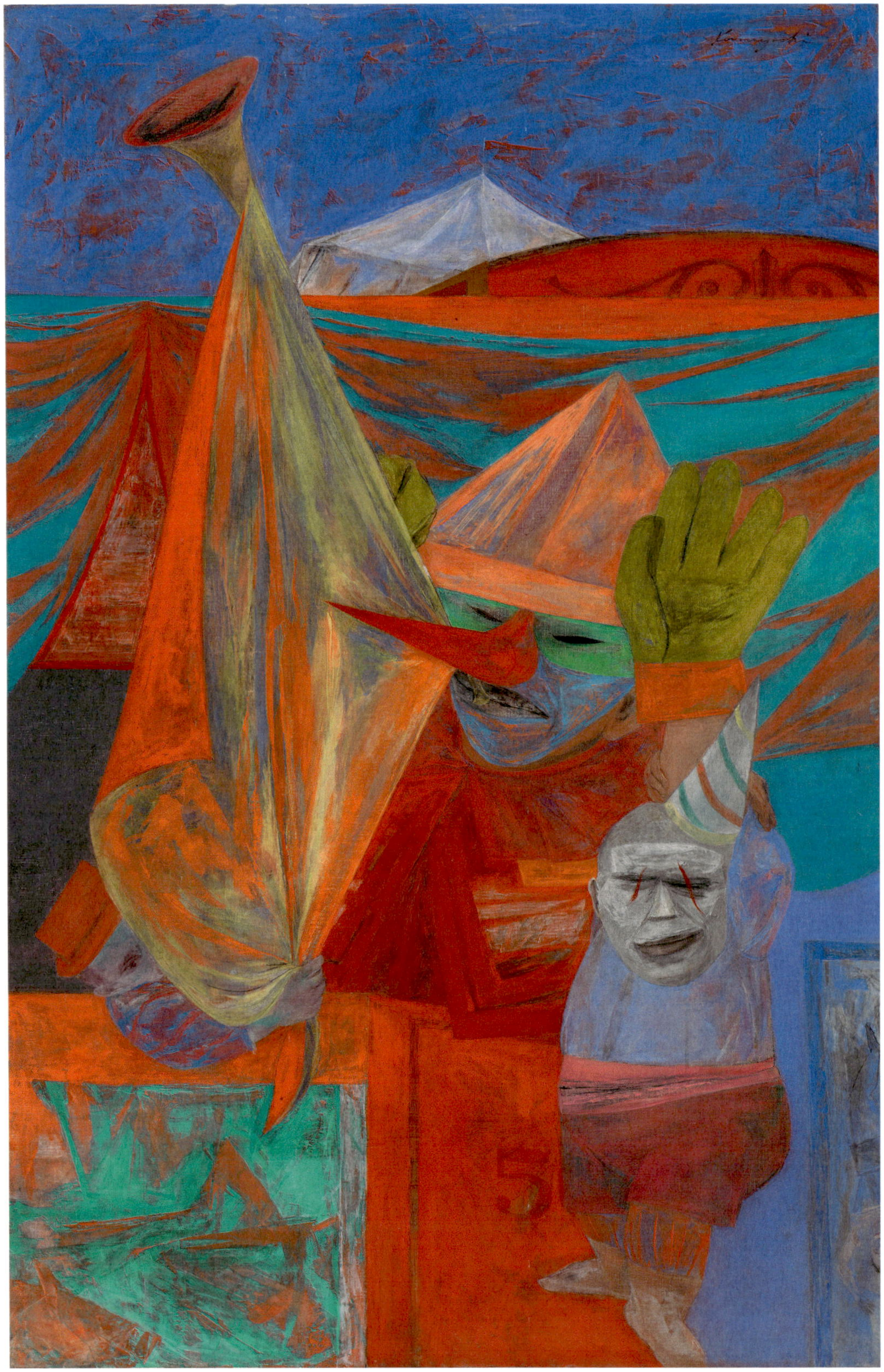

62
Fakirs
1951
50 ¼ × 32 ¼ in.
Smithsonian American Art Museum, Gift of the Sara Roby Foundation, 1986.6.93

63
Mr. Ace
1952
46 × 26 3/10 in.
Fukutake Collection,
Okayama, Japan

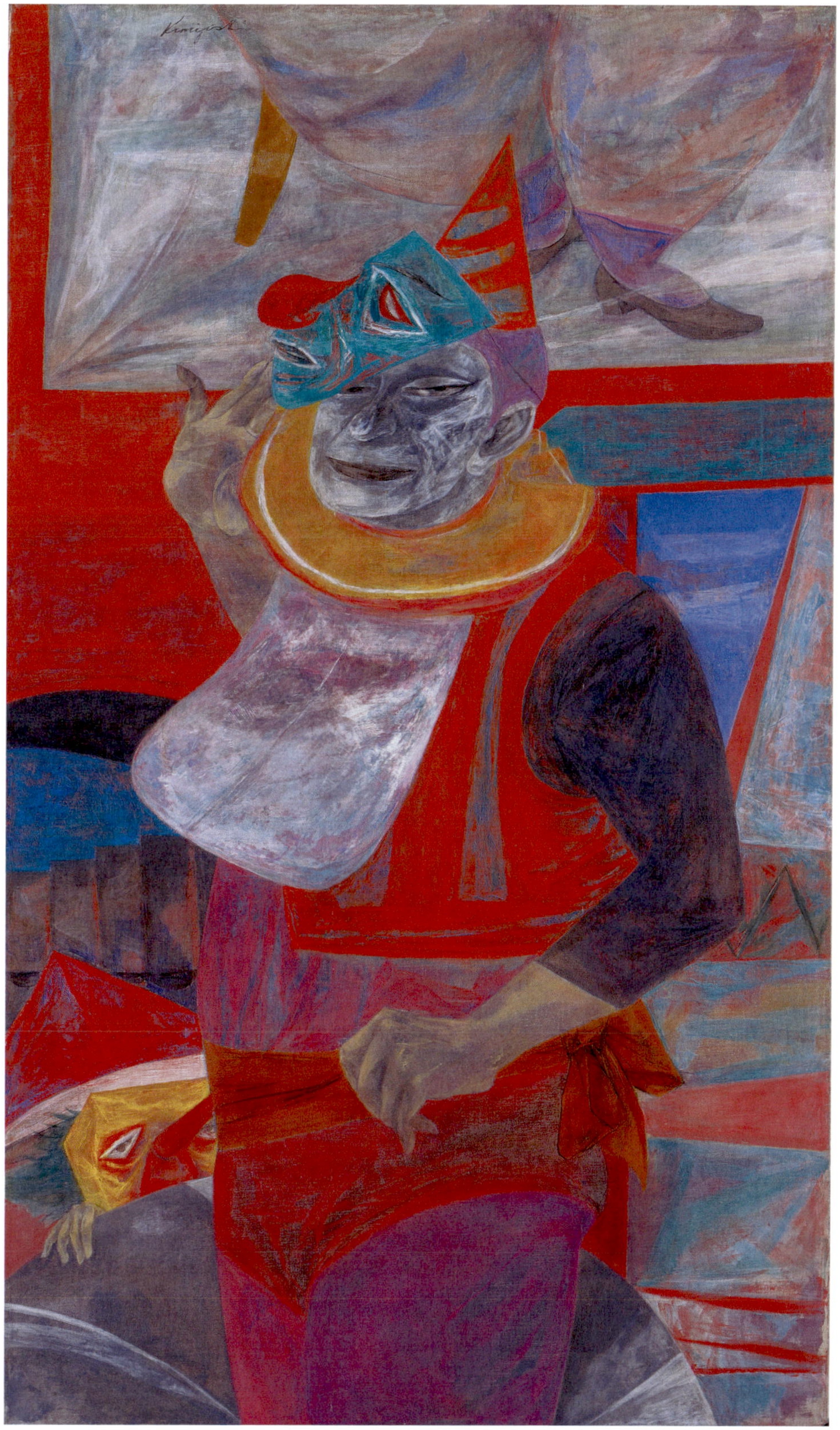

64
Fish Head
1952
ink and wash on paper
22 × 28 in.
Metropolitan Museum of Art, New York; Rogers Fund, 1953

65
Work at Dawn
1952
pen and ink and brush and ink on paper
sheet: 18 ½ × 28 ¼ in.
Whitney Museum of American Art, New York; Gift of Sara Mazo Kuniyoshi in honor of Lloyd Goodrich

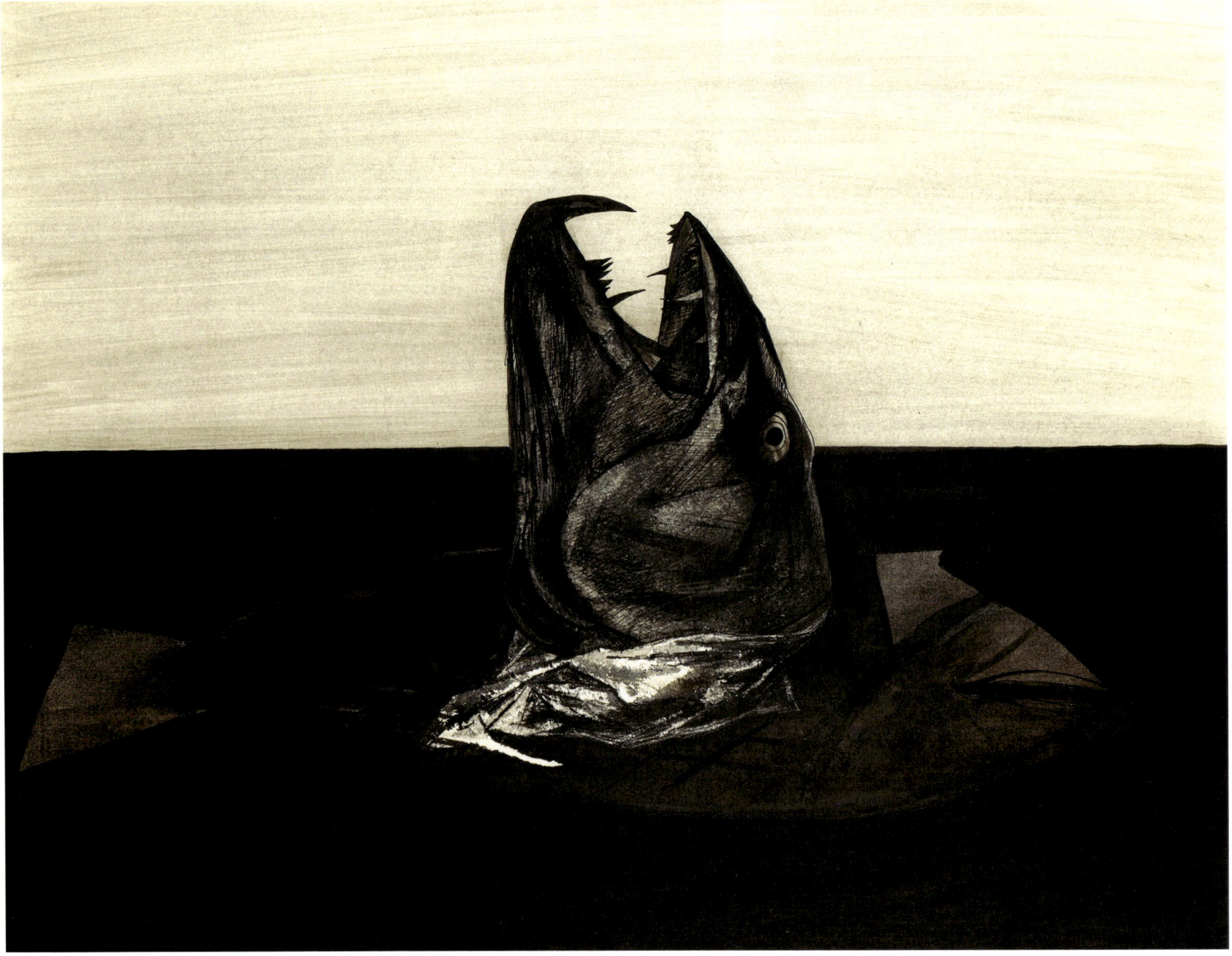

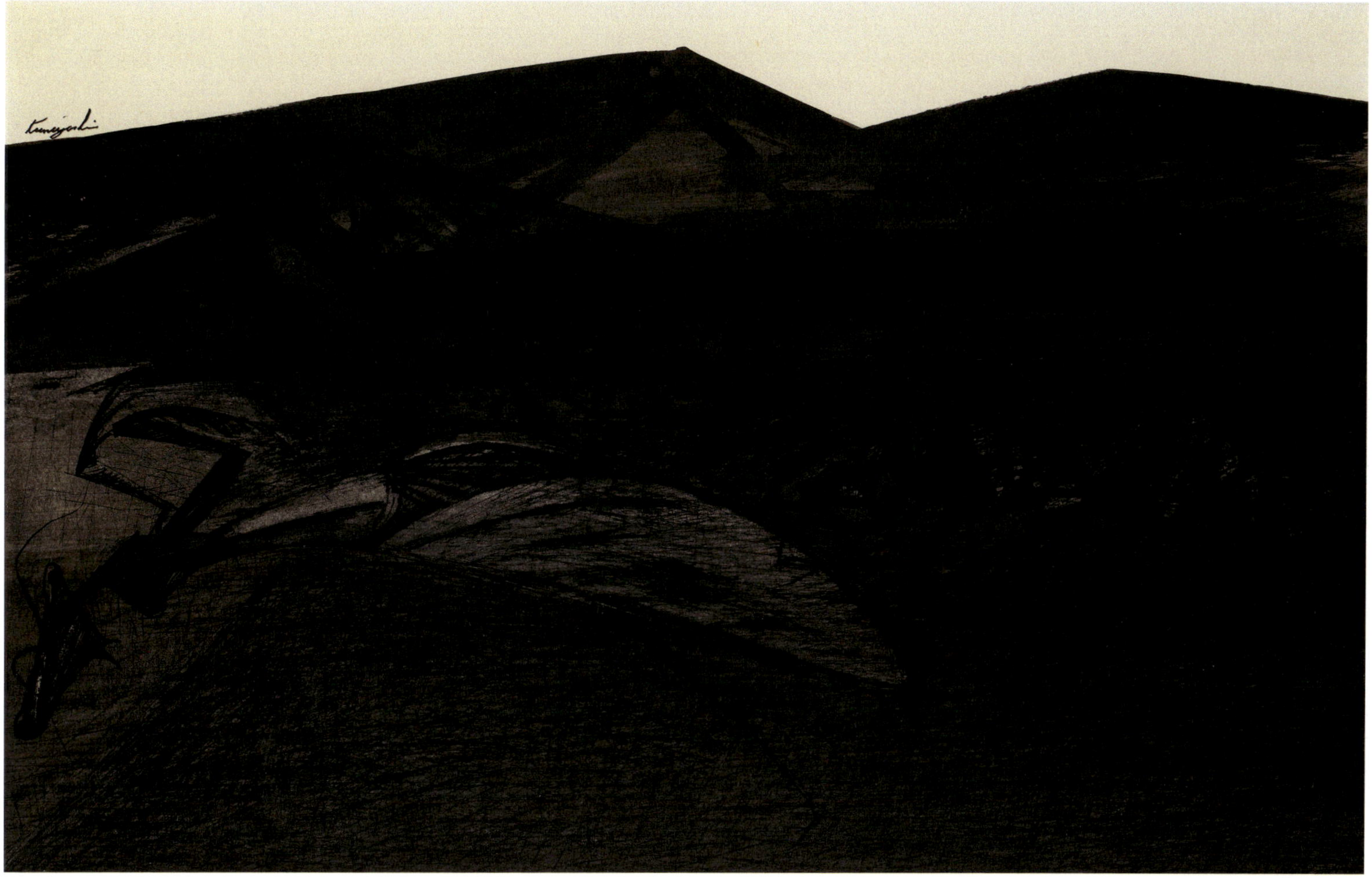

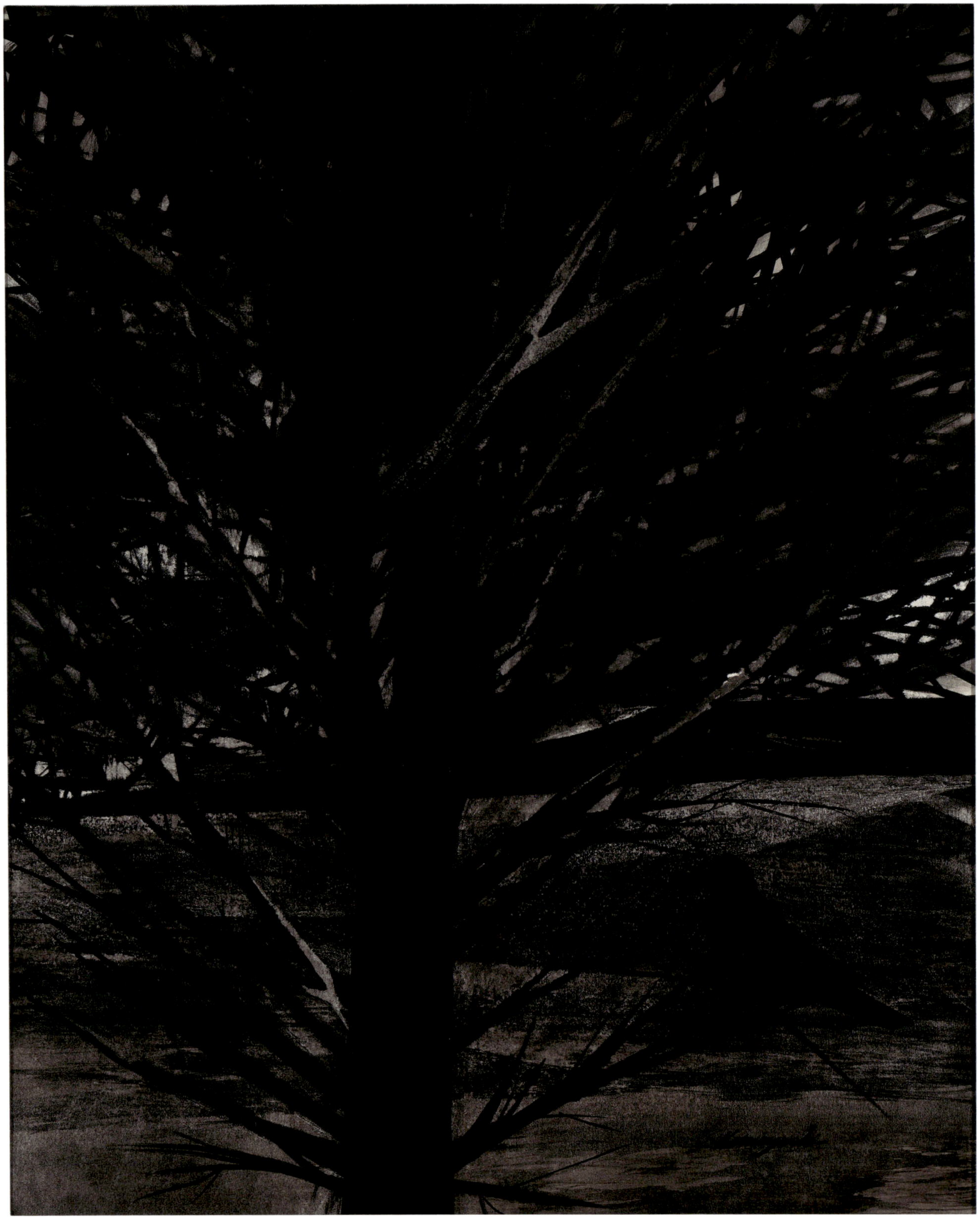

66
Old Tree
about 1953
ink on paper
image: 28 ½ × 22 ⅝ in.
image with mat:
33 ¼ × 27 ½ in.
Delaware Art Museum,
Wilmington; Special
Purchase Fund, 1953

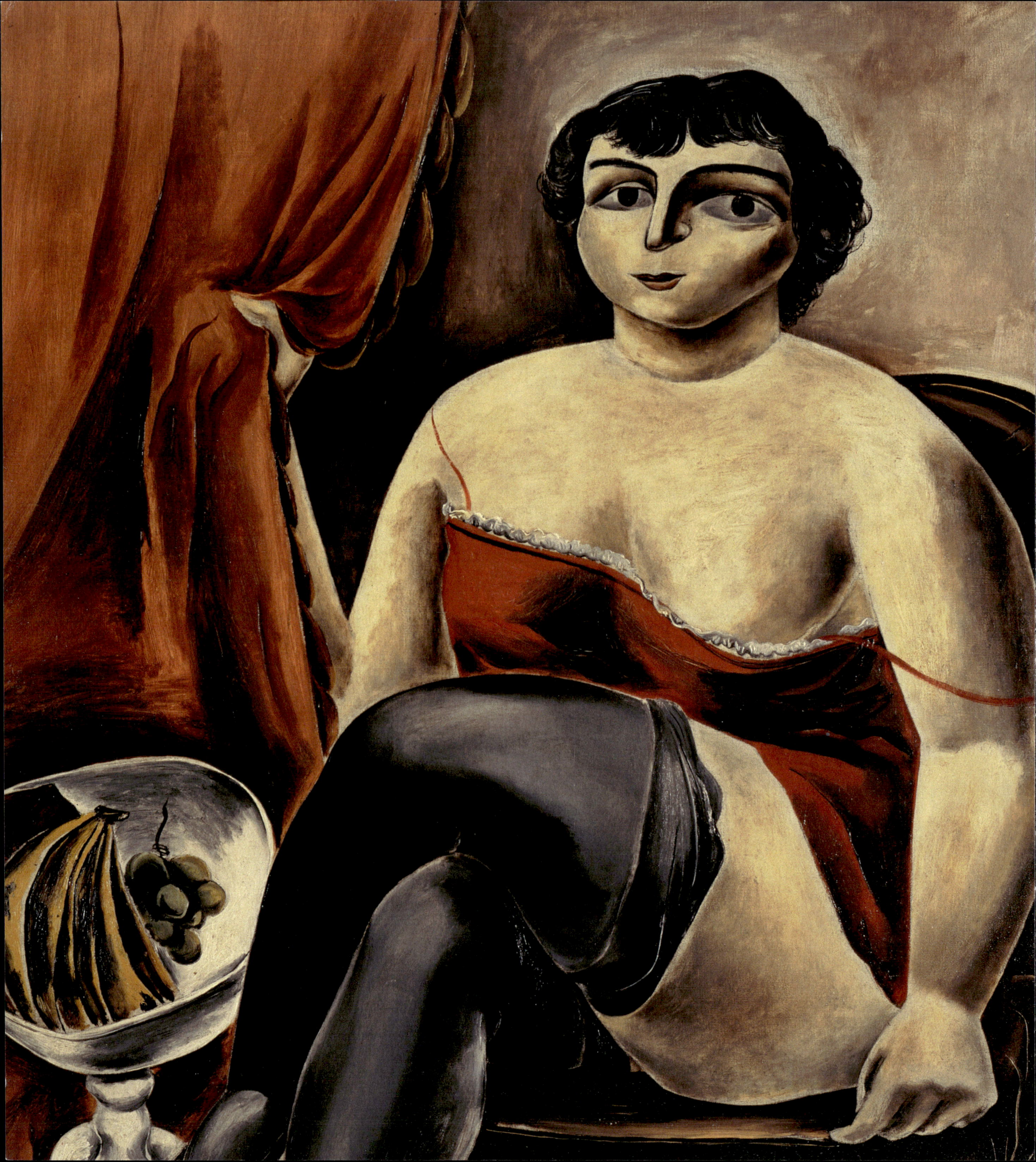

Chronology

1889
Yasuo Kuniyoshi is born September 1 at Nakaizushi, Okayama City, Okayama Prefecture, Japan, an only child to Ukichi and Ito Kuniyoshi. His father ran a general shop and later became head of a *rikisha* (rickshaw) men's union.

1896
Enters Okayama primary and secondary public schools.

1904
Enrolls at Okayama Prefectural Industrial High School to study textiles and dyeing.

1906
Travels alone by ship to North America; arrives in Vancouver, British Columbia, on July 27 and travels by train to Seattle, Washington.

1907–10
Begins public high school in Los Angeles, then attends the Los Angeles School of Art and Design for three years, working in a hotel and during summers picking fruit in Fresno and the Imperial Valley.

1910
Moves to New York. During his first year in the city, he receives food and lodgings from a Japanese artist who was a friend of his father's in exchange for cleaning his studio. Studies briefly at the National Academy of Design and the Henri School.

1914–16
Studies with Homer Boss at the Independent School, where he befriends Stuart Davis.

1916
Enters the Art Students League and studies painting under Kenneth Hayes Miller. Makes etchings with the encouragement of Peggy Bacon.

1917
Receives a scholarship from the Art Students League and meets Toshi Shimizu there. Louis Bouché introduces Kuniyoshi to the Penguin Club, an association of progressive artists. Attends the league's summer landscape painting school in Woodstock, New York, studying with John Carlson and Walter Goltz.

Shows *Modern Crucifix* (now known as *Crucifixion*) and *Homeward* at the Society of Independent Artists.

1919
Marries Katherine Schmidt, a fellow student at the Art Students League, in Ogunquit, Maine, and begins working as an art photographer to support himself. Spends his summers until 1924 in Ogunquit, with the support of Hamilton Easter Field.

1920
Completes studies at the Art Students League.

1921
Daniel Gallery on West 47th Street exhibits two pictures by Kuniyoshi. This is his first affiliation with the gallery, which would represent him for the next ten years.

1922
First lithograph, *Milking the Cow*, printed by George Miller. William Murrell publishes a short monograph on Kuniyoshi. Death of Hamilton Easter Field.

1924
Organizes exhibition *Portraits and Religious Works* for the Whitney Studio Club.

1925
With Schmidt visits Italy (Cremona, Padua, Venice, Ravenna, Florence, Assisi, Perugia, and Siena); winters in Vence, in the South of France.

1927
Makes twenty-two lithographs, printed by George Miller at the Art Students League.

1928
With Schmidt, makes second and last trip to Europe, visiting Spain and then Paris, where he makes lithographs at Atelier Desjobert.

1929
Paris with his friend Jules Pascin, then returns to New York; with Schmidt, builds a summerhouse in Woodstock, New York.

Five pieces featured in *Paintings by 19 Living Americans*, the second exhibition of the newly opened Museum of Modern Art, New York, which is criticized for including non-Americans like him in the show.

1930
March–April: Last solo show at Daniel Gallery before Charles Daniel closes his gallery the following year.

1931
Moves with Schmidt from their Brooklyn residence to 30 East 14th Street in Manhattan. Visits Japan to see his ailing father and has three shows of his paintings and lithographs, in Okayama City, Tokyo, and Osaka.

Receives an honorable mention for *Odd Objects on a Couch* (1930) in the 30th Annual International Exhibition at the Carnegie Institute, Pittsburgh.

1932
Returns from Japan in February; he and Schmidt divorce. Commissioned by Donald Deskey to paint murals in the women's restrooms in Rockefeller Center Music Hall after Georgia O'Keeffe abandons the project.

1933
Teaches at the Art Students League, as he will until his death in 1953. First solo exhibition at the Downtown Gallery.

1934
Wins one of four painting awards at the 15th Annual Exhibition at the Los Angeles Museum, Exposition Park, and awarded Temple Gold Medal at the 129th Annual Exhibition, Pennsylvania Academy of the Fine Arts.

1935
Marries Sara Mazo on June 29; that summer, Kuniyoshi wins a Guggenheim Fellowship and they honeymoon through the Southwest and Mexico. More than one hundred American artists protest Kuniyoshi's exclusion from the first exhibition of the Municipal Art Center, New York, due to his not being a U.S. citizen, leading to his inclusion in the show.

1936
Becomes an officer of the American Artists' Congress. Under Kuniyoshi's chairmanship, the congress sponsors *Against War and Fascism: An International Exhibition of Cartoons, Drawings and Prints* at the New School for Social Research.

1937
Sets up a photography darkroom in his Woodstock studio.

1939
Elected president of An American Group, an informal association of progressive artists; serves as president until 1944.

Awarded first prize for *Weathervane and Objects on a Sofa* (1933) in the American Section of the Golden Gate Exposition in San Francisco, and second prize for *Lay Figure* (1937–38) in the Annual International Exhibition at the Carnegie Institute.

1940
Autobiographical essay, "East to West," appears in the February issue of *Magazine of Art*.

1941
Separates from his wife, Sara Mazo. During the summer travels by car to Taos, Colorado Springs, Nevada, and Los Angeles. After Japan attacks Pearl Harbor in December, Kuniyoshi's status changes from "resident alien" to "enemy alien."

1942
Writes two speeches for broadcast by shortwave radio to Japan as U.S. war propaganda. Holds a retrospective exhibition of his works at the Downtown Gallery to benefit United China Relief.

Artists for Victory: An Exhibition of Contemporary American Art is held at the Metropolitan Museum of Art, New York. Although Kuniyoshi is president of An American Group, a sponsor of the exhibition, he cannot participate because only American citizens are eligible.

1944
Reunites with wife Sara Mazo.

Founder of the Arts Council of Japanese Americans for Democracy.

Room 110 wins first prize out of 311 paintings exhibited at *Painting in the United States, 1944* at the Carnegie Institute; receives the J. Henry Scheidt Memorial Prize for *End of Juanita* (1942) in the 139th Annual Exhibition at the Pennsylvania Academy of the Fine Arts and the Purchase Prize for *Nevadaville* (1942) at the 4th Biennial Exhibition at the Virginia Museum of Fine Arts, Richmond.

1945
Awarded the Norman Wait Harris Bronze Medal for *Headless Horse Who Wants to Jump* in the 56th Annual Exhibition at the Art Institute of Chicago.

1946
The U.S. State Department purchases Kuniyoshi's *Circus Girl Resting* (1925) for its international exhibition, *Advancing American Art*, organized to foster goodwill through cultural exchange, but in the United States the painting becomes the object of scorn in the press and for conservative political opponents of the project.

1947
Elected the first president of the new Artists Equity Association, created to promote artists' rights.

Look, It Flies! (1946) receives fifth prize in the 2nd Exhibition of La Tausca Art Competition at the Riverside Museum, New York.

1948
Becomes the first living artist to receive a retrospective exhibition at the Whitney Museum of American Art.

Kuniyoshi ranked third after John Marin and Max Weber in *Look* magazine feature of the ten most outstanding contemporary American painters as determined by a poll of American museum directors and curators. The other artists cited after Kuniyoshi were, in order: Stuart Davis, Ben Shahn, Edward Hopper, Charles Burchfield, George Grosz, Franklin Watkins, and, tied for tenth place, Lyonel Feininger and Jack Levine.

This Is My Playground (1947) receives fifth prize in the 3rd Exhibition of La Tausca Art Competition, Riverside Museum, New York.

1949
Guest instructor at Mills College in Oakland, California, during the summer. Travels through the western and Southwestern United States; designated an honorary associate of the National Institute of Arts and Letters.

1950
Guest instructor at the University of Minnesota, Duluth, during the summer.

Fish Kite receives third prize in *American Painting Today: A National Competitive Exhibition*, at the Metropolitan Museum of Art.

1951
Guest instructor at Ohio State University in the summer.

1952
Selected to represent the United States at the 26th Venice Biennale at the American Pavilion along with Alexander Calder, Edward Hopper, and Stuart Davis.

1953
With Raphael Soyer and other artists, creates the art magazine *Reality: A Journal of Artists' Opinions* to defend representational art.

Dies of cancer in New York on May 14, after a long illness.

1954
Kuniyoshi's Posthumous Exhibition, National Museum of Modern Art, Tokyo

1969
Yasuo Kuniyoshi, University Gallery, University of Florida, Gainesville

1975
Yasuo Kuniyoshi (1889–1953), a retrospective organized by the University Art Museum, University of Texas, Austin; show travels to venues in the United States, Japan, and Canada.

1983
Yasuo Kuniyoshi: Artist as Photographer, Edith C. Blum Art Institute, Bard College, Annandale-on-Hudson, New York

1986
Yasuo Kuniyoshi, Whitney Museum of American Art at Philip Morris

1989
Yasuo Kuniyoshi, a one hundredth anniversary retrospective organized by the Kyoto Museum of Modern Art

2003
At Woodstock: Kuniyoshi, Woodstock Artists Association, Woodstock, New York

2004
Yasuo Kuniyoshi, National Museum of Modern Art, Tokyo

2006
Kuniyoshi in Japanese Collections, Okayama Prefectural Museum

2013
I Am an American!: Yasuo Kuniyoshi in New York, 1916–1953, Selected Works from the Fukutake Collection, Benesse House Museum, Naoshima and Yokusuka Museum of Art

Selected Bibliography

PRIMARY SOURCES

Archives of American Art, Smithsonian Institution, Washington, DC

Yasuo Kuniyoshi Papers, 1921–1993
Katherine Schmidt Papers, Circa 1921–1971
Oral History Interview with Katherine Schmidt, 8–15 December 1969, by Paul Cummings

Archives of the Philadelphia Museum of Art, Pennsylvania

Yasuo Kuniyoshi Papers, 1931–1932

Whitney Museum of American Art Archives, New York

Yasuo Kuniyoshi artist file, including Lloyd Goodrich's 1948 interviews with the artist, Lloyd Goodrich Artists Correspondence, 1917–1978

Woodstock Artists Association and Museum Archives and Library, Woodstock, New York

WRITINGS BY YASUO KUNIYOSHI

"Art and Artists in Japan." *Arts Weekly*, April 23, 1932, 150.

"The Artist and the War." *Common Ground* 4 (Spring 1944): 33–35.

"East to West." *Magazine of Art* 33 (February 1940): 72–83.

"Universality in Art." (Art Students) *League Quarterly* (Spring 1949): 7–8.

"What About the Artist?" In *The First Woodstock Art Conference: Statements and Discussions from the Conference on the Artist and His World, Held at the Art Students League of New York, Woodstock, New York, under the Auspices of the Woodstock Art Association, August 29–30, 1947*, edited by John D. Morse, 7–10. Woodstock, NY: Woodstock Art Association and Artists Equity Association, 1947.

Yasuo Kuniyoshi. New York: American Artists Group, 1945.

EXHIBITION CATALOGS

Bloodgood, Josephine. *At Woodstock: Kuniyoshi*. Woodstock, NY: Woodstock Artists Association and Museum, 2003.

Boston University Art Gallery. *Yasuo Kuniyoshi Retrospective Exhibition*. With a foreword by Ben Shahn. Boston: The Gallery, 1961.

Goodrich, Lloyd. *Yasuo Kuniyoshi*. New York: Whitney Museum of American Art, 1948.

Goodrich, Lloyd, and Atsuo Imaizumi. *Kuniyoshi: Catalogue of Kuniyoshi's Posthumous Exhibition under the Auspices of the National Museum of Modern Art, Tokyo, and the Mainichi Newspapers*. Tokyo: National Museum of Modern Art, 1954.

Ishii, Ayako, ed. *Japanese and Japanese American Painters in the United States: A Half Century of Hope and Suffering, 1896–1945*. Tokyo: Nihon Terebi Hōsōmō, 1995.

Kuraya, Mika, and Masaaki Ozaki, eds. *Kuniyoshi: A Retrospective*. Tokyo: National Museum of Modern Art, 2004.

Moriyasu, Osamu, et al. *Kuniyoshi Yasuo ten* [Kuniyoshi in Japanese collections]. Okayama, Japan: Okayama Prefectural Museum of Art, 2006.

Myers, Jane. *The Shores of a Dream: Yasuo Kuniyoshi's Early Work in America*. Essays by Jane Myers and Tom Wolf. Fort Worth, TX: Amon Carter Museum, 1996.

National Museum of Modern Art, Kyoto, ed. *Yasuo Kuniyoshi: [100th Anniversary of His Birth . . .]*. Essays by Susan Lubowsky, Alexandra Munroe, Takeo Uchiyama, and Tom Wolf. [Japan]: Nippon Television Network Corp., 1989.

Ozawa, Yoshio. *I Am an American! Yasuo Kuniyoshi in New York, 1916–1953: Selected Works from the Fukutake Collection*. Okayama, Japan: Benesse Holdings, 2013.

Riehlman, Franklin. *Yasuo Kuniyoshi: Artist as Photographer*. Essays by Franklin Riehlman, Bruce Weber, and Tom Wolf. Annandale-on-Hudson, NY: Edith C. Blum Art Institute, Bard College, 1983.

University Art Museum. *Yasuo Kuniyoshi, 1889–1953: A Retrospective Exhibition, February 9–March 23, 1975*. Essays by Alexander Brook, Donald Goodall, Paul Jenkins, and Hideo Tomiyama. Austin: University Art Museum, University of Texas at Austin, 1975. Traveled to Japan with a separate catalog.

University Gallery. *A Special Loan Retrospective Exhibition of Works by Yasuo Kuniyoshi*. Essay by Lloyd Goodrich. Gainesville: University Gallery, University of Florida, 1969.

Whitney Museum of American Art. *Yasuo Kuniyoshi: Whitney Museum of American Art at Philip Morris, April 11–June 19, 1986*. Essays by Lloyd Goodrich, Susan Lubowsky, and Tom Wolf. New York: The Museum, 1986.

Woodstock Artists Association. *Yasuo Kuniyoshi: 1893–1953*. Woodstock, NY: The Association, Artists Equity Fund, and Art Students League of New York, 1956.

SECONDARY SOURCES

Brook, Alexander. "Yasuo Kuniyoshi." *Arts* 5 (January 1924): 24–27.

Chang, Gordon H., Mark Dean Johnson, and Paul J. Karlstrom, eds. *Asian American Art: A History, 1850–1970*. Stanford, CA: Stanford University Press, 2008.

Davis, Richard Allen. *Yasuo Kuniyoshi: The Complete Graphic Work*. San Francisco: Alan Wofsy Fine Arts, 1991.

Francis, Jacqueline. *Making Race: Modernism and "Racial Art" in America*. Seattle: University of Washington Press, 2012.

Frost, Rosamund. "Kuniyoshi, American of Two Decades." *Art News* 41 (May 15–31, 1942): 19, 25.

———. "What the War Has Meant to Kuniyoshi." *Art News* 44 (April 1–14, 1945): 25.

Fukutake Publishing Co., Ltd. *Yasuo Kuniyoshi. A Course of Glory Followed by a Neo-American Artist*. Okayama, Japan: Fukutake Publishing, 1990.

Greenhalgh, Adam. "Yasuo Kuniyoshi's *Cows in Pasture*," *Gastronomica: The Journal of Food and Culture* 9 (Summer 2009): 15–21.

Hoshino, Mutsuko. "Yasuo Kuniyoshi and Abstract Expressionism: Why Did the Painter Defend 'Non-abstract Forms'?" *Tsukuba Studies in Art and Design*, no. 8 (2004): 91–100. In Japanese with an English abstract.

Iwasaki, Yoshikazu. *Japanese Artists Who Studied in U.S.A. and the American Scene*. Tokyo: National Museum of Modern Art, 1982.

Laurent, Robert. "Memories of Yas." *College Art Journal* 13 (Autumn 1953): 6–9.

Levin, Gail. "Between Two Worlds: Folk Culture, Identity, and the American Art of Yasuo Kuniyoshi." *Archives of American Art Journal* 43, nos. 3–4 (2003): 2–17.

Louchheim, Aline B. "Kuniyoshi: Look, My Past." *Art News* 47 (April 1948): 46–48.

Murrell, William. *Yasuo Kuniyoshi*. Woodstock, NY: William M. Fisher, 1922.

Ozawa, Ritsuko, ed. *Bulletin of the Yasuo Kuniyoshi Museum*. Okayama, Japan: Benesse Corp., 1992–2002.

Ozawa, Ritsuko, and Kazuma Suzuki, eds. *Yasuo Kuniyoshi*. Okayama, Japan: Fukutake Publishing, 1991.

Ozawa, Yoshio. *Hishō to kaiki: Kuniyoshi Yasuo no seiyō to tōyō* [Flight and return: Yasuo Kuniyoshi, west and east]. Okayama, Japan: Nihon Bunkyō Shuppan, Heisei 8, 1996.

———. *Hyōden Kuniyoshi Yasuo: genmu to saikan* [Yasuo Kuniyoshi: Dream and colors]. Okayama, Japan: Fukutake Publishing, 1991.

———. *Kuniyoshi Yasuo: Hyōden* [Yasuo Kuniyoshi biography]. Tokyo: Shinchōsha, Shōwa 49, 1974.

———. *Yasuo Kuniyoshi: neo Amerikan ātisuto no kiseki* [Yasuo Kuniyoshi: A trajectory of the neo-American artist]. Okayama, Japan: Fukutake Publishing, 1991.

Pollock, Lindsay. *The Girl with the Gallery: Edith Gregor Halpert and the Making of the Modern Art Market*. New York: Public Affairs, 2006.

Salpeter, Harry. "Yasuo Kuniyoshi: Artists' Artist." *Esquire*, April 1937.

Sokol, David M. "The Founding of Artists Equity Association after World War II." *Archives of American Art Journal* 39, nos. 1–2 (1999): 17–29.

Tepfer, Diane. "Edith Gregor Halpert and the Downtown Gallery Downtown, 1926–1940: A Study in American Art Patronage." PhD diss., University of Michigan, 1989.

Terakado, Rintarō, ed. *Ishii korekushon kenkyū: Kuniyoshi Yasuo, 2* [Yasuo Kuniyoshi: Ishii collection studies 2]. Essays by Cecile Whiting, Bert Winther-Tamaki, and Omuka Toshiharu. Tsukuba, Japan: University of Tsukuba, 2013.

Tomiyama, Hideo. *Kuniyoshi Yasuo*. Tokyo: Kōdansha, Shōwa 49, 1974.

Wakayama Kenritsu Kindai Bijutsukan. *Amerika no naka no Nihon: Ishigaki Eitarō to senzen no tobei gakatachi* [Japan in America: Eitarō Ishigaki and other Japanese artists in the pre–World War II United States]. Wakayama, Japan: Museum of Modern Art, 1997.

Wang, ShiPu. *Becoming American? The Art and Identity Crisis of Yasuo Kuniyoshi*. Honolulu: University of Hawaii Press, 2011.

———. "Japan against Japan: U.S. Propaganda and Yasuo Kuniyoshi's Identity Crisis." *American Art* 22 (Spring 2008): 28–51.

———. "Masks That Reveal/Faces That Conceal: Kuniyoshi's Postwar Imagery." In *Yasuo Kuniyoshi: The Origin of the Benesse Art Site Naoshima*. Naoshima, Japan: Benesse House Museum, 2013.

Wolf, Tom. "The Late Drawings of Yasuo Kuniyoshi." *Drawing, The International Review*, published by the Drawing Society, New York (January–February 1992): 100–104.

———. *Yasuo Kuniyoshi's Women*. San Francisco: Pomegranate Artbooks, 1993.

Yamaguchi, Taiji. *Amerika bijutsu to Kuniyoshi Yasuo: kaitakusha no kiseki* [Yasuo Kuniyoshi and American art: A trace of the frontiersman]. Tokyo: Nihon Hōsō Shuppan Kyōkai, 2004.

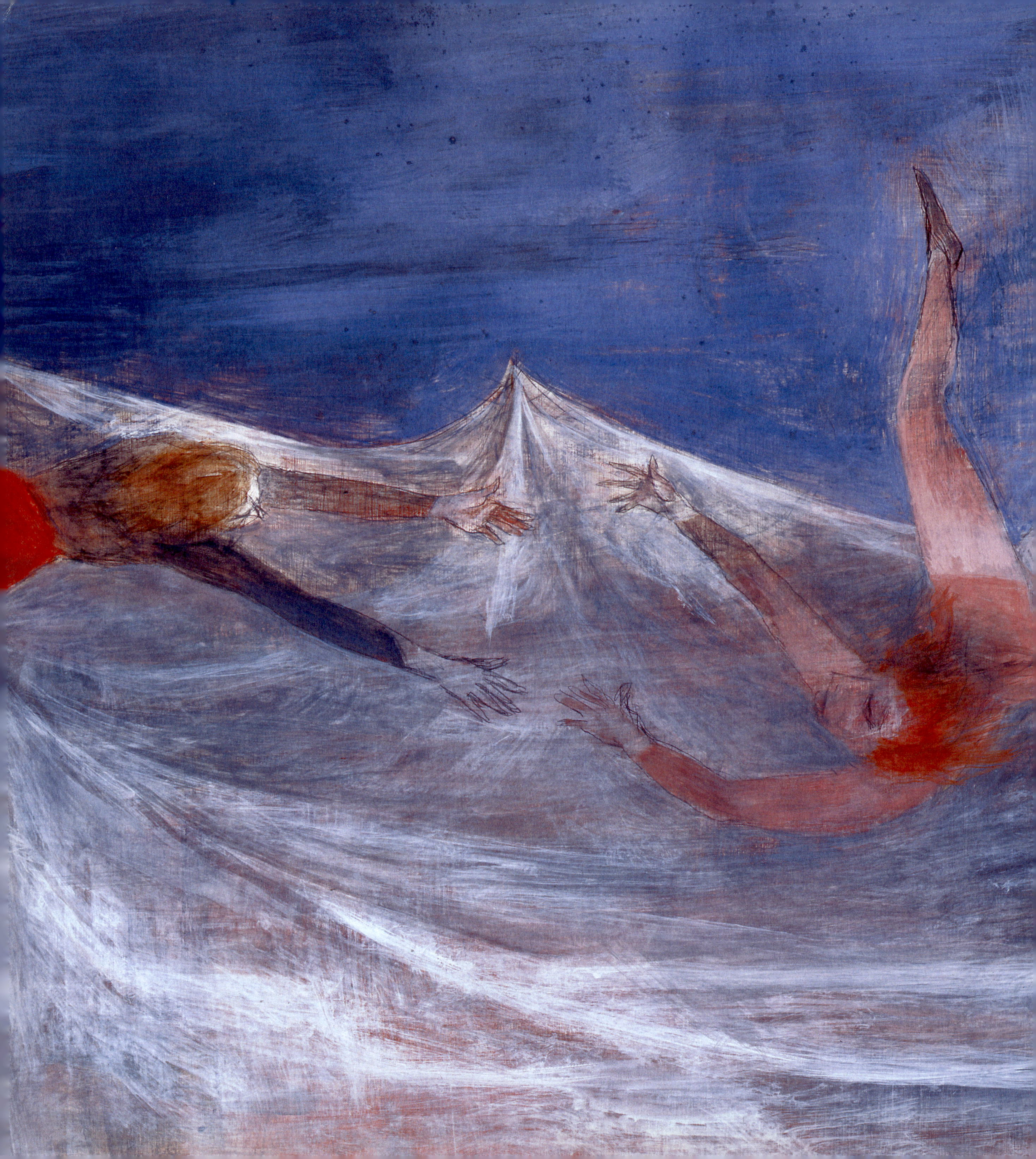

Acknowledgments

It has been a truly rewarding experience working on *The Artistic Journey of Yasuo Kuniyoshi* with the highly professional staff of the Smithsonian American Art Museum. Joann Moser, senior curator of graphic arts, has been great as my co-curator. I developed the idea for the exhibition and catalog in partnership with her, and she has been professional and supportive every step of the way, while also curating her own online supplement to this exhibition, *Kuniyoshi's Circle*. Elizabeth Broun, director, was behind the project from day one, and has given invaluable advice and leadership. Her comments on the first draft of my essay were extremely helpful, as were those by the two anonymous readers. Rachel Allen, deputy director, coordinated the logistics of this initiative from start to finish.

In the Publications office, headed by Theresa Slowik, Mary Cleary's editing has been essential to making my essay lucid and readable, and I thank Jessica Flynn for her elegant book design. Amy Doyel has been extremely helpful securing images and permissions, as has Jennifer Bauman with research, Eunice Park Kim with the exhibition design, Jo Ann Gillula and all in the External Affairs department with audience outreach, and Melissa Kroning and her staff in the Registrars office with processing the many loan requests.

I worked with the artist's late widow, Sara Mazo, for many years and we became good friends; she was always generous and supportive of my endeavors and I am very sorry that she is no longer with us to enjoy the results of this project, which would have pleased her greatly.

Ritsuko and Yoshio Ozawa, the leading Kuniyoshi experts in Japan, have for many years generously shared their information and expertise with me. In Japan, Naruhisa Hirose, Mutsuko Hoshino, Hayato Sakurai, Katsumi Senoo, Hiroya Sugimura, and Hal Hisey have always taken the time to help me out with my research, and have contributed their expertise to it. My research and writing for this catalog were made possible by a grant from the Fukutake Foundation, and Kumiko Ehara and Kenjiro Kaneshiro have been supportive and helpful throughout. Soichiro Fukutake of the Fukutake Foundation is the leading collector of Kuniyoshi's work; his continual support and that of his staff have been essential to the success of this exhibition and its catalog.

In the United States my friend Midori Yamamura has been a consistent help with her camaraderie, insights, and translating. ShiPu Wang, who has written an essential book about Kuniyoshi, has always been a supportive and encouraging colleague. I also thank Daniel Belasco, Marilla Consolini, Erin Coryell, Stephen Diamond, Bruce Dorfman, Susan Elvin-Cooper, Michael Gotkin, Tyuki Imamura, Emily Jones at the Archives of the Woodstock Artists Association, Dr. Herbert Kayden, Dale and Akiko Kleps, Jennifer Tobias at the library of the Museum of Modern Art (New York), Minoru Yasuda, Marian Yoshiki-Kovinick, and Reiko Yoshimura of the Freer Gallery of Art for their generous assistance and contributions to my work on this project. Jeanette McDonald at Bard College has consistently helped me with all my endeavors. My late friend, Franklin Riehlman, was my partner in Kuniyoshi studies for many years; when I go through my files I find entries in his hand, and I am very sorry that he is not with us to see the realization of this exhibition and catalog. There are many people who helped in significant ways, and I am sure to leave some out. Throughout this project and long before, my life has been immeasurably enriched by my family, Cheryl, Jonah and Raphael.

T. W.

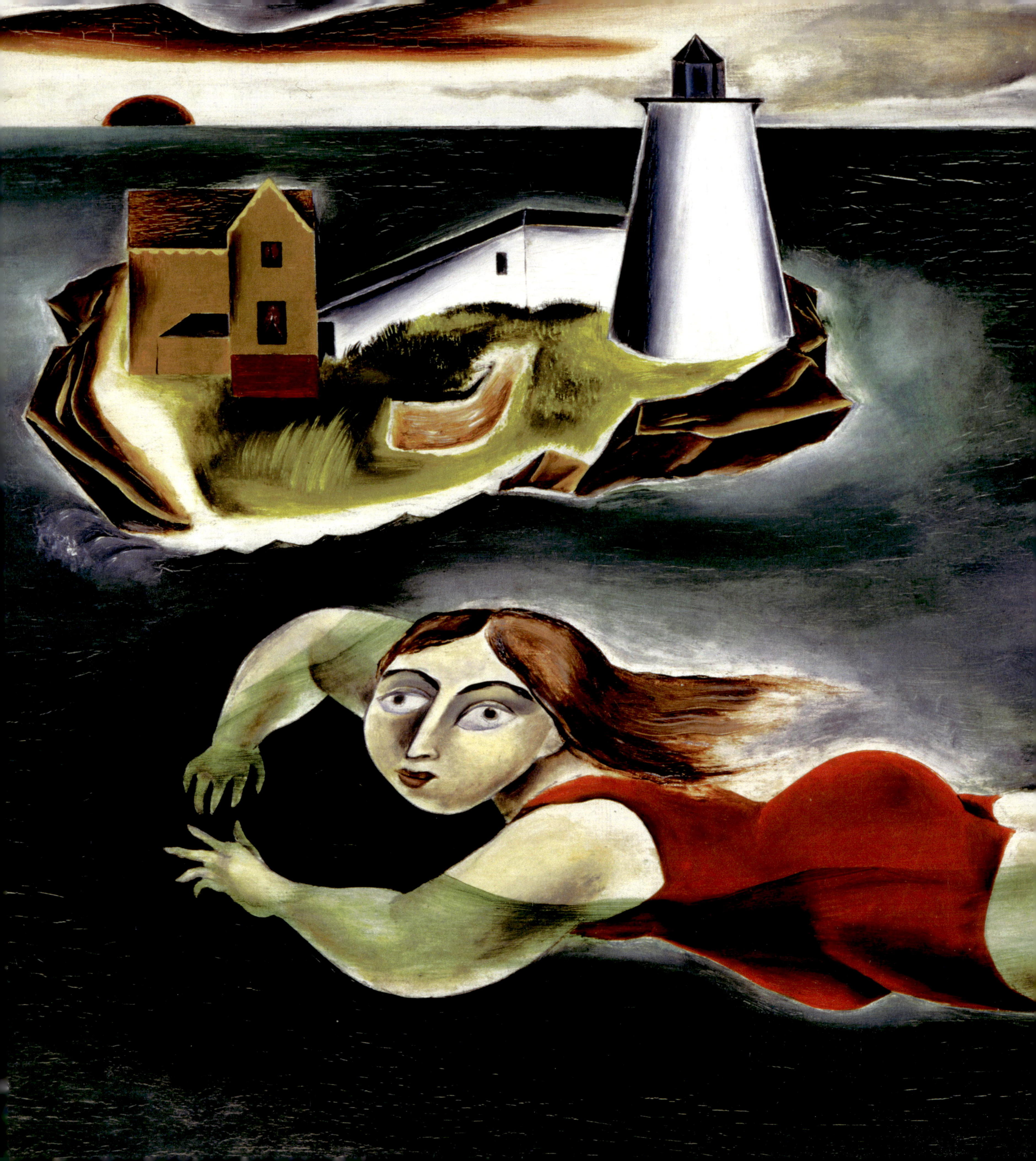

Index

Page numbers in *italics* indicate illustrations. All artworks are by Kuniyoshi unless otherwise noted.

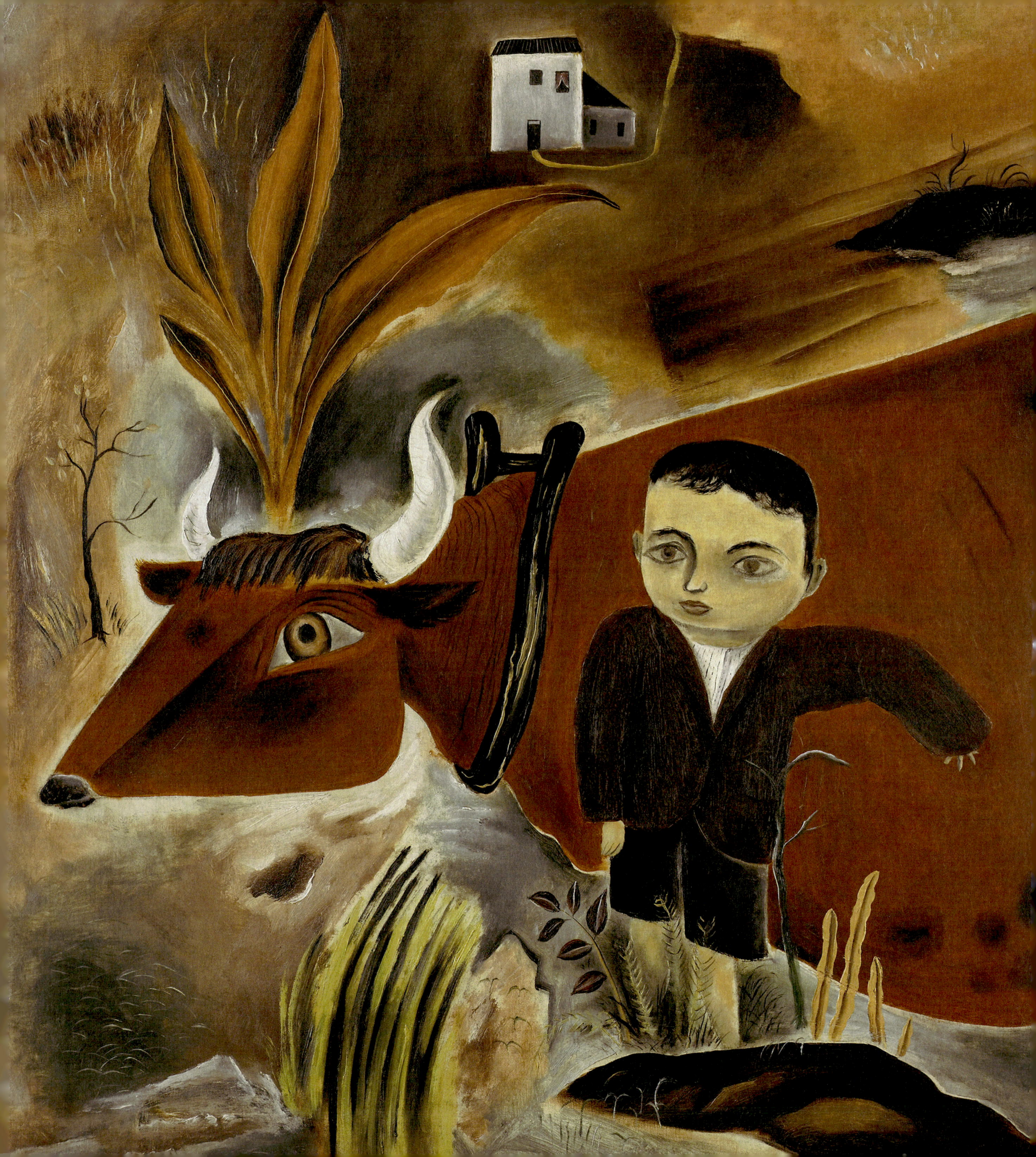

Image Credits

Unless otherwise specified, images were obtained from the collection or owner noted in the captions.

Additional photography credits and copyright notices: Figs. 4, 17, 24, 42; pls. 17, 19, 30, 35, 65: Digital image © Whitney Museum of American Art; figs. 6, 12, 73; pls. 23, 64: Image copyright © The Metropolitan Museum of Art. Image source: Art Resource, New York; fig. 8: courtesy private collection; fig. 10; pwl. 34: Courtesy Bridgeman Images; fig. 11: Photo by Martine Beck-Coppola © RMN-Grand Palais (Musée d'Orsay) / Art Resource, New York; fig. 13: Art © 2015 Calder Foundation, New York / Artists Rights Society (ARS), New York. Digital image © Whitney Museum of American Art; fig. 18: Image courtesy Fukutake Collection, Okayama, Japan; fig. 19: reproduced from Guy Pène duBois, "Art By the Way," *International Studio* 77 (July 1923): 352; figs. 23, 26, 40: Image courtesy private collection / photograph by Soichi Sunami; fig. 25: Image courtesy Conner-Rosenkranz, LLC; fig. 28: Image © The Frick Collection; figs. 30, 32; pls. 8, 20, 29: Digital image © The Museum of Modern Art / Licensed by SCALA / Art Resource, New York; fig. 31: Courtesy Bridgeman Images / © 2014 Artists Rights Society (ARS), New York / ADAGP, Paris; fig. 34: Art © Estate Bernard Karfiol, Courtesy Forum Gallery, New York. Digital image © The Museum of Modern Art / Licensed by SCALA / Art Resource, New York; fig. 36: Philadelphia Museum of Art, Archives, Kuniyoshi Papers, box 1, folder 9; fig. 38: Photograph by Robert W. F. Gray / Image courtesy private collection; fig. 39: Image courtesy private collection; fig. 41: Art © Estate of Max Weber / photo courtesy The Jewish Museum, New York / Art Resource, New York; fig. 44: Image courtesy private collection; fig. 46: Photograph by Soichi Sunami; fig. 47: Image courtesy private collection; fig. 49: Photo by Lee Stalsworth; fig. 50: reproduced from Henry M. Lester, ed., *Leica 1937 Photo Annual* (New York: Galleon Press, 1936), 124; Courtesy Kuniyoshi Library, Woodstock Artists Association and Museum Archives; fig. 54: Photo by Katherine Wetzel © Virginia Museum of Fine Arts; fig. 58: reproduced from ShiPu Wang, *Becoming American? The Art and Identity Crisis of Yasuo Kuniyoshi* (Honolulu: University of Hawaii Press, 2011), 83; fig. 59: Art © Estate of Ben Shahn / Licensed by VAGA, New York, NY, photograph by Joshua Nefsky; fig. 60: Photography © The Art Institute of Chicago; fig. 61: National Archives ID: 534126/local ID: 179-WP-277; Art © Estate of Ben Shahn / Licensed by VAGA, New York, NY; fig. 64: reproduced from Franklin Riehlman, Tom Wolf, and Bruce Weber, *Yasuo Kuniyoshi: Artist as Photographer* (Annandale-on-Hudson, NY: Edith C. Blum Art Institute, 1983), 66; fig. 65: Art © 2014 Estate of Reginald Marsh / Art Students League, New York / Artists Rights Society (ARS), New York; fig. 66: Art © Estate of Ben Shahn / Licensed by VAGA, New York, NY. Digital image © The Museum of Modern Art / Licensed by SCALA / Art Resource, New York; fig. 69: Art © Estate of Philip Guston; fig. 70: Photo by David Allison; fig. 72: Photograph © 2014 Museum of Fine Arts, Boston; pls. 2, 27, 62: Photography by Gene Young, Smithsonian American Art Museum; pl. 6: Photography by Mildred Baldwin, Smithsonian American Art Museum; pl. 9: Photo by Carlos Silva; pl. 12: Photograph by Amon Carter Museum of American Art; pls. 18, 32: Photography by Mindy Barrett, Smithsonian American Art Museum; pls. 22, 53: Photo by Cathy Carver; pls. 37, 38, 45: Image courtesy National Museum of Modern Art, Tokyo; pl. 57: Image © The Cleveland Museum of Art.